BROOK, Barry S. and others, comps. Perspectives in musicology. Norton, 1972. 363p ll bibl 78-103964. 15.00. ISBN 0-393-02142-4

In 1971, when CUNY instituted its doctoral program in musicology, 15 internationally known musicologists were invited to deliver a series of lectures on the present state of musical scholarship and to point up problem areas within the discipline that needed exploration. *Perspectives in musicology* is a compilation of these lectures together with excerpts from some of the discussions that took place during the seminars with doctoral students.   Included among the lecturers were Gustave Reese, Friedrich Blume, Vincent Duckles, François Lesure, Emanuel Winternitz, Edward Lowinsky, H. C. Robbins Landon, Milton Babbitt, Paul Henry Lang, Gilbert Chase, Mantle Hood, Frank Ll. Harrison, etc.— in short, a "Who's who" of musicology today.   The lectures encompass a variety of topics: lacunae in musicological research, archival research, iconology of music, secret chromatic art, musicology and related disciplines, non-Western musicological studies, to mention but a few. Most of the lectures included a bibliography, and Brook, one of the editors of this volume, has included a 12-page selected bibliography on "Musicology as a discipline."   This set of lectures is a very healthy contribution, for unlike many festschriften

Continued

BROOK

whose contents are uneven in worth, this series is uniformly of high calibre. The lectures read well and, more importantly, they hold interest. Although musicology is considered a graduate discipline, this book belongs on all academic library shelves.

Perspectives in Musicology

Contributors

LUIZ HEITOR CORRÊA DE AZEVEDO

MILTON BABBITT

FRIEDRICH BLUME

GILBERT CHASE

VINCENT DUCKLES

FRANK LL. HARRISON

MANTLE HOOD

GEORG KNEPLER

H. C. ROBBINS LANDON

PAUL HENRY LANG

FRANÇOIS LESURE

EDWARD E. LOWINSKY

J. H. KWABENA NKETIA

GUSTAVE REESE

EMANUEL WINTERNITZ

PERSPECTIVES IN MUSICOLOGY

The Inaugural Lectures of the Ph. D. Program in Music
at the City University of New York

EDITED BY

BARRY S. BROOK
EDWARD O. D. DOWNES
SHERMAN VAN SOLKEMA

W · W · NORTON & COMPANY · INC ·
NEW YORK

Copyright © 1972 by W. W. Norton & Company, Inc.

FIRST EDITION

Library of Congress Cataloging in Publication Data

Brook, Barry S   comp.
  Perspectives in musicology.

  Bibliography: p.
    1. Music—Addresses, essays, lectures. 2. Musicology—Addresses, essays,
lectures. I. Downes, Edward, 1911–   joint comp. II. Van Solkema,
Sherman, joint comp. III. Title.
ML55.B77   780   78–103964
  ISBN-0-393-02142-4

1 2 3 4 5 6 7 8 9 0

Contents

Plates

Introduction

*I*N *1915*, the lead article in the inaugural issue of the *Musical Quarterly* was entitled "On Behalf of Musicology." Its author, Waldo Selden Pratt, described the newly coined word—which had not as yet appeared in any English dictionary—as "more ingenious than euphonius, more curious than alluring," and "as much a hybrid word as 'sexology.'" He nonetheless accepted the term and used it thirty-six times in his sixteen-page article—cautiously adding thirty-six sets of quotation marks. The word gained currency with considerable difficulty. Lexicographical Philistines derided it, coining such parallels as danceology, artology, even paintingology.

Nor was the discipline itself any more readily accepted. It was not until 1930 that the first chair of musicology was established in this country, at Cornell University. It was occupied by the late Otto Kinkeldey, revered dean of American musicologists. It is appropriate to point out here that Kinkeldey was a graduate of the College of the City of New York (now the City College), the oldest branch of the City University, and that this university's new "chair" in musicology is the fortieth in the country.

The City University lecture/seminar series has had two goals: one was to herald—with subdued fanfare—the inauguration of the university's doctoral program in musicology; the second and major, objective was to provide our fledgling doctoral students with the opportunity of hearing and exchanging ideas with a number of visiting scholars, including seven from abroad, exploring with them the state, the methods, the theories, and the lacunae of musicological research today. In intent, this last concern—with lacunae—resembles that of the famous challenge made in 1900 by David Hilbert of Göttingen to the International Congress of Mathematicians. Hilbert divided the field of mathematics into a dozen major areas and set down some twenty-three fundamental problems in need of solution. In 1900, Hilbert was probably the only mathematician able to range over his entire field. Such a probing survey would be impossible in our day for one man—even in so young a discipline as musicology.

In the planning of the series, "musicology" was thought of in the broadest of terms—historical, systematic, ethnological. Particular attention was given to some relatively little-developed aspects of our discipline—the archival, the iconographical, and the interdisciplinary. Fifteen distinguished scholars, representing a wide spectrum of musicological interests, were invited to lecture and to conduct informal seminars on specifically designed topics. For the present publication, the series' rather ponderous original title, "Perspectives and Lacunae in Musicological Research," was abridged to read "Perspectives in Musicology"—a title that better fits, perhaps, both the contents of the volume and the size of its cover.

All but the initial lecture (and concert) of the series took place at the City University Graduate School (formerly Graduate Center)in Manhattan, facing the New York Public Library. At the turn of the century, the Graduate School building, which today houses most of the University's Ph.D. programs, was a hub of musical life; it contained a leading concert room, Aeolian Hall, as well as numerous studios and managerial offices. In addition to the Graduate School, the City University of New York currently comprises ten senior colleges and professional schools, six community colleges. The four oldest senior colleges, City College (founded in 1847), Hunter College, Brooklyn College, and Queens College, participate in the doctoral program in music, offering master's-level courses on their campuses. Doctoral seminars are conducted at the Graduate School, with the exception of those in iconography and organology, which are held at the Metropolitan Museum of Art.

The "Perspectives" series was organized as follows: the lectures were open to the university community and to members of the American Musicological Society. They were delivered on Friday afternoons during the academic year 1968–69, at intervals of two to three weeks. The following mornings, the guest lecturers led closed three-hour seminars, attended by the enrolled students, a few resident faculty members, and an occasional guest. Reading lists having been provided in advance by the lecturers, seminar discussions usually revolved around both the lectures and the readings, although tangential subjects were by no means excluded.

Two addresses were not followed by seminars, that by Emanuel Winternitz, of the Metropolitan Museum of Art, and the initial "Inaugural Lecture" by Gustave Reese of New York University (not to be confused with the City University of New York). Professor Reese's address, given on the afternoon of October 12, 1968, was followed in the evening by an inaugural concert by the New York Pro Musica, under the direction of John R. White, in a program of English medieval and Renaissance music.*

---

* The New York Pro Musica was in residence at the City University during 1968–69, giving a series of concerts and workshops on five campuses. For the final lecture

No doctoral program in musicology—nor, indeed, in any other discipline —could have been more auspiciously launched.

During the year, on nonlecture Fridays, the students participating "for credit" met with Professor Sherman Van Solkema, coordinator of the seminar, for more discussion, clarification, and follow-up. Students were expected to explore the "lacunae" that lecturers may have pointed to or hinted at, and then to prepare specific studies, on their own, of the unmapped terrain of their choice. (These student papers will be published by the City University in a photo-offset paperback under the title *Lacunae in Musicological Research.*)

Since the sequence of the lectures as they occurred depended more on the coordination of crowded calendars rather than on any logical succession of topics, the original sequence has been considerably altered. The lecture topics seem to divide themselves into two types: the first, historically oriented; the second, more concerned with ethnomusicology and with other disciplines. Since none of the invited scholars had any specific knowledge of what the others were planning to say, it is interesting to observe that several themes recurred again and again. The three most prominent were: first, that the prevailing dichotomy between historical and ethnomusicological research is artificial and damaging to the growth of our discipline, or, to quote Jacques Handschin—as several speakers did —the proper subject of musicology is man; second, that extensive cultivation of some of the means and methods—e.g. hypothesis building and testing—long standard in other more established disciplines, plus the expansion of interdisciplinary research, will be required before musicology attains its full potential; and third, despite its youthful lack of balance and its many current lacunae, musicology as a discipline is expanding and maturing at an increasing pace in many countries and—to quote especially our foreign visitors—nowhere more rapidly than in the United States.

The sections in this volume marked "Discussion" represent, as a rule, both the Friday-afternoon question periods and the Saturday-morning seminars for thirteen of the fifteen lectures. These were taped and transcribed, and then editorially distilled to about one-sixth of their original length. Where appropriate, the lecturer's suggested advance reading list and other bibliographical materials are appended. Thanks are due to Laura Rosenthal for help in transcribing the tapes; manuscript preparation was largely in the capable hands of Carlene Price; Vered Cohen's research assistance was invaluable in the preparation of the Selected Bibliography printed at the end of the volume.

A sincere expression of gratitude is proffered to a distinguished mathematician and brilliant administrator, who succeeds in being at the same time a devoted humanist and a great lady, Mina Rees, president of the

---

in the series, Edward Lowinsky's *"Secret Chomatic Art* Re-examined," the New York Pro Musica provided the live—and quite astounding—musical illustrations.

Graduate Division of the City University of New York; without her sympathetic support, this rather unconventional series of lecture/seminars—and hence this volume—would not have come into being.

Barry S. Brook,
Executive Officer, Ph.D. Program in Music
The City University of New York

MARCH, 1971

Participants

Lecturers

LUIZ HEITOR CORRÊA DE AZEVEDO

Professor Catedrático, Escola Nacional de Música, Universidade do Brasil

MILTON BABBITT

William Shubael Conant Professor of Music, Princeton University; Director, Columbia-Princeton Electronic Music Center

FRIEDRICH BLUME

Professor Emeritus of Music, University of Kiel; Editor, *Die Musik in Geschichte und Gegenwart*

GILBERT CHASE

Director, Inter-American Institute for Musical Research, Tulane University

VINCENT DUCKLES

Professor of Music, and head, Music Library, University of California at Berkeley

FRANK Ll. HARRISON

Oxford University; Visiting Professor, Princeton University; now Professor of Ethnomusicology, University of Amsterdam

MANTLE HOOD

Professor and Director, Institute of Ethnomusicology, University of California at Los Angeles

GEORG KNEPLER

Professor of Music, Humboldt University, Berlin

H. C. ROBBINS LANDON

Buggiano, Italy; Adjunct Professor, City University of New York, Spring, 1969

PAUL HENRY LANG

Avalon Professor of Music, Columbia University; editor, *The Musical Quarterly*

FRANÇOIS LESURE

Conservateur-en-chef, Département de Musique, Bibliothèque Nationale, Paris

EDWARD E. LOWINSKY

Ferdinand Schevill Distinguished Professor of Music, University of Chicago

J. H. KWABENA NKETIA

Professor and Director, Institute of African Studies, University of Ghana

GUSTAVE REESE

Professor of Music, New York University

EMANUEL WINTERNITZ

Curator, Crosby Brown Collection of Musical Instruments at the Metropolitan Museum of Art; Visiting Professor of Music, City University of New York

City University Doctoral Faculty, 1968–69

Barry S. Brook
Luther A. Dittmer
Edward O. D. Downes
Philip Alan Friedheim
H. Wiley Hitchcock
William B. Kimmel
H. C. Robbins Landon,
   Adjunct Professor
Edward R. Lerner

Siegmund Levarie
George Perle
Ruth Halle Rowen
Felix Salzer
Boris Schwarz
Sherman Van Solkema
Emanuel Winternitz,
   Visiting Professor

Students

Edward Berlin
David M. Bushler
Vered Cohen
Emily Ellis
Genette Foster
Bea Friedland

Barbara Hampton
Benjamin Harms
Gene Hayden
Jeffrey Hest
Elise Jorgens

Michael Leavitt
Drora Pershing
Howard M. Schott
Roberta Singer
Linda Solow

Guests

Rose Brandel
Donaldson Byrd
Walter Gerboth

Elise Kirk
Barbara Krader
Stoddard Lincoln

John B. MacMillan
Eric Werner

Perspectives in Musicology

Perspectives and Lacunae in Musicological Research: Inaugural Lecture

GUSTAVE REESE

A SOMEWHAT raw young student recently asked me who the first American musicologist was. "Was it," he inquired, "Dr. Otto Kinkeldey?" There was something particularly fortunate and fitting in the coincidence that Otto Kinkeldey's name should have been raised in this manner so shortly before the present inaugural occasion, for a portion of the education of this distinguished musical scholar was obtained at the City College of New York, from which he was graduated with a B.A. in 1898. We may take it for granted that he would be pleased by the fact that a Ph.D. program in music is being inaugurated today at the City University of New York. Perhaps we may look back upon him as somewhat in the nature of a patron saint.

I could have answered the young student by saying that musicologists existed before the term "musicology" was introduced. Certainly, Burney and Hawkins were musicologists in the eighteenth century, though they would have been surprised to learn this. If Guido Adler was correct in maintaining that all peoples who can be said to possess an art of music also possess a science of music, even though it may be undeveloped as a scientific system, the first musicologist in our country may well have been an Indian. Actually, I informed the student that Dr. Kinkeldey did indeed occupy the first chair of musicology set up in an American university—a chair that was established at Cornell in 1930—but that certainly there had been musicologists in the land before him. He himself had held in the highest esteem his older contemporary, O. G. Sonneck, who had become the first chief of the Music Division in the Library of Congress in 1902 and the first editor of the *Musical Quarterly* in 1915, and who, before his death in 1928, had produced a considerable and most valuable output of scholarly writings, including the basic pioneer works on American music up to 1800.

Although Kinkeldey's American elders included nobody else of similar musicological distinction, other workers in the field did exist. The International Musical Society, founded at Leipzig in 1899, gave rise in this country to a national section in 1907, and this section held annual meetings (in conjunction with the Music Teachers National Association) until, in 1914, the outbreak of World War I led to the dissolution of the parent organization. The presidents of the section were Albert A. Stanley, from 1907 to 1911, and Waldo S. Pratt thereafter. Stanley, a professor of music at the University of Michigan, compiled an extensive catalogue, published in 1918 and 1921, of the collection of 1400 musical instruments given to the university in 1898 by Frederick Stearns of Detroit. Stanley's name is perpetuated in that of the Stanley String Quartet, the quartet-in-residence now functioning at the university. Pratt is remembered especially for his *History of Music*, first published in 1907 and twice revised, his *New Encyclopedia of Music*, and his studies of the French Psalter. The American section of the International Musical Society was represented by delegates at the Musical Congresses of Vienna (1909), London (1911), and Paris (1914), and by articles printed in the *Sammelbände* and the *Zeitschrift* of the society, both O. G. Sonneck and Otto Kinkeldey making valuable contributions. When, therefore, the chair of musicology was established at Cornell in 1930, it was not in the nature of an artificial graft upon the cultural life of the country. If musicology had not been a rampantly luxurious growth before that, it had at least put forth some healthy shoots. Only a few years later, political conditions were to send to our shores a large number of superbly gifted and trained scholars, whose contributions to the development of American musicology can hardly be overestimated. But if what they encountered here in the field of musicology was not on the large scale of what they had left, it could at least lay claim to being a small growth of promise and of quality.

The scene that the newcomers found here included the early stages of what has since proved to be a major force in the musicological life of the country. In January, 1930, Kinkeldey and four colleagues had met in New York for the purpose of forming a purely local society, the New York Musicological Society, and they were soon joined by some other scholars in the vicinity. Papers were read at frequent intervals, and the length of the discussions that ensued may be deduced from the following sentence, quoted from the society's *Bulletin*, No. 1. "Meetings (all but one) were held at the residence of Mrs. E. F. Walton, who invariably provided refreshments some time after midnight."

From these modest beginnings grew, with the help of some judicious prodding on the part of Harold Spivacke and sage counsel provided by Carl Engel, the American Musicological Society, organized in 1934 on a national scale, to replace the local New York group. In identifying the man chosen as the first president of the organization, we return once more to Otto Kinkeldey. In the thirty-four years since the society was founded, it has flourished like the Biblical green bay tree. There is no need to recount numerous details regarding its growth.[1] At its annual meeting held in December, 1969, the Treasurer reported a membership of about 2700. The society is divided into sixteen local chapters, operating throughout the country. It has magnitude not only in the size of its membership, but also in the quality of the scholarship by which it is represented. Its *Journal* is one of the best musicological periodicals printed anywhere and exemplifies, in concentrated and varied form, the excellence shown by American musicologists in their individual publications, large and small, appearing in other media.

If, then, the chair established at Cornell was not an artificial graft upon American musical life in 1930, the CUNY doctoral program in music is very clearly not such a graft today, but a wholly normal growth rising out of favorable, fertile soil. The inauguration of the program is another manifestation of the growth of musicology in American universities, an expansion the rapidity of which must be considered among the most remarkable developments on the American academic scene. Seven universities offered Ph.D. degrees in our discipline in 1931, as Oliver Strunk reported in "The State and Resources of Musicology in the United States," which appeared in 1932.[2] Today, the universities—including CUNY—that offer the Ph.D. in musicology are thirty-eight in number. In an excellent survey, entitled "The State of Musicology at American Universities,"[3] Merellyn M. Gallagher presents a formidable array of statistics, and with acknowledgment to Miss Gallagher I shall avail myself of some of them.

In the 1930s, the number of Ph.D. degrees granted annually in musicology averaged 2.4; this had risen to 26.3 by the mid 60s. In 1932, the Music Department at Cornell, so important in the history of American musicology, granted its first doctorate; the fourth edition of Helen Hewitt's *Doc-*

1. See *Bulletin of the American Musicological Society*, I (June, 1936), 1; and Barry S. Brook, ed., *American Musicological Society, Greater New York Chapter* (New York, 1965), Prologue, p. 1.

2. Oliver Strunk, "The State and Resources of Musicology in the United States," *Bulletin of the American Council of Learned Societies*, XIX (1932).

3. Merellyn M. Gallagher, "The State of Musicology at American Universities," *Student Musicologists at Minnesota*, II (July, 1967), 1–51.

toral Dissertations in Musicology (1965) lists, as completed or in process, 1204 dissertations. If we reflect upon these statistics, certain questions come to mind. What are the reasons for this amazing expansion? Is it paralleled in other disciplines? What patterns of consistency and change are discernible in it? What has been the impact of the development of musicology in America upon the discipline as a whole? What can we predict in the way of further growth and achievement?

To attempt to answer all or even a few of these questions with so much as a semblance of completeness would extend this talk beyond reasonable limits. Some of the questions have already been considered at length by Frank Harrison, Claude Palisca, and Mantle Hood in their book, *Musicology*.[4] I shall, therefore, restrict most of my remaining comments to some observations on the statistics just mentioned, and on similar ones, and to a few prognostications about the future of musicology, especially in American universities.

What kind of training in musicology has been offered by our universities? Some information can be obtained from the curricula that have been offered over the years. Further insight may be obtained from an examination of the subject matter of the dissertations produced over these same years. As for consideration of the ultimate quality and success of this training, this can be better assessed by a close inspection of the published achievements of our younger American-trained scholars than in a talk like this, but it may nevertheless be ventured here, as an incidental comment, that the outlook encourages the expectation that the younger scholars will continue upon the path of their elders and that their efforts will be as distinguished, and perhaps more so.

Since musicology was introduced in the American university, emphasis in the curricula has always been on the historical aspects. The related, so-called systematic fields of music psychology, esthetics, and acoustics have steadily declined over the years as primarily musicological subjects. The collective total number of semester hours offered in these fields by our present music departments is lower than ever before, in spite of the great increase in the number of such departments. The reason for this decline is not elusive: with the growing specialization of interest and the increasing sophistication of research methodology, musicology and three of the disciplines with which it once had especially close ties have tended to go their separate ways—music psychology reverting to the psychologist, esthetics to the philosopher, and acoustics to the physicist. Such specialization has affected the subdivisions of historical musicology itself. There are 70 per cent more general surveys of music history for graduates today than there were in 1931, but a chart in Miss Gallagher's paper shows that the total number of departments offering Ph.D. degrees have increased 500

4. Frank Ll. Harrison, Claude Palisca, and Mantle Hood, *Musicology*, Princeton Studies in Humanistic Scholarship in America (Englewood Cliffs, N.J., 1963).

per cent. In contrast with the relatively small gain in the general surveys, the number of surveys of individual periods has increased 1100 per cent. Moreover, concurrently with these surveys of individual periods a huge number of specialized seminars and lecture courses have been conducted on topics ranging from early Christian chant to the Masses of Josquin to the symphonies of Beethoven to the music of our own time.

The emphasis on historical musicology in lecture offerings is not unnaturally paralleled in the dissertations. Indeed, the statistics show that dissertations on early music—medieval, Renaissance, Baroque—have always been in the majority, consistently comprising about 60 per cent of the total. If we consider the vast increase in the number of dissertations submitted, this particular statistic is quite striking. The total number of dissertations accepted between 1940 and 1949—that is, 63—is slightly over 80 per cent of the number of dissertations written between 1960 and 1965 on the Renaissance alone. The reasons for this concentration on earlier periods are many. The large and enormously beneficial influx of foreign scholars trained in the classical musicological tradition of Adler and Chrysander must be regarded as a decisive influence. But the simple fact that so much spadework obviously remained to be done had its effect also, coupled with an increasing, but fortunately only temporary, academic reaction against much of the more familiar music of the recent past.

Although historical musicology dominates scholarly study in our departments and in spite of the previously mentioned decline of certain areas as subdivisions of systematic musicology, the systematic portion of our discipline has been coming back with considerable vigor. First, with the great increase in specialized lecture courses and seminars, growing attention has been paid to methodology—that is, to the *technique* of musical research. This may be observed not only in the many "Introduction to Musicology" courses—of which, incidentally, there were only two in 1931—but also within the subject courses themselves. Another area in which systematic studies have made a substantial gain is, obviously, ethnomusicology. As of the present, this gain is only spottily distributed among our universities, but in such a place as the University of California at Los Angeles the advance is a remarkably large one. Ethnomusicological courses are being offered in twelve of our universities, and of this number seven offer more than one course. A marked rise in interest is discernible also in scholarly investigation into problems of music *theory*, as is shown by recent musicological dissertations in that area. The role of theory as a tool for historical research and as a discipline worthy of scholarly investigation for its own sake is undergoing re-examination. This fact, mentioned both by Miss Gallagher and by Lewis Lockwood,[5] points to at least a partial reintegration of the historical and systematic sides of musicology, a

5. Lewis Lockwood, review of *Musicology* by Harrison, Palisca, and Hood, *Perspectives of New Music*, III/1 (1964), 119–27.

rapprochement that is bound to work, in the main, to the advantage of both.

The fact that musicology, as a consciously organized discipline, is still young is in many ways a boon. For both the student and the mature scholar, it means that there is no shortage of attractive and important subjects awaiting investigation. The Ph.D. candidate in musicology is not in the least hard-put to find a subject interesting to himself, to his faculty advisers, and to a somewhat wider, though necessarily select, reading public. In spite of the enormous activity in the field, gaps continue to exist in great profusion, and they provide ample opportunities not only to individual researchers but also to the university departments that provide the main centers in which they work.

We have just tried to place in perspective the remarkable development that has brought American musicology to its present healthy state. If we now try to place in perspective what lies ahead of us, we might well include a brief survey of examples of the lacunae in musicology that confront—and thereby provide opportunities for—the international band of musical scholars, among whom our own researchers have been laboring so devotedly. The present series of lectures, "Perspectives and Lacunae in Musicological Research," will provide ample opportunity to call attention to such lacunae in greater detail, and only a brief mention of a somewhat random sampling will be undertaken here.

The lacunae exist in practically all subareas of our larger field. If we go far back in time, our curiosity is piqued by an unusual possibility, brought to our attention in a book by Walter Kaufmann, *Musical Notations of the Orient* (1967).[6] We learn from Kaufmann that the earliest Chinese musical notation known to be extant dates from the T'ang dynasty (618–907), but that most early Chinese music comes to us from the Sung dynasty (960–1279); he mentions also, however, the possibility that notated music may be found on bones, shells, stones, etc. Over 23,000 "oracle bones," as they are called, have come down to us, and Kaufmann applies the term "pre-Confucian" to them—that is, "earlier than 500 B.C." These are yet to be completely examined and deciphered, and Kaufmann believes that there is reason to hope that, somewhere in the pile, examples of musical notation will be found, as well as on bronzes of the Chou dynasty, which ended in 249 B.C. What fascinating possibilities!

By comparison, further recoveries of ancient Greek music would seem to be rather unremarkable. But what a huge gap extends before us in this section of our music history! How maddening it is that, of all the music that was once sung and played in connection with the plays of Aeschylus, Sophocles, Euripides, and Aristophanes, only a tiny fragment of music for the *Orestes* of Euripides has been found. Of course, we must be resigned

6. Walter Kaufmann, *Musical Notations of the Orient: Notational Systems of Continental East, South, and Central Asia* (Bloomington, 1967).

to the fact that this gap may never be narrowed, no matter how hard scholars may exert themselves. But scraps of ancient Greek music do continue to be found from time to time, and we may hope that the end has not yet been reached.

Numerous scholars have engaged in intensive research in connection with the music of the Middle Ages, and yet many lacunae remain. Indeed, the whole question of the origins and provenance of the Gregorian repertoire—and of its troublesome relative, the "Old Roman" chant—remains very much unsettled. Moreover, only recently new findings and queries have made us feel that a chapter of music history that we once considered close to the truth must be regarded as superseded—for example, the one dealing with the music of the medieval tropes.

Problems like these, dealing basically with liturgy and plainsong, affect various polyphonic works of the Middle Ages and early Renaissance. For example, even if we have modern transcriptions of Alleluias of the Perotinus period and later that are correct with regard to pitch and perhaps with regard to rhythm, do we always know just how these pieces should be performed? Normally, at the end of an Alleluia there is a return to the beginning, with a certain modification that need not concern us now. But, if an Alleluia is followed by a sequence, the return is not made. Now, as is well known, practically all sequences were ousted from the liturgy at the time of the Council of Trent in the 1560s. Great skill and industry have been and are being directed toward the task of recovering the discarded sequence repertoire. But, until we know, for example, just which Alleluias were followed by sequences in the various local uses—and by which sequences—over a period of approximately four hundred years, we shall not be certain of how to round off the performance of the various Alleluias of these centuries. Does this or that Alleluia end with a return to the beginning or lead directly into a plainsong performance? Some work has been accomplished in finding the proper answers, but much remains to be done. Such questions as these might be supplemented by many further ones of a more or less similar nature.

Notwithstanding all the skill and devotion that have gone into the study of the rhythm of what is inaccurately called Gregorian chant, we can hardly claim that we have as yet sailed entirely out of the sea of doubt into a safe harbor. And much the same thing can be said about the rhythm of medieval secular monophony—the music of the troubadours, trouvères, and minnesingers. These several problems of rhythm may simply be among the puzzles that will never be solved, but we shall not know if we do not continue to try, and success has certainly rewarded efforts that have been made with regard to certain aspects of the notation of medieval rhythm that misled investigators of about a hundred years ago—and less.

Of the lacunae that confront us when we enter the fourteenth century, a most perplexing one involves the instrument referred to as the *echiquier*

in some French manuscripts and is called by more or less similar names in
Spanish, English, and German sources. Since we have several references to
this instrument, it seems odd that we have only a vague idea of its nature.
We are satisfied that it was a stringed keyboard instrument—but with
regard to more precise details, as Sybil Marcuse observes in her dictionary
of musical instruments, "the puzzle remains unsolved."[7] Perhaps there is
hiding somewhere a clearer reference to the instrument or even drawings
illustrating its construction, such as those of a number of keyboard instruments that the fifteenth century has left for us.

If we turn to fourteenth-century Italy, we wonder why we have what
might be described as a full-blown flower that seems never to have been a
bud. We have next to nothing to show the early formative stages of the
magnificent body of highly developed polyphonic music that comes to us
from *trecento* Italy. Tentative attempts have been made to explain this
gap, and we may have to be satisfied with them. But we cannot be sure
that they clinch the matter. One might be ready to concede that this
corpus was based on earlier music in other countries, notably France, but
the style is strikingly different and, even more remarkable, the specifically
Italian form of notation in which this music is written down not only differs considerably from earlier French notation but is highly developed in
the very earliest examples that we have.

Even more puzzling is the fact that we have absolutely no lute music
antedating the sixteenth century and the further fact that the earliest
examples of such music that reach us are written down, like Italian *trecento* music, in a highly developed form of notation. The appearance of
lutes in art works of earlier centuries shows, of course, that lute music
must have existed at least in sound. But the highly developed notation of
the oldest surviving examples makes one strongly suspect that lute music
existed also in writing at some earlier stage.

To be sure, the lacunae affecting *trecento* music and lute music can be
satisfactorily filled only if further sources are discovered. But new sources
do turn up from time to time, even though not as often as one might wish,
and lacunae such as these should be viewed not just as vexing but also
as stimulating.

In 1954, Thurston Dart published an article, "Renaissance Music: Some
Urgent Tasks for Scholars,"[8] in which he catalogues many lacunae in our
knowledge of fifteenth- and sixteenth-century music. It is a sign of the
diligence of the musicological fraternity that since 1954 many of the tasks
mentioned by Dart have been undertaken. But numerous problems remain
virtually untouched. For example, we know next to nothing about where
and from whom the early printers, and especially Petrucci, acquired the

7. Sybil Marcuse, *Musical Instruments: A Comprehensive Dictionary* (Garden City,
N.Y., 1964), p. 91.
8. Thurston Dart, "Renaissance Music: Some Urgent Tasks for Scholars," *Renaissance News*, VII (1954).

material they published. Such information would be useful in evaluating the merits of different printed sources when editing a piece and in providing possible clues to the solution of problems of dating and chronology. Also, our knowledge of the interpolations of laude, carols, and other paraliturgical compositions into liturgical contexts is far from adequate. Knowing the purpose for which a composition was written can often tell us much about why it was written in a certain style and how it should be performed. In addition, we still lack many bibliographical tools, among the most useful of which would be an index of motet text-incipits. The value of such a tool in controlling the vast body of sixteenth-century motets would be immense—for example, in locating composer attributions for works that are anonymous in some sources and in solving problems of date and provenance.

The many gaps in our knowledge of the authentic performance practice of Renaissance and other early music are so well known that there is no need to describe specific examples. Robert Haas, in his *Aufführungspraxis*,[9] tried to be inclusive with regard to early music, but it is perhaps symptomatic of the situation in this field that Frederick Dorian, in his *History of Music in Performance*,[10] begins with a chapter entitled "From Renaissance to Baroque" and allots to it only 23 pages out of a total of some 350.

Leaping ahead in time, a glance at the recent musicological literature will reveal that the subject of Baroque and Classical ornamentation, both melodic and rhythmic, is very much with us. This is amply shown by the controversy over *notes inégales*, which in this country involves Michael Collins, Robert Donington, Frederick Neumann, and Sol Babitz.[11] I hesitate to classify such an extensively treated subject as representing a lacuna, but the definitive solution to the problem may not yet have been reached.

In the special field of Mozart ornamentation, brave efforts have been made by Eva and Paul Badura-Skoda in the book *Interpreting Mozart on the Keyboard*,[12] but, as any thoughtful and informed performer can testify, much work remains to be done. It would be a relief if musicology could help put an end to the situation in which, for example, in a single

9. Robert Haas, *Aufführungspraxis* (Wildpark-Potsdam, 1931–32).

10. Frederick Dorian, *The History of Music in Performance* (New York, 1942).

11. Sol Babitz, "Restoring Baroque Inequality," *American Recorder*, IX/1 (Winter, 1968), 7–8; *id.*, "Concerning the Length of Time that Every Note Must Be Held," *Music Review*, XXVIII/1 (Feb., 1967), 21–37; *id.*, "Notes Inégales: A Communication," *Journal of the American Musicological Society*, XX/3 (Fall, 1967), 473–76; Michael B. Collins, "*Notes Inégales*: A Re-examination," *ibid.*, 481–85; Robert Donington, "A Problem of Inequality," *Musical Quarterly*, LIII/4 (Oct., 1967), 503–17; Frederick Neumann, "External Evidence and Uneven Notes," *ibid.*, LII/4 (Oct., 1966), 448–64; *id.*, "The French *Inégales*, Quantz and Bach," *Journal of the American Musicological Society*, XVIII/3 (Fall,1965), 313–58.

12. Eva and Paul Badura-Skoda, *Interpreting Mozart on the Keyboard*, trans. Leo Black (London, 1962).

performance of Mozart an appoggiatura is inserted in a particular context in one passage but omitted in another passage in which the context is exactly analogous.

An immense amount of work remains to be done on musical sources from the nineteenth century. Most of the Beethoven sketchbooks have scarcely been touched. We are not even sure how many sketchbooks exist at present—according to the last count, there appear to be about fifty. Of these, only a handful have been transcribed.[13] While they have been used often by Beethoven scholars such as Nottebohm as sources of information on style and text-critical problems, they still await analysis in depth with regard to the light they can throw on Beethoven's creative process, a subject treated in a limited fashion in Paul Mies's excellent *Die Bedeutung der Skizzen Beethovens zur Erkenntnis seines Stiles.*[14] To give other examples from this "forgotten" century: quantities of complete but unpublished works of Mendelssohn are extant in the Staatsbibliothek in East Berlin.[15]

With regard to a composer as comparatively recent as Wagner we are not precisely certain as to what he had in mind when he conceived what we have come to call the Wagner tuba—a fact that has been brought to light by some recent, unpublished research by Professor Martin Bernstein.

In our own country, as mentioned earlier, O. G. Sonneck put the subject of early American music up to 1800 on a firm musicological foundation. Since his day, some excellent research has been done on individual developments after 1800, but no extensive survey for this later period has yet appeared that is similar to Sonneck's in depth.

Mention must be made of the recent rise of a whole store of new musical resources with the development of electronic music. What problems for the scholar are implicit in the electronic medium cannot as yet be formulated comprehensively. But it is clear that this new medium, together with the techniques created for its manipulation, is giving rise to a new musical style with which the scholar must come to terms. And the possibilities for acoustically oriented research are many. The revolution in research techniques brought about by the development of modern data-

13. Joseph Schmidt-Görg, *Beethoven. Ein Skizzenbuch aus dem Jahren 1819–20* (Bonn, 1952); Dagmar Weise, *Beethoven—ein Skizzenbuch zur Chorfantasie Op. 80 und zu anderen Werken* (Bonn, 1957); id., *Ludwig van Beethoven: ein Skizzenbuch zur Pastoralsymphonie Op. 68 und zu den Trios Op. 70, 1 und 2* (Bonn, 1961); N. L. Fishman, ed., *Kniga eskizov Beethoven za 1802–1803 gody*, 3 vols. (Moscow, 1962); Karl L. Mikuliez, ed., *Ein Notierungsbuch von Beethoven aus dem Besitz der preussischen Staatsbibliothek zu Berlin* (Leipzig, 1927); Gustav Nottebohm, *Zwei Skizzenbücher von Beethoven aus dem Jahren 1801 bis 1803*, ed. Paul Mies (Leipzig, 1924); Joseph Kerman, ed., *Ludwig van Beethoven: Autograph Miscellany from ca. 1786–1799. British Museum Additional Manuscript 29801: ff. 39–162. The "Kafka Sketchbook,"* 2 vols. (London, 1971).

14. Paul Mies, *Die Bedeutung der Skizzen Beethovens zur Erkenntnis seines Stiles* (Leipzig, 1925).

15. *Leipziger Ausgabe der Werke Felix Mendelssohn Bartholdys*, ed. Internationalen Felix-Mendelssohn-Gesellschaft (Leipzig, 1960–).

processing equipment and of computer technology is beginning to make itself felt in an important way. The significance of the computer for work in the new electronic media as well as problems connected with traditional music cannot be overstressed. It will aid greatly in filling in the lacunae before us and may well open up new and hitherto unsuspected areas of inquiry.

This hodgepodge list of lacunae suggests the extent of the enormous task still facing the musicologist in working within his chosen discipline. The solution of such problems is his proper pursuit and must take prece-dence over other activities in the field of music that are connected with that discipline. But the rather aloof attitude occasionally adopted by and attributed to the musicologist is, I believe, something that will have to be modified in the future. It should be possible for the scholar to work with his colleagues from the other branches of music without neglecting his primary tasks or compromising his own standards. There is much evidence to show that his cooperation has been increasingly sought in recent years.

In 1957 a remarkable monograph was published by Manfred Bukofzer, *The Place of Musicology in American Institutions of Higher Learning*.[16] Many of his ideas have, in the short span of eleven years, become such current coin that a reader encountering the essay for the first time today may well fail to understand why it made such a strong impression when it first appeared. In a way, this is in itself a tribute to Bukofzer's keen fore-sight. He held, and rightly, that the university graduate school, with its emphasis on musicology, and the conservatory, with its emphasis on composition and performance, play roles that are not necessarily antagonistic, but *are* distinct. The great, richly endowed conservatories, such as Juilliard in New York, and Curtis in Philadelphia, continue to flourish. But it is a plain fact that many conservatories are losing their independence; universities are providing havens for so-called "Schools of Music"—that is, for conservatories. Thus, we increasingly find on the American scene a situation in which a body of musicologically oriented faculty and students and a body of faculty and students dedicated to performance are thrown together under the same roof. Peaceful co-existence between these schools and the more musicologically oriented departments may not always be easy to achieve. But the fact is that the practical and the scholarly branches of music are going to be thrown together more and more, and some form of cooperation between them must be achieved. And, if safeguards are adopted, there is no reason why this cooperation should not be workable, and even beneficial.

Not so long ago, as we all know, many professional musicians and music

16. Manfred Bukofzer, *The Place of Musicology in American Institutions of Higher Learning* (New York, 1957), a contribution to a series sponsored by the American Council of Learned Societies.

students tended to look down upon musicologists as pedants far removed from the mainstream of musical activity and too much concerned with words. Reciprocally, musicologists tended to be suspicious of the intellectual powers of the performers. It would be too optimistic to claim that these attitudes no longer exist at all. But there has been some drawing together. I was gratified to observe this at Juilliard during a class conducted recently in a course for students working for the Doctor of Musical Arts. I was explaining to the students what goes into the making of a fine, scholarly edition—among other things, the tracking down and comparing of sources. They listened with unmistakable interest when I gave them some examples of how a table of variants is drawn up. Trying to wind up the session, I stressed how useful it might be to them as performers to know about the variant readings of some particular passage and added that they could always go to a musicologist friend and ask him to read a table of variants for them. They did not like this at all and asked, "Why can't *we* learn to read a *Revisionsbericht* for ourselves?" Naturally I was delighted by this reaction and tried to satisfy their wishes.

There is no need to maintain a strict dichotomy between performer and scholar. Certainly I have not been trying at Juilliard to make musicologists out of pianists, violinists, and composers, but rather, within the framework of a music-literature course, to let them have a clearer idea of what musicology is and why it should be of interest to them for cultural and even for practical reasons. This year I have asked my Juilliard students to read Arthur Mendel's article, "The Service of Musicology to the Practical Musician."[17] We need more bridges between the practical and scholarly sides of music. These bridges are being built on the American university scene. To quote Denis Stevens: "To most European observers, such an arrangement is hair-raising and heretical. Yet when they observe from a closer vantage point and for a reasonable period of time, they generally admit that the system works much better than seemed possible."[18]

At the risk of seeming repetitious, I should like to say that increasing the ties between conservatories and departments of musicology need have, to my way of thinking, nothing to do with any attempt to water down musical scholarship. The closer ties should, rather, result in greater service rendered by musicology and increasing recognition received by it.

The situation is somewhat similar in connection with a field that has, with, I am afraid, sufficient justification, been a bugaboo to many musicologists in the past. I refer to the field of music education. In this regard I shall refer, in the main, to only two events. One is the appearance of the Fall-Winter, 1966, issue of *Current Musicology*, in which there are no

17. Arthur Mendel, "The Services of Musicology to the Practical Musician," in *Some Aspects of Musicology* (New York, 1957), pp. 1–18.

18. Denis Stevens, review of *Musicology* by Harrison, Palisca, and Hood, *Musical Times*, CV (Feb., 1964), 112.

fewer than six articles dealing with the relationship of musicology and music education.[19] The mere existence of these papers, including contributions by such respected colleagues as Claude Palisca, Barry Brook, and Frank D'Andrea, shows that at least some educators are ready to enlist the help of the musicologist and that at least some musicologists are willing to give that help.

The other event is the institution of the Yale Seminar on Music Education by Professor Palisca in 1963. This seminar, an extended meeting of leading figures from various fields of music, is a fine example of the sharing of insights and specialized knowledge by scholars and educators. An outgrowth of this seminar is the Juilliard Project, designed to assemble and edit simple music of the finest quality and make it available in the teaching of pupils in the elementary grades in our schools. In this project, such men as Paul Henry Lang and Professor Palisca have participated together with performers, composers, and educators in a common program of action. The music prepared through this project has not yet been published [1969], and it is too soon, therefore, to know what effect its availability may have. But such a project clearly indicates that the American musicologist of the future is almost certain to be called upon more frequently than were his predecessors to contribute his skills and knowledge to work lying outside the field that is most essentially his own.

From time to time I alluded in passing to the problem of maintaining standards of excellence, above all in our universities. In 1955 the Committee on Graduate Standards of the American Musicological Society published a report in the society's *Journal*. Recommendations were made regarding the nature of the training of the student, training not only in music and musicology but also in ancillary fields such as history, a subject in which those of us who teach have often found the student to be lamentably uninformed. But no effort was made to induce our institutions of higher learning to adopt these guidelines. With the great increase in the number of graduate students in recent years and the expansion of the activities of musicologists, the problem has become more acute, as Professor Brook points out in his review of the question, "On Graduate Study and Standards in Musicology." Not insignificantly, this article appeared among the papers on musicology and music education mentioned earlier. Can we, or should we, impose a set of standards on our university graduate schools, perhaps by a system of accreditation? As Professor Brook

19. Austin Clarkson, "Introduction: Music Literacy and the Teaching of Music in School, College, and University," *Current Musicology*, II (1966), 129–35; Alexander L. Ringer, "Musicology and the Future of Music Education," *ibid.*, 136–39; Frederick D. Mayer and Jack Sacher, "Toward a Rapprochement of Musicology and Music Education: Some Practical Considerations," *ibid.*, 140–44; Claude V. Palisca, "The Challenge of Educational Reform," *ibid.*, 145–50; Frank D'Andrea, "Music Education Needs Musicology," *ibid.*, 151–55; Barry S. Brook, "On Graduate Study and Standards in Musicology," *ibid.*, 156–60.

points out, there is need for, and room for, much debate before the whole question of standards can be resolved. At the very least, the question should be aired from time to time. That in itself might be enough to encourage the maintenance of a high academic level.

It must be apparent from all of the foregoing remarks that there is much work to occupy the musicologist's attention both inside and outside his immediate field. Musicology is currently in a fortunate position, considering the tremendous influx of graduate students attracted to musical scholarship. While I occasionally wonder how much expansion within our discipline there can ultimately be, there is certainly at present and is going to be in the foreseeable future—assuming, of course, that our world remains intact—ample opportunity academically and economically for young scholars. Indeed, many of us who are called upon to recommend such scholars can testify to the fact that the number of openings available often exceeds the supply [1969]. Therefore, if CUNY is entering a field within which there will be keen competition from well-established departments, it can do so with the confidence that its graduates will be able to join a flourishing academic community. Considering its faculty, its position within a great university complex, and the facilities of a great metropolis that are at its disposal, we may be confident that the graduate department in music and musicology at CUNY will quickly find its own style and make a major contribution to the fields of music and musical scholarship. If some of the 23,000 oracle bones mentioned earlier were available for consultation here today, I am sure that they would predict a brilliant future for the newly instituted doctoral program at CUNY.

Musical Scholarship Today

FRIEDRICH BLUME

MUSICAL scholarship, in the broadest sense of the phrase, is the sum total of all research in and knowledge of music. This would appear to be a simple definition. But it is not. Recent controversies have shown that there is no generally accepted definition. Even if we assume that the words "research" and "knowledge" have the same meaning for all of us (which is probably not true), there remains the one great undefined factor: music. If we could agree on what we mean by music we could more easily agree on what we mean by musical scholarship.

For my present audience I need not explain why the term music defies definition. Music consists of sounds but is not identical with the sounds. The ways in which sounds combine, successively or simultaneously, consonantly or dissonantly, their colors, and their progressions are manifold. The material of sounds offered by nature needs screening and limiting and only this screened and limited material fits our concept of music. This is what may be called the physical basis of music, a real basis, for music cannot be thought of without this material. It is what canvas and paint are to the painter; it is what language, with all its nuances, its fluctuations, and inflections, is to the writer. And just as canvas and paint are not the picture and the language is not the poetry, so the sounds with all their parameters are not the music but only the substance through which music may materialize.

Although music is embodied in physical sound, it rests on a spiritual basis. The two spheres are inseparably interwoven into a single entity.

15

The scholar, therefore, has the choice between two approaches to music. He may set out from the physical substance and explore the sounds and their organization, or he may set out from the mental processes of shaping this substance. But neither of the two ways of access can afford to disregard the other, because the two spheres are indissolubly fused. If, on the one hand, music cannot exist without the sounding material (with all its transformations and transfigurations), it cannot, on the other hand, exist without the human mind (with all its power of self-assertion and self-reliance). Permit me a variation on a well-known dictum: shaping power without sounding substance is empty; sounding substance without shaping power is blind.

This is the crux of all problems of musical scholarship. The Janus-headed nature of music is inherent in the art. The ancient Greeks knew this and so did the Romans and all later theorists. The definitions of Ptolemy and Aristides Quintilianus mirror the abyss that separates the two approaches to music in the Hellenistic epoch and in succeeding eras. The well-known definition of St. Augustine—"musica est scientia bene modulandi"—is copied from Aristides, and the one by Boethius—"musica est facultas differentias acutorum et gravium sonorum sensu ac ratione perpendens"—rests on Ptolemy. The latter emphasizes that the attributes of the sounds ought to be distinguished and perceived by the senses *and* by reason. The conflicting views have been handed down all through the Middle Ages into the Age of Humanism and the Enlightenment. The gulf between the two approaches is a fundamental fact of "Musical Scholarship Today."

Since I have the honor of talking to you on this subject, I feel bound to explain at the outset that I feel unable to cope with the physical aspect of musicology. I am an historian. My business is the world of music as represented in works of art, or, I may say, my business is the human mind as represented in the music it has created. Present musicology is, to a wide extent, the knowledge of this world of music. It is, by tradition, primarily a branch of history—"eine geisteswissenschaftliche Disziplin" as we say in German, which by no means implies any deprecation of the scientific approach. As I mentioned before, the two approaches are closely interwoven with each other. But each has developed into a vast separate field with its own aims and methods, and it is obviously impossible today for one person to command both of them. So you will understand and, I hope, will pardon me for restricting myself to the field of history where I feel at home and for not talking on matters I know only secondhand.

Musicology, in this sense of the word, means knowledge of and research in the field of empirical music, no matter how far we may extend our concept of "music." It embraces all fields of musical activity in all periods of history and all peoples and nations. Our present knowledge begins with Chinese, Sumerian, and Egyptian music of several thousand years B.C. and ends, at least theoretically, with the music of our present day as far as it is possible to consider the music of one's own period from an historical point of view. It comprises the world of monophonic and polyphonic music, from simple African chants to the highly stylized tunes of Japanese Noh singers or the melodic intricacies of Arabian soloists. It comprises orchestral music from the Indonesian gamelan and the Japanese gagaku to the orchestra of Richard Strauss and Gustav Mahler. It comprises primitive canon and parallel heterophony as well as the sophistications of Jan Ockeghem or J. S. Bach. The world of musical works of art is immense; the techniques and styles of music are of an overwhelming variety. It goes without saying that the history of music itself is closely connected to the history of the knowledge of music. An enormous bulk of writing on music and musicians, on theory and esthetics has been handed down to us. Together with the music itself, this is a formidable mass of historical sources that we possess today. It would be good to emphasize at the outset that knowledge of the single sections of this vast heritage is today highly specialized. When I was young, we could fancy it possible to reach in due time a certain command of the whole territory, or at least something like a tolerable survey. In the present state of scholarship in music history it is hardly possible to be up to date in more than a few tiny areas.

The beginner in the study of historical musicology should make his start with two fields of fundamental learning: with music and with languages. When I say "with music," this seems to be a truism. But it is not. In my long career as a professor of musicology I have learned that a good many students lack this basis. They confuse "reading musicology" with "learning music." The consequence is that they find themselves unexpectedly involved in the questions of medieval modes before having a command of harmony, or entangled in the niceties of the *chiavette* before ever having learned how to read normal clefs. First of all it is, in my view, absolutely essential that a beginner in musicology have a fairly ample knowledge of the music existing in a certain field and that he be able to sing or play this music. It is not too important whether the chosen field is the music of the Netherlanders of the fifteenth century or the music of German Romanticism or Italian Baroque. For obvious reasons, it is desirable and useful to know the literature of music from Haydn to Brahms in any case. But whatever field he may choose, it is indispensable that the beginning student of musicology have a thorough knowledge of the music in his chosen field. It is of paramount importance for him to have a firm basis in one field, because this assures a standard by which to measure all other music he may come to know in the course of his studies. The one sort of music he knows and loves and of which he has a well-founded concept will serve him as a key to others. I have often observed that students who lack this firm basis and who have no inner connection with any sort of music at all never achieve an understanding for the more uncom-

mon and more distant kinds of music. Time and again I have told my own
students that anyone who lacks this firm basis is likely to be one of those
wretched musicologists who can describe in detail the construction of a
Machaut motet or analyze the serial structure of a twelve-tone piece, but
have never experienced the meaning of any music.

The young student must be amply acquainted with the field he has
chosen and must be able to play or sing the compositions. Nobody will
expect him to play the Tchaikovsky Violin Concerto like Jascha Heifetz
or sing Figaro's "Non più andrai" like Renato Capecchi. But he must be
able to recreate the music he has chosen as best he may, as his basis, and he
cannot do without some experience in ensemble performance, in choral
singing, chamber music, and so on. If he lacks this practical experience he
will later be one of those narrow-minded pedants who are unable to look
beyond their writing desks. And I assure you from a long experience that
they are a poor lot. Close contact with the world of practical music is one
of the fundamental requirements for all study in the history of music.

Close contact with the practice of music includes solid knowledge of
the elements of music (*solfège*, *Elementarlehre*), of harmony, of thor-
oughbass (is it not humiliating if a man who has taken his Ph.D. in musicology proves unable to improvise an accompaniment over a thorough-
bass?), and of at least the basic types of counterpoint. Some of this may be
learned in undergraduate college training, and so may clef reading, score
reading, score playing, and so on. But every student should understand
clearly and unequivocally that it is sheer nonsense to set out on a study of
the history of music unless these foundations have been laid. I have no
desire to become involved in questions of the training of present-day
American students who are (I am convinced) all solid practical musicians.
With respect to German students, however, I feel bound to take a strong
stand on this subject.

Second only to the knowledge of music is the command of languages.
There are not many fields of academic studies where knowledge of languages is as indispensable as in musicology. I will pass over the Slavic or
the Asiatic or African languages, which may be regarded as a matter for
specialized studies, and I will leave aside Greek and Spanish, desirable as
they may be. But in any case at least five languages are indispensable to
the student of the history of Western music—that is, Latin, English,
French, Italian, and German.

Latin is the language of writers on music, from the Middle Ages right
down into the seventeenth and eighteenth centuries. Almost 90 per cent of
all composed music from time immemorial down into the age of Humanism, and perhaps 50 per cent of all composed music from the fifteenth to
the eighteenth century, rests on Latin texts. I have often told my students
that a musicologist without at least a tolerable command of Latin is out of
place and had better change his craft. I recently had the opportunity of

attending a seminar in a German university where excerpts were read from fifteenth-century writings: the professor was a distinguished man, his assistants were well versed in the language, and his students were nice fellows, but their Latin was poor and I doubt if more than a few of them were able to follow the class.

In musicology English is, of course, as fundamental as it is in any other field of learning, and it has indisputably become one of the primary modern languages in our discipline. I am sure that most young students today are aware of this fact, but I know quite a number of middle-aged and even younger musicologists from various countries, some even in outstanding positions, whose English does not permit them to keep up to date with current literature or to participate in international discussions.

French is required primarily for historical reasons. The importance of French vocal music, especially French opera from the seventeenth century on, requires sufficient command of the language, and the ample French literature on music from Mersenne and Rameau on into the twentieth century peremptorily demands perfect understanding.

Italian does not (at least in Europe) belong to the normal curriculum of high schools and is, therefore, often neglected. But what is musicology without the Italian language? Italian lyric poetry from Petrarch to Tasso and Marini, Italian opera and oratorio libretti from Rinuccini and Chiabrera down to Arrigo Boito, Luigi Illica, Luigi Pirandello, and Luigi Dallapiccola are the background to one of the most important areas in the whole history of music, and Italian theorists writing in their mother tongue, from Pietro Aron and Giovanni Maria Lanfranco right into our own days, have provided the most valuable contributions to musical scholarship. I know by experience that many middle-aged and younger musicologists do not really know Italian. But this means that they have no access to the immense fields of frottola, lauda, or madrigal, no understanding of the huge complex of Italian opera over almost four centuries: in a word, to the student of the history of music this is plainly impossible.

Finally, with regard to my own language, I do not, of course, want to advance any exaggerated arguments for learning German. But I must admit I hardly see how any reasonable study of musicology can be imagined without it. Even if we leave aside seventeenth- or eighteenth-century German opera or church cantata or the vast field of the German lied of the Renaissance and the Baroque eras, even if we leave all medieval German or the history of Protestant church music to the specialists, there remains the great era of Romantic lied and opera from Schubert and Weber to Hugo Wolf and Richard Strauss. And it should not be forgotten that in the period beginning with August Wilhelm Ambros, Friedrich Chrysander, and Philipp Spitta, and far into the twentieth century, Germany was the cradle of modern musicology and that it still maintains a remarkable standard of scholarship alongside the United States, although, in my view, your country has overtaken us in the last two decades. Nevertheless, the standard German literature on the history of music will remain indispensable for some time to come. This means that German must be added as the fifth language to the above-mentioned four.

Well, let us assume that our young student, well equipped with experience in musical practice and sufficient knowledge of languages, sets out to train in the history of music and to become a scholar himself some day. The first serious hurdle he meets usually is bibliography. No sooner does he set foot in a library than he is confronted with awe-inspiring masses of works on music of all kinds and periods and with still more intimidating masses of music. At first he feels entangled in a labyrinth. But he will soon learn that bibliography has long been and today more than ever is a major field of scholarly work. Music bibliography has made considerable progress in recent decades. Catalogues of libraries, archives, and other collections have been compiled; publishers' catalogues, inventories of different kinds of music have been published, some primarily for practical use, some with the heavy weight of an ample scholarly apparatus (one of the most remarkable I know is of American origin—Howard Mayer Brown's *Instrumental Music Printed before 1600: A Bibliography*. The International Musicological Society and the International Association of Music Libraries are jointly wrestling with the largest project in existence: the *Répertoire International des Sources Musicales* (RISM). This aims at cataloguing the sources of music and writings on music, printed and manuscript, all over the world, from ancient times up to 1800, in two voluminous series—one listing the sources alphabetically under the names of authors (in some fifteen to twenty volumes), the other listing the sources in particular fields, such as Gregorian chant, medieval polyphony, or printed theorists, etc. (also in fifteen to twenty volumes). Of this latter series, nine volumes have so far appeared or are in press. An amazing number of specialists are working in about forty countries and trying to give us as complete a picture as possible of all sources of music or musical writings that have been preserved over the entire world through the long history of music.

The abundance of bibliographies in existence, including RISM, is a considerable relief to all students of the history of music. These bibliographies smooth the way toward the sources of any music or any older writings a scholar may look for, provided he does not surpass the borderline of the year 1800. I have often been asked why we did not enlarge the scope of RISM into the nineteenth century where, so far, bibliography is in an almost desperate situation. The obvious reason is that amplifying the field even for a mere three decades (say, until the death of Beethoven) would mean doubling the amount of time, work, money, and personnel we require for the completion of the entire RISM project up to 1800. RISM has its circumscribed field, and a bibliography of the sources of music and musical writings in the nineteenth or twentieth century must be left to our grandsons.

A less satisfactory situation obtains, to date, in the bibliography of music since 1800: in the current listing of modern music and the cataloguing of re-editions of old music within, say, the last eighty or one hundred years, including current and cumulative listing of current publications. As a special case we may add the bibliography of modern photographic reprints of all sorts of out-of-print sources of all periods. Our young student will soon find himself at a loss if he tries to trace an article or a book on a given subject published in, say, 1963, or to get hold of a modern edition, published in 1912, of some Baroque trio sonatas, or to make sure whether a reprint exists of Artusi's *Discorso secondo* of 1608. Whether he happens to find a library able to give him the information he needs or whether some journal or special catalogue contains what he is looking for is largely a matter of luck.

As to the current listing of literature on music, the situation is not at all unfavorable. We had the older current bibliographies in the *Peters-Jahrbücher*, and the *Verzeichnis des musikalischen Schrifttums* by Kurt Taut, later continued by Wolfgang Schmieder. They are not complete but give a reasonable survey from the early years of our century up to 1960. But there we come to a dead end. It is true that Schmieder's *Verzeichnis* is being continued, but it lags far behind. The large new project, outlined and directed by Professor Barry S. Brook of the City University of New York, the *International Repertory of Music Literature* (RILM), begun in 1967, covers all significant current literature and has developed far-reaching plans. We all wish Professor Brook a successful continuation of this important project. It should prove an invaluable aid to all sorts of musicological research, which, without a current bibliography of the literature, will soon find itself in a jungle.

Much less encouraging are the prospects for a bibliography of re-editions of old music. This is a vast field, much more extended and complicated than any outsider might expect. Some years ago the International Musicological Society started preparations for such a project but the difficulties proved insurmountable. Since the field of re-editions of old music today is a complete muddle, a bibliography would seem to be an urgent challenge to musicologists of the years to come. In my view at least, it is ridiculous that although for many decades we have had a flourishing industry of re-editions in many countries, the musicologist who wants to find out what actually exists is like the knight errant, condemned to roam about for the rest of his days in search of the adventure of meeting the specter of this or that early re-edition.

The truth is that bibliography has long been neglected in music. There remains much to do. The soil is better prepared now than it was some twenty or fifty years ago. An immense amount of preparatory work has been done. International cooperation has been secured, at least to a considerable degree. Nevertheless, even today, when it comes to particular fields, the student of the history of music finds himself forsaken. Thus when he begins to study the music of earlier periods and to use the re-editions, the so-called *Denkmäler-Ausgaben*, the *Gesamtausgaben*, etc., he will find himself in fresh trouble. First, he will realize that most important fields in the history of music are by no means as well covered by re-editions as he would have expected; and second, he will discover that the methods of transcription and editing vary among the nations, among the kinds of music, among editors, etc., in a confusing way.

Moreover, no old music, whatever the period, can be performed as it is written or printed in the sources, but always requires transcription by the scholar. The musicians of ancient times did not do us the favor of writing music the same way. Many different notations were used; even in more recent times, say in the eighteenth century, when notation approached our present style, instrumental scores were very rare and we are compelled to make scores from parts before we can read the work. This problem is augmented by the fact that, for example, in older periods the matching of the words to the notes was not specified as exactly as we do today, and by hundreds of smaller details.

But the most unpleasant hurdle is the fact that editors, regardless of nationality, seem unable to establish conventions on the methods of transcribing and reprinting. I have been a musicologist now for approximately fifty years, and throughout my whole life I have experienced these controversies over methods, controversies that are fundamentally irrelevant and out of place. Any scholar who has been responsible for many editions knows that no modern editorial practice, however refined it may be, does complete justice to older notation; and, of course, the older the music, the greater the problem. It is mere fancy to believe that even comparatively recent music, such as Haydn or Bach, can be rendered with perfect adequacy in modern notation without distorting the music and affecting the spontaneity of its performance. Transcription always requires compromise, and it is about the extent and the mode and the admissibility of compromise that editors cannot come to terms with each other. The result is, for the transcriber, that even editions of music of closely related fields and composers apply different methods of transcription and, for the reader and performer, a confusing motley of methods, where uniformity would easily be possible and would much better serve the purpose. I have always been unable to understand why the editors of the present *Gesamtausgaben* of the works of Bach, Handel, Mozart, and Beethoven found it impossible to apply the same editorial rules to all of them. There is a comparative edition of these rules, recently published by the German Gesellschaft für Musikforschung; when you look it up you will see that everybody tills his own soil in his own way.

Another difficulty our young student will meet is that although some fields in the history of music are well covered by re-editions, by the national *Denkmäler*, by *Gesamtausgaben*, etc., and by a host of special series or single editions, other very important fields are very sparsely served, as for example, seventeenth- and eighteenth-century opera, church music of the same era of all denominations, early symphony, early string quartet, early solo lied, etc. We are in sore need of the works of such composers as Caldara and Conti, Campra and Destouches, Theile and Förtsch. We wait eagerly for modern editions of printed music of five centuries and countless music manuscripts of all ages. We will certainly not disregard what musicologists have achieved in the realm of editions in recent decades; I am full of admiration of what many of them have done. But I find myself unable to understand why it should be more important to publish the hundredth or two-hundredth edition of the *Well-Tempered Clavier* or the fiftieth *Don Giovanni* than all those important works in the history of music which are as inaccessible to the student today as they were when I began to study the history of music with Hugo Riemann and Johannes Wolf. It is not the fault of the single scholar; it is the fault of the present school of thought, which is on the wrong track and causes editing to miss its primary aim, which should be to unearth and to make accessible as much as possible the important music of the past.

Here we land on controversial ground. The present trend in editing old music aims at concentrating on the few well-known "great masters" and at the most sophisticated methods of source criticism and source interpretation. Historical tradition is in the foreground of interest. The sources and the tradition sometimes seem to be more interesting than the work in question. This might be all right if this attitude did not devour manpower, time, and financial means to a degree that ruins the rest. And "the rest" means the overwhelming number of important composers between and around the so-called "great masters." Many an important project cannot make headway because energy and means are pre-empted by what is, in the scholarly sense, of minor importance. (This may be less true of the state of affairs in the United States than in Germany.) The attitude is closely connected with the predominance of philological thinking in present musicology. The philological processes have been brought to the utmost degree of perfection. They lay claim to the prevailing activity of the scholar, and this is the reason why the business of editing old music today requires so much manpower, time, and money. We have seen many a fine result of modern editing in the last fifteen or twenty years. Nevertheless I say again that we are on the wrong track with this trend: first, because musical scholars should be far more interested in editing unknown works and little-known masters than in the endless repetition of the well known; and second, because philological methods have reached a bias toward superperfection as an end in itself, which is fundamentally worthless. Thorough study of the sources of our musical heritage is necessary; nobody will doubt it. But when it becomes an end in itself, "philologism" blocks progress and diverts us from what is really worthwhile.

The student will soon be aware of these facts. He will probably try to avoid the traps and to find his own way into historical research. He will look for a topic on which he can settle but will soon be puzzled when he realizes that the majority of historians are concentrating on a few fields of investigation while large areas are scarcely cultivated or almost deserted. There are fashions in the study of all branches of history. In music history, the polyphony of the Middle Ages, organum, discantus, motet, and the various forms of secular music are as familiar a playground of scholarly competition as are seventeenth-century early monody or opera, while neighboring fields like the German lied or instrumental music of the same period are neglected. There are, of course, at all times distinguished scholars in other areas. But in some fields, there is mass competition and, consequently, a high degree of specialization, while certain areas are disregarded for decades. The number of highly specialized writings on Bach or Mozart appearing at any given time is immense, whereas we find no more than a handful of studies on some of the most urgent and attractive problems rising in the areas surrounding these two masters. Here we meet with a state of affairs similar to the one in the field of music editions: every button on Bach's waistcoat has been described, and we know the most irrelevant facts and persons in Mozart's environment, down to the charwoman who polished his staircase and the copyist who happened to write the second-oboe part in a symphony. But when it comes to, say, the pupils of Bach or the church composers around Mozart, not only do we lack editions of their music, but in many cases we have neither catalogues of their works nor even the most elementary biographical data about them.

If I may mention a practical experience of my own: there are more than a thousand musicians listed in Eitner's *Quellenlexikon* with a few compositions and a few dates, musicians who in their days apparently enjoyed a certain reputation, but whom I have been unable to include in MGG because as a rule nobody has taken the pains to work on them. Of their lives and works and activities, we know no more than Eitner knew seventy years ago—and in many cases even less, because Eitner's sources have meanwhile disappeared. This holds good for musicians of the fifteenth and sixteenth centuries and far into the eighteenth and nineteenth, which are the worst of all.

In musical scholarship, the nineteenth century has long been the Cinderella, an unrecognized area on the historical map, and only in recent years have scholars set out to explore this "dark continent." Fundamental results have been reached and published by eminent young scholars in the German series *Studien zur Musikgeschichte des 19. Jahrhunderts*, a large-scale project, twelve volumes of which have appeared and another twenty or thirty are expected. This seems to me a model of how neglected areas of music history should be tackled. Similar projects should be developed for similar areas, and young scholars should be guided to settle on one of them, singly or in teams. Every scholar tends to find areas and problems that suit his personal taste and ability. Nobody should interfere with this individual choice of subjects; but individualization should be guided toward systematic exploration of the important neglected areas. It is sometimes pitiful to observe how highly motivated young scholars are induced to concentrate on less and less pertinent details in a field which has been plowed again and again. Here the state of affairs is similar to the situation in the area of re-editions: you can easily fill a large bookshelf with writings on the *Well-Tempered Clavier*, you can fill libraries with the literature on Richard Wagner, but when you look for information on Ignaz Pleyel's piano trios or on Anton Reicha's keyboard fugues, you are at a loss. It is my strong conviction that young music scholars should rather investigate the backgrounds of the few great masters, the "Zwischen- und Vorformen," as Guido Adler called them—the music between and before that of the great masters. Research of this kind has become indispensable for well-grounded surveys in many an important field. I certainly do not underrate the work of industrious scholars in cutting paths through these large thickets. But in many areas of history the number of existing sources is far from exhausted. Compared to the vast quantity of, say, Italian operas and oratorios of the seventeenth and eighteenth centuries, the extent of our knowledge is slight. Compared to the huge mass of Italian madrigals of the sixteenth and seventeenth centuries, the amount of research is still tiny. In view of the great number of early Classical symphonies, present knowledge of the field is hardly more than a first approach. And there are dozens of such large fields that need investigation.

On the other hand, there are, of course, outstanding examples of well-explored fields. William S. Newman's *History of the Sonata Idea* and Ludwig Finscher's work on the string quartet, for example, are models in that they combine an extended knowledge of the "Zwischen- und Vorformen" with research on great masters. But we have to admit that in large areas of history too many details are still lacking, even though we have countless scattered facts in hand. We look in vain for the scholars who have the courage to integrate the facts and the details with our present understanding of great figures in order to produce a comprehensive picture of a given field.

Here we reach an important characteristic of present music scholarship: the striking shortage of comprehensive works on great persons or important subjects. I would guess that at least 80 per cent of all writings on music appearing in the present time are essays published in special journals and dealing with more or less specialized questions. Of the remaining 20 per cent, by far the majority are small booklets or pamphlets, which likewise have to do with some special aspect of a given field or simply are popular writings. Comprehensive books on major subjects—which are both learned and readable—Paul Henry Lang's *George Frideric Handel* or Eric Werner's *Mendelssohn*, for example—are outstanding models, but rarities. In the endless array of new titles listed in every number of *Notes*, you will find hundreds of titles concerning specialized subjects or questions of sophisticated erudition but only in exceptional cases a book or an article on a major subject of general interest. The great era of the musical biography seems to be over, and so, too, the era of the comprehensive histories of music, whether in universal descriptions or according to nations or periods. The Norton History of Music (begun in 1943), which contains the eminent volumes of Gustave Reese and Manfred Bukofzer, is not yet complete. The *New Oxford History of Music* (begun in 1954) makes slow headway. Large-scale attempts at histories of the single forms or genres of music (such as Hermann Kretzschmar's seventy-year-old series *Kleine Handbücher nach Gattungen*) seem today quite unimaginable. The sum total of research into the history of music has multiplied during these last fifty years, the amount of knowledge has remarkably increased; but the results have accumulated in impenetrable masses of tiny fragments. The vast field of "Musical Scholarship Today" looks like a bombed area, and it is extremely difficult, not only for the layman, but for the scholar as well, to find one's way through the rubble. The reason is obvious: the enormous amount of knowledge acquired within the last decades makes scholars cautious and renders book writing a neck-breaking venture. We have lost the courage of our convictions and the courage to make errors. We dare not risk drawing conclusions from the present state of knowledge. It is my personal view that major achievements are impossible in history without such courage. Dealing only in minutiae will continue to lead to more minutiae and not to the understanding of history.

It should always be kept in mind that the starting point and the final aim of all musical scholarship should be music. This, again, sounds like a truism but is not. Hans F. Redlich put it in simple words in his Percival Lecture for 1963–64: "One of the main raisons d'être of musicology was, is and will be in the future, the recovery of great music of the past." What we most urgently need in music scholarship today, apart from the editing of great music of the past, is wider access to these works of art, without anxiety for utmost security of detail or fear of falling into philological traps. I should prefer a new readable book on the Italian Renaissance that integrates music into the wider spiritual context of the age to a dozen learned studies enumerating minute details that only provoke the next author to enumerate yet other details. I should prefer this book even if it contained a good many errors of detail. Errors can be corrected and nothing is so subject to error as outrageous perfectionism. In most cases, errors in detail do not alter a picture very much if this picture is based on broad historical insight.

We should never forget that music is not the unique domain of the musician and the musicologist. It is the cultural heritage and the common property of all men, and interest in music, fortunately, is found throughout the world. Inquiring into music and writing its history makes sense only if it helps pave the way to the understanding of music by many. Scholarship will always have its own internal problems to take care of. It will need publications not necessarily of interest or even accessible to the general public. But it seems to me a real danger of present scholarship in music that so many students lock themselves up in the "ivory towers" of their particular needs and forget that, compared to the impact of music in our social life and the role played by music in humanity, these needs are mere trifles. Musicology should always be aware of the fact that it cannot exist (or, at least, that its existence grows senseless) unless it maintains contact with the wide range of people seriously interested in music.

This, I think, is what "Musical Scholarship Today" means or should mean (leaving aside the study of the physical aspect of music): musical scholarship deals with the history of music and musicians. Its principal aim is to study and unearth music of all periods—music that is characteristic of the thought and the spirit of these periods. It is concerned not only with the "Great Masters" and with the most outstanding works of art but with vast masses of music still hidden under the debris of time. Musicology clears the path to knowledge of the techniques and forms of all music, and it tries to make its meaning understood—the meaning this music had for its contemporaries and the role it played for later ages. Historical musicology tries to establish the connection between periods and schools and between the forms and functions of music, and so tends to integrate music into the social life and the spiritual thought of an age. It is also an important task of historical musicology to compare the styles of the works of art of different ages and to convey a notion of the worth and significance of these styles to us who are born centuries later.

The continuing debate on methods of attaining these goals is necessary and valuable, no doubt; no branch of scholarly research can do without a body of tested, well-developed techniques. But questions of method should not be overrated. To edit old music is a necessity; *how* it is to be edited is a minor problem—a question of second rank. To build catalogues and bibliographies is urgent; but *how* to do it is an internal question of the craft. To disentangle paleographical complexities is essential in order to be able to read old music, but this, too, is a matter of craft. To inquire into the subsidiary details of the sources—the watermarks and the writing tools, the copyists and the handwritings—in order to restore the music to its precise shape is a useful objective, but it should not become an end in itself. The same holds true for many other branches of musicological craftsmanship.

Musicology today tends to confuse two things which should be kept strictly separate: the minutiae of the *craft* and the loftier aims of *scholarship*. "Scholarship in Music" means to restore and illumine the great music of all ages.

DISCUSSION

SCHOTT: In both Germany and the United States we have very formalistic systems of education on the university level. In the United States, particularly, we have rather sharply defined sequences of seminars and lectures in many fields and in their subdivisions. But when I look at the great examples of musicological scholarship in the past—such as the work of Eitner, Riemann, or Einstein—I have the impression that the breadth of their interests and their ability to integrate their specialties into a vast perspective were not developed through a rigidly organized curriculum. Can you identify the additional factors that enabled them to achieve such breadth and perspective?

BLUME: A prescribed sequence of lectures, seminars, or colloquia has never really existed for any humanistic field of study at German universities. I am speaking of the practice from approximately 1900 to 1960; recent "reforms" of German universities may have changed this traditional practice. Most great German musicologists of the past began as students of practical music, after which they went to the university and studied philosophy, history, art history, Germanic languages and literature, and similar subjects. Musicology as a formal field of study hardly existed at that time. The musicologists were often self-taught in the areas of music history and music theory. Some scholars, such as Jahn, Spitta, Abert, and others, came from the outside, so to speak, from other disciplines such as theology or classical philology. This explains the breadth of their interests and their capacity to integrate their musicological research into a "vast perspective." I consider it of fundamental importance that a musicologist be a well-trained practical musician, and that he combine his study of musicology with as wide a study of languages and of the other humanities as possible. I personally began with the study of medicine and then later studied other things along with music and musicology, especially the history of art and philosophy.

MISS FOSTER: In this country at least, the performer who wants to study musicology often finds it difficult to gain admission to graduate programs, although one of the stated aims of musicology is to coordinate scholarship and performance. One problem is that a performer cannot afford to spend the time required by the prescribed courses of study if he wishes to maintain the status of an expert performer. Perhaps special programs, tailored to the needs of the serious performer of older music, should be set up within our graduate musicological departments. I wonder if you have any solutions to suggest.

BLUME: Coordinating the study of practical music with graduate musicology should be easier in America than in Germany, because in the United States the training in practical music and the study of musicology are often to be found at the same university and under one roof. In Germany, practical music is studied at conservatories and professional schools, which have nothing to do with the university, while musicology is studied at the university. Thus one area of study tends to exclude the other, although the division is not as sharp as it was twenty or thirty years ago. In the universities of the United States it seems to me that it should be quite possible for the performer to train himself in both aspects of his art. You may envy us our practical musicians who study musicology; we envy you the many excellent practical musicians you have at your universities.

VAN SOLKEMA: May we turn to the problem of how the young musicologist arrives at his major field of study in musicology? In the sciences, the young scholar often finds his research direction by becoming an apprentice to an older man whose work he admires. But in musicology it is often a subject area itself that first engages the student's interest, as a result of either chance or a deliberate search. Would you tell us something about how your own students have arrived at their own fields?

BLUME: I have always been particularly happy when my students have chosen their own fields of specialization and subjects for their dissertations, particularly when they have been guided by their own favorite fields of activity or their professional activities. One of my students, who for years had been a volunteer worker at an opera house, found himself a subject in the history of opera. Another, a professional organist at one of the large churches, turned to the study of ancient organ music. A third began as a cantor at a Protestant church and subsequently developed a great interest in the polyphony of the sixteenth century. I myself have only rarely suggested a field of specialization to students, because no one ever does excellent work in a field for which he has no natural inner inclination. It is important at first to obtain a secure footing in *one* special area, to become a native, so to speak, of that area; then the breadth of musicological interests develops almost of its own accord.

BUSHLER: Professor Blume, in your lecture you mentioned certain topics that are as yet unexplored. Can you tell us why they are unexplored?

BLUME: If you have in mind the many musicians listed in Eitner's *Quel-*

lenlexikon who have not yet been investigated, research on such personalities often meets very great difficulties. This is true not only for older
epochs, but at least equally so for the nineteenth century. Biographical
records are often difficult or impossible to find. Many historical documents have been displaced or destroyed. Primary sources for the composer's works may be dispersed from Capetown to Bethlehem, Pa., and from
Leningrad to Coimbra. Long traditions frequently confuse one personality
with another and are full of false attributions of works. Contradictions
among sources frequently prove insoluble. There are countless reasons
why it has been impossible to find solutions to this or that problem up to
our day. Furthermore, there are fads in research: many areas and many
epochs have been long neglected. Until quite recently, the nineteenth century has been virtually *terra incognita* from the scholarly point of view.

BROOK: You have suggested in your lecture that we are not yet ready
for a definitive book on the Classic era. But it seems to me that an interim
book, if one could call it that, collecting and integrating our present
knowledge, would be immensely valuable for both students and scholars.
Would you agree that such a book might be feasible today, or, as your
articles in MGG imply, do you believe that the Romantic and Classic eras
should not be separated?

BLUME: I do, indeed, believe that, in the perspective of the great epochs
of music history, the Classic era cannot be separated from the Romantic
era. Classicism and Romanticism gradually developed divergences within a
common concept of style. And we still lack too much factual information
to be able to undertake a comprehensive history of the epoch. We have
many recent and excellent studies on single composers, single categories of
works, and so forth. Many of these are by American researchers. However, we still lack the perspective to write a history of so vast a mass of
musicians and works. Furthermore, if such a history is to prove satisfying,
it must present music as a reflection of the spiritual and intellectual developments of the eighteenth and nineteenth centuries. Who feels himself
adequate to such a task? All this need not prevent us from writing a book
on the development of Classic music from, say, the sons of Bach to the
young Beethoven. An interim book of this kind would doubtless be
immensely valuable. But who has the courage to risk even this much?

VAN SOLKEMA: Could you distinguish for us the styles of German,
French, English, and American musicology as you see them?

BLUME: I can certainly attest that national styles of musicology do
exist. Please believe the editor of an encyclopedia, who has worked for
twenty-five years with almost 2,000 collaborators from more than forty
nations, when he tells you that the differences are very great! The
demands of courtesy must prevent him from characterizing these individual differences. I will say that American musicology has made enormous

advances during the last ten years or so. Your scholars have been comprehensive and far-seeing in their choice of fields; they have been broad in their approach, and thorough in their methods without being narrow or pedantic; they have courageously attacked problems long in need of investigation.

Musicology at the Mirror:
A Prospectus for the History
of Musical Scholarship

VINCENT DUCKLES

W HEN a discipline begins to be concerned with its
own image in history, it may well be accused of entering an Alexandrian
Age, guilty of that excess of introspection which marked the closing years
of Hellenistic culture. Has musicology reached that point? One is tempted
to think so in view of the proliferation of works on methodology, system-
atics, theory, and historiography that have appeared in recent years. There
is a disposition to regard speculation of this kind as a "bad thing," as Leo
Treitler implies when he speaks of "a rattling of skeletons in the halls of
humane learning."[1] I am not so sure that all we hear is the sound of dry
bones. It is true that abstract thought often comes between the investigator and his essential object, which in our case is music. It is difficult
enough to justify the existence of musicology itself, which is committed
to ideas *about* art and must depend upon the alien medium of language to
convey its findings; but when we confront historiography, the history of
musicology, we seem to be involved in an endless regression from the realities of musical experience, building a chain of words about words, and so
on *ad infinitum*.

In spite of these recognized obstacles, I propose to stress some of the

1. Leo Treitler, "On Historical Criticism," *Musical Quarterly*, LIII/2 (April, 1967),
188–205.

values to be gained from the study of the history of music scholarship, and to outline a prospectus for bringing into review some of the principal areas of music-research activity that have occupied scholars in the past two hundred fifty years or so. I shall present this prospectus as a work in progress, conscious of the fact that its patterns may change as the investigation develops. But I also have another purpose in view, and that is to extend an invitation to those of you who may be attracted to the historiography of music as a field for further study. There are definite insights to be gained from subjecting our own discipline to the scrutiny of historical method. A doctor should have no qualms about taking his own medicine; no more should the historian hesitate to hold his activities up to the mirror of history. To speak of a mirror in this connection may seem a trifle misleading. A mirror presumably gives us a reflection of things as they *are*. But we are concerned here with an investigation of musicology as it *was*, or as it appears in the process of becoming what it is. In this light the mirror metaphor is apt enough if we remind ourselves that all historical investigation is conducted in the present, that the facts of history as we apprehend them are facts as of 1969, and that the historian's effort to relive the past is largely an illusion. What seems to be an antecedent phenomenon as we look back on it is actually a consequent event viewed from the platform of our present experience. The shape of music scholarship as we see it emerging in the past is the result of the state in which we find it today. We are engaged in the process that Arthur Mendel has described as "retrodiction," the interpretation of the past in the light of the present.[2] It is important, therefore, to take a close look at some of the strands that determine the pattern of music scholarship as we know it.

There are many ways of approaching the history of our discipline. One would be to take the viewpoint of the sociologist and recount the development of the institutions that support advanced study and research in music. This would involve tracing the gradual admission of music history as a legitimate field for advanced study in the university, the establishment of professorships in music, research institutes and libraries, learned societies, and scholarly publication. Another approach is allied to the history of ideas, the analysis of currents of thought, many of them shared by other disciplines, that provide the context for scholarly endeavor in music: the impact of the so-called "scientific method," of sociological method (*Geisteswissenschaft*), of esthetics, and of the philosophy of history. Still another avenue might consist in breaking down the composite structure of musicology into its constituent elements, a method adopted by Guido Adler, tracing the separate developments not only of historical studies but of theory, acoustics, esthetics, notation and paleography, analysis and crit-

2. Arthur Mendel, "Evidence and Explanation," in *Report of the Eighth Congress of the International Musicological Society, New York, 1961*, II (Kassel, 1962).

icism. Or one could adopt an approach that is essentially bibliographical (or, if you prefer, philological) and study the increasing control that has been gained over the primary source materials, the refinement of editorial techniques, the classification and evaluation of writings on music.[3] This last interest might take as its model Johann Nikolaus Forkel's *Allgemeine Literatur der Musik* (1792), which, far from being a mere bibliography of music literature, can tell us more about the state of musical learning in the late eighteenth century than any other single document of its time. Finally, the history of the discipline might be recounted through a discussion of specific "breakthroughs" in research, the illumination of selected historical problems, such as Kiesewetter's analysis of the contribution of the Netherlands composers, Winterfeld's similar treatment of the Venetians, Ludwig's analysis of the *ars antiqua* sources, the Pirro-Schweitzer discussion of the symbolic content of Bach's music, or the recent revision of the Bach chronology.

There is something to be said for each of these approaches; in fact they must all be brought into an harmonious relationship before our understanding of the whole is complete. Each represents a particular set of questions to be asked of the data. Yet there is another way of framing our inquiry that stimulates a more vivid response, at least in my own imagination. This is to place the emphasis on the scholar himself, or rather on the learned musical mind as it has functioned and changed from one age to the next. One cannot speak of musicology per se much before the beginning of the twentieth century, but one can examine musical erudition as it exists in any age or time. Expressed in these terms, the basic question is: What is the character of musical learning, and who are the individuals that best represent it? The danger in such an approach, focusing as it does on the scholar as a person, is that our narrative will be reduced to a series of biographical sketches. Obviously the investigation must go deeper than that. What the scholar is and does depends upon the role that music plays in human culture, upon the changing meanings that have accrued to the art in society.[4]

There are few constant factors in the profile of scholarship. Learning means different things in different periods of history. A scholar is defined in one respect by his attitude toward his discipline, and in another by the attitude his contemporaries take toward him. The character of scholarly repute has changed radically over the years. This leads one to the conclusion that the criteria used to define musical erudition must be fairly broad

3. See Friedrich W. Riedel, "Zur Geschichte der musikalischen Quellenüberlieferung und Quellenkunde," *Acta Musicologica*, XXXVIII (1966), 3–27.

4. Among the few studies that have been devoted to the cultural meaning of music are Kathi Meyer's *Bedeutung und Wesen der Musik. Teil I: Der Bedeutungswandel der Musik* (Strasbourg, 1932), and Hermann Pfrogner's anthology of writings on *Musik, Geschichte ihrer Deutung* (Munich, 1954).

and elastic. There was a time when all musical learning was identified with the church. In other periods the mark of the learned musician was possession of a thorough knowledge of the music of the ancients. During most of the seventeenth and eighteenth centuries a place of honor was reserved for mathematicians and specialists in the growing science of acoustics.[5] Sometimes pedagogical interests come to the fore. Rameau is a case in point. And who is to say, for example, that Leopold Mozart, Quantz, or C. P. E. Bach were not erudite musicians in view of their mastery of the performance practices of their time and their ability to organize and communicate a complex body of knowledge.

If every age has its image of the learned musician, we need not resign ourselves to complete relativism in this matter. Certain large-scale patterns can be observed that give the narrative a developmental, even evolutionary, cast. Scholarship is cumulative; it is a pyramid made up of men standing on each others' shoulders; a meaningful continuity can be traced from one achievement to the next. Likewise, there is a point in the history of European learning where the current that leads to the so-called modern age begins to move with unmistakable energy. The precise position of the divide will always be subject to dispute since we are dealing with a complex cultural phenomenon here, not unlike the identification of the beginnings of the Renaissance, the Baroque, or the Classic eras. Yet there was something new on the horizon of scholarship about the middle of the seventeenth century, the quality of which has been suggested by the historian David Knowles.

> The 17th century, or more exactly the period from about 1630 to 1730, was a golden age of scholarship. The great and absorbing theological controversies of the Reformation, in which almost all the great minds of the age had been engaged, were now near spent, and a period of relative peacefulness began; throughout Europe a generation of highly educated and civilized men, full of curiosity and appreciation of the history and writings of the distant past, was able to review the treasures, printed and unprinted, that had been assembled in the great libraries and collections of Europe. The spirit of the age, which witnessed so many triumphs of mathematical discovery and the first great advances in natural science, showed itself in the humane disciplines as an influence in the direction of criticism and analysis.[6]

Music played its part in this new humanism we call the Enlightenment, although its participation was somewhat slower than in the other arts. Mersenne and Kircher, for example, were influenced by it yet they

5. See Karl Gustav Fellerer, "Zur musikalischen Akustik im 18. Jahrhundert," in *Zum 70. Geburtstag von Joseph Müller-Blattau*, Saarbrücker Studien zur Musikwissenschaft, 1 (Kassel, 1966), pp. 80–88.

6. David Knowles, *Great Historical Enterprises* (London, 1963), p. 38.

remained scholars of an older, pre-rationalistic tradition. Their knowledge was vast but uncritical.

The modern spirit in music scholarship can be clearly recognized by the end of the seventeenth century. It manifested itself in a variety of ways, four of which I would like to select for emphasis: (1) musical learning became increasingly secular; (2) it was informed by a new sense of history; (3) it was motivated by broad didactic purposes; and (4) it modeled itself on "philological" methods. Let me expand briefly on each of these characteristics.

1. To say that scholarship became increasingly secular means more than to suggest that it became free of the controls of the church. What secularization implies is the absence of any ax to grind, freedom from commitment to anything but the pursuit of knowledge for its own sake. This is, of course, a concept that came into existence at least as early as the Renaissance, but it reached a new level of significance during the Enlightenment. In place of any single institution, church or state, to whom the scholar addressed himself or whom he represented, there grew a community of cultivated minds, a kind of cultural universe that extended across national boundaries. It was at this point that the international character of scholarship became fully recognized. The men who truly represented the Enlightenment were an entirely different breed from the tradition-oriented scholars mentioned above (Mersenne and Kircher). Men like Roger North in England or Sébastien de Brossard in France had no vested interest in any academic tradition and approached music with a lively curiosity and fresh vision. They took their cue from Descartes and were prepared to be skeptical of everything save the power of human reason to bring order out of the chaos of experience.

2. By suggesting that these rationalistic scholars were informed by a new sense of history, I do not mean to imply that the preceding eras were necessarily unhistorical or anti-historical in outlook. Their concept of history was of a different order. The men of the Enlightenment were among the first to conceive of time as an homogeneous, on-going, irreversible process. Their sense of history was governed by chronological thinking. Most of us would take this for granted, but there are implications here worth pursuing beneath the surface. As Siegfried Kracauer points out, when history is experienced as a continuous, unending flow of events, the date of any given event in the continuum is a "value-laden fact."[7] Continuity becomes equated with progress. The more remote an event is in time, the less it shares in the perfection attributed to the present. We are just beginning to become aware of the limitations of the chronological view and the degree to which our historical thinking is shaped by it.

7. Siegfried Kracauer, "Time and History," in *Zeugnisse Theodor W. Adorno zum 60. Geburtstag* (Frankfurt, 1963), pp. 50–64.

There are other ways of viewing history, and this is not the place to give them detailed consideration. I would suggest, however, that Kracauer's concept of "the manifold spaces of time" is an illuminating one. He holds that certain kinds of events, most conspicuously works of art, occupy positions in time that do not depend wholly on chronology. Works of art impose their own systems of relevance on the observer. The new and the old can exist simultaneously at any given instant. Strauss and Schoenberg, for example, were contemporaries, yet they lived in different historical worlds. However, these speculations did not concern the eighteenth-century historian. For him the idea of history as a flowing stream, gaining in significance and value as it moved, was a liberating concept, through which historical thought broke free of the static confinement of Biblical authority and myth.

3. Knowledge, for the Enlightenment, was not a commodity to be hoarded; it was intended for the free use of society. Reason was the instrument through which man could learn to control his world. Most of the learned men of the time took their teaching function very seriously. The culmination of this didactic impulse is represented by the great French *Encyclopédie*, edited by Diderot and his colleagues, which made France the center of the intellectual life of Europe for half a century. The musically informed readers to whom the *philosophes* addressed themselves were known variously as *dilettantes* or *Liebhabern*, terms referring to individuals that were definitely a cut above what we in the twentieth century refer to as the musical amateur. The members of this rapidly expanding group of cultivated men and women were ready to dispute the merits of the Italian versus the French opera, or to discuss the common esthetic features of painting, music, and poetry. In Germany they subscribed to the new journals of music criticism that issued from Berlin, Hamburg, and Leipzig: Mattheson's *Critica Musica*, Marpurg's *Historisch-kritische Beyträge*, or Hiller's *Wöchentliche Nachrichten*. In England they patronized such groups as the Madrigal Society or the Academy of Ancient Music, and added their names to the subscription list for Burney's *General History of Music*. Throughout Europe there was a growing separation between the kind of learning regarded as useful to the professional (*Fachlehre*) and that which was intended for public consumption. This did not represent a lowering of standards, but rather a liberalizing and humanizing of the approach. Charles Burney's statement in the Preface to his history is much to the point:

> My subject has been so often deformed by unskilful writers, that many readers, even among those who love and understand music, are afraid of it. My wish, therefore, is not to be approached with awe and reverence for my depth and erudition, but to bring on a familiar acquaintance with them, by

talking in common language of what has hitherto worn the face of gloom and mystery, and been too much "sicklied o'er with the pale cast of thought."

Thus did the music scholars of the Enlightenment establish a broad base of communication between themselves and the cultivated laymen, a base which in the nineteenth century could grow to support the institutional structure of modern musicology.

4. The term "philology" has two distinct meanings that are often confused. It stands for a discipline devoted to the study of language, its origins, relationships, transformations, and in this respect it leads quite naturally into what we now call the study of linguistics. But in a more general sense it implies a method of humanistic research based on a critical study of the sources. Its purpose is to organize the sources, clarify and compare them, and its outcome frequently takes the form of a critical edition or highly detailed inventory (Ludwig's *Repertorium* is one of the best examples of the latter product). As might be expected, philology, as a method, is often employed by philologists, as students of language, and many of these scholars work in areas adjacent to music history; a natural sharing of procedures is to be expected. Philological method is sometimes confused with "scientific" method. What the two have in common, however, is simply the detached, empirical approach to knowledge that is the *sine qua non* of all research activity as we know it.

The methods of philology received their definitive expression in the work of the Benedictine fathers of the Congregation of Saint Maur in Paris in the late seventeenth century. The most notable figure in this group was Dom Jean Mabillon (1632–1707), whose masterpiece, *De Re Diplomatica* (1681), established the techniques for criticizing manuscript documents of all kinds. For the next one hundred years or more, the Benedictines of Saint Maur, or Maurists as they were called, issued a succession of scholarly works in diplomatics, lexicography, liturgical history, and bibliography, which, according to David Knowles, "may well remain for centuries to come, the most impressive achievement of co-operative, or at least co-ordinated, scholarship in the modern world."[8] The Maurists did not survive the French Revolution, but the energy of their work generated a spark that leaped across the years to activate the Benedictines of Solesmes in their philological investigation of the sources of plainchant.

A long and distinguished line of source-oriented research can be traced from Mabillon to the present day. Belonging to the tradition are Migne's great series of Latin and Greek texts, *Patrologiae cursus completus*, the Dreves and Blume *Analecta hymnica*, and Chevalier's *Repertorium Hymnologicum*, all tools of more than passing utility for music scholarship. Even more direct contributions to music research are such works as Ger-

8. Knowles, *op. cit.*, p. 61.

bert's and Coussemaker's editions of medieval theory texts, Juste-Adrien-Lenoir de La Fage's *Essais de diphthérographie musicale* (1864), and, of course, the crowning accomplishments of Robert Eitner in his *Quellenlexikon* and *Monatshefte für Musikgeschichte*.

The reasons for this eighteenth- and nineteenth-century empasis on source studies are clear. Music scholarship, a late starter among the humanities, could not proceed about its essential business, the historical study of music, until it had liberated the evidence contained in countless scattered documents. This has called for much painstaking, thankless work. The philologists are still with us, and much remains for them to do. They have new devices, such as the computer, to call to their assistance. Their function, however, is to implement the final step in the research process, to serve as a means to an end, the achievement of an understanding of a musical work in its historical context.

Thus far, my purpose has been to establish a setting for a study of the history of music scholarship in the modern era (ca. 1700 to the present). The time has come to offer a more detailed prospectus indicating how such a study might be organized. The field is vast enough to allow for a variety of different approaches. Some kind of scaffolding is required to support the weight of the data which is derived from a review of almost the entire range of scholarly activity in music and an assessment of the work of scores of erudite musicians. The prospectus I have to offer is in seven parts; it might be described as seven variations on a theme or seven different ways of telling the same story. I propose to describe the headings briefly, and then take up each in turn for somewhat fuller commentary.

I. The music of the ancients as a proving ground for historical method. A discussion of the efforts to separate fact from myth with respect to the music of the early Greeks.

II. Chant reform as an impetus to scholarship. Application of the techniques of philology and paleography to the study of liturgical music. (Similar patterns could be traced in the development of studies in the Lutheran chorale.)

III. The discovery of world music. First steps toward an understanding of primitive and non-Western musics. The beginnings of ethnomusicology.

IV. The discovery of national song. The emergence of folk-music scholarship in the major European countries.

V. The revelation of music history. The unfolding by historians of the musical life of the past.

VI. The arts of custodianship. The role of collectors, librarians, and bibliographers in assembling, preserving, and organizing the documents of early music.

VII. National approaches to music scholarship. The development of native traditions in the major European countries, their supporting institutions, academies, learned societies, research institutes, journals, and editorial activity. Music in higher education.

1. The Music of the Ancients

Unless one is a student of scholarship he should be advised to stay away from the subject of early Greek music. The historiographer is one of the few who have a valid reason to concern themselves with the futilities of this particular area of speculation. For him the study of ancient music as it emerged from the mire of centuries makes a fascinating narrative of the triumph of mind over myth. From the Middle Ages onward, Greek theory had been called upon to serve as the rationale for a variety of anachronisms. I need mention only one of the most familiar—the creation of an esthetic basis for opera in the seventeenth century, based on a misunderstanding of the nature of Greek drama. The scholars of the Enlightenment were at a loss to explain the apparent discrepancy between the rich culture of antiquity revealed in its architecture, sculpture, and literature, and the poor, fragmentary survivals of Greek musical practice. "What the ancient music really was," said Burney, "is not easy to determine; the whole is now become a matter of faith; but of this we are certain, that it was something with which mankind was extremely delighted." The aura of that delight persisted long after the experience of the art had vanished. The skepticism of the Age of Reason had eroded much of the myth of Greek musical supremacy by Burney's time, but he and his contemporaries were still burdened with two heavily loaded questions: (1) Did the Greeks know harmony or part music? (2) How does one account for the Greek doctrine of ethos, the belief in the powerful effects the modes were reputed to have on human behavior? Every eighteenth-century historian addressed himself to these questions, and the pros and cons of their argument were summarized by Burney in his *Dissertation on the Music of the Ancients*, a vivid piece of historiographical writing. Through the general confusion and speculation, a fine line of pure scholarship can be traced in the writings of Pierre-Jean Burette (1665–1747), who contributed a series of papers on Greek music to the *Mémoires de l'Académie des Inscriptions*. Martini, Marpurg, Burney, Hawkins, and Forkel were all indebted to his basic research.

A new phase in Greek music studies came into being in the early nineteenth century with August Böckh's edition of Pindar (1811). According to Riemann, the end of dilettantism in this field came with Johann Friedrich Bellermann's *Die Hymnen des Dionysios und Mesomedes* (1840) and Karl Fortlage's *Das musikalische System der Griechen* (1847). French scholars also made some valuable contributions, notably A.-J.-H. Vincent, who wrote numerous articles on Greek music in contemporary journals and tangled with Fétis on the question of the Greeks' use of harmony, and François Louis Perne (1772–1832), whose enthusiasm for antiquity was such that he transcribed the complete score of Gluck's *Iphigénie en Tauride* into Greek notation.

Thus one can pursue the study of ancient Greek music down to the present day through Rudolf Westphal, François Gevaert, Hermann Abert, to R. P. Winnington-Ingram, Otto Gombosi, and Edward Lippmann. Throughout history the field has retained its fascination, not only for scholars but for composers as well, a fascination compounded of admiration for the Greek cultural heritage and the lure of the unknown. In so far as it brought the disciplines of classical philology into music scholarship, it has served as a proving ground for modern historical method.

II. Chant Reform as an Impetus to Scholarship

Like the music of the ancients, the music of the church suffered long from uncritically held assumptions on the part of its savants. The scholarly study of the chant as carried out under the aegis of the church has always been subject to the pressures of orthodoxy. This has been a source of strength as well as weakness. On the one hand, it has enjoyed the prestige and stability that only an institution such as the church could provide; and on the other, it has suffered from periods of dogmatism and a general resistance to change. The history of plainchant has been marked by a series of reforms designed to make it comply with the esthetic or devotional requirements of the liturgy. The church has always resisted the historical approach, although the expressed aim of many of these reforms was to preserve or restore the purity of an earlier practice. It is only within the last seventy-five years that the ideals of critical, scientific research have influenced the editing of the authorized books of the chant.

First to come to mind when we think of the application of critical methods to the chant is the work of the monks of Solesmes under the leadership of Prosper Guéranger, Joseph Pothier, and André Mocquereau. But Peter Wagner, in reviewing progress in research on the neumes, begins his account as early as 1615, when Michael Praetorius dealt with the subject in his *Syntagma musicum*.[9] The next high point in the chronicle of pre-Solesmes investigation was Dom Jumilhac's *La Science et la pratique du plain-chant* (1673), a work inspired by the same scholarly environment that produced Mabillon's achievements—the Congregation of Saint Maur in Paris. Another Benedictine scholar must be mentioned, Martin Gerbert, abbot of Saint-Blasien, who collected and copied numerous documents of liturgical music, most of which were destroyed in the burning of the cloister in 1768. Much valuable information was preserved, however, in his great history of sacred music, *De cantu et musica sacra* (1774). French writers maintained an interest in chant reform throughout

9. See Peter Wagner, "Geschichte der Neumenforschung," in the introduction to his *Einführung in die gregorianischen Melodien*, II, *Neumenkunde*, 2nd ed. (Leipzig, 1912).

the eighteenth century, the chief works being by Guillaume Nivers (*Dissertation sur le chant grégorien*, 1683), the Abbé Jean Lebeuf (*Traité historique et pratique sur le chant*, 1741), and the Abbé Poisson (*Traité théorique et pratique du plainchant*, 1750). More than one hundred and fifty years after the publication of Dom Jumilhac's treatise, mentioned above, it was reissued in Paris (1847) with a supplement and commentary by Théodore Nisard (the Abbé Normand) and A. Le Clercq, creating an extraordinary interest in problems related to the chant, in which Fétis, La Fage, Félix Clement, and Jean-Louis-Félix Danjou all participated. A memorable controversy was carried on between Fétis and Kiesewetter concerning the origin of the neume forms in the famous Saint-Gall Codex 359. In spite of their enthusiasm for the subject, French scholars did not play a decisive role in plainchant reform until the end of the nineteenth century. The field was quietly usurped by the Germans under the leadership of Karl Proske (1794–1861) of Regensburg, and later Franz X. Haberl (1840–1910), who had the weight of the Caecelian movement and the authority of the Vatican behind them. Their effort to sustain the tradition of the *Editio Medicea* was misguided scholarship, but they provided a foil to set off the achievements of the Benedictines of Solesmes when they began their work. This is not the place to review the brilliant contributions to research made by the Solesmes monks. That ground has been well covered in a recent series of articles by Dom P. Combe appearing in *Etudes grégoriennes*.[10]

III. The Discovery of World Music

Mantle Hood, writing in 1963, suggests that the discipline we call ethnomusicology came into existence about eighty years ago. This may be true in the strict sense, as it would be true of musicology itself, but the earlier scholars gave more attention to primitive and non-Western music than we generally give them credit for. We tend to underestimate the receptivity of the eighteenth-century historians to the concept of world music. In the comprehensive historical schemes of men like Padre Martini, Burney, La Borde, and Forkel, there was ample place for consideration of the music of the Egyptians, Jews, Chinese, Turks, and even the West and East Indians. Hawkins was one of the few who could not project his imagination beyond the European sphere. "Of what importance," he asks in the Preface to his history, "can it be to enquire into a practice that has not its foundation in science or system, or to know what are the sounds that most delight a Hottentot, a wild American, or even a more refined Chinese?" Most of Hawkins's contemporaries, however, were more than

10. Dom P. Combe, "Le Réforme du chant et des livres de chant grégorien à l'abbaye de Solesmes (1833–83)," *Etudes grégoriènnes*, VI (1963), 185–234; and "Préliminaires de la réforme grégorienne de S. Pie X," *ibid.*, VII (1967), 63–145; VIII (1967), 137–98; IX (1968), 47–100.

curious about the prehistoric origins of music and sought to account for them within a universal pattern. Forkel's philosophy of history, for example, was based on an anthropological concept, the assumption that primitive man developed powers of musical expression concurrently with his conquest of speech. But if Forkel's general attitude was hospitable to an ethnic view, he was unable to follow through its implications. For one thing, the data he had to work with was far too limited. Travelers such as James Bruce, the African explorer who supplied Burney with information on Egyptian music, were not trained observers. For another, the music historians of the Enlightenment were committed to an idea of Progress that rendered them incapable of evaluating the music of other cultures in objective terms. Yet in spite of this, the report of Père Joseph Amiot, a French missionary in Peking, on the nature of Chinese music was a work of considerable merit.[11] Likewise, Sir William Jones's monograph, *On the Musical Modes of the Hindoos* (1784), was one of the first "scientific" studies of East Indian music. Early in the nineteenth century the French government issued its twenty-volume set, *La Description de l'Égypte* (1809–26), initiated by the Emperor Napoleon and for which Guillaume-André Villoteau furnished the observations on Egyptian music, one of the first authentic attempts at ethnomusicological field work. More and more information on ethnic music began to appear in the periodicals and popular histories of music. William C. Stafford's *History of Music* (Edinburgh, 1830) devotes 166 of its 387 pages to ethnic material, treating music of the Burmese, Siamese, Singhalese in Asia as well as of a number of African provinces. The information is superficial but the direction of interest is clear. In 1831 Gottfried Wilhelm Fink wrote what may well be the first popular book on ethnic music, *Erste Wanderung der ältesten Tonkunst als Vorgeschichte der Musik* (Essen, 1831), in which he engaged in some rather fantastic speculation on the migration of scales and melodic devices from ancient China and India to various parts of Europe, including Scotland. The man who took the study of primitive music out of the realm of the quaint and curious was François-Joseph Fétis. He believed that the history of music is inseparable from the study of the characteristics of the races that cultivated it, and that the historian must avail himself of the help afforded by anthropology, ethnology, and linguistics.[12] He was, however, unable to grant true artistic value to the music of the non-Western peoples since it lacked the "system" (that is, harmony and polyphony) displayed in European music. Yet Fétis did much to prepare the

11. Joseph Amiot, *Mémoires sur la musique des Chinois, tant anciens que modernes* (1779). Much of the information in this work found its way into La Borde's *Essai sur la musique ancienne et moderne* (1780) by way of another French priest, the Abbé Foussier.

12. See Emile Haraszti, "Fétis, fondateur de la musicologie comparée," *Acta Musicologica*, IV/3 (1932), 97–103.

ground for Carl Stumpf, Erich von Hornbostel, and Otto Abraham, who a generation later brought "comparative musicology" into its own.

IV. The Discovery of National Song

On Burney's German tour in 1772, he encountered in Vienna a certain M. L'Augier, whom he praised for "a most refined and distinguishing taste" and remarked that "he has heard national melody in all parts of the world with philosophical ears."[13] M. L'Augier was not the only musician of the late eighteenth century whose ears were tuned philosophically to the strains of national melody. He lived in a time that was marked by the upsurge of interest in folk music and folk culture throughout Europe. As a trend this was something quite distinct from the ethnological, although the two strands merged toward the end of the nineteenth century. The folksong movement was a chapter in its own right, closely tied to developments in the field of literature, and part of the broad cultural stream that led into the Romantic era.

In England Bishop Percy and Joseph Ritson turned their attention to the relics of ancient poetry and song well before the end of the eighteenth century. Edward Jones collected and published the music of the Welsh bards; Edward Bunting devoted himself to Irish folk music, as did James Johnson to Scotch. A high point in the study of English national song was reached some fifty years later in the work of William Chappell, although opinion is still divided as to where he drew the fine line that separates folk from popular elements. He was joined by a group of colleagues that included Edward F. Rimbault, J. W. Ebsworth, Hales, and Furnivall, whose research is embodied in the thirty volumes of Percy Society publications that appeared between 1840 and 1851. These were followed by a more specialized group of investigators, such as Frank Kidson, Lucy Broadwood, and others, whose work is linked directly with that of Cecil Sharp and the English Folksong Society.

In Germany the study of folk music was pursued with no less fervor but more sentiment. German culture in the early Romantic period was permeated with nostalgic feeling for "das Volk," a feeling that manifested itself in a fascination with folk tales and legends, folk crafts and customs, folk dance and song. Folk elements invaded literature and the fine arts, producing in music, along with other hybrid forms, the artful simplicity of "Lieder in Volkston" or "das volkstümliches Lied." Another major line of influence stemmed from the educators, Pestalozzi, Pfeiffer, and Nägeli, who found in folksong an ideal instrument for training young children in music and morals.[14]

J. G. Herder (1744–1802) was one of the major instigators of the

13. *Dr. Burney's Musical Tours in Europe*, ed. Percy A. Scholes (London, 1959), II, 86.

14. See Julian von Pulikowski, *Geschichte des Begriffes Volkslied im musikalischen Schrifthem* (Heidelberg, 1933).

movement through his writings and his collections of folk poetry. The idea of folksong as "an expression of the voice of humanity" was basic to his own philosophy and of profound influence on contemporary thought. All of this ideological interest was accompanied by vigorous activity on the part of the collectors, Carl Ferdinand Becker, Ludwig Erk, and Franz Böhme. Similar collecting industry was displayed in other parts of Europe, by Andreas Berggreen in Copenhagen, and by Weckerlin and Tiersot, both librarians at the Conservatoire in Paris. In Russia, Poland, Hungary, and Czechoslovakia, the collecting and study of folk music contributed to the crescendo of nationalistic feeling that had so obvious an effect on the art music of the late nineteenth century.

V. The Revelation of Music History

The study of the gradual unfolding of our knowledge of the musical past is in many respects the central concern of the historian of music scholarship. It has not been a smooth and continuous process. Quite the contrary. One generation of scholars may be attracted to some particular sequence of historical events, the next will direct its attention elsewhere. Often the choice is a matter of esthetic preference. A focal point of interest for the eighteenth-century historians was the question of who invented counterpoint. Sometime later the work of Guido d'Arezzo was subjected to close scrutiny in an effort to determine who established the principles of modern musical notation. Often a single work will start a current of interest that mounts into a flood, as did Giuseppe Baini's biography of Palestrina (1828), which joined Anton Thibaut's *Über Reinheit der Tonkunst* (1825) in elevating the "pure" sixteenth-century style to the highest level of musical value. All of us have observed the fluctuations in Bach and Mozart scholarship in our own time, the Schütz renaissance of the early twentieth century, the spectacular emergence of Monteverdi as a major composer. Fashions in historical interest change sharply. Some twenty years ago it seemed to me that every musicologist of any worth was working on fifteenth-century studies, and the gods of the musical pantheon were Bukofzer, Besseler, Handschin, and Reese. These shifting patterns of emphasis are not altogether fortuitous. Each generation of music historians finds in the past what it seeks in the present, and the historiographer, in attempting to understand these patterns and their relationships to a given place and time, is himself engaged in sharpening a new tool of historical analysis.

VI. The Arts of Custodianship

The role of the librarian, the collector, the bibliographer, and the editor has been touched upon by a few writers but never fully elaborated.[15] The

15. See, for example, A. Hyatt King's *Some British Collectors of Music* (Cambridge, 1963), for a survey of the activity of British music collectors from the late seventeenth century to the present.

work of these specialists is usually regarded as auxiliary, yet how many major contributions to research have been made by men who were nominally in charge of a music collection. One thinks of Anton Schmid in Vienna, Wilhelm Altmann and Johannes Wolf in Berlin, Jules Écorcheville in Paris, William Barclay Squire in London, and Oscar Sonneck in Washington, to mention only a few. Their accomplishments were in keeping with the long-standing European tradition of the scholar-librarian, and their activity reflects the prevailing nineteenth-century interest in philological, archival studies.

In the eighteenth century a scholar's power could almost be measured by the strength of his library. Pepusch, Burney, and Hawkins in England, Walther, Forkel, and Gerber in Germany, Padre Martini and Sébastien de Brossard, all possessed magnificent personal music collections that have since been dispersed or assimilated into major European libraries. In the nineteenth century a new species of private collector emerged, best represented by Aloys Fuchs in Vienna, Georg Pölchau in Berlin, and Fortunato Santini in Rome. For these men, collecting was an end in itself, and they pursued their calling with energy and devotion. When the full story of their work has been told, we will recognize how much scholarship is indebted to them, particularly for assembling and preserving the priceless autograph manuscripts of Bach, Beethoven, Mozart, and Haydn. The late Paul Hirsch was one of the last great representatives of this group.

Bibliography is another form of collecting, involving the selection and ordering of the documents on which our knowledge of the art and its history are based. Bibliography can serve very specific purposes, as, for example, the appended list of references to a dissertation, or it can aim at comprehensiveness. The dream of the perfect, comprehensive, bibliographical tool for research has haunted scholars from Brossard to Barry Brook. The chronicle of their search, leading through Forkel and Eitner to the latest efforts at computerized control, is an important aspect of our narrative. The same thing could be said of editorial activity, another form of custodianship. The chief outcomes of the philological method are the critical editions, the *Denkmäler* and *Gesamtausgaben*. Scholarship is powerless without them. The work of an editor is like that of the technician who prepares a biological specimen for examination under a microscope. Throughout the nineteenth century one can follow a procession of editorial activity of increasing refinement. Some of the first sets were Commer's *Collectio operum musicorum Batavorum* (1844–58), Proske's *Musica divina* (1853–64), and Maldeghem's *Trésor musical* (1865–93). In 1851 the Bach Gesellschaft was founded. In 1862 publication was started on the complete editions of Beethoven and Palestrina. From this point onward, the energy of scholarly publication was such that it could not be interrupted by two world wars.

VII. *National Approaches to Musical Scholarship*

Nationalism is a dangerous subject to bring into a discussion of scholarship. It brings to mind the all-too-frequent abuses and distortions that occur when research is pursued along chauvinistic lines. But just as there are recognizable national styles in music composition, so are there national styles—perhaps one should say "national traditions"—in scholarship that develop as a result of local tastes, habits of thought, and institutional structures. No one can fail to observe that, as musicology matures and moves toward the last quarter of the twentieth century, national distinctions become less and less pronounced. The situation is not unlike that which prevails in the field of the composer, which Walter Wiora views as entering into its "Fourth Age," an age dominated by what he calls "global industrial culture."[16] But while one may view with some concern those trends toward consolidation and uniformity in musical art, the forces that tend toward internationalism in scholarship cannot be anything but welcome.

My purpose in directing attention to national traditions in this area is not to draw invidious comparisons between one country and another, but to recapitulate the development of musicology in more precise and concrete terms. There is much of interest to be found in observing the changing roles played by nations in the development of the discipline over the past two hundred and fifty years. France was the focal point for European intellectual life throughout most of the eighteenth century. England's contribution was most significant in the last quarter of that century, in the brilliant historical accomplishments of Burney and Hawkins, along with the work of the Georgian estheticians led by Charles Avison and John Brown. Germany came into its own in the early nineteenth century, largely because it was able to supply the institutions through which the new discipline could find its home in the structure of society. Johann Nikolaus Forkel at Göttingen became the prototype of the academic musical scholar. He bore the title of "academic music director," as did Daniel Gottlob Türk at Halle, who in 1808 was designated "Professor der Musik." These were the first of a long line of scholars whose work enjoyed the stimulus and the protection of the German university system, men such as Carl Breidenstein at Bonn, Joseph Frölich at Würzburg, A. B. Marx at Berlin. Finally, in 1870 Eduard Hanslick became the first music professor, *ordinarius*, at the University of Vienna.[17]

Another source of vitality on the nineteenth-century German scene was provided by the critical journals, of which the *Allgemeine musikalische Zeitung*, edited by Johann Friedrich Rochlitz in Leipzig, is the outstand-

16. Walter Wiora, *The Four Ages of Music* (New York, 1965), pp. 149 ff.

17. See Werner Friedrich Kümmel, "Die Anfänge der Musikgeschichte an den deutschsprachigen Universitäten," *Die Musikforschung*, XX (1967), 262–80.

ing example. The Leipzig journal served as the model for another of the same title edited by A. B. Marx in Berlin, and for *Cäcilia*, edited in Mainz by Gottfried Weber. Journals of this kind provided an avenue through which the results of research could be reported to the general public, along with musical activity of all kinds. Their level of intellectual content was remarkably high, and they were linked by a chain of communication so that reviews of publications and events originating in any one capital were soon spread throughout the whole of Europe. In Paris the czar of musical journalism was François-Joseph Fétis, who held a virtual monopoly over musical opinion through his *Revue musicale* and its successor *La Revue et gazette musicale*. England had only one comparable journal in the *Quarterly Musical Magazine and Review*, edited by Richard Mackenzie Bacon from 1818 to 1828.

Details could be multiplied indefinitely as we trace the varying paths that led to the establishment of research institutes, learned societies, academies and conservatories. And within this framework of institutions there developed a new type of professional musician, the musicologist. The professional aspect of his work has been resisted in certain countries, notably England and Italy, almost up to the present day. I think it is safe to say that musicology achieved its full definition and acceptance as an international discipline in the work of American scholars.

Barry Brook has reminded me that the central theme of this series of lectures is "Perspectives and Lacunae in Musicological Research." I hope I have succeeded in some degree in placing in perspective a particular field of research that is in itself riddled with lacunae. The historiography of music has been a comparatively unknown territory for investigation. Its novelty lies more in the approach than in the subject matter involved. Some thirty years ago, Warren Allen wrote his famous *Philosophies of Music History* (New York, 1939), a work that has both the virtues and defects of a pioneer study. Nothing comparable has been done since that time, at least in English. In recent years German scholars have turned their attention to problems of an historiographical nature. A leader in this direction was the late Wilibald Gurlitt, whose monographs on Riemann and Fétis are models of their kind.[18] Among those who have pursued similar interests are Carl Dahlhaus and Walter Wiora, and the current series published under the title *Studien zur Musikgeschichte des 19. Jahrhunderts* (Regensburg, 1965–) contains several volumes pertinent to our subject.

It is important to recognize that investigation in this area is concerned

18. See Wilibald Gurlitt, *Hugo Riemann (1849–1919)* (Mainz, 1951); also "Hugo Riemann und die Musikgeschichte," in *Musikgeschichte und Gegenwart*, Beihefte zum Archiv für Musikwissenschaft, II (1966), 103–22, and "François-Joseph Fétis und seine Rolle in der Geschichte der Musikwissenschaft," *ibid.*, 123–39.

not only with the "breakthroughs" and brilliant achievements, but with the "blind alleys" and "dead ends" as well. As the historian Herbert Butterfield has said: "Let us by all means study the perversions of history, and in particular hunt out their origins. . . . It is important to discover, furthermore, how far men tend to become intellectual victims of the technical procedures they habitually follow." This remark leads me to suggest one major contribution which the historiographer should be able to make, if he has pursued his study of human error dispassionately and objectively, and that is to form some judgment on the present state of health and a prognosis for the future well-being of his discipline. There is certainly no more reason for the music historiographer to stop short of judgment on his own time than for the writer of a general history of music to stop short of a discussion of the contemporary scene. Having said this, I shall promptly beg the question, for the present at least, because of lack of time to cover it adequately. I will simply remind you that we are entering into an era where the technical procedures for research are becoming vastly complex and demanding, and that we should welcome these new devices for their mind-expanding propensities as well as guard against them lest we become their intellectual victims.

DISCUSSION

HARMS: Do you accept the common definition of historiography as a history of history?

DUCKLES: In general I do, but to me it means more than the history of history. It is the history of methods and procedures that might be applied to things which ordinarily are not treated historically. It involves having a philosophy of history and an esthetic point of view. We are often faced with presuppositions and moral overtones, but these contribute to the interest in investigating earlier ideas.

DITTMER: In the last two hundred years we have faced the problem of philosophy in general history—with Hegel, Spengler, Toynbee, and so forth. I have two questions: Is it possible to have a philosophy of *music* history, and, if we do have such a philosophy of music history, do we thereby lose our objectivity?

DUCKLES: I think our position would be no different from that of any other discipline. I think that all music historians operate with a philosophy of music history, whether they are aware of it or not. Part of the interest of this kind of investigation is to reveal these philosophies, to see what the implications are and how they relate to other humanistic studies.

DITTMER: But can there be specifically a philosophy of music history?

In thinking of musical style, for example, can we predict a pattern, beyond the fact that change is always present in musical style?

DUCKLES: At that level, you are not dealing with what I would consider a philosophy of history. I would not consider the philosophical assumptions behind music history to be different from those behind art history, for example. When you are dealing with different media, of course, you use different terms and you isolate different elements for discussion. No, I do not think there is a particular and unique kind of philosophy of music history.

DITTMER: There are certain philosophies of music history that seem to work against an objective viewpoint. To take an example, the Spenglerian theory proposes a morphological approach to music history: that a style is born, matures, and has within itself the seeds of self-destruction. If we subscribe to such a theory we would tend not to view history objectively.

MRS. HAMPTON: It seems to me that historiography by definition suggests a greater objectivity. Yet we do have a basic set of prejudices. All of us are conditioned by them very thoroughly, although we may not question our own objectivity.

DUCKLES: I find that to be one of the most absorbing aspects of this kind of study. One is continually searching one's mind to see what presuppositions may lurk there. One's philosophy of history is basic to an investigation of this kind, and I approach it with some trepidation because it is a field that professional philosophers work and argue in. Nevertheless I think every musicologist has to come to terms with the concepts that control his idea of history.

DITTMER: Obviously we will never be completely objective about anything. We do the best we can to describe things as they are. What we do not have in the social sciences is what the natural sciences have—repeatability. We can not verify general principles by repeating an experiment.

DUCKLES: "Wie es eigentlich gewesen ist"—this is the basis of the nineteenth-century historical approach, the attempt to tie it up with scientific method. But I would like to return to a point that fascinates me, although I am not qualified to develop it. I am interested in the idea that there are many kinds of historical movements, including non-chronological ones. We are embedded in the idea of history developing through time. There are other ways of looking at history, which are characteristic of the late sixteenth and early seventeenth centuries. Is this kind of speculation of any interest? I have the feeling that we are at the end of a period of historical analysis that is focused on the idea of chronology, of one thing developing out of another. This is the teleological approach. But we are now getting into a period where history is conceived of in a different way. I think that this is not unrelated to developments in contemporary esthetics and in contemporary music, where chronological time ceases to be as significant as it used to be.

MISS FOSTER: In a non-chronological approach, would you be suggesting that there is some sort of closed equilibrium—that there may be a certain number of elements which seem to be constant throughout any age, such as the desire for order, the desire for pure expression in Classicism and Romanticism, and so forth? I believe that in all periods we will find all of these things, and a problem of the chronological approach is that we tend to ignore the minority.

DUCKLES: Yes, I think you are on the track of the kind of analysis that puts us into a new realm. I consider the point of such an article as Siegfried Kracauer's "Time and History" to be that the values of works of art are not determined by chronology. They have their own spheres of meaning and relevance, which is why old and new works and contemporary works representing old and new points of view can have significance for us at the same time.

GERBOTH: I see difficulties in a non-chronological approach. If we aren't to examine each work in relation to an evolutionary or chronological approach, how shall we relate works to one another?

DUCKLES: I do not think we can abandon the chronological approach altogether. There must be a merger of the two points of view. When we consider Strauss and Schoenberg, of whom I spoke in my lecture, our judgment of "location" in two different historical worlds depends on our knowledge of chronology. I hesitate to speak as an authority in this area of nonchronological approaches, but I do think the framework of ideas has to be brought into the picture.

MISS FOSTER: Could you clarify the distinction you made in your lecture, between eighteenth-century information designed for professional use and information for the cultured public?

DUCKLES: I think that most of the contributions that lead in the direction of modern musicology were not made by professionals, but by dilettantes, by part-time lawyers or public officials. Professional musicians were so involved in their own professional life that for them it was a kind of cult or guild—a matter of keeping secrets within one's own group. The dilettantes, on the other hand, welcomed ideas from every source. That is why it is important to make the distinction between professional knowledge on the one hand and the dilettantes' liberal, humanistic learning on the other.

VAN SOLKEMA: Do we know whether the amateurs of the seventeenth or eighteenth century had any kind of influence on professional musicians? Did the professionals actually take note of their books, or were they read only by other amateurs?

DUCKLES: One finds various kinds of books in the eighteenth century. In the area of musical journalism, I think that Hiller's *Wöchentliche Nachrichten*, with its weekly reports and reviews of events in music, represents the first periodical addressed to the public—the amateurs—and it is at a very high level if you contrast it with Scheibe or with Mattheson's earlier publications, which were designed mainly for professionals. The obviously technical treatises on mathematics and acoustics were designed for people with highly specialized knowledge. One thing that makes Hiller's periodical so interesting is that he has a long series of articles describing the essential music library for the *Liebhaber*. He goes through a whole series of titles, including some of the rather technical treatises, but all are recommended for the library of an amateur. This amateur, of course, is not just an amateur musician, but an amateur philosopher and humanist. Mattheson's *Der volkommene Kappellmeister* has elements of both, but I would say it is directed more toward the professional than the amateur. It contains the kind of knowledge you would need to conduct the musical establishment of a wealthy patron or a town.

BROOK: May I turn to another point related to our discussion with Milton Babbitt on how to talk about a piece of contemporary music [see page 151]? It seems to me that your subject and his are not unrelated. Does the analysis of music fit into the four basic trends of modern music-scholarship, or might it not be a fifth approach?

DUCKLES: I think it might be considered an expansion of the "philological" method I referred to. The procedures of analysis are very closely related to what is regarded as "musical meaning"—what music means to a given generation. The question of determining what meaning music had for people of the eighteenth century, or any earlier time, is a rather hazy subject to get hold of. There are a few writers who have attempted to handle this question, but not many. Kathi Meyer has written a book called *Bedeutung und Wesen der Musik*, published in 1932, and there is an anthology by Hermann Pfrogner, *Musik: Geschichte ihre Deutung*. The Pfrogner is interesting as an anthology of the writings of musicians of different periods, selected because they reveal something about the meaning music had to each individual in his time. I think the study of such writings is closely related to the problem of tracing different approaches to analysis.

BROOK: Nevertheless, I feel that what analysts themselves describe as analysis differs from what the estheticians think of as meaning in music.

DUCKLES: Let me ask you a question related to analysis. Do you think it is possible for analysis to proceed without reference to history?

BROOK: No, I do not. But I do think by examining terminologies and techniques that analysts have developed, we can better understand how they relate to each other. (Some, of course, appear to live in a world completely divorced from anything around them.) Taken together, the various analytic approaches themselves constitute an aspect of contemporary intellectual history.

READING LIST

Bibliographical Note

The literature of music historiography is vast and widely dispersed. Very few works are to be found that cover the field systematically or comprehensively, but a large number contain information related to particular aspects of our study. For example, most of the entries cited in *RILM Abstracts* under the headings No. 20 ("Historical Musicology: The Discipline") and No. 30 ("Ethnomusicology: The Discipline") are relevant. The items listed below have been selected for their usefulness, and they include some of the most recent studies that have bearing on our subject.

It will be noted that German scholars have been very active in this field in recent years. Much of the impetus has come from the work of the late Wilibald Gurlitt (represented below). Important statements have also been made by Walter Wiora and Carl Dalhaus. Readers are invited to explore the writings of these scholars, only a few of which have been cited here, for further insights into "Die Geschichte der Musikwissenschaft."

Allen, Warren D., *Philosophies of Music History* (New York, 1939; reprint, New York, 1962).

> Written some thirty years ago, this work, in spite of many deficiencies, remains the only full-scale study of music-history writing in English.

Haraszti, Emile, "La Musicologie, science de l'avenir," in *Histoire de la musique, ed.* Roland-Manuel (Paris, 1963), II, 1549–92.

Harrison, Frank Ll., Mantle Hood, and Claude V. Palisca, *Musicology*, Princeton Studies in Humanistic Scholarship in America (Englewood Cliffs, N.J., 1963).

> See particularly Pt. I, Ch. 2 (by Harrison), and Pt. II, Ch. 2 (by Palisca).

Heinz, Rudolf, *Geschichtsbegriff und Wissenschaftscharakter der Musikwissenschaft in der zweiten Hälfte des 19. Jahrhunderts*, Studien zur Musikgeschichte des. 19. Jahrhunderts, 11 (Regensburg, 1968).

Kümmel, Werner F., *Geschichte und Musikgeschichte, Die Musik der Neuzeit in Geschichtsschreibung und Geschichtsauffassung des deutschen Kulturbereichs von der Aufklärung bis zu J. G. Droysen und Jacob Burckhardt*, Marburger Beiträge zur Musikforschung, 1 (Marburg, 1967).

——— "Die Anfänge der Musikgeschichte an den deutschsprachigen Universitäten," *Die Musikforschung*, XXX (1967), 262–80.

Riedel, Friedrich W., "Zur Geschichte der musikalischen Quellenüberlieferung und Quellenkunde," *Acta Musicologica*, XXXVIII (1966), 3–27.

Westrup, Sir Jack A., *An Introduction to Musical History* (New York, Harper and Row, 1964; first published in England in 1955).

Not a history of music, but a survey of the problems of writing music
history.
Wiora, Walter, "Musikwissenschaft," *Die Musik in Geschichte und Gegenwart*, IX, 1192–1220.
The article incorporates discussions of "Musikwissenschaft als historische
Disziplin," and "Die Entwicklung der musikgeschichtlicher Forschung,"
by Hans Albrecht.

Historical Esthetics

Goldschmidt, Hugo, *Die Musikästhetik des 18. Jahrhunderts* (Zürich-Leipzig,
1915).
Schäfke, Rudolf, *Geschichte der Musikästhetik in Umrissen* (Berlin, 1934; 2nd
ed., Tutzing, 1964).
Serauky, Walter, *Die musikalische Nachahmungsästhetik im Zeitraum von 1700
bis 1850* (Münster, 1929).

Musical Meaning in History

Meyer, Kathi, *Bedeutung und Wesen der Musik* (Strasbourg, 1932).
Pfrogner, Hermann, *Musik, Geschichte ihrer Deutung* (Leipzig-Munich,
1954).
An anthology of writings by music theorists and estheticians, arranged
chronologically.

The Approach Through Biography

Guido Adler:
Adler, Guido, *Wollen und Wirken aus der Leben eines Musikhistorikers*
(Vienna, 1935).
Charles Burney:
Scholes, Percy, *The Great Dr. Burney*, 2 vols. (Oxford, 1948).
François-Joseph Fétis:
Gurlitt, Wilibald, "François-Joseph Fétis und seine Rolle in der Geschichte
der Musikwissenschaft," in *Musikgeschichte und Gegenwart* [collected
essays by Gurlitt], Beihefte zum Archiv für Musikwissenschaft, II (1966),
123–39.
First printed in the proceedings of the IMG Kongress, Lüttich, 1930.
Wangermée, Robert, *François-Joseph Fétis, musicologue et compositeur*
(Brussels, 1951).
Johann Nikolaus Forkel:
Edelhoff, Heinrich, *Johann Nikolaus Forkel: Ein Beitrag zur Geschichte der
Musikwissenschaft* (Göttingen, 1935).
Sir John Hawkins:
Scholes, Percy, *The Life and Activities of Sir John Hawkins, Musician Mag-
istrate and Friend of Johnson* (Oxford, 1953).
Raphael Georg Kiesewetter:
Kier, Herfrid, *Raphael Georg Kiesewetter (1773–1850): Wegbereiter des
musikalischen Historismus*, Studien zur Musikgeschichte des 19. Jahrhun-
derts, 13 (Regensburg, 1968).

Hugo Riemann:
  Gurlitt, Wilibald, *Hugo Riemann (1849–1919)* (Mainz, 1951).
  ——— "Hugo Riemann und die Musikgeschichte," in *Musikgeschichte und Gegenwart* [collected essays by Gurlitt], Beihefte zum Archiv für Musik-wissenschaft, II (1966), 103–22.
Jacob Gottfried Weber:
  Lemke, Arno, *Jacob Gottfried Weber. Leben und Werk*, Beitrage zur Mittelrheinischen Musikgeschichte, 9 (Mainz, 1968).

Some Recent Papers on Music Historiography

Dalhaus, Carl, "Historismus und Tradition," in *Zum 70. Geburtstag von Joseph Müller-Blattau*, Saarbrücker Studien zur Musikwissenschaft, 1 (Kassel, 1966), pp. 46–58.
Grout, Donald, "Adaptation as a Hypothesis in the History of Music," in *Festschrift Walter Wiora* (Kassel, 1967), pp. 73–78.
——— "Current Historiography and Music History," in *Studies in Music History: Essays for Oliver Strunk* (Princeton, 1968), pp. 23–40.
Treitler, Leo, "On Historical Criticism," *Musical Quarterly*, LIII/2 (April, 1967), 188–205.

Archival Research: Necessity and Opportunity

FRANÇOIS LESURE

*I*T *IS* a real pleasure for European librarians and archivists to serve as guides to the young (and not so young) Americans who each year come to prepare dissertations or pursue their research. Generally, they quickly become familiar with the organization or lack of organization found in libraries. The world of archives, on the other hand, seems to impress them as a very mysterious fortress, the entrance of which they cannot even approach. I do not claim that I shall give you any magic key; but I will offer a general survey of what has already been found and what one might expect to find in archival repositories. Since the situation is quite different for each country, I can only define briefly the general principles of archives in several countries of western Europe, and give more precise examples for those which I know the best—that is, the archives of France.

Since recent music dictionaries and encyclopedias offer no articles on this subject, it is not surprising to find that some researchers often have difficulty in recognizing the difference between libraries and archives. Even the recent useful handbooks by Vincent Duckles and Ruth Watanabe[1] fail to mention the subject of archives. Almost every week,

---

1. Vincent Duckles, *Music Reference and Research Materials: An Annotated Bibliography*, 2nd ed. (New York, 1967); Ruth T. Watanabe, *Introduction to Music Research* (Englewood Cliffs, N.J., 1967).

56

requests of the following type arrive at the Bibliothèque Nationale: "Would you please send me all the information you have on the life and career of composer X, on whom I am writing my thesis." To this type of request there can be only one response: "Please consult the standard encyclopedias and other reference tools first. To get beyond what is given there, you must inquire of the archives in the various cities where your musician pursued his career."

Actually, the distinction between library and archive is not always absolute. Many ancient European institutions house documents that they acquired by sheer chance; from a strictly administrative point of view, some of these should have gone to other repositories. During a recent congress of archivists, the participants were forced to admit that, because of the ways history has molded their collections, they could not arrive at a clear definition of the boundaries between libraries and archives. Furthermore, in several countries, librarians and archivists have the same professional training, and in Spain and Portugal they are even united in a single administration. And I understand that in the United States the distinction, where it exists at all, is relatively recent.

Not infrequently, musical manuscripts are to be found in archives (not to mention the manuscript fragments that are sometimes discovered used as stiffening in the bindings of archival registers). To cite but a few examples: there is an important manuscript dating from the end of the fifteenth century in the archives of the German city of Heilbronn; an extensive collection of printed eighteenth-century music in the departmental archives of Agen; numerous censored or forbidden operas and songs as well as drawings of operatic costumes in the French national archives and in each of the French departmental archives with small libraries specializing in local history.

Conversely, many libraries hold important archival material. A whole series of account books of the royal household, gathered from dispersed collections and very important for the history of music, is found in the manuscript department of the Bibliothèque Nationale, as well as in stray ecclesiastical archives (notably the chapter registers of Parisian churches) and among the considerable quantity of materials gathered by private collectors or genealogists. Examples of anomalies of this type could be multiplied. We might add that collections of letters or the notes and papers of scholars may be conserved just as well in archives as in libraries. The situation may be deplored, but it is not desirable that it be changed. The principle of respecting a collection's location is a wise one and avoids time-consuming conflicts between administrations. The archivist should not alter that which history has assembled or dispersed. This opinion was not shared by Napoleon who, in his mania for organization and centralization, tried to effect the massive transfer of archives in Europe, a move that was soon canceled by the treaty of Vienna. In the course of one of these transfers, entire wagon-loads of Venetian musical archives were lost in the fires of military campaigns.

Before beginning a research trip or before writing for information, one should consult the archival guides that exist for certain countries or certain specialties. These guides usually contain a history of the depository and of its collections, a summary of the latter's contents, and a list of all of its available research tools: inventories, directories, card files, etc. To begin with, there is the *Guide international des archives*, with an introduction by Charles Samaran (Paris, 1934). This is supplemented by the *Bibliographie sélective des guides d'archives*, published in 1953 by R. H. Bautier in the *Journal of Documentation* (vol. IX) and by the same author's *Annuaire international des archives* (Paris, 1955). In German, there is the work of Adolf Brennecke, *Archivkunde, ein Beitrag zur Theorie und Geschichte des europäischen Archivwesens* (Leipzig, 1953).

In each country, the organization of archives obviously reflects the history of that country. Where political centralization occurred recently, as in Germany or Italy, the federal or national archives will also be recent, and older documentation will be found in each province or state. On the other hand, where centralization came relatively early, as in France, the national archives will be much richer. This principle operates at all levels. The archives of a state theater, for example, are in principle conserved in the national archives, while the archives of a theater administered by a city will have been directed toward the municipal archives.

Of the existing national guides to archives, whose consultation I cannot too strongly recommend, I mention only several of the most important:

1. Great Britain: Sir Hilary Jenkinson, *Public Record Office: Guide to the Public Records*. I, Introductory (London, 1949), which is non-analytic, but only a general orientation.
2. Italy: R. Piattoli, *Guida storica e bibliografica degli archivi e delle biblioteche d'Italia* (6 volumes, 1932–40), for the provinces of Prato, Pistoia, Cava, Aquila, and partially for Rome; and *Gli archivi di stato italiani* (Bologna, 1944), a general panorama which includes, for each region, a brief description of the resources, a bibliography, and an index. These two works are complemented by the studies published regularly by the *Rassegna degli archivi di stato* since 1950 and by the *Publicazioni degli archivi di stato*, inventory-outlines or guides.
3. Netherlands: Graswinckel, *De Rijkarchieven in Nederland* (The Hague, 1953).
4. Sweden: Ingvar Andersson, *Libraries and Archives in Sweden* (Stockholm, 1954), more a general introduction than a true guide.
5. Switzerland: *Archives, bibliothèques et autres centres de documentation en Suisse*, 3d ed., compiled by Robert Wyler (Berne, 1958), a sort of yearbook.

6. Spain: L. Sanchez, *Bibliografía de archivos españoles y de archivistica* (Madrid, 1963), entirely bibliographic.

7. France: *Guide du lecteur aux archives nationales* (Paris, 1966), and *Etat des inventaires des archives nationales, départementales, communales, et hospitalières* (Paris, 1938). These two works are complemented by the special guides of which I shall now speak.

To my knowledge, the only guides that orient the researcher toward archives of musical interest concern the holding of the Archives Nationales of Paris: Henri de Curzon, *État sommaire des pièces et documents concernant le théâtre et la musique conservés aux archives nationales* (Besançon, 1899, extracted from *Bibliographe moderne*), and Mireille Rambaud, *Les Sources de l'histoire de l'art aux archives nationales* (Paris, 1955). The latter is particularly useful. Several repositories of local archives have been able to publish special guides. This is the case in France for the departmental archives of Aube, Doubs, Île-et-Vilaine, the Vendée, and the Haute-Vienne.

In our field, archival research has never really been organized. At the end of the last century and the beginning of this one, there was some activity in Europe, due to the scholarly movement promoted by learned societies of a more or less provincial character. Doctors, notaries, priests, or, indeed, archivists themselves used their leisure to burrow into the holdings of archives in their regions and to publish the results in local journals. Their tendency was to isolate only a few documents relating to known persons. These would be utilized in an elegant literary trapping, stylish at the time, but deprived of their historical and social context. This practice gave a false idea of the discoveries and encouraged neglect of information that since then may have been revealed as useful. Although the results of this movement (see, for example, Jules Écorcheville, "La musique dans les sociétés savantes de la France," in *Bulletin français de la SIM*, Feb. 15, 1907). The evolution of the modern world has brought about the virtual disappearance of this type of erudite amateur, who, until the Second World War, could be profitably questioned about precise details of regional history.

Without claiming to present a complete account of archival publications relating to music, I would like to mention the paths followed in several European countries since the last century. At the very beginning, these efforts very rarely seem to have been the work of academicians or of real musicologists, but often of cultivated musicians or distinguished amateurs.

For Italy I might mention the names of Francesco Caffi (1778–1874), Antonio Bertolotti (1847–93), Count Valdrighi (1827–99), Giuseppe Radiciotti (1858–1931), Angelo Solerti (1865–1907), and Giovanni Tebaldini (1864–1952). Along with a number of others, they were the first in their country to explore the collections that furnished the history of music with the necessary guidelines, although they lacked a feeling for method and left much to be gleaned by subsequent generations. For this reason the work of Msgr. Raffaele Casimiri calls for special recognition from musicologists. From 1924 to 1943, a period of nineteen years, he breathed life into the quarterly journal *Note d'archivio per la storia musicale* and "stuffed" it, not only with studies developed with the help of documents, but also with the documents themselves, when they were worthy of publication. Thus he published the famous *Diarii Sistini* of the Vatican library, from which Baini, Haberl, and Celani had earlier made only arbitrary selections. He also devoted individual monographs to such cities as Urbino, Fermo, and Udine. More recently a younger generation, including Ulisse Prota-Giurleo, Claudio Sartori, and Remo Giazotto, have more or less followed in his footsteps. Aware of the fact that only an infinitesimal part of Italian archives has as yet been searched, the Giorgio Cini Foundation of Venice has for several years been promoting the publication of a series of documents on the organ and on church chapels, in the form of local monographs. In so doing, this foundation has in a way taken over the role played by dilettante scholarship in the nineteenth century and serves the same function as do scientific research foundations in other countries.

In Great Britain, the proper path was taken early. In 1909 H. C. de Lafontaine published *The King's Music*, with the help of the "Calendars of State and Treasury Papers." Then, through the medium of *The Musical Antiquary*, W. H. Grattan Flood published in 1912–13 the "Entries Relating to Music in the English Patent Rolls of the Fifteenth Century." Unless I am gravely mistaken, these two scholars have not really been followed until comparatively recently. Today, such scholars as Frank Harrison, Thurston Dart, Michael Tilmouth, and Alan Tyson understand the necessity of drawing on archives in order to place their respective studies on solid bases.

In France, it was in the field of opera and comic opera that publication of archival musical texts was inaugurated. Between 1877 and 1894, Emile Campardon, a former student of the École des Chartes (a school in Paris for the study of paleography and auxiliary sciences of history), drew on the holdings of the Archives Nationales for his two studies: *Les Spectacles de la foire*, and *L'Académie royale de musique au XVIIIe siècle*. His example was surpassed, however, by Michel Brenet in 1910 with *Les Musiciens de la Sainte-Chapelle du Palais*, an admirably critical assemblage of all the widely dispersed documents on the subject. Her example was not emulated, but her book has been, and continues to be, constantly used by all those who have to deal with sacred music of the period. If she had not carried out her work in a systematic way, and if she had been satisfied to choose only the most prominent names, others after her would have had to leaf through thousands of pages of registers all over again. How many scholars have only superficially tilled the virgin soil of a source, and thus made their successors waste precious hours. I have the impression that this is somewhat the case, for example, with the Archives of the Duomo in Milan and of the Archivio di stato in Florence, both of whose resources are considerable; each searcher stays several weeks in order to glean enough material for an article, then abandons to others the trail just traced.

On another level of ideas, imagine the case of André Pirro, who spent a good part of his life in the archives. He would record information on the labels from mineral water bottles, on tobacco wrappers, or on the backs of invitations to his colleagues' funerals. From time to time he would draw from these treasures the details he needed for his articles, always of an exceptional documentary richness, and for his *Histoire de la musique de la fin du XIVᵉ siècle à la fin du XVIᵉ* (Paris, 1940). Naturally, I have the deepest admiration for the work of Pirro, but the fact that he had an aversion to publishing full texts is heartbreaking, since in the end musicology gained relatively little from his previous discoveries and from the innumerable number of documents that he studied.

In calling for the publication of such documents I do not suggest pursuing an indiscriminate course. There are, of course, many texts that are not at all worthy of being published or even analyzed. This is especially true for the modern period, where the enormous mass of preserved documents justifies or even necessitates a selective approach. It is precisely this selection that is the duty of the musicologist, and he must do it rigorously.

In order to clarify my suggestion, I would like to contrast two recent French publications. The first is the series *Recherches sur la musique française classique*, which has been appearing since 1960. The series is accumulating analyses of all sorts of documents related to musicians of Paris and Versailles, but without any preestablished plan. Some of these documents will, of course, be useful. The second publication is the first volume of the collection of *Documents du minutier central concernant l'histoire de la musique, 1600–1650*, issued by the Archives Nationales in 1967, through the efforts of Madeleine Jurgens. This work seems to me to be a model of its type. The complete study of this period will occupy six or seven volumes, but the first one gives a good idea of the results that may be expected from such an undertaking. Everything is included: composers' biographies, the functioning of musical institutions, popular music, the making and sale of instruments, the musical taste of Parisians as shown by the inventories of their libraries, even the history of music publishing. Musicians appear in these documents not only as private individuals, but also in their professional capacities, including details such as apprenticeship and guilds of instrumentalists, hiring of organists with specifications of their duties, information about music or dance lessons. Certain documents judged to be of greater importance are published in their entirety; others are given only in résumé.

Perhaps some will consider much of what is offered in this volume as of little real value for music history. Such a view would be valid if we believed that music history should limit itself to recording the lives of great composers and establishing the circumstances surrounding the appearance of the best-known masterpieces. But for those who are interested in such sociological questions as musical taste, instrumental performance, or music's place in society, this publication, when completed and enlarged, will furnish musicologists with a gold mine of useful information. Furthermore, its exhaustiveness will make quite unnecessary any return to the original source at a later date.

Having thus cast an eye on some current projects, I would now like to take you into an archival depot, in order to study how it is organized and how it may be utilized. In consulting the yearbooks cited above, you will discover that in Germany and Italy the archives are greatly dispersed; that in Spain very few of the ancient archives have accomplished any reorganization (two good examples are the Archives of the kingdom of Castile at Simancas and those of Aragon in Barcelona); that in France the organization of archives is strongly centralized and arranged in a hierarchy; and that everywhere one must be aware of a complex mosaic of national, regional, municipal, religious, and charitable institutions that reflect the history of each country; and finally, that certain family archives are of considerable size and importance (as those of the Fürstenberg and Hohenlohe families in Germany).

All archival collections consist of groupings (*fonds* and *séries*) corresponding to their origin, which may be administrative, corporative, legal, commercial, institutional, familial, or from other sources. Naturally, the musicologist must begin by abandoning any hope of finding the card catalogues that he customarily uses in libraries—that is to say, in American libraries. Instead, written or printed inventories are usually available. These are often very sketchy and may furnish, for example, little more than the limiting dates of the collections. But sometimes they may be very detailed, particularly if they date back to the era when archivists were not burdened with administrative tasks and had time to explore their riches, or even to exploit them. The immense series of printed inventories of French departmental and municipal archives thus present all the possible variants between the two concepts. Some series have valuable indexes of personal and place names. One example of a very detailed inventory is that of the *département* of the Somme, where the archivist of Amiens, Georges Durand, was himself interested in music and missed no opportunity to call attention to sales of organs, to lawsuits over defamatory songs, to post-mortem inventories of instrument collections, and to many other items relating to music. Since many archival inventories are still not published, the musicologist may profit from the working tools in the manuscript that the archivist has at hand.

Ecclesiastical archives present particular problems, from the legal as well as the technical viewpoint. These archives are especially valuable for the insights they add to our understanding of sacred music. Very little is really known about the circumstances under which religious music was incorporated into the liturgy. Too often there is a tendency to consider Masses and motets as self-sufficient works, while they were actually composed under conditions that must be defined, just as we strive to describe the events that accompany the appearance of secular works. In 1961, at the International Musicological Congress here in New York,[2] I attempted to direct attention to the need for studying the archives of the ancient choir schools (*maîtrises*). Having been unsuccessful then, I am trying once more.

The situation is simple only in France where, following the Revolution and the subsequent separation of church and state, ecclesiastical archives were confiscated and placed in various public archives. In the national archives they now form series L and LL, while in the departmental archives they form series G for secular clergy and H for monastic orders. In Belgium, state archivists have the right to inspect archives belonging to bishoprics, seminaries, and churches, and to invite parish priests to deposit their registers in governmental archives. In Hungary and Yugoslavia the state also exercises control over ecclesiastical archives. In England quite a few agreements exist between church and public institutions for the deposit of their archives, often very well preserved since their founding. Frank Harrison's studies of English religious music of the fifteenth century have thrown a brilliant light on these riches.

Because of canon law, the church is generally not very eager to relinquish possession of its archives. If it has done so in certain cases, it results from the lack of personnel qualified to maintain records and from the fact that the archives are, in fact, often badly classified and kept under unfavorable conditions. In Italy and Spain, it is still difficult to gain access to certain collections—the Roman archives of the Jesuit monastic order, for example, have been inaccessible for a long time.[3]

Besides ecclesiastical archives, where several generations of scholars will be able to find thesis topics, musicology should seek revitalization in many other directions. Some imagination may be required to discover them. For

2. François Lesure, "The Employment of Sociological Methods in Musical History," *Report of the Eighth Congress of the International Musicological Society, New York, 1961* (Kassel, 1961), I, 337–40.

3. A useful guide in this area is that of Victor Carrière, *Introduction aux études d'histoire ecclésiastique locale*, 3 vols. (Paris, 1936–40).

example, the bankruptcy records in the archives of the Seine explain the economic processes of some firms engaged in instrument making and music publishing. These would have to be included among the materials for an economic history of music.

For the history of opera, since the ancient archives of theaters so often burned with their buildings, complementary sources must be discovered. Among the latter, diplomatic correspondence is an excellent one which has been little utilized. Diplomats of past days were also very much interested in artistic matters, and would inform their governments of local novelties. By reading the correspondence of Florentine residents of Paris, together with that of the French minister of foreign affairs, Henry Prunières was able to rewrite completely the history of Italian opera in France during the seventeenth century.[4] As for the complex situation with regard to theater archives in various countries, the recent international directory published by André Veinstein[5] will resolve many problems.

Bibliographers must for once learn to leave their libraries and stop ignoring the help available in archives. The accuracy of the London registers of Stationers' Hall permitted Alan Tyson to establish the priority of certain English editions of Clementi and Beethoven and to fix the dates of plate numbers of London music publishers for the first half of the nineteenth century. In Paris the registers of the *dépôt légal* (copyright deposit) are preserved in the Archives Nationales for the years 1811 to 1912 in the Paris region, and from 1849 to 1885 for provincial publications.

When speaking of archives one is not speaking only of the fourteenth, sixteenth, or eighteenth centuries. It is rather typical that studies on the nineteenth century rarely involve research in archives. This type of source may appear unnecessary to the scholar who for this period has available in abundance newspapers, personal reminiscences, and correspondence. Probably the profusion of sources and the fact that the era is relatively close to our own give a feeling of security, which creates a danger of succumbing to the superficial and neglecting to follow all available paths of research. Perhaps this is why, until rather recently, most of the best musicologists have been medievalists, and why so many of the nineteenth-century "specialists" have been journalists.

It is, therefore, not superfluous to call attention to the problem of recent and contemporary archives, those which have just been formed or are being constituted under our very eyes. One might cite, for example, the archives of concert societies, of record manufacturers and music publishers, of radio and television stations, or of musical-instrument makers. Too often in the past these have suffered a sad fate, even though in many

4. Henry Prunières, *L'Opéra italien en France avant Lulli* (Paris, 1913).

5. André Veinstein, ed., *Bibliothèques et musées des arts du spectacle dans le monde*, 2nd ed. (Paris, 1967).

cases they offer much of real interest. To those among you who in the future may have some role in this kind of enterprise, I take the liberty of suggesting that you act for the benefit of future generations and see to it that at the appropriate time these sources of documentation be deposited in public archives. If the papers and documents of the earliest record manufacturers had not been allowed to fall into the hands of trash collectors, we would not be lamenting their loss today. Similarly, a few years ago, the archives of the Ballets Russes of Diaghilev were dispersed beyond recall. Still another example: Hector Berlioz, trying to assure that his works and papers would be transmitted to posterity as a unit, presented them to one of the oldest Parisian concert societies, stating in his accompanying letter that there was no better institution in the world to receive them. But several years ago, a part of these very archives were retrieved from the wastebasket just in time—and I speak literally!

Another source of unexploited documents is publishing firms; contracts between composers and publishers may often reveal aborted projects or unexpected modifications made in works whose geneses were otherwise believed to be well known. Even labor-union records may be a source of interesting information on the working conditions of performers or instrument makers.

Now, let us have a look at the approach followed most frequently by young musicologists: biographical research. For those who have not found a broader thesis topic growing out of their personal interest, the monograph on a specific composer, of minor or medium stature, remains the classical doctoral road, even though it may not be the most profitable for musicology. In carrying out this work, the student soon discovers the relativity of our existing information about his man (with all the dictionaries repeating the same errors), and usually undergoes his first battle with archival records. Biographical research may turn out to be easy or difficult, depending on the means that are initially available. Certain guides perfected for the genealogists may be useful in this respect: in English, the old guide by Richard Sims,[6] and in French, that of Jacques Meurgey.[7] Those who succeed best in this type of activity have the temperament and the instincts of a detective: their search may often lead them far afield. From the *état civil* (birth and death registers), they may progress, depending on the vagaries of musical careers, to ecclesiastical archives (maîtrises) or to those of the king's household, the conservatories or the universities, or may even take an oblique turn toward military documents or legal proceedings (nearly always very well preserved), if not toward police records (as has been fruitful for more than one attractive singer or

6. Richard Sims, *A Manual for the Genealogist* . . . , 2nd ed. (London, 1888).

7. Jacques Meurgey, *Guide des recherches généalogiques aux Archives Nationales avec une étude sur les recherches biographiques aux Archives de la Seine* (Paris, 1953).

dancer during the eighteenth century). In any case, notarial records must always be consulted—this is a relatively new source of documentation about which I should like to say more.

Today the notary is a person whose door we enter only on rare occasions. The situation was quite different during the fifteenth to the seventeenth centuries. Then, he was relied upon for the most ordinary daily activities, such as engaging musicians, ordering instruments, or signing a contract with a printer or dancing teacher, etc. One is not surprised to find, therefore, at Avignon, in an act notarized in 1449, a list of *basses danses* that a student expected to learn from his music teacher.[8] In certain countries, like Portugal, Hungary, and Denmark, the notarial profession was controlled by the church. In those countries strongly influenced by Roman law, these archives are very old, sometimes dating back to the fourteenth century. Elsewhere, as in the north of France, they rarely go back beyond the fifteenth or even the sixteenth centuries. Until relatively recent times notarial records were preserved in the office of each notary. In many cities, the public archive has become the recipient of the ancient notarial archives, thus creating a concentration of such sources. (These archives usually comprise documents that the notary no longer needs in the exercise of his functions.) Thanks to this concentration, which has been effected most notably in Venice and in Paris as well as in many of the French departmental archives, scholars may search with ease through an extremely rich mass of documentation. Notarial sources will often fill major gaps in public archives, and give a more vibrant picture of the life of the period.

In larger cities, where the number of notaries was great, it may be complicated to track down information about a specific individual. In such instances, without a good point of departure, there is a danger of leafing in vain through hundreds of document-crammed folders. The location of the person's home might provide a good clue, if he used a local notary. Valuable advice concerning Parisian notaries may be found in the guide by Mireille Rambaud and in the volume published by the Minutier Central, both cited above. Another possible source of help is series Y of the Châtelet of Paris, which contains the registrations (*insinuations*) of certain notarized acts and also provides alphabetical tables for the period from the sixteenth to the eighteenth century; one may find the name of the person's notary and then be able to proceed to the registers of the Minutier. There, the first document to be sought should be the inventory of the person's estate (*inventaire après décès*). This act usually furnishes, among other information, the list of contracts made during his lifetime and is thus the

---

8. Published most recently by Daniel Heartz, "A Fifteenth-Century Ballo: Roti bouilli joyeux," in *Aspects of Medieval and Renaissance Music: A Birthday Offering to Gustave Reese*, ed. Jan LaRue (New York, 1966), p. 372.

key to all biographical research in notarial archives. In the last analysis, there is no domain of historical musicology not served by this source.

Most of the documents we have discussed present difficulties of decipherment in varying degrees. First of all, there is the problem of language. Almost all texts emanating from the Catholic church, until at least the seventeenth century, are in Latin. Public and private documents, depending upon the country and locality, are very often also in Latin until the sixteenth century; thereafter they are in the vernacular.

The beginner is even more likely to be discouraged by the difficulty of understanding the handwriting. It is an error to assume that the oldest documents are the most difficult to read, and that the more recent they are, the easier to decipher. Those who are accustomed to medieval documents written by professional scribes (the *Libraria*) know that reading them is relatively easy, once the code of abbreviations has been assimilated. Similarly, scribes of the major administrative institutions, who write in the official registers, almost always have a legible handwriting. The same is not true of other copyists, especially beginning with the fifteenth century; daily handwriting (the *epistolaris*) takes on a cursive aspect, which becomes even more pronounced in the course of the sixteenth century, especially in notarial documents. From this point of view the first half of the seventeenth century is sometimes described as the "paleographer's inferno." There are, however, so many specific exceptions that this evolution should not be oversimplified.

There is only one way to learn how to read archival documents: practice! Manuals of paleography do, of course, exist,[9] and several schools offer training in this auxiliary science of history. However, the value that may be gained from such training instruction is ineffective without prolonged and repeated practice. Even after long experience, each new type of document requires an initial period of orientation. Nevertheless, I do not believe that this should discourage young American musicologists. Many have already been successful despite the difficulties.

I have yet to speak of the problem of transcription and publication of archival documents. Although musicological source documents have been published for more than half a century, the situation remains quite anarchistic. Some scholars adopt a puristic attitude and reproduce only what they see. This is taking the easy road; it seems very desirable to me that we arrive at a codification, an official agreement on transcription practices. In this connection we might emulate the philologists and the publishers of literary texts, who have come to agreement on certain principles, at least

9. For example, Maurice Prou with Alain de Boüard, *Manuel de paléographie latine et française*, 4th ed. (Paris, 1924); Lewis Steig, *An Introduction to Palaeography for Librarians* (Chicago, 1938); Guilio Battelli, *Lezioni di paleografia*, 3rd ed. (Città del Vaticano, 1949); and A. C. Floriano, *Curso general de paleografia* (Oviedo, 1946).

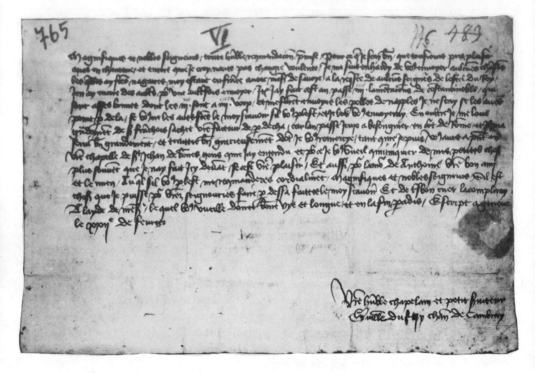

Florence, Archivio di Stato, Mediceo avanti il Principato, VI, old number 783, new number 776.

for medieval texts.[10] These same principles may be applied to musicological documents—but with greater flexibility, since literary considerations are not involved; this is especially true for the modern era.

A transcription is not a facsimile. It must be remembered that up to the eighteenth century scribes followed no rules with regard to punctuation, accents, or capitalization. To normalize these secondary details of orthography in our transcriptions is not to deform the original. Editorial principles should not be left to the arbitrary decision of each transcriber, who might more profitably concern himself with understanding the text's vocabulary and syntax. Too often, an overly pious respect for a text only hides lack of understanding of that text. The simplest intellectual honesty should prescribe that we publish nothing we have not understood.

That is why a transcriber who is concerned about his readers should attempt to recreate the correct phrasing and pronunciation; he should

10. I refer here to Paul Meyer, "Instruction pour la publication des anciens textes français," *Bibliothèque de l'École des Chartes*, LXXI (1910), 224–33; Mario Roques, "Règles pratiques pour l'édition des anciens textes français et provencaux," *ibid.* LXXXVII (1926), 453–59; and Clovis Brunel "A propos de l'édition de nos textes français du moyen âge," *Bulletin de la Société de l'histoire de France* (1941), 67–74.

Guillaume Dufay, to Piero and Giovanni de Medici in Florence. Geneva, the 22nd of February [1454].

Magnifiques et nobles seigneurs, toute humble recommandacion premise. Pour ce que je sçay bien que tousjours pris plaisir avés en chanterie et encore, comme je croy, n'avés pas changié voulenté, je me suis enhardy de vous envoyer aulcunes chansons, lesquelles ay faictes nagaires, moy estant en France avoec monseigneur de Savoye, a la resqueste de aulcuns seigneurs de l'ostel du Roy. J'en ay encore des aultres pour une aultre fois envoyer. Item j'ay fait cest an passé iiii lamentacions de Constantinoble qui sont assés bonnes: dont les iiii sont a iiii voix, et me furent envoyés les parolles de Napples. Je ne sçay se les avés point par dela. Se vous ne les avés, faictes le moy scavoir, s'il vous plest, et je les vous envoyeray. En oultre je me loue grandement de sire Franchois Sachet, vostre facteur de par decha, car l'an passé j'eux a besongnier en court de Romme et il m'a servi bien grandement et traittié bien gracieusement, dont je vous remercye tant comme je puis. Vous avés a présent en vostre chapelle de Saint Jehan de bonnes gens comme j'ay entendu et pour ce je vous vueil communiquier de mes petites choses plus souvent que je n'ay fait icy devant, se c'est vostre plaisir, et aussi pour l'amour de Anthoine, vostre bon ami et le mien, anquel, s'il vous plest, me recommanderés cordialment. Magnifiques et nobles seigneurs, s'il est chose que je puisse pour vostrez seigneuries faire par dessa, faittes le moy scavoir et de tres bon cuer l'acompliray à l'ayde de Nostre Seigneur, lequel vous vueille donner bonne vye et longue, et en la fin paradis. Escript a Genève le XXIe de fevrier.

> Vostre humble chapelain et petit serviteur
> Guillaume Dufay, chanoine de Cambray.

spell out all abbreviations, add missing punctuation, standardize capitalization according to modern usage, and reconstitute the paragraph structure according to the internal logic of the text. In my opinion the above procedures represent the minimum obligation of the transcriber, and do not in any real sense violate the orthography of the original.

For languages, like Italian and French, that have accents, the problem is more complex. If I do not dare to give you advice on the subject of Italian, here at least are some rules that may be adopted for French. The only indispensable phonetic sign is the acute accent, especially for the final syllables (such as *pie–pié*, *livre–livré*, or *tombe–tombé*). In indicating it when it is absent, the transcriber adds nothing of his own, but only restores to the word its true contemporary pronunciation. And above all, he is then providing a correct text, instead of a bastardized transcription that remains fifty-per-cent facsimile. In the latter case, he would merely be passing on to the user some of the difficulties of decipherment that he himself experienced.

These simple rules, which come from the philologists, are valid for archival documents; their application in the publication of texts with music from the fifteenth and sixteenth centuries is eminently suitable, whether the originals are in manuscript *or printed*. The same rules may be extended to documents dating from after the sixteenth century, by those who hesitate to make a total modernization.

American musicologists are at some disadvantage in doing archival work in Europe. You are not on the spot to begin with and you are generally less familiar with the source materials for which there are few equivalents here. However, the recent work of some of your compatriots, like Robert Stevenson (on Morales), Lewis Lockwood (on Vincenzo Ruffo), and Frank D'Accone (on Florentine composers of the Renaissance), may serve as excellent examples for others. These scholars have followed the precept that nothing replaces direct and personal contact with the original sources.

It seems to me that, in Europe at least, a thesis topic is chosen more to permit the candidate to demonstrate his abilities than to fill a gap in our knowledge. I concede that a topic restricted to archival research provides limited opportunity to assess the over-all talents of a candidate who must be granted a diploma if he is later to become a teacher. As a result, the publication of musical archives is neglected on two fronts: historians have no particular reason to be interested in music, and musicologists do not usually consider it an essential part of their task. However, the fact that so many professors and candidates seem to have such difficulty in finding valid topics for dissertations can derive only from a poor appreciation of the sources still remaining to be explored. To both these groups I dare suggest some subjects that are immediately available in France:

1. Monographs on the *maîtrises* of the cathedral of Notre Dame of Paris (a subject large enough to be divided in two), or of Bordeaux, Toulouse, Avignon, or Besançon, for each of which there exists an almost complete series of documents. These are subjects which involve musical sources as well, but are not recommended for those who have no knowledge of Latin.

2. Music at the court of Lorraine at the end of the fifteenth and in the sixteenth century (starting with the archives of Meurthe-et-Moselle in Nancy).

3. Music at the French court during the sixteenth century. The account books of the king's musical establishments, dispersed in various locations, should be reassembled and published in a critical edition.

4. Popular concert life in Paris during the nineteenth century.

5. History of the Opéra during the Restoration (based on Series O of the Archives Nationales).[11]

6. History of the Théâtre italien during the Restoration (based on the same series).

11. See J.-G. Prod'homme, "État alphabétique sommaire des archives de l'Opéra," *Revue de musicologie*, XIV (1933), 193–205.

Musicology is a totality. I suggest that it requires all kinds of approaches if it is to become a mature, humanistic discipline. One cannot deny that archival research, in its present state, is one of musicology's most neglected aspects—one need only compare the paucity of archival publications that have appeared in the last twenty-five years with the large quantity of bibliographical studies and scholarly editions of music. In stating this I have no desire to distract you from what remains the essential element of our task, the music itself. But some among us harbor the singular belief that we must not ignore the social and historical context in which musical works are born; if we do, we shall never arrive at determining the creative processes of each age, at distinguishing the fashionable from the original, or the followers from the innovators. Perhaps in the past there was insufficient discipline and rather too much dilettantism. It is up to us, henceforth, to be more exigent and more efficacious.

DISCUSSION

BROOK: In order to structure this seminar, may I suggest three main areas for discussion? First, Monsieur Lesure, may I ask you to describe in detail how one might pursue an archival investigation of an individual composer? Second, how should archival research be pursued as part of the profession of musicology, and how should its results be published? Third, text transcription. The solutions you suggested in your lecture may seem sacrilegious to musicologists accustomed to the pious approach used in the trancription of music.

Could we start with a composer on whom you have done a great deal of work, Clément Janequin? Would you describe how your archival work on Janequin proceeded?

LESURE: The beginning of my research on Janequin was not typical. On my first day in the Minutier Central of the Archives Nationales, in the very first register opened, I found the will, the *testament*, of Janequin. Needless to say, this was the lone discovery of the sort in my career. It was a very good start. The will permits one to learn the names of different persons connected with him, and the *exécuteur testamentaire*. I had the further good fortune to meet an archivist in Bordeaux who had discovered some *actes* in the departmental archives there relating to his youth. Janequin's life now had a beginning in Bordeaux and an end in Paris. And the middle soon became less mysterious. Janequin's name was found in Angers, thanks to another archivist, Monsieur Levron, who discovered, also in notarial archives, several *actes* that permit us to learn a little of the middle period. With these three sources providing precise names and dates, it was very easy to extend the research to ecclesiastical archives and to the archives of the Châtelet de Paris.

VAN SOLKEMA: Could we also ask you to take up a "nonmiraculous"

case? Suppose you wished to investigate the background of a minor sixteenth-century composer, Cléreau, for example, or Passereau. How would
you set about it without a miracle?

LESURE: Passereau is very difficult. All the information about Passereau
is quite wrong, and one doesn't know where to begin. The sole solution in
this instance is to await the systematic publication of all the sixteenth-century *actes* of the Minutier Central. In the meantime, it is wasteful to
search for months or years without any initial facts. What Fétis has written—to wit, that Passereau was curator of Saint Jacques de la Boucherie—
is impossible to verify. Passereau is apparently not his family name, and it
is senseless to search under it in the Minutier Central. It is probably his
nickname. It is always possible, of course, to find out something by
chance.[12]

Cléreau is easy because we have a starting point. We can go to Toul or
Nancy, because we know from other sources that he was in these cities.

BUSHLER: I would gather that in archival research much depends on
being on the scene. You chanced upon Janequin's will and happened to
meet a Bordeaux colleague with further information. Can we pursue such
research from the United States? If you write to an archivist, will he do
any searching for you? Don't you have to go there yourself?

LESURE: You can always write to an archivist if you have a *piste* to start
with. I do not recommend preparing a questionnaire and sending it out to
twenty archivists to see what will happen. You may develop an hypothesis and ask the archivist to verify it, but it is necessary to send him
something to go by.

MRS. HAMPTON: With notarial records, you can start with the name of
the notary and the area in which he operated. I have noticed that civil and
ecclesiastical archives are not as well organized and I suppose they are
even more difficult to work with.

LESURE: It is necessary to have a precise idea of the classification of the
archives. In France it is relatively easy because the same classification
system is used in all *archives départementales*; these are the principal
archival repositories, aside from the Archives Nationales in Paris. You
know, for example, as I mentioned in the lecture, that the categories G
and H contain ecclesiastical records. You locate things by *paroisse*, by
year, and so forth, plus some good luck of course. In Italy I think there is
a similar sort of classification, but their archives are not as centralized or as
consistent as in France.

HARMS: How complete is the Minutier Central in Paris? In your preface to the first volume of *Documents du Minutier Central*, you state that

12. As the volume was going to the printer, chance did, indeed, come to rescue
Passereau from virtual anonymity. His identity and background have been uncovered
in the archives of the Cathedral of Bourges.

the notaries began functioning at the end of the fifteenth century, that in 1928 the French government passed a law providing for a notarial depository in the National Archives, and that some notaries did not deposit their minutes into the Minutier Central. Were these important notaries?

LESURE: No. Some notaries resisted, but very few. At the present time the bulk of notarial archives up to varying dates in the second half of the nineteenth century are deposited in the Minutier. We have, for example, the *inventaire après décès* of Chopin conserved there (it has not been published!). While each notary's *étude* may not be complete, because documents were destroyed during civil wars and other disasters, in general the Minutier is very well preserved and accessible. In the *départements* it is not always the same as in Paris, because in certain cases there has been greater resistance on the part of the notaries. But more and more, in all of France, notarial records are becoming available.

BROOK: It may clarify things to say that the notary must be able to produce on appropriate demand all the papers which concern his client. The *étude* of a notary is his office and, by implication, the documents it houses. An *étude* may exist for two or three centuries. A *minute* is a notation by the notary. It is not an official public record, but a provisional document used to prepare an official act.

LESURE: The *minute* is the first document written down by the notary or his scribe. It remains in his office. The collected *minutes* have become the basis of the Minutier Central. The contractees are each given a copy of the official *acte*, which they keep—a marriage contract for example, with seal and wax. Often the notary preserves a copy of the *acte* itself only in registers, not in individual sheets.

MRS. JORGENS: You mentioned that from the fifteenth through the seventeenth centuries, people made numerous transactions through the notary. After the seventeenth century, is there some other archival source that is more important for biographical detail than the notarial records?

LESURE: Notarial records have diminished in importance, but they have not been replaced in function. It is impossible to pick a precise date when the notarial archives become no longer very interesting, archivally speaking. But I think that it was during the seventeenth century that the transformation began—it is difficult to explain it in a few words—it was based on the evolution of private and social life.

You always have, of course, the *état civil* and the *Châtelet*. But these sources are most effectively used in conjunction with the *notaire*.

BROOK: The notarial minutes, because they record in detail so many important events having to do with a family, give a more complete picture, a more living picture, than the more formal documents that you might find, say, in a birth or marriage certificate on file at the *état civil*.

LESURE: This is true. For example, I remember an *acte* in Avignon:

when two men make a bet on the birth of a child—boy or girl?—they go before the notary to put down the precise conditions of the bet.

SCHOTT: If one is not able to go to a particular archive with precise initial information, are there dependable specialists that one can engage? I realize there are genealogical research people who can be hired to justify somebody's *titre de noblesse*, but are there similar services on which a scholar can rely?

LESURE: Most of the researchers in the archives are, indeed, genealogists. I don't think that similar specialist services are available for scholarly research. It is a pity. The state-employed professional archivist usually has no time; the other personnel in the archives are not competent. I deplore the fact that, in writing a dissertation on a minor musician, young scholars often lose many weeks seeking the impossible. That is why I favor publications such as those of the Minutier Central.

VAN SOLKEMA: Can you tell us anything about the schedule of publication of volumes for before 1600 and after 1650?

LESURE: I estimate that six volumes will be required for the seventeenth century alone. It will take ten years. It is a very rich documentation.

MRS. HAMPTON: I noticed that Madame Rambeau has also published a volume on art from 1700 to 1750, with a chapter on music.

LESURE: This is true. But unfortunately, it is only a selective rather than a systematic book like that of Madame Jurgens. For us it is useful, nevertheless, because it contains many detailed eighteenth-century documents.

SCHOTT: You indicated that the Minutier Central now houses practically all the documents from Parisian notaries' offices through 1900. I have in mind the testament of Alkan, who died in 1880. Would it be reasonable to expect that so recent a document would be located there?

LESURE: Yes, I think the chances are good. Since it is a private paper rather than a public document, the scholar would have to secure the notary's permission to publish it; notaries today are usually quite cooperative.

BROOK: May we now turn to our second main topic: how does archival research relate to the musicological profession, and how should its results be published? How valid, for example, is the review, by W. H. Auden, of Deutsch's *Mozart: A Documentary Biography*,[13] describing it as:

> An unbook, unwritten by, it would seem, an anal madman. . . . I say madman because the theory of Truth presupposed by such an undertaking as this is insane. . . . To think, that is to say, to compare one object with another, to ask their value and meaning, is to falsify. The only function of the human mind is, as it were, to photograph the objects which the hand has succeeded in collecting. . . . By the law of Probability, such senseless industry, if pursued over a long enough period, can hardly fail to unearth some

13. Otto Erich Deutsch, *Mozart: A Documentary Biography* (Stanford, 1965).

new documents of genuine interest. . . . But why, for the sake of a few nuggets, should any reader be expected to sift through tons of detritus. . . .[14]

Auden polarizes "collecting" and "thinking," and proceeds, with a wave of his waspish wand, to dismiss the validity of systematic documentation —precisely what Monsieur Lesure has been advocating here. Auden's viewpoint is unfortunately not unique. His review infuriated me. I could not refrain from sending a letter to the editor which I would like to quote in part, not only because it is appropriate to our discussion, but because it was never printed:

> To the Editor of the *New York Review of Books*:
> What next, Billy Graham on Tennessee Williams? . . . W. H. Auden's admiration for Mozart, and his genuine gift for translating libretti, hardly qualify him to pass judgment on a basic volume of Mozart scholarship, nor do they grant him license to make irresponsible and ignorant assumptions about Professor Deutsch's methods, objectives, and "theory of Truth." "Anal madman" indeed! Without such "madmen," books like the Köchel Catalogue would never have appeared, the Mozart letters would never have been gathered, the Mozart iconographies would never have been assembled. Indeed, museums of any kind would hardly exist. The detritus of ancient Carthage can become the delight of the modern curator. By whose "senseless industry" did Auden come to learn whatever facts he values about Mozart?
> Otto Erich Deutsch needs no defense; he is one of the great scholars of our time. He has singlehandedly dramatized and fulfilled the need for complete documentation, iconography, dating, authentication, and thematic cataloguing of a single composer's life and output.

HARMS: Isn't Auden really talking about people who view collecting as an end in itself?

BROOK: That may be, but he does so by a frontal attack on a discriminating and thinking bibliographer. Deutsch was a man who fully recognized the coexistent need for analysis, esthetic interpretation, and historical perspective. Auden's unthinking assumption to the contrary is insulting.

LESURE: Yes, indeed. I think that it is not only the nature of the research which is put into question by Auden, but, by extension, also the value of history itself. In France we have often read satires by detractors of the significance of history.

MRS. JORGENS: On the subject of the publication of archival research, I couldn't understand why Madame Jurgens chose to reproduce some documents in their entirety—for example, agreements between musicians to perform together over a period of time—while other documents are presented in résumé.

LESURE: I think that is easy to explain. A contract between ten instru-

---

14. W. H. Auden, review of *Mozart: A Documentary Biography* by Otto Erich Deutsch, *New York Review of Books* (Aug. 5, 1965), 12.

mentalists that contains details of the constitution of the orchestra—one
man playing *all* basses, another playing the dessus de cornet *and* the basse
de viol—is very useful. This kind of selection will always be a little
subjective, but I think Madame Jurgens has been reasonable and judicious
in her choices.

BROOK: On getting things published, I like the Royal Musical Association *Research Chronicle*'s practice. As general editor of the series, Thurston Dart put it this way in his preface:

> During the course of his investigations every musical scholar inevitably
> accumulates large quantities of musicological raw material—lists, indexes,
> catalogues, calendars, extracts from newspapers, new fragments of biograph-
> ical information, and so on. . . . The R.M.A. Research Chronicle, it is hoped,
> will serve to circulate some of the more worthwhile material brought to
> light during the course of such investigations. . . .[15]

Let us turn to the third main topic: transcription of archival texts and
how this compares with the transcription of music. Monsieur Lesure has
advocated that the transcriber of verbal texts should follow existing principles and make certain changes in accents, punctuation, and so forth,
instead of copying out the original exactly. Do you accept this? I suggest
that some musicologists may not. In other disciplines, overly pious transcription is rare; the transcriber helps the reader as much as possible without violating the text.

HARMS: Does this imply that in transcribing a document from the 1600s
one would change all the spellings to modern spellings?

LESURE: Not at all. You transform only that which is lost, the *respira-
tion*, the punctuation. If you find an error in spelling, you must keep it as
evidence of the earlier times. For the modern period, it is more difficult.
Debussy, for example, didn't know how to spell. In editing his letters, do
we keep his obvious errors?

HEST: Would it not be possible to use brackets, as in scholarly editions
of music? It would seem to me that prejudices or ignorances of the transcriber would easily creep into his transcription.

LESURE: Not if basic principles are observed. As I have said, these principles have been widely accepted in archival work and have been followed
successfully for many years. It would be very useful to adopt them for
archival texts about music and also for underlayed texts. In performances
of ancient music, I have often noticed that if the text is not properly
accented, the singer who is not knowledgeable in the language sings the
words quite stupidly.

BROOK: We could use a similar set of principles for the transcription of
music. The purist approach has often resulted in overedited music and in
the wasteful production of hundreds of pages of *Revisionsberichte*. If a

15. *RMA Research Chronicle*, I (1965), verso of title page.

Mass, for example, has twenty different "authentic" sources, the experienced scholar-transcriber should be relied upon to decide which version or combination of versions is closest to the composer's probable intentions. His critical edition, equipped with only the essential brackets, question marks, and footnotes, will represent his best thinking. Should he also be expected to spend months indicating every last variant dot, ligature, and copyist's error in a long *Revisionsbericht*, or should he rather devote his time to transcribing more Masses according to a reasonable set of basic principles upon which most scholars could agree?

DITTMER: In the transcription of fifteenth-century music, we have quite a few ligatures that are apparently meaningless. We still indicate their presence by some kind of mark, with the thought that someday we may discover that they were significant. Those transcriptions that have these indications will then be valuable, and those which do not will be less so.

LESURE: I agree. It is important to indicate the existence of ligatures. But for archival texts, it is absolutely useless to know that there are abbreviations in the text and to take pains to designate them in italics; it is, after all, an historical question, not a poetic or philological one.

May *I* ask a question? Do you have schools of paleography in this country, or here in New York City?

BROOK: There may be occasional individual courses but to my knowledge, there is no school in the United States that resembles your École des Chartes, which is specifically designed to train archivists and paleographers. The extent of paleographical work and of archival collections in this country is summarized in *A Guide to Archives and Manuscripts in the United States*,[16] compiled by Phillip Hamer and published under the auspices of the National Historical Publications Commission, established by Act of Congress in 1934 to promote better control, utilization, and unification in the handling of our archival resources. The *Guide* contains a number of references to little-known, musically important collections.

LESURE: From a quick glance at Mr. Hamer's *Guide*, it seems that you do not make the same distinction we do between archives and manuscript collections in libraries.

BROOK: Could you define the difference?

LESURE: Let me give you two examples: the receipt from a king's finance office for a musician's salary belongs in the archives; it is an official document. A personal letter from Gabrieli to the duke of Ferrara is material for the library; it is a personal document. Even if the letter is from a familial archive, it does not normally belong in the archives unless the family places it there.

VAN SOLKEMA: Could you describe what is happening in France today with regard to archival research or musicological research in general?

16. Phillip Hamer, *A Guide to Archives and Manuscripts in the United States* (New Haven, 1961).

LESURE: We have few musicological researchers in France and, as you may know, little goes on outside of Paris. We do not have the extraordinary activity that you have developed here in your universities. However, there is no parochialism of subject; now and then we even try to push a student into archival work.

MRS. FRIEDLAND: Monsieur Lesure, I have a question relating to sociology. In your article "Musicologie et sociologie,"[17] you make a plea for the larger, contextual view of music history. You take a very firm stand against what you called *dessèchement de la méthode "historisante,"*—the drying up of historically oriented method—which is the *reductio ad absurdum* against which I think Auden was inveighing in his misguided review of Deutsch's work. I agree completely. But I would question whether the references you cite in that article successfully use this kind of approach. I refer specifically to two books, Ernst Meyer's *English Chamber Music*[18] and Edward Lowinsky's *Secret Chromatic Art in the Netherlands Motet.*[19] In your discussion of Meyer's book you laud the author for his larger aim, but suggest that he sometimes falls prey to oversimplification. I cannot see that there is enough *internal* evidence, for example, for his deduction that the violence and ferment in Italian choral music at the turn of the sixteenth century was directly attributable to the intervention of the Counter Reformation, whereas in England at that time—without the same religious impetus—the music was of a quiet, more private sort. This is a broad and largely unsupported generalization that I suspect may have been made by sifting and selecting examples. My question is this: How can we take facts accumulated in our research and in the context of a rigorous scholarly approach try to place them within a larger sociological framework, without falling prey to making statements that appear unsupported and possibly unsupportable?

LESURE: You are correct in employing the word *dessèchement*, and, of course, archives do not liberate us *a priori* from the drying up of musicological method. I seem, in fact, to be holding two conflicting viewpoints: in the article you cite from the *Revue musicale* I present an avant-garde attitude, whereas in this discussion we are dealing essentially with a question of method. I would like to try to show that the two approaches must ultimately be joined together. To begin with, I exclude the use of the term sociology because the more it is used, the more I fear this word is abused. I personally have been somewhat discouraged by the lack of progress made in music sociology, in the sense of strict sociology. I think that

17. François Lesure, "Musicologie et sociologie," *Revue musicale*, CXXI (1953).

18. Ernst H. Meyer, *English Chamber Music, the History of a Great Art from the Middle Ages to Purcell* (London, 1946).

19. Edward Lowinsky, *Secret Chromatic Art in the Netherlands Motet*, trans. Carl Buchman (New York, 1946).

this particular problem is too general and would require too much time for us to go into here. Today, I believe it essential to return to a period of synthesis, a period of broad general ideas that would set in motion a discussion of great value to the advancement of learning. You know how much Lowinsky's book was criticized at the time—Meyer's also, by the way. I believe it is extremely useful to launch provocative ideas, no matter how shocking they may seem at first, in order to arrive ultimately at greater understanding. This is the kind of venture musicologists have only too rarely undertaken. And now, how can these problems of archives help us to speak about "sociology" and "music sociology"? I believe that Lowinsky's *Secret Art*—and his other work as well—offers a good example of just that. He begins with a specific body of source material and proceeds to extract from it a maximum of inference; and if he may seem at times to go beyond the maximum, that is infinitely preferable to remaining strictly within the confines of the evidence in fear, pious or not, of saying a single word not immediately provable by one's documentary sources. I believe that if by starting with a certain group of archival materials, say from Notre Dame, one could succeed in telling the story of such a great choir school, even for only a limited period, and if one could try to solve each problem that came up (for example, the training of Cantor A, the voyages made by Cantor B), one could illuminate one corner of our knowledge and penetrate into the life and musical mentality of the people of that period.

READING LIST

Carrière, Victor, *Introduction aux études d'histoire ecclésiastique locale*, 3 vols. (Paris, 1936–40).

Dunan, Elisabeth, *Archives nationales . . . Inventaire de la série A5³⁷*, I (Paris, 1971).

Jurgens, Madeleine, *Documents du Minutier central des notaires relatifs à l'histoire de la musique (1600–1650)*, I (Paris, 1968).

Rambaud, Mireille, *Les sources de l'histoire de l'art aux Archives nationales* (Paris, 1955).

The Iconology of Music: Potentials and Pitfalls

EMANUEL WINTERNITZ

*I*CONOLOGY of music deals with the lessons that pictures can teach the music historian. A more sophisticated definition would be: the analysis and interpretation, by the historian of music, of pictorial representations of musical instruments, their players, singers, groups of performing musicians, and all other kinds of musical scenes.

Iconology is not an easy tool to use; it requires a skilled hand. We cannot simply look at a painting showing string instruments and say "no drones," or look at an angel concert in painting or sculpture and say "five strings plus seven singers and two trumpets." Things are usually much more complex.

As documents of the past, pictures have two enormous advantages over verbal descriptions or contemporary reports in treatises: first, pictorial representations often show a precision of detail that words cannot convey; second, pictures often reveal facts of detail that contemporary writers neglect to describe because they take them for granted. Social historians of the year 3000 could not learn from Hemingway or T. S. Eliot whether a lady in 1968 used to enter a taxi with her head or her behind first; but movies, Kodak snapshots, and caricatures will provide precise evidence. The same is true of the interesting things we expect to learn from iconography: the shape and stringing of instruments; playing technique; the grouping of instruments in church, court, and home; the proportions among strings, brass, woodwinds, etc.; and—a very large topic—the social status of instruments and their players as well as the environment of performances.[1]

Before the invention of photography, most visual depictions occurred in works of art. Since an artistic portrayal of an object may differ in many ways from a realistic sketch or a snapshot, familiarity with the many time-bound artistic styles of the past and with the idiosyncrasies of the individual artists is necessary in order to translate its altered image, its style-bound rendering, into information that the music historian can accept as reliable "visual evidence" for his own purposes—for instance, for the study of performance practice. We have only to think of the various forms of perspective as practiced in various artistic climates, from Egyptian wall paintings to Renaissance intarsias to Baroque cupola frescoes, to immediately become aware of some basic differences in rendering instruments or players.

An awareness of these variable degrees of pictorial realism is needed today more than ever, since we are faced with the question of how far computers can be of help for the aims of musical iconology. No doubt they can be enormously useful for many tasks; but we cannot—or, rather, should not—naïvely feed into them visual data from various periods of style for the purpose of inventory without previously examining the data critically from many angles, a few of which I shall try to demonstrate here.

Rather than take the time to summarize what iconology has given us in the past or what remains to be done, or to outline a system of musical iconology, I feel that it will be more appropriate to show a few examples of iconology at work—in short, a sort of demonstration by a series of sample vivisections.

I will begin by illustrating three pitfalls, to sharpen and instruct our eyes: first an error by Renaissance artists and archeologists; second, a blunder by a famous eighteenth-century historian of music; and third, a misinterpretation by one of the greatest musicologists of our times.

Our first example deals with an error committed by Renaissance artists dealing with mythological subjects of Greek and Roman antiquity. Looking at a Renaissance relief from about 1480 (Pl. 1a), we recognize Apollo and his rival Marsyas, surrounded by their instruments, among which is Apollo's lyre—but is it a lyre? It is clearly patterned after ancient Greek and Roman lyres as they appear in statues, reliefs, wall paintings, and vase paintings, but with this important exception: it has a fingerboard for stopping the strings. Greek and Roman antiquity used chiefly open strings; lyres, kitharas, and harps had open strings, but no fingerboard, that ingenious device which makes stopping possible and thus provides a single string with the capacity to produce different pitches.

1. A subject recently approached in an original way in a book by François Lesure, *Music and Art in Society* (University Park, Penn., 1968).

The error committed by the sculptor of our relief (and by many others) was not a willful falsification of history. Renaissance musical archeologists imputed the invention of the bowed fiddle (a fingerboard instrument) to Sappho. Their erroneous belief was encouraged by the way Greek and Roman sculptors rendered the strings. In full, round sculptures, the strings are never shown; even in reliefs, they are not incised or three-dimensionally indicated, for the simple reason that all of these reliefs had painted details in colors, and the painter had obviously less difficulty showing strings than the sculptor.

In a very few cases, a set of strings was condensed into a sort of band, as in this ancient Roman relief from the Palazzo Spada (Pl. 1b), but such depictions are exceptional and usually turn out to be Renaissance restorations or even fakes of ancient works. Thus, an historical phenomenon as fundamental as the evolution from open-string to stopped-string technique is blurred by errors of Renaissance artists and pseudoarcheologists—errors that later misled modern art and music historians.

To turn to our second pitfall: Charles Burney, in his famous *General History of Music*, devotes no less than forty pages to praising the ingenuity of the Egyptians as musicians and instrument makers. His eulogy is inspired by the representation, on an Egyptian obelisk, of what he thought was a lute, and Burney observes that the use of pegs and neck, enabling the player to elicit many tones from one string, is symptomatic of a highly progressive musical culture. Burney's chapter includes a very large engraving of an Egyptian "lute" (Pl. 2a), based on a drawing made under his very eyes from the Egyptian obelisk lying in the Campus Martius in Rome. He also devotes almost two pages to the explanation of this instrument. This drawing then found its way into Forkel's *Allgemeine Geschichte der Musik*.[2] This "lute," however, is only a very common Egyptian hieroglyph, meaning "good," which uses an ideogram based on the shape of the windpipe joined to the heart!

The third pitfall concerns a crucial organological question, the first documentation of the string bow in the Occident. The evidence for this was believed to exist in one of the drawings in the Utrecht Psalter, dated about A.D. 800 in the Carolingian era (Pl. 2b). It was Curt Sachs, a giant in our field and many others, a pioneer on whose shoulders we all stand, who committed this error in his *Handbuch der Musikinstrumentenkunde*, published in Leipzig in 1920. In his illustration, Sachs showed only about a third of the length of the stick in the hands of the psalmist. The Latin text of the Psalter, Psalm 108, "et dividam Sicimam et convallem tabernaculorum dimeciar" (I will divide Sichem and mete out the valley of the tabernacles) leaves no doubt about what is illustrated: the psalmist is using a measuring rod to survey the ground for the temple. Well, even Homer

2. Johann Nikolaus Forkel, *Allgemeine Geschichte der Musik*, 2 vols. (Leipzig, 1788, 1801), I, Ch. 2, p. 83.

nodded, and there were no quick xeroxes at the time of Sachs's handbook.[3]

Let us turn, then, from our examples of pitfalls to some larger historical problems that may be illuminated with the help of iconology, problems such as the evolution from open strings to stopped strings and bowing; the importance of drone music in the face of developing polyphony; the grouping of instruments into large or small orchestras producing loud or soft music; and the changing social status of instruments and their symbolic connotation—religious, erotic, political, as the case may be. To do this, I should like to submit to you not microscopic details, but whole landscapes seen with an astronaut's eye, or—if we drop the metaphor—a comparison of material from several centuries in one glimpse, as it were. In this connection it will be helpful to be aware of one basic phenomenon: the stubborn force of tradition. For example, at the same time that saxophones are played in nightclubs of modern Athens or Cairo, pipes with double reeds are played not too far away in the lonesome mountain valleys of Macedonia or in the swamps of the Nile delta.

To trace the survival of the aulos, or, rather, the diaulos, in reed pipes or similar instruments, a large number of illustrations are available from many periods. I will offer here only six illustrations covering six centuries. The first (Pl. 2c) shows various double pipes from the tenth and eleventh centuries. I will not go into a discussion of whether all these double pipes are reed pipes. The second (Pl. 3a) shows two musicians from the beautiful miniatures of the *Cantigas de Santa Maria*, commissioned by Alfonso the Wise of Castile in the second half of the thirteenth century and preserved in the Escorial. Here we have, beyond doubt, separate double-reed pipes. Our next illustration (Pl. 3b), from the famous frescoes by Simone Martini in Assisi, about 1330, shows two separate double-reed pipes. In the High Renaissance, Pollaiuolo's famous bronze monument to Sixtus IV in Saint Peter's (Pl. 4a) shows the allegorical figure of Musica playing an organ and surrounded by other instruments, among which there is a double recorder with pipes of different lengths. Such depictions of double pipes were probably made with conscious reference to the ancient heritage.

One tondo in the Palazzo del Tè in Mantua by Giulio Romano shows the sacrifice of a bull accompanied by the inevitable double pipes as represented in countless ancient Roman reliefs of sacrifices—or so it seems at first glance. On closer inspection (Pl. 4b), we find that Giulio Romano has brought the design nearer to his time; what appears to be a double pipe is in fact two separate shawms, each played by a separate player. Another

3. It is amusing to note that another author since then, Friedrich Behn, who had facsimiles available and saw the entire drawing, concluded from the excessive length and clumsiness of the stick, that the bow must have *just* been invented (*Musikleben im Altertum und frühen Mittelalter* [Stuttgart, 1954], p. 33n).

attempt to adapt the ancient reed pipe to a later age can be seen in Ruben's famous procession with the drunken Silenus (Pl. 5a), which shows recorders. Rubens, as an erudite connoisseur of ancient art, obviously replaced the ancient diaulos with the double recorder of his time.

The survival of the aulos is a subject that also throws a light on the perpetuation of the drone in wind music. We shall return to the drone and its function in string music a little later.

Our next demonstration of the force of tradition may be called "the survival of the kithara." This offers us a lesson on atrophic or afunctional elements in the shapes of instruments. The gist of the matter is the amazing fact that the cittern, usually traced back to Elizabethan times, is nothing more than an outgrowth of the ancient Greek kithara, by way of a slow and often almost imperceptible process of modification. This evolution, spanning more than one and a half millennia is so surprising because it leads from an instrument with only open strings (which cannot be stopped) to an instrument whose strings run over a fingerboard, permitting stopping.

Citterns of the seventeenth century often had small, inconspicuous buckles, sometimes in the form of scrolls, at their shoulders. These protuberances were entirely nonfunctional. What, then, is their significance? As soon as we bring ourselves to interpret them as being atrophic remnants of the arms of the ancient kithara, their meaning becomes clear. A systematic scrutiny of visual representations of Renaissance, medieval, and even earlier instruments confirms the hypothesis beyond any doubt, for if we step back in time, we find an unbroken line of visual representations in intarsias, sculpture, and book illuminations, revealing that the further back we go, the bigger and more conspicuous the buckles appear, until in the Utrecht Psalter (of Carolingian origin) we find actual kitharas side by side with "fingerboard kitharas"—that is, instruments that retain the shape of kitharas with arms, but have a long neck with frets for stopping, while the arms carry no yoke and are, therefore, nonfunctional.

But even this is not the end of the search, since we know that the Utrecht Psalter was copied from earlier models, probably originating in the sixth century; thus, it was written and illustrated at a time when the ancient kithara with functional arms was still in fashion.[4]

One by-product of this investigation is a clarification of the origin of the fingerboard: the grafting of fingerboards onto instruments of the lyre or kithara type. This transition from instruments with open strings only (one string, one tone) to instruments that provide for stopping (many tones from one single string) was the essential step that made possible the later development of bowed strings.

4. I have sketched this story here in brief because I gave a detailed account of it, with many illustrations, in the chapter "The Survival of the Kithara and the Evolution of the English Cittern: A Study in Morphology" in my book, *Musical Instruments and Their Symbolism in Western Art* (New York, 1967).

My third example of the force of tradition concerns another large problem, the persistence of drone music from the Middle Ages to the present day. We have touched upon the drone before, apropos the diaulos and double pipes, but have not mentioned another heir of the double pipe, the bagpipe. The bagpipe is a somewhat mechanized form of double, triple, or even quadruple pipes. It is also a wind counterpart of the mechanized drone instrument in the realm of strings: the organistrum and its successor, the hurdy-gurdy (*vielle à roue, ghironda, lira tedesca, Drehleier, Umblaufenden Weiber Leier*). Simultaneous occurrences of both these specialized drone instruments can be documented in pictures through the centuries, in both the mainstream and side currents of music, in sacred art and folk art, in court entertainment and *fêtes champêtres*, up and down the social ladder. This evidence is particularly interesting for the study of the Middle Ages, when the organum and its instrumental vehicle, the drone, were important elements in the origin of Occidental polyphony. Again, I will show only a very small selection from the enormous material.

In the thirteenth century, from the *Cantigas*, we see two hurdy-gurdy players (Pl. 5b), and the largest of the many bagpipes represented in the *Cantigas* (Pl. 6a), with a double chanter and two double drones. The hurdy-gurdy and bagpipe also occur together in the marginal miniatures of the Luttrell Psalter (ca. 1340) in the British Museum (Pl. 6b). A fourteenth-century angel concert of the school of Giotto in Pistoia shows a hurdy-gurdy with six strings and a bagpipe of considerable size with an enormous oboe chanter and a large drone (Pl. 7a). Skipping over some four centuries to Watteau's *L'Accordée de village* (about 1735), we find our two drone instruments as the only providers of music for this pastoral (or should we say pseudopastoral?) dance (Pl. 7b). The ultimate *rapprochement* of *vielle à roue* and musette can be demonstrated from one page in Bordet's *Méthode raisonnée* (Paris, ca. 1755; Pl. 8), one of the many instruction books of the time that treat both instruments together. We learn from this page that the compass and the tuning of the drones as well as of the chanterelles of the vielle and musette are virtually identical.

Leaving the subject of the force of tradition, we turn now to another topic and another technique, the examination of a single group of illustrations at a single point in time: illustrations of the twenty-four Apocalyptic Elders (Rev. 4:4)[5] in twelfth-century Spain and France. These are among the earliest musical subjects in medieval art, the only earlier ones being the shepherds with their pipes in Nativity scenes and King David, who, as musician par excellence of the Judeo-Christian tradition, inherits the role and image that Orpheus had enjoyed in antiquity.

What can we learn from the twelfth-century Apocalyptic Elders con-

5. An examination of the Elders in painting and sculpture, chiefly as early documentation of bowing, is found in Werner Bachmann's excellent book, *Die Anfänge des Streichinstrumentenspiels* (Leipzig, 1964).

cerning the technique of string instruments? Do we find evidence of plucking or of bowing? And what about drones? Do we find evidence of (a) inner drone strings—that is, drones between the other strings, with which the bow cannot therefore avoid contact—or (b) marginal drones —that is, drones that can be avoided by the bow if the other voice or voices do not require them, but are also available for stopping—or (c) drone strings outside the neck running through the air, and available only as open strings, each producing only one tone?

Turning to our illustrations, the first (Pl. 10a) shows a page from the Beatus manuscript from Saint-Sever (8878) in the Bibliothèque Nationale. This beautifully colored miniature depicts the Redeemer and the four living creatures surrounded by the twenty-four Elders, each holding in one hand a typical vielle of the time and a golden vial in the other. The text, Apocalypse 4:6, says: "Viginti quatuor seniores ceciderunt ante agnum et habebant singuli citharas et fialas aureas, plenas odoramentorum, quae sunt orationes sanctorum. . . ." Since one hand is occupied holding the bowl full of odoramenta, the incense, and, therefore, only one hand can be devoted to the instrument, it is difficult to ascertain whether the instrument was to be plucked or bowed.

Let us turn to illustrations of the Elders in *sculpture*—for instance, in the portal tympanum of the Church of Saint Pierre in Moissac, 1120. The Elders are arranged in three rows, fourteen in the bottom row, and higher up, five left and five right (Pl. 9a). All the Elders hold bowls; the vielles or fidulae vary greatly in shape and in number of strings from one to five.

Were the vielles bowed? Plate 9b shows two Elders, the one on the left holding a pear-shaped fidula with five strings (grouped two and three), the other holding a cucumber-shaped instrument with one string. What about the bows? The left Elder has one; the right doesn't. The left Elder's bow arm clearly is bowing, although the sculpture is damaged and most of the bow is missing. What, then, is the conclusion? Is only one of the twenty-four bowing? Or did the sculptor (who, we must assume, followed strict orders from the ecclesiastical authorities) show one Elder with a bow to make clear that only the presence of the bowls prevented the twenty-three others from holding bows, too? We are inclined to embrace the second hypothesis.

Now to the problem of drone strings—an important one in a period of incipient polyphony and in view of the existence of organum music. Are there visible drones? In vielles that have no less than five strings, we would certainly expect them, and this would be quite interesting in view of the tuning prescriptions for vielles given by Jerome of Moravia, who prescribed three accordaturas in his *Tractatus de Musica*: one with the drone as a marginal string, a second eliminating the drone, and the third shrinking the number of five strings to four and tuning them by a fourth,

a fifth, and another fifth. But no drone string outside the neck is mentioned.

The next step would have been toward drones running outside the
fingerboard or the neck (and thereby optional, like those of the heir of
the vielle, the lira da braccio), but Jerome's *Tractatus* was written at least
150 years after the Moissac tympanum. Would it not, therefore, be interesting to find outside drones—that is, open strings never to be stopped and
only optionally touched, permitting melodies without the drone as early
as 1120? Let us bear in mind that a sculptor would find it difficult to
render strings running through the air. If we turn to poorer churches,
which could only afford wall paintings, we find in Saint-Martin de Fenollar, a small church in Roussillon in the Pyrenees, a painted representation
of the Apocalyptic Elders (Pl. 10b). The painter had, indeed, no trouble in
rendering such characteristic drones.

Let us now turn to my last group of problems: the symbolism of musical instruments. I will try to illuminate briefly three kinds of such symbolism: religious symbolism, number symbolism, and finally an especially
interesting case in which the portrayal of a musical instrument by a great
Renaissance painter served two functions—allegorical and archeological
—simultaneously.

Let us begin with the religious symbolism in a small picture of the
Virgin and Child by Geertgen tot Sint Jans[6] (Pls. 11a & 11b). Geertgen,
not more than a dozen of whose works are known, was probably born in
Leiden and died at the age of twenty-eight; he lived and worked in Haar-
lem, and his whole known oeuvre dates from the decade between 1485
and 1495.

Geertgen's painting of the Virgin and Child is a visionary work of great
originality, unforgettable to anyone who has ever seen it, because of its
poetry and its miraculous luminosity. The Child shakes two large jingle
bells and is in excited motion, almost dancing, with His right leg up in the
air and both large toes turned up.

The Virgin is surrounded by an enormous number of angels, neatly
grouped into distinct concentric ovals. The outermost oval and the corners of the panel are filled with twenty-three angels playing musical
instruments that represent a nearly complete instrumentarium of the time,
even including three keyboard instruments: organ, clavicytherium, and
clavichord.

Does this heavenly orchestra depict an actual orchestra? Two observations help to answer our question. Geertgen's organization of the angels in
concentric rings or ovals, sharply distinct in their function, evidently
alludes to the revolving heavenly spheres (one need only focus on the

6. A detailed analysis of this painting can be found in my book, *Musical Instruments and Their Symbolism in Western Art, op. cit.*, pp. 139 ff.

lower part of the ovals to see how the angels there, floating in nearly hori-
zontal position, partake in the rotation). These rings clearly depict,
according to the angel doctrine of the time, the celestial spheres developed
originally in the writings of the Babylonians and Pythagoreans, and later
in Plato's *Timaeus* and *Politeia* and Cicero's *Dream of Scipio*.

A second observation helps us further. The Child, shaking the jingle
bells, looks down to the side and, in the line of His gaze, one of the musical angels in the outer ring is intently returning His glance. It is the only
angel whose eyes, notwithstanding the minuteness of the whole representation, are so distinctly rendered as to make their direction unmistakable.
And it is this very angel who shakes a smaller pair of jingle bells toward
the Child. The rapport between the two pairs of jingles is clearly inspired
by the Areopagitic and Thomistic doctrines, especially Thomas Aquinas's
Summa Theologiae, I, Questio 105, which discusses the difference between
corporeal contact and incorporeal contact—that is, the form of contact by
which God, being incorporeal, touches creatures. Here, in the picture, the
musical consonance between the inner and outer tintinabula is used as a
poetic symbol of this spiritual contact. Thus, Geertgen's picture is rich in
theological and poetic symbolism, but offers little to the historian of performance practice.

Geertgen's picture, harking back to medieval tradition, can profitably
be compared to angel concerts such as in the *Ascension of the Virgin* by
the so-called Master of the Saint Lucy Legend, a Flemish painter who
worked about 1480. There, Mary's ascension into heaven is accompanied
by two pairs of angels singing an *Ave Regina*, and by an instrumental
ensemble composed of loud instruments (one trumpet, three shawms) and
soft ones (lute, vielle, harp, organetto)—that is, eight instruments against
the small vocal body of four voices. But at the top of the painting, the
clouds open, and near the throne of the Trinity we see two groups of
angels: on the left, eleven singers in two groups, six and five, each group
singing from a book with music, and on the right, six instrumentalists,
playing three recorders, a small lute, a dulcimer, and a harp—all "soft"
instruments.

In the outer heaven, the four singers would be drowned out by the
eight instruments, but in the inner heaven, the reality of the instrumental
group in terms of earthly practice is beyond doubt, and numerous parallels are to be found in fifteenth-century paintings.[7]

Let us turn now to symbolism of numbers. I will confine myself to the
number nine, which is the number of the heavenly spheres, of the angelic
choirs and, in antiquity as well as in the many renascences of ancient
thought, of the Muses.

From the Middle Ages, we choose a picture from a Florentine choir

7. A detailed analysis of this painting, with many illustrations, can be found in *ibid.*,
pp. 145 ff.

book of 1350, today in the Cleveland Museum of Art (Pl. 12a). On top of the page, we see nine angels in a row, symmetrically arranged and representing the nine heavenly choirs. Corner pairs of angels play four trumpets, clearly overpowering the soft string instruments in the middle. In brief, an allegorical, not a realistic, depiction.

Very schematically—indeed, pedantically—arranged are the nine homogeneous groups of angels in Lorenzo Costa's *Adoration of the Child Jesus* in Venice (Pl. 12b). Imagine how this heavenly orchestra, or rather, these nine heavenly double orchestras, would sound; secular ears, at least, might not deem the sound heavenly.

For an example of number symbolism as applied to the Muses of pagan mythology, let us turn to Raphael's *Parnassus*, one of the frescoes in the Segnatura in the Vatican. Apollo on the top of Parnassus plays a lira da braccio with nine strings: seven melody strings and two bordoni (the usual number at that time was five plus two). The number nine is clearly symbolic of the nine Muses, whose leader Apollo is and who are flanking him in the fresco.

And now, since we are already in Raphael's *Parnassus*, let us select our last "vivisection" from there. In the fresco, the Muse Euterpe holds a strange instrument (Pl. 13a) with the mouth cup and general shape of a trumpet, but a strangely small and flat bell. Even stranger are the bulb beneath it and the four dark protuberances growing out of the tube: features recalling the Greek aulos, or rather, its ancient Roman counterpart, the tibia. What is the meaning of this strange composite instrument?

In the last compositional preparatory sketch for the fresco, Euterpe holds no trumpet, but an unmistakable double pipe, or diaulos. Raphael, who was familiar with the literature of the ancients and in continual touch with humanists, must have known Euterpe's attributes: "dulceloquis calamos Euterpe flatibus urgit" (the sweet-voiced Euterpe excites the pipes with her breath). From where did Raphael take this shape? As I have explained in my study *Archeologia musicale del rinascimento nel Parnaso di Raffaello*,[8] Raphael was deeply interested in the musical instruments of the ancients. In that study, I presented a lucky discovery—that Raphael, in the midst of his preparations for the fresco, changed all of his plans under the impact of a recently found Sarcophagus of the Muses, now in the Museo Nazionale delle Terme in Rome. All of the instruments on this sarcophagus, with one exception only, were taken over by Raphael into his fresco—in the same order from left to right, with amazing precision!

Only one of these instruments has not been transplanted precisely, and for good reasons: the tibia. I have made detail photographs (Pl. 13b) of the Euterpe on the sarcophagus, and we can distinguish clearly the cup-shaped protuberances, four of which must have existed still unbroken

8. *Archeologia musicale del rinascimento nel Parnaso di Raffaello*, Rendiconti della Pontificia Accademia Romana di Archeologia, XXV/2 (1952–54).

when Raphael saw the sarcophagus shortly after it came to light. These four protuberances still exist today.

In view of this archeological precision, why the nonsensical fusion of the tibia, a reed instrument, with a trumpet? (When I say "nonsensical," I mean in terms of acoustics.) Archeological precision meant much only to the initiated, the humanists and archeologists of the time—the *dotti*, as the Italians say—and Euterpe, according to ancient iconography, had to have her traditional attribute, the reed pipes. On the other hand, Raphael's fresco of *Parnassus* was intended as a celebration of the great poets from Homer up to the painter's contemporaries. The allegorical instrument for Fame or Glory was, of course, the trumpet. It was Raphael who ingeniously combined here two aims into one single instrument: on the one hand, reverence for the ancients and archeological fidelity, which was the great intellectual fashion of his time; on the other hand, homage to the great poets by using the traditional symbol of fame.

In closing, one further point: iconological research in music has a very important by-product. It helps to free musicology from that isolation into which so many specialized branches of research have fallen in our over-specializing times. It makes us study music within its social-cultural context, uniting it with its sister arts, particularly the visual arts. Quoting a saying of the Starets Zosima, "They have divided the world into hundreds of parts, and have forgotten how they hang together."

READING LIST

Kinsky, Georg, *History of Music in Pictures* (New York, 1930).

Lesure, François, *Musica e Società* (Milan, 1966); *Musik und Gesellschaft im Bild* (Kassel, 1966); *Music and Art in Society* (University Park, Penn., 1968).

Winternitz, Emanuel, "The Visual Arts as a Source for the Historian of Music," in *Report of the Eighth Congress of the International Musicological Society, New York, 1961* (Kassel, 1961).

——— *Musical Instruments and Their Symbolism in Western Art* (New York, 1967).

——— Articles in *Die Musik in Geschichte und Gegenwart* (Kassel) on Orpheus, X (1962); Theorbo, XIII (1966), Lira da Braccio, VIII, (1960); and Leonardo da Vinci, XIII (1966).

——— *Gaudenzio Ferrari, His School and the Early History of the Violin* (Milan, 1967).

Secret Chromatic Art
Re-examined

EDWARD E. LOWINSKY

W HEN the *Secret Chromatic Art*[1] appeared in
1946 it was hailed by scholars such as Jack Westrup,[2] François Lesure,[3]
Alfred Einstein,[4] and Charles van den Borren,[5] and it was rejected, indeed
condemned, by others such as Leo Schrade,[6] Marcus van Crevel,[7] and
Willi Apel.[8] Its acceptance in the mainstream of musicological literature
was slow. Although van den Borren had given over three pages of his
history of Netherlandish music[8a] to a discussion and defense of the theory,
in Gustave Reese's *Music in the Renaissance* of 1954 it rated no more than

1. Edward E. Lowinsky, *Secret Chromatic Art in the Netherlands Motet*, Columbia
University Studies in Musicology, 6 (New York, 1946; repr., New York, 1967).

2. J. A. Westrup, review of *Secret Chromatic Art* by Lowinsky, *Music and Letters*,
XXVII (1946), 268.

3. François Lesure, review of *Secret Chromatic Art* by Lowinsky, *Revue musicale*,
CCXXI (1953), 7–8.

4. Alfred Einstein, review of *Secret Chromatic Art* by Lowinsky, *Notes*, III (1946),
283-84.

5. Charles van den Borren, "Y avait-il une pratique musicale ésotérique au temps
de Roland de Lassus?," *Revue belge de musicologie*, II (1948), 38–43.

6. Leo Schrade, "A Secret Chromatic Art," *Journal of Renaissance and Baroque
Music*, I (1946), 159–67.

7. Marcus van Crevel, "Secret Chromatic Art in the Netherlands Motet?" *Tijdschrift der Vereeniging voor Nederl. Muziekgeschiedenis*, XVI (1946), 253–304.

8. Willi Apel, review of *Secret Chromatic Art* by Lowinsky, *Musical Quarterly*,
XXXII (1946), 471–76.

8a. Charles van den Borren, *Geschiedenis van de muziek in de Nederlanden*, 2 vols.
(Antwerp, 1948), I, 268–71.

a footnote;[9] but in Donald Grout's *A History of Western Music* of 1960 it was given a full page of text and a music example,[10] the idea was discussed, the technique explained, and the theory was considered as essentially correct with extreme probability.

Recently, unbeknown to its author, the *Secret Chromatic Art* was reprinted, and last year a book on symbolism in Netherlandish music appeared, in which the theory of the secret chromatic art, as well as its critics, was subjected to a lengthy and detailed analysis and accepted as basically sound, even though the writer differed on certain cases of application.[11]

In the years since the publication of the book, I have turned my attention to other topics, without, however, losing interest in the problem. In my monograph on *Tonality and Atonality in Sixteenth-Century Music*,[12] I constructed a wider framework for the phenomenon, theoretically and historically. In two articles on *Fortuna* compositions by Josquin and by Greiter, I demonstrated both the use of a bold modulatory technique and its justification by symbolic purposes.[13] In two further papers I explored Willaert's chromatic "duo" of 1519, found that it was a quartet, and discovered that not only was it the fountainhead of the whole chromatic movement in theory and in compositional practice, but that its effects were still felt in the seventeenth century.[14] In a study on the concept of genius, I laid a philosophic foundation for the acceptance of extraordinary artistic means by the Renaissance musician, who concedes to genius the use of exceptional means.[15] I wrote an introduction to a facsimile edition of Vicentino's great work, *L'antica musica ridotta alla moderna prattica*,[16] the chief work on Renaissance chromaticism, much bolder than anything undertaken by the composers of the secret chromatic art and yet pub-

9. Gustave Reese, *Music in the Renaissance* (New York, 1954; rev. ed., 1959), p. 353, n. 78.

10. Donald Jay Grout, *A History of Western Music* (New York, 1960), pp. 186–87.

11. Willem Elders, *Studien zur Symbolik in der Musik der alten Niederländer* (Bilthoven, 1968), pp. 165–91.

12. Edward E. Lowinsky, *Tonality and Atonality in Sixteenth-Century Music* (Berkeley-Los Angeles, 1961; 2nd rev. printing, 1962).

13. Edward E. Lowinsky, "The Goddess Fortuna in Music, with a Special Study of Josquin's *Fortuna dun gran tempo*," *Musical Quarterly*, XXIX (1943), 45–77; and "Matthaeus Greiter's *Fortuna:* An Experiment in Chromaticism and in Musical Iconography," *ibid.*, XLII (1956), 500–519, XLIII (1957), 68–85.

14. Edward E. Lowinsky, "Adrian Willaert's Chromatic 'Duo' Re-examined," *Tijdschrift voor Muziekwetenschap*, XVIII (1956), 1–36; and "Echoes of Adrian Willaert's Chromatic 'Duo' in Sixteenth- and Seventeenth-Century Compositions," in *Studies in Music History: Essays for Oliver Strunk*, ed. Harold Powers (Princeton, N.J., 1968), pp. 183–238.

15. Edward E. Lowinsky, "Musical Genius—Evolution and Origins of a Concept," *Musical Quarterly*, L (1964), 321–40, 476–95.

16. Nicola Vicentino, *L'antica musica ridotta alla moderna prattica*, with a Postface by Edward E. Lowinsky, *Documenta Musicologica*, XVII (Kassel, 1959).

lished in 1555, the same time the secret chromatic motets appeared in print.

Other scholars explored the phenomenon. Alfred Einstein gave a comprehensive picture of chromaticism as used in the Italian madrigal.[17] Kenneth Levy wrote an interesting study on Costeley's chromatic chanson of 1558, first printed in 1570.[18] Henry W. Kaufmann published Vicentino's *Opera omnia*[19] and wrote a book on the composer,[20] the archchromaticist of the century. Joseph Kerman investigated chromaticism in the English madrigal.[21]

Many more musicological enterprises could be listed, but the net effect of the work done since 1946 has been to uncover an increasingly large and impressive context of ideas, theory, and practice that show the secret chromatic art to have grown in a fertile soil of chromatic experimentation and discussion.

It seems time, therefore, to re-examine the theory of the secret chromatic art and its criticism, in the light of the new evidence accumulated.

There are special reasons for opening the subject again at this occasion. One has to do with the initiator of the present lecture series, the other with the audience of young musicologists for whom it was arranged in the first place. Professor Barry S. Brook, with that imagination and broadmindedness that characterize his enterprises, offered me the opportunity of having the lecture illustrated by that incomparable group of musicians, the New York Pro Musica, founded by the unforgettable Noah Greenberg, and carried on with zest and artistic vision by John Reeves White. In all the talk on secret chromatic art, the sound of the music was almost forgotten. To have the New York Pro Musica sing a few works of the secret chromatic art in both the diatonic and the chromatic versions and to have these works performed together with other chromatic works and experiments was a temptation not to be resisted.[22]

The second consideration relates to the future development of musicology and musicologists. If we compare the prevailing working methods of

17. Alfred Einstein, *The Italian Madrigal*, 3 vols. (Princeton, N.J., 1949).

18. Kenneth Levy, "Costeley's Chromatic Chanson," *Annales musicologiques*, III (1955), 213–63.

19. Nicola Vicentino, *Opera omnia*, ed. Henry W. Kaufmann (Rome: American Institute of Musicology, 1963).

20. Henry W. Kaufmann, *The Life and Works of Nicola Vicentino (1511–c. 1576)* (Rome: American Institute of Musicology, 1966).

21. Joseph Kerman, *The Elizabethan Madrigal: A Comparative Study*, American Musicological Society, Studies and Documents, No. 4 (1962).

22. I am deeply indebted to Barry S. Brook and to John R. White for their efforts, finally crowned by success, to make available a recording of the music performed in illustration of my lecture (Decca Records, forthcoming). I beg the reader to remember that the music was, and is, the chief *raison d'être* for undertaking a re-examination of the secret chromatic art on this occasion, and I wish to thank the musicians and the director of the New York Pro Musica for their splendid cooperation.

musicologists with those of scientists, physicists in particular, we come to the surprising conclusion that it is the humanistic discipline that resists, indeed suspects, the use of hypothesis and theory, and that it is science today which celebrates the triumph of theory and hypothesis. One of the most important scholarly arts, how to construct a sound, coherent, responsible, and logical hypothesis, is hardly considered, let alone taught, in our discipline.

As soon as one enters the realm of hypothesis and theory, one enters the realm of controversy. Ideas are always controversial. But in musicology the term "controversial" is used as a pejorative, or at any rate as a cautionary, word. In commenting upon my *Tonality and Atonality in Sixteenth-Century Music*, an eminent musicologist wrote: "brilliant but controversial." "But" shows the lifted finger of caution—and caution and factuality are considered the chief virtues of a true scholar. Caution and factuality *are* scholarly virtues, but without imagination they are like wingless birds, unable to soar aloft and command vaster views of land and sea. And when they are used, as they have been, to fight the imaginative formation of theory and hypothesis, then they are abused. Facts in themselves are meaningless and uninteresting. The facts assembled about a composer's biography, for example, are interesting chiefly in relation to the composer's significance. The importance of a composer rests less on facts than on the intangible of how we experience and evaluate his music, a process so personal that it will always remain controversial. Judgments of value, central in the writing of the history of art, rest more on intuition and personal taste than on scholarship.

The function of hypothesis is to explain what remains otherwise inexplicable, to make sense of what seems contradictory, to bring meaning and order, logic and causality into a conglomeration of facts without discernible connections. History cannot be written by adding fact to fact. The human mind wishes to grasp the connection of things. Far from being content with the "what," it aspires to the "how," it grapples with the "why," it searches beyond the surface of the phenomenon for its roots. A factual approach to history isolates the events; hypothesis connects them. The factual approach leaves the events inanimate; hypothesis breathes life into them. To record facts takes precision; to formulate an hypothesis calls for imagination. It also calls for discipline of the highest order. Without discipline it is not possible to marshal and to verify the facts needed, to connect them in a logical fashion, to reason with lucidity and cogency. The stranger the phenomena, the greater the need for imaginative hypothesis. Any hypothesis is valid until a better hypothesis takes its place. Better is that hypothesis that rests on a broader basis of verifiable facts, that explains more phenomena, that has less need to distort them or leave out significant parts of them or ascribe them to error or chance.

The factual approach is favored by those who seek certainty above all, who believe certainty to be the very purpose of scholarship. The hypothetical approach is favored by those who seek meaning above all, who know how to live with uncertainty as a price to be paid for deeper understanding. The factual and the hypothetical approach enrich each other; true scholarship suffers when one or the other approach is dogmatically rejected. New facts call for new explanations; a new hypothesis in turn inspires the search for new facts. At its best, a good hypothesis sends the scholar in the right direction to discover the unknown facts that the hypothesis postulates. It is well known that some of the greatest discoveries in physics in this century have been the consequence of new hypotheses. The fructifying effect of imaginative and responsible use of hypothesis still remains to be tapped in much of humanistic scholarship, and particularly in the field of musicology.

If scholarship without the use of hypothesis remains inadequate, it is to be preferred to the irresponsible construction of wild hypotheses, based on unverifiable (or demonstrably wrong) facts, ignoring inconvenient facts, connecting them illogically, and lacking a cogently reasoned framework of thought. Worst of all is the hypothesis that falsifies facts to prove its validity. There should be a sensible proportion between the effort expended in working out an hypothesis and the illumination it affords. An elaborate hypothesis that explains little is worth little. The abuse and the wrong use of hypothesis are not reasons for doing without its illuminating force; they are reasons for refining the use of one of the most valuable tools in the search for truth and understanding.

Imaginative hypothesis has no claim upon being beyond the pale of criticism. But the critique must not deny the *raison d'être* of hypothesis itself. In speaking to the coming generation of musicologists, I wish to stress the vital importance to scholarship of imaginative, well-reasoned, carefully buttressed hypothesis. I also wish to encourage youthful scholars to bear with fortitude criticism, controversy, and occasional abuse in the service of an idea they believe in. A good theory, in the course of time, will assert itself.

Whether the secret chromatic art is a good theory depends on a number of criteria. Does it rest on a solid factual basis? Does it explain phenomena that otherwise would remain inexplicable? Does it fit in logically and relate meaningfully to other musical phenomena of the time? Does it make sense in a larger cultural perspective?

Let us begin with a concise definition: secret chromatic art, at home in the Netherlandish motet of the mid-sixteenth century, denotes a technique of modulation[23] without the full notation of the accidentals ordinarily used to chart the course of a modulation. Its basis is the age-old practice of singing and playing unnotated flats and sharps according to a coherent

23. On the use of the term "modulation" for the purposes of understanding harmonic processes peculiar to sixteenth-century music, see *Secret Chromatic Art*, pp. 15–16.

set of rules divided into the two famous categories of *causa necessitatis* and *causa pulchritudinis*.[24] The former operates in the secret chromatic art with special stringency. The most important of its rules demands that accidentals be used to avoid imperfect intervals such as the diminished or augmented fourth, fifth, and octave. This set of rules, first called *musica falsa*, then, in the time of the *Ars nova*, pioneered as *non falsa sed vera et necessaria*—Philippe de Vitry's words[25]—established itself in the fifteenth and sixteenth centuries under the name of *musica ficta*, a term already used by Prosdocimus de Beldemandis, in his *Tractatus de Contrapuncto* of 1412. At times writers also spoke of *musica colorata*; more frequently they used the term *coniuncta* synonymously with *musica ficta*.

Mostly, *musica ficta* has to do with the raising or lowering of one single note. But, as early as 900 in the *Scholia enchiriadis*,[26] the B♭ of the *tonus peregrinus*, in the opinion of Oliver Strunk, calls for an E♭ in organum at the fourth and fifth (Ex. 1). "Only on this basis," asserts Strunk, "do the

Ex. 1 From the *Scholia enchiriadis* (after Strunk, *Source Readings*, p. 128)

Nos qui vivimus, benedicimus Domino,   ex hoc nunc et usque in saeculum.

examples illustrating the organum at the fourth become intelligible."[27] The example illustrates another point of interest: the scribe, in the beginning, leaves both B♭ and E♭ without accidentals. He relies on the musician's knowledge of the *tonus peregrinus* to flat the B and on his knowledge of perfect consonances to intone E♭ against B♭. Already the very infancy of polyphony reveals the presence of that element of ambiguity that has marked—or, shall we say, plagued—the long, vicissitudinous career of *musica ficta*. The reason for omitting the B♭ in the beginning may very well have been the fear of having to write down the E♭.[28]

24. For an exposition of the principles of *musica ficta*, see the writer's Introduction to *Musica nova*, ed. H. Colin Slim, Monuments of Renaissance Music, 1 (Chicago, 1964), pp. viii–xxi.

25. Philippe de Vitry, *Ars nova*, ed. Gilbert Reaney, André Gilles, and Jean Maillard (Rome: American Institute of Musicology, 1964), p. 23.

26. Oliver Strunk, *Source Readings in Music History* (New York, 1950), pp. 126–38.

27. *Ibid.*, p. 128, n. 3.

28. See Gustav Jacobsthal, *Die chromatische Alteration im liturgischen Gesang der abendländischen Kirche* (Berlin, 1898). This book, heatedly rejected at the time of its appearance, is generally accepted today; it is a model of careful construction of an important hypothesis.

Without the element of fear—fear of impairing the purity of a carefully constructed system of tones and of modes, a fear whose intensity fluctuated in precise proportion to the changing philosophies of music—there would have been no *musica ficta*, and certainly no secret chromatic art.

A vast array of theoretical writings on *musica ficta* removes all doubt that the system is not limited to the raising or lowering of one single note but that it sanctions, indeed requires, such chain reactions as are postulated in the theory of secret chromatic art. A few examples from sixteenth-century theory will illustrate the point.

Andreas Ornitoparchus includes a chapter on *musica ficta* in his *Micrologus* of 1517.[29] In an example of *musica ficta* for one voice in tenor clef without key signature, the writer progressively uses B♭, E♭, and A♭ (Ex. 2). Each time the new flat is reached by the leap of a fourth or a

Ex. 2 Ornitoparchus, *Micrologus*, fol. C5ᵛ

fifth, accounting for the unmelodious character of the example, which has the aspect of a bass line. The principle is stated in the accompanying text, which we quote in Dowland's translation:

> Marking fa in [i.e. writing a flat before] ♭fa♮mi, or in any other place, if the Song from that [tone] shall make an immediate rising to a Fourth, a Fifth, or an Eight, even there fa must necessarily be marked, to eschew a *Tritone*, a *Semidiapente* [a diminished fifth], or a *Semidiapason* [a diminished octave]. ...[30]

29. Andreas Ornitoparchus, *Musice Active Micrologus* (Leipzig, 1517), fol. C5ᵛ.

30. John Dowland, *Andreas Ornitoparcus, His Micrologus or Introduction* (London, 1609), p. 25.

Just as important, for our purposes, is another principle so self-evident that it is not discussed by Ornitoparchus or any other writer. In the example there are a number of unmarked flats that are not reached by the skip of a perfect interval, such as the fourth, eleventh, fifteenth, seventeenth notes, etc. No one would think of debating the need for flatting these tones, because the context so clearly demands them. This self-evident principle of the tonal coherence of a phrase is central to an understanding of the secret chromatic technique, in which the efficacy of flats or sharps in governing the harmonic progression vanishes at the cadence point or, to put it differently, is confined to the context of a phrase.[30a]

What Ornitoparchus shows in a monodic example Georg Rhau, in his *Enchiridion utriusque musicae practicae*,[31] demonstrates in a four-part phrase, as awkward in harmony as the former was in melody, but clear in its bearing on *musica ficta* (Ex. 3). The bass has a key signature of two flats, but the other voices have none, to demonstrate more clearly the need for *musica ficta*. Again flats are introduced before B, E, and A by the leap of a fourth or a fifth, and again the self-evident principle of tonal coherence within the phrase calls for the repetition of flatted notes, without the leap of a perfect interval and without benefit of accidentals. But now we encounter a new application of the *musica ficta* rule, the application by vertical consonance—something expressly denied by some musicologists on the ground that sixteenth-century musicians, having before them only the individual part-books, could not possibly take into account the voice leading of other parts. In Rhau's example, the soprano passes directly from F and G to A♭ because the harmonic progression, founded on a bass going from E♭ to A♭, renders the use of A♮ impossible.

To make certain that the reader understands the necessity of introduc-

---

30a. The principle of tonal coherence of a phrase was less in need of theoretical discussion since it had its roots in the notation of Gregorian chant. In medieval chant books a flat refers to the whole phrase, and often to the whole line; that means if the phrase contained more than one B, the flat affected all of them. The old manuscripts are bolder in this respect than the modern *Liber usualis* and the other Vatican editions which follow the practice of using one flat per phrase, the phrases being marked off by small vertical strokes. One example among many is the Gradual *Christus factus est pro nobis* (*Liber usualis*, p. 669). The *Liber* uses three flat signs for the five Bs occurring in the phrases *ad mortem, mortem autem crucis*. The Sarum Gradual, however, employs only one single flat, notated in the middle of the line before the first note B, for this whole passage, which is written on one line (see W. H. Frere, *Graduale Sarisburiense* [London, 1894], pl. 235). Proof of the extension of the flat sign even beyond the line is provided by the Introit *Lux fulgebit hodie* (*ibid.*, pl. E), where a flat appears in the middle of the second line on the word *deus* and extends to the second note (B) on line 3, followed after two notes by a natural sign for a group of notes demanding the *subsemitonium modi* (ADCCB♮CA) for the following phrases and requiring it also for the ending on a Mixolydian cadence. The *Liber* version (p. 403) presents an interesting variant reading which, however, confirms the flat and natural signs of the Sarum reading.

31. Georg Rhau, *Enchiridion utriusque musicae practicae* (Leipzig, 1520), fol. f iii.

Ex. 3 Rhau, *Enchiridion*, fol. f iii

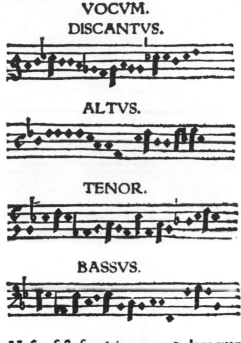

Musica ficta fingit in quacunque claue quam
cumque vocem, consonantiae causa.

Aliud

ing *musica ficta* in one voice because of the harmonic context, Rhau follows his example with the remark:

> Musica ficta fingit in quacunque clave quamcumque vocem, conson-
> antiae causa.
> (*Musica ficta* feigns on any key any tone [flat or sharp] for the sake
> of consonance.)

And he adds to the example of *musica ficta* in the flat region another one using sharps (Ex. 4).[32] In this example, too, the sharps are reached either

Ex. 4 Rhau, *Enchiridion*, fol. f iii[v]

by the melodic skip of a fifth, as in the soprano, or by the harmonic interval of a fifth, as in tenor and alto. The principle of tonal coherence of the phrase operates here also. Once the first F is raised to F♯, the whole

32. Ibid., fol. f iii[v].

phrase is construed with F♯.[33] Nor should it be argued that we do not deal with genuine *musica ficta* inasmuch as accidentals are used. Theorists, in their discussions of *musica ficta*, always use accidentals. How else could they clarify the meaning and effects of *musica ficta*? Moreover, the term *musica ficta* comprehends all chromatic alterations, written and unwritten.

In 1538 the Spanish theorist Gonçalo Martinez de Bizcargui brought out a new edition of his *Arte de canto llano y contrapunto y canto de organo*.[34] He shows that at times even in plainchant musicians use the principles of *musica ficta*—something expressly denied by some scholars. A melody without key signature on the responsory text *Omnis sapientia a Domino Deo est* (Ex. 5) descends by triadic motion from F to B,

Ex. 5 Martinez de Bizcargui, *Arte de canto llano*, fol. d ii[v]

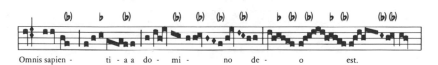

expected to be sung as B♭, for the melody ascends over D to a notated E♭ and maintains the two flats throughout.[35] Martinez places his flats above the melody; the flats in parentheses are added by the present writer. In another example, the responsory *Versa est in luctum cithara mea*

33. Rhau, like many of his contemporaries, uses a flat for lowering, a natural sign for raising a note. In the Guidonian hand, B♭, the only chromatic note, is indicated by a flat, B♮ by the natural sign. In the system of solmization the flat is always sung as *fa*, the natural sign as *mi*. Since any sharp in the hexachord system must be solmizated as *mi*, it was possible, in a basically diatonic music, to make do with a flat for lowering and a natural sign for raising a note. To the degree that music became more chromatic, it became necessary to distinguish between a sharp and a natural sign.

34. Gonçalo Martinez de Bizcargui, *Arte de canto llano y contrapunto y canto de organo* (Saragossa, 1538). The original edition, much smaller, appeared in 1508.

35. *Ibid.*, fol. d ii[v].

(Ex. 6) begins with A, goes in skips or in stepwise melodic progressions of the fourth and fifth to B♭, E♭, and ends on the tones A♭, G, F.[36]

Ex. 6 Martinez de Bizcargui, *Arte de canto llano*, fol. d iiii

Again, Martinez considered the first flat to the note B so obvious that he did not indicate it.

The same author, in the plainsong *Sancte Erasme martyr inclite* (Ex. 7),

Ex. 7 Martinez de Bizcargui, *Arte de canto llano*, fol. d v^v

36. *Ibid.*, fol. d iiii.

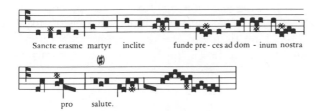

shows the use of F♯, C♯, and G♯, produced in each case by a strict application of the subsemitone principle—that is, raising the lower note in three-note progressions involving the lower auxiliary tone.[37]

Finally, Nicolaus Listenius, in his *Musica* of 1537, in an *Exemplum Cantus Ficti* already quoted in the *Secret Chromatic Art*, carries the principle of chain reaction from B♭ to D♭ (Ex. 8).[38]

Ex. 8 Listenius, *Musica*, fol. b 4ᵛ

From Ornitoparchus, Rhau, and Martinez de Bizcargui to Listenius, the principles and techniques of *musica ficta* are the same. The theorists explain them in written commentaries, since notation alone does not furnish adequate guidance; their examples and commentaries provide incontrovertible proof of the existence of the principles postulated in the *Secret Chromatic Art*. This is what I consider the factual basis of the theory of secret chromaticism.[39]

37. *Ibid.*, fol. d vᵛ.

38. Nicolaus Listenius, *Musica* (Wittenberg, 1537); facsimile of the 1549 edition by Georg Schünemann (Berlin, 1927), fol. b 4ᵛ.

39. This is one point on which I have changed my opinion. In the second chapter of the *Secret Chromatic Art* (p. 15) I wrote: "For the purposes of this study the term 'chromaticism' is used to designate not only a succession of half-tone steps but also those departures from the diatonic system that are not provided for by *musica ficta*. This includes the introduction of A flat—which actually is on the borderline between the old *musica ficta* and the new chromaticism—D flat, G flat, C flat." Now, on the basis of a much broader knowledge of theoretical writings, I would rephrase that sentence as follows: "For the purposes of this study the term 'chromaticism' is used to designate not only a succession of half-tone steps but also those departures from the diatonic system that are provided for by *musica ficta*, particularly by its more advanced adepts such as Hothby, Ramos de Pareja, Aron, Spataro, Gonçalo Martinez de Bizcargui, Listenius, and others." The *musica ficta* practice of the "musical avant-garde" was sufficiently removed from everyday *musica ficta* practice to justify, particularly in the Netherlandish music of the mid-sixteenth century, the concept of a "secret chromatic art," with its practical, musical, religious, and philosophical implications.

If we now examine the following bass line against the background of the preceding theoretical testimony, we must conclude that it is, if anything, clearer and more compelling than any of the foregoing theoretical examples (Ex. 9). For one thing, it has a key signature of two flats,

Ex. 9

thereby securing the first triadic motive. Moreover, the A♭ of the second descending triad is clinched both through the use of the triadic motive and of sequence. The skips, which go up a fourth to D♭ and down a fifth to G♭, tie the whole modulation into a well-formed chain that can be broken only by disregard of contemporaneous *musica ficta* theory.

This phrase is the bass part to the first modulation in the initial measures 5–13 of Clemens non Papa's *Fremuit spiritu Jesu*, published in 1554 (Ex. 10).[40] It could have figured in any of the text books on theory that we just examined; it goes only one step beyond the D♭ of Listenius. But the

Ex. 10 Clemens non Papa, *Fremuit spiritu Jesu*, mm. 5–13

40. Modern edition in Eduard Reeser, *Drie Oud-Nederlandsche Motetten* (Amsterdam, 1936), pp. 13–28 (transposed a major third higher), and Jacobus Clemens non Papa, *Opera omnia*, ed. K. Ph. Bernet Kempers, XIV (Rome: American Institute of Musicology, 1966), 32–40.

dry and awkward school examples of Georg Rhau and the monodic examples of the other writers are here transformed into a five- and six-part polyphony of rare beauty and a modulation marvelous in the logic and expressiveness of its development and *dénouement*.

Clemens presents in tones the story of Christ's miraculous resurrection of Lazarus. The words to which he set the modulation, "and Jesus groaned in his spirit," are taken from the Gospel of John (11:33), where the story is told of how Jesus saw Mary fall down at his feet weeping about the death of her brother Lazarus: "When Jesus therefore saw her weeping, and the Jews also weeping which came with her, he groaned in the spirit, and was troubled." John's story goes on. Jesus asks: "Where have ye laid him? They said unto him, Lord, come and see. And Jesus wept." Christ's tears are "painted" in another secret chromatic modulation. This time Clemens uses another technique. The whole motet is built over the ostinato call sung by the second soprano: "Lazare veni foras" (Lazarus, rise!). These are the words Jesus speaks in calling his dead friend to life. The ostinato, *sol mi mi mi fa re ut*, framed by the interval of a fifth, appears throughout in two hexachords, *molle*, on F, and *durum*, on C. Only once, at the words "et lachrimatus est Jesus" (and Jesus wept), does the ostinato begin on B♭. If we solmisize it *sol mi mi mi fa re ut*, we obtain B♭, G, G, G, A♭, F, E♭, inducing another modulation, as logical and as expressive as the first one, and as flawless in its resolution into major at the cadence, but this time emphasizing the minor harmonies (Ex. 11).

My critics have gone to great lengths arguing that identical solmization in ostinato repeats cannot be taken for granted. In this they are right. A number of ascending and descending ostinati, the so-called *pes ascendens*

Ex. 11 Clemens non Papa, *Fremuit spiritu Jesu*, mm. 63–74

et descendens, change their solmization with each step. The critics, however, overlook a few significant points:

(1) In this work the ostinato appears not as a *pes ascendens et descendens* but, with one exception, only in the soft and hard hexachords, in
which the solmization remains identical.

(2) This particular short ostinato motif, framed as it is by the interval

of a perfect fifth, sounds poor, and goes against the rule that forbids the diminished fifth, if read diatonically.

(3) Why, if Clemens did not wish to have a modulation here, should he have started the ostinato on B♭ at all? Why should he have risked confusing the singers of the ostinato who, singing the repeated melody in one and the same solmization throughout, would of course want to intone it in that same solmization at this point? This central question was never posed, let alone answered, by my critics.

The first discussion of Clemens non Papa's motet occurred in my dissertation on Orlando di Lasso's Antwerp motet book.[41] The printer's ink was scarcely dry when the first controversy over secret chromaticism took place.[42] The Dutch critic conceded that the modulations were magnificent, that they helped suggest in tones the emotion expressed in the text, but, he concluded, "such chromaticism was not possible at the time of Clemens non Papa."[42a]

Over thirty years have passed since that debate went into print. Today there is hardly anyone conversant with the researches of the last generation who would doubt that such chromaticism was indeed possible and practiced at the time of Clemens non Papa and even before. But the critic's honest admission of the artistic superiority of the chromatic version raises a fundamental question. We shall deal with it later on.

It may be taken as axiomatic that in the vocal music of the Renaissance extraordinary means are always chosen for the representation of extraordinary events, emotions, or ideas. Clemens used his magnificent modulations to depict Christ's emotion in the presence of Lazarus's death and the mourners' laments. Hubert Waelrant, in his motet on Saint John's prophecy of the coming of Christ, *Venit fortior me post me*, uses a double modulation, first to flat, then to sharp keys, to express the miracle of baptism by the Holy Spirit.

Waelrant, younger than Clemens, and from his first works on inclined toward the modern style of humanistic declamation and expressive setting of the text, uses a technique different from that of Clemens and more advanced. Instead of initiating his modulation by the traditional use of fourths, fifths, and triadic motives, or by the transposition of motives, he

41. Edward E. Lowinsky, *Das Antwerpener Motettenbuch Orlando di Lasso's und seine Beziehungen zum Motettenschaffen der niederländischen Zeitgenossen* (The Hague, 1937), pp. 70–72.

42. Reeser, *Drie Oud-Nederlandsche Motetten*, p. [ix]. See also Edward E. Lowinsky, "Zur Ausgabe der Motette 'Fremuit spiritu Jesu' von Clemens non Papa," *Tijdschrift der Vereeniging voor Nederl. Muziekgeschiedenis*, XV (1937), 106–8.

42a. During a dinner offered to the foreign guests at the International Josquin Festival-Conference, June, 1971, Professor Reeser made a charming speech recalling our one-time controversy and relating how Felix de Nobel, some years ago, with his Netherlands Chamber Choir, performed Clemens non Papa's Lazarus motet in both versions, diatonic and chromatic. The chromatic version sounded marvelous. "Today," he concluded, "perhaps, I would decide in favor of the chromatic version."

relies on false relation. As other "forbidden" intervals, false relations can and have been used as conscious artistic means. That they are not intended here is clear from the musical context and the concordance between music and text (Ex. 12). Musically speaking, the false relation between E♭ in

Ex. 12 Waelrant, *Venit fortior me*, mm. 14–31

*Orig.: in

the soprano and E♮ in the alto in measures 18–19 makes little sense, since it occurs in the context of a clear and undiluted F major with simple triadic harmonies. If Waelrant wanted a diatonic reading, he would have written an E♮ in the soprano at measure 18, for there is no artistic justification for the temporary disturbance created by the isolated E♭. Anything exceptional in a work of art needs consequence to justify itself. Without consequence there is no justification for the single false relation in measure 18.

The F♯ written in the tenor of measure 26 makes even less sense, if Waelrant did *not* intend a modulation. For then he would have committed the further blunder of repeating, in direct succession, the motive of measures 24–25 with its ear-catching rise of a minor sixth, a conspicuously inelegant repetitiousness to which so fastidious a craftsman as Waelrant would hardly fall victim.

The text speaks of baptism, which is the sacrament that most profoundly transforms man, without which he can achieve neither forgiveness of sins nor salvation. It is this transformation that Waelrant means to express in the symbol of the harmonic change. To begin with the last modulation to the sharp keys: the chromatic reading takes the motif of the ascending minor sixth (soprano, mm. 24–25) and changes it to the triumphant, mystically transformed melody with the leap of an ascending major sixth (m. 26), doubly remarkable in view of the reticence on the part of sixteenth-century composers to use such a skip. In the preceding modulation to the flat keys, on the other hand, the clear F major is transmuted via C minor and A♭ major into the dark and expressive hues of F minor. The two works by Clemens non Papa and Hubert Waelrant suffice to illustrate the sound, the techniques, and the expressive and symbolic purposes of the secret chromatic art. To understand their historical position they must be placed into the context of preceding as well as contemporaneous chromatic music—chromatic not in the sense of the Italian madrigal, but of the modulatory techniques of the works by Clemens non Papa and Hubert Waelrant. By necessity, I must refer to my own previous research and let you hear and consider compositions discussed at length in publications covering the last twenty-five years.

If Waelrant can conceive of the transforming power of baptism in terms of stunning modulations to the flat and sharp keys, it is because he continues, and develops, a tradition that was started by Josquin des Prez in his *Fortuna dun gran tempo*. Here was a symbol in sounds fully equivalent to the innumerable presentations of Fortuna in painting and architecture. In the visual arts, Fortuna is often presented turning a wheel, throwing down the king on top, raising another one from the ground, crushing one under the wheel, and lowering a fourth figure in decline.[43] To sym-

43. See, for example, the illumination from a codex in the Biblioteca Nazionale Centrale, Florence, reproduced in Lowinsky, "Matthaeus Greiter's *Fortuna*," *loc. cit.,* Fig. 1, between pp. 506 and 507.

bolize her extreme instability, she is also depicted standing precariously on a globe, partly immersed in water, and blown by the wind.[44]

Josquin conceived of depicting Fortuna's eternal mutability through a system of modulations ranging from C major to F minor; Fortuna's coyness is expressed in a melody and rhythm of exceeding grace and lightness; the ill-starred ending of Fortuna's game is suggested in the dark color, the low tessitura, and the retarded pace of the ending in minor.[45] To the genuine musical symbolism was added a musical-verbal pun, for what we call modulation was then called *mutatio*, and this is the same term that the philosophers and poets used for Fortuna's changeability. Helen Hewitt discovered a passage in which the poet and musician Jean Molinet, a contemporary and, indeed, an admirer of Josquin, speaks of the incredible things that Fortuna does "par sa fainte musique," by her use of *musica ficta*,[46] a surprising literary confirmation of the "chromatic" interpretation of Josquin's *Fortuna*, the more precious for the precise concordance of time and cultural provenance.

Josquin was also the first composer to use modulation to express deepest sorrow. Recently I suggested that Josquin's *Absalon fili mi*,[47] the lamentation of David over the death of his son Absalom, was composed in 1497, on the occasion of an event so terrible that it gripped all of Rome, indeed, all of Italy, and shook the reigning Pope Alexander VI to the very marrow of his bones, causing him to refuse food and drink for three days, and to confess, in open consistory, in the presence of cardinals and ambassadors, his sinful conduct, promising reform—reform of the church from the head down to its smallest members. The event was the murder of the duke of Gandia, the oldest son of the pope, and the apple of his eye.[48]

Josquin's setting of David's dirge over the death of his son Absalom belongs to a tradition of memorializing contemporary events in a work of art by using Biblical analogies. The unusual means chosen by Josquin—the extremely low tessitura for four men's voices with the bass reaching down to contra B♭, the unprecedented key signature of B♭ and E♭ in the two upper voices, E♭ and A♭ in the tenor, and E♭, A♭, and D♭ in the bass, the modulatory harmony alternating restlessly between the centers

44. As in the engraving by Nicoletto da Modena, *ibid.*, Fig. 2, between pp. 506 and 507.

45. Modern edition in Lowinsky, "The Goddess Fortuna in Music," *loc. cit.*, 51–53, and Helen Hewitt, *Harmonice Musices Odhecaton A* (Cambridge, Mass., 1942), pp. 375–76.

46. Helen Hewitt, ed., *Ottaviano Petrucci, Canti B, Monuments of Renaissance Music*, 2 (Chicago, 1967), p. 57.

47. Modern edition by Helmuth Osthoff, *Josquin Desprez*, 2 vols. (Tutzing, 1962–65), II, 382–84.

48. Edward E. Lowinsky, "Josquin des Prez and Ascanio Sforza," in *Il Duomo di Milano. Congresso Internazionale, Atti*, ed. Maria Luisa Gatti Perer, 2 vols. (Milan, 1969), II, 17–22.

of B♭ major, E♭ major, F minor, and B♭ minor; the powerful and grating dissonance patterns and appoggiaturas emphasizing the semitone in varying combinations, and finally the astonishing modulation at the end, descending by triadic motives from B♭ major to E♭, A♭, D♭, and using G♭, cadencing in B♭ minor on the words of David: "I shall descend into the underworld weeping"—these extraordinary means chosen by the most imaginative composer of the time were meant to give expression to the passionate mourning of a man no less emotional for his being the supreme head of the church.[49]

Both Josquin's *Fortuna* and his lamentation of David over Absalom, though completely dissimilar in mood and character, are related through the use of the novel technique of modulation. Both are works of perfection. Whenever a new technique is invented by a great artist, one finds contemporaneous efforts at absorbing and practicing the new technique in works more experimental than artistically successful. This is true for the new technique of modulation. *Canti B* contains a work by Brumel, *Noé, noé, noé*, which, in the introduction to Helen Hewitt's edition, I have interpreted as such an experiment.[50]

In the light of the preceding theoretical and practical examples, there is no difficulty in understanding Brumel's design as an experiment in *musica ficta*. Without such interpretation it would be very difficult to account for the extremely dry and pedantic character of the lengthy final passage of an otherwise lively and animated piece of music by a talented composer, who does not usually write in such mechanical fashion. A triadic motive in descending sequence, used in strict fourfold canon at the octave and the fifth, creates a modulatory chain reaction similar to the one in Josquin's *Absalon fili mi* (Ex. 13).[51]

The chromatic interpretation of Brumel's *Noé, noé, noé* finds a surprising illumination and corroboration in a composition that appeared one hundred and twenty years after *Canti B*. Romano Micheli's *O voi che sospirate* was published by the composer in the year 1621.[52] Micheli's composition is one of the strangest and most incredible *tours de force* in the

49. For a recent recording of *Absalon fili mi*, see Nonesuch H-71216, performed by the University of Illinois Chamber Choir under the direction of George Hunter.

50. Edward E. Lowinsky, Introduction to *Ottaviano Petrucci, Canti B, op. cit.*, pp. xi–xiv.

51. In the Introduction to vol. 2 of *Monuments of Renaissance Music*, the question was raised as to which of the two compositions might have been composed earlier. In the absence of a date for Josquin's work, the question was unanswerable. The assumed date of 1497, which fits both the evolution of Josquin's style and an extraordinary historical event, makes it possible—though not mandatory—to assign priority to the older master, an assumption the more easily accepted as it accords with his character as one of the great innovative geniuses of music.

52. The composition has been reprinted in Lowinsky, "Echoes of Adrian Willaert's Chromatic 'Duo,' *loc. cit.*, 186–90.

Ex. 13 A. Brumel, *Noé, noé, noé*, mm. 39–57

1) Greifswald E♭ 133 has E-flat.
2) Bologna Q 18 has E-flat.

history of music. At a time when Italian monody had triumphantly superseded Netherlandish counterpoint, Romano Micheli took unto himself the protectorate of counterpoint and canonic art, presenting it to the musical world as the achievement of the Roman school of composition, elevating it to the state of an esoteric religion, and assuming himself the role of its high priest. Ideas and models of the work go back to Marenzio and Adrian Willaert. Micheli emulates and tries to surpass both—Marenzio, by setting the same text and using modulation; Willaert, in outdoing the still celebrated chromatic "duo" by going not once but twice through the circle of fifths, once descending in fifths, then ascending by fourths. Unprecedented is the technique used by Micheli: a strict canon for six parts that can also be read in inversion, thereby changing major to minor.

The means used for the first modulation through the circle of fifths are so similar to Brumel's procedures that one might suspect Micheli of having had a copy of Petrucci's print before him and having included the Netherlandish master among his models. For Brumel preceded Micheli in combining triadic motion, descending sequence, and canon. Unlike Brumel, Micheli wrote down every accidental from B♭ to C♭, F♭, and even one

B♭♭, leaving the fate of the further modulations in the circle of flat keys in the hands of the singers (Ex. 14). However, what was a transitory passage in Brumel becomes a seemingly unending solfège of modulation in Micheli's hands. With Baroque exaggeration, the Roman master seized upon an old device, creating a paradoxical fusion of technical genius and musical boredom.[53]

Ex. 14 R. Micheli, *O voi che sospirate*, mm. 14–20

53. Under the direction of John White, in the fresh tempi for which the New York Pro Musica is famous, the work not only reveals harmonic ripeness and extraordinary sonorous beauty, but an unexpected animation. Here is a case in which a spirited performance almost overcomes the effects of an overdose of constructivism.

I have saved Willaert's chromatic "duo," now known to be a quartet, for strategic reasons.[54] This short, ingenious work, which fascinated musicians and theorists for almost two centuries, may be considered the foundation of the whole chromatic movement. I confine the illustration to the "duo," which is the form in which the epoch-making piece entered into theoretical discussions, remaining there from Spataro's correspondence in 1524 till at least 1690 in the work of Angelo Berardi, *Arcani musicali svelati* (Musical Mysteries Unveiled).[55] Unlike his predecessors, Willaert leads only the tenor voice through the circle of fifths, using the technique of skips and melodic progressions of fourths and fifths (Ex. 15). He insures the correct interpretation of his chromatic example by writing out the accidentals for all flat notes from E♭ (B♭ appears in the signature) to C♭, stopping short, however, of writing F♭ and double flats. By keeping the other voices in the original Dorian mode, he was able to equate the final D with the chromatic part's E♭♭, proving thereby the necessity for equal temperament. To justify his unprecedented undertaking he chose for it verses from Horace in praise of inebriety (Epistles, I, 5).[56]

Finally, in this parade of Renaissance *tours de force* of Netherlandish and Italian vintage, we come to the work of a German, Matthaeus Greiter, a one-time priest who became a Protestant, married, and wrote German chorales and secular German songs—only two and a half dozen of his works are extant. We do not know of any other chromatic experiment in German music before the arrival of Orlando di Lasso at the court of Munich in 1558. It is a riddle how Greiter, in the conservative climate of Germany, could have conceived of a composition that begins in F major and by stepwise degrees in the circle of fifths finishes half a tone lower in F♭ major.[57] Even more astonishing is that he did it in a piece in which experimental skill is matched by musical talent. Since the work is published in a theoretical treatise, every accidental is clearly written, down to the last C♭, F♭, and even B♭♭. And the topic of Greiter's composition is Fortuna. The piece, although undoubtedly instrumental, is accompanied by the distichs from Ovid's *Tristia* (5.8.15) on *Fortuna volubilis*, "changeable Fortune, wandering in uncertain steps, never staying still in one place." It is the first instrumental composition with a definite symbolic intent that carried its "program" with it. It took two centuries for this form of instrumental music to become popular.

54. Modern edition in Lowinsky, "Adrian Willaert's Chromatic 'Duo' Re-examined," *loc. cit.*, 33–36.

55. See Lowinsky, "Echoes of Adrian Willaert's Chromatic 'Duo,'" *loc. cit.*, 198–200.

56. The New York Pro Musica illustrated the modulatory passage in the duo setting, in which it was published and debated in the theoretical discussions of the sixteenth and seventeenth centuries, and then performed the work in the four-part setting in which I have reconstructed the bass, since only the three upper parts have survived.

57. Modern edition in Lowinsky, "Matthaeus Greiter's *Fortuna*," *loc. cit.*, 505–8.

Ex. 15 A. Willaert, *Quid non ebrietas*, soprano and tenor, mm. 11–39

Greiter uses as a *cantus firmus* the opening motive of the famous *Fortuna desperata* song (*ut ut re mi re ut*) in systematic transposition, marking every transposition with only the new flat needed—first E♭, then A♭, then D♭, and so on—implying in the new accidental, according to Renaissance usage, all accidentals introduced before. The three remaining voices are written with the same system of key signatures; nothing is left to speculation.

Great turning points in the history of the arts, aside from the inevitable controversy between old and new, are usually marked by an intensification of intellectual effort, shown both in the concentration of the artist on technical and stylistic problems and in theoretical discussions of the esthetic and technical issues involved. Such turning points often occur contemporaneously in more than one art; they are ordinarily the expression of deep, underlying social and cultural changes, strains, and stresses. The theory of the secret chromatic art was hard enough to accept in itself. What made it even more difficult to accept, at least in the eyes of some scholars, was that its author connected musical techniques with social events. Chromaticism, he claimed, was frowned upon by the church; the composers of the secret chromatic art were inclined to Reform, if they were not outright heretics. The suppression of new ideas by the Inquisition was said to be a pervasive strand of the fabric of contemporaneous intellectual life; the fear of detection on the part of reform-minded musicians living in the Netherlands under the Spanish yoke was claimed to be a prime factor in the secrecy in which the new art was shrouded.[58] The curious ambivalence in the secret chromatic art, which allowed a diatonic interpretation, but whose chromatic realization was infinitely more expressive, was said to be a unifying bond in the intellectual make-up of the whole epoch. The book ended with a chapter on "the meaning of double meaning in the sixteenth century."[59]

The manuscript of the *Secret Chromatic Art* was finished in 1943. At that time I was not familiar with the concept of mannerism, then rather recently developed by art historians. This concept, since then much debated and variously interpreted, was coined to give a common denomination to new trends in visual representation—exaggerated expression, distortion of classical line and proportion in the service of a depiction of tension, struggle, and stress. Art historians transferred the term from painting and sculpture to architecture; from the visual arts it was taken into the field of literature. Some scholars incorporated it into a sociological analysis that took into account social and religious conflict. Recently it has also been borrowed by musicologists, who, however, have rarely undertaken

58. See the chapter on "Religious Background of the Secret Chromatic Art," in Lowinsky, *Secret Chromatic Art*, pp. 111–34.

59. Lowinsky, *Secret Chromatic Art*, pp. 135–75.

the primary task of defining musical mannerism in clear technical and stylistic terms. In my social and cultural analysis of the secret chromatic art I had unwittingly created, imperfectly to be sure, my own theory of mannerism—without, of course, the name, and without its technical and stylistic application to the visual arts.

All of this added to the novelty of the theory and accounted for both the vehement character of some of the critiques and the reluctance of other scholars to accept the social implications of the new theory. Nobody doubts the existence of strong heretical movements in the sixteenth century. They are too well documented, and they have resulted in new denominations still in existence today. Few would question that the heretical movements had their own literature and their own songs. For some reason, never explicitly stated, the critics of the secret chromatic art could not accept the connection drawn there between a bold new musical technique and bold new religious ideas judged to be heretical by the orthodox. Only three years after the *Secret Chromatic Art* was published, Henry A. Bruinsma completed a dissertation on the "Souterliedekens," in which the relationship between the Netherlandish psalm songs and the heretical movement was documented with irrefutable evidence.[60] The "Souterliedekens" were proven to be translations from the Luther Bible, which had been published in Flemish by Liesveldt in Antwerp, the center of the heretical movement in the Netherlands.[61] This translation was promptly condemned by the Inquisition. In 1536 the Bibles of Liesveldt were publicly burned; in 1545—that is, at the beginning of secret chromatic technique—Liesveldt was beheaded because he had printed in one of his Bibles that "the salvation of men comes alone through Jesus Christ"[62] —an idea that I have shown to be a pervading issue in the motet texts of Hubert Waelrant.[63] Protestantism of all persuasions did away with the veneration of Mary and the saints; Christ alone was Savior. Anyone uttering such a conviction immediately branded himself as a dangerous heretic in the eyes of the Inquisition.

There is a prevailing fashion in our treatment of the history of music that one might call—not too irreverently, I hope—the theory of the Immaculate Conception. In Pfitzner's opera *Palestrina* (Act I, Scene 5) occurs a scene in which the heavens open and angelic choirs sing; the inspiration for the Pope Marcellus Mass that supposedly saved church music from being banned from the divine service pours down into the composer's mind and guides his pen as he writes the score. Similarly, there is a theory of the history of music as a sequence of styles uninfluenced,

60. Henry A. Bruinsma, "The *Souterliedekens* and Its Relation to Psalmody in the Netherlands," Ph.D. diss. University of Michigan, 1949.
61. Lowinsky, *Secret Chromatic Art*, pp. 130–33.
62. Bruinsma, *op. cit.*, p. 99.
63. Lowinsky, *Secret Chromatic Art*, pp. 121–26.

one would almost say untainted, by real life. I take it to be axiomatic that any creative utterance of man is at once the expression of an individual and the symbol of the society in which he lives. Anthropologists, and their musical confrères, ethnomusicologists, have embraced this view as their working hypothesis; its fruitfulness has been shown in many applications. Many scholars have shown its application to historical musicology. In the secret chromatic art I found a fascinating demonstration of how the *geistesgeschichtliche* treatment of music history—which, after all, goes back to Wilhelm Dilthey, August Wilhelm Ambros, and Carl von Winterfeld—illuminated and explained what otherwise would have remained an oddity in the history of musical technique. The Netherlands, oppressed by Spanish domination, was seething with rebellion—social, political, religious—at the time of the flowering of the secret chromatic art. Ten to fifteen years later the ferment broke out in open conflict. The secrecy of the new technique was intimately related to the conspiratorial character of the growing heretical movement. Writing out the unusual modulations, in addition to making explicit the chromaticism, would have drawn attention to the texts and the text passages that I have shown to be inspired by heretical ideas, for the utterance of which Liesveldt and many other religious martyrs were executed.

But, said my critics, the soundness of the theory of secret chromatic art should stand not on sociological interpretation, not on cultural background, but on the validity of the musical result. Granted—but the validity of the musical result cannot be proven or disproven on such grounds as whether an ostinato motive must *always* be transposed literally, whether imperfect fifths *always* are to be perfected, and whether a false relation *always* has to be avoided. The demand of my critics that the rules invoked for secret chromatic constructions be shown to be inviolable rests on their failure to come to terms with three basic premises:

(1) There are no rigid, mechanically enforceable rules in sixteenth-century music—or anywhere else, for that matter.

(2) Whether a given rule applies depends on one thing, and one thing only: the musical context.

(3) Ambivalence is an essential part of the theory. The diatonic reading, though artistically and expressively inferior and often technically defective, is not impossible. The chromatic reading exhibits not only musical logic and fluency; it is infinitely more eloquent. It is a reading for the expert, the initiate.

From the first Dutch critic, who conceded the artistic and expressive superiority of the chromatic reading of *Fremuit spiritu Jesu* but contended that such chromaticism was impossible at that time, not a single critic has come forward to deny the musical viability of the chromatic readings. This implies that my critics believe it possible to impose chromatic constructions upon diatonic passages in sixteenth-century scores.

But the same critics have complained about the limited number of works in which the secret chromatic art survives.

Now I wish to pose these two questions:

Why, if the chromatic readings were willfully imposed by me, did I not create a larger repertory?

Why, if one can construe chromatic readings at will, did none of my critics come forward with another repertory of secret chromatic works? [63a] Why, for example, not choose the works of Palestrina and prove that it is possible to impose chromatic readings wherever one likes? If it can be done with the works of Clemens non Papa who, according to Bernet Kempers, never wrote a chromatic passage, why not in Palestrina? What more effective argument against the theory of secret chromatic art could there be than the proof that anybody can make his own secret chromatic art?

The answer is that chromatic constructions by modern editors not intended by sixteenth-century composers would have to meet so many conditions that their fortuitous coincidence may safely be ruled out:

63a. In the article "Verwante Sequensmodulaties bij Obrecht, Josquin en Coclico" (*Tijdschrift der Vereeniging voor Nederl. Muziekgeschiedenis*, XVI [1941], 119), M. van Crevel, taking his point of departure from my interpretation of Clemens non Papa's Lazarus motet and Josquin's Absolom motet in my dissertation on Lasso's Antwerp motet book, proposed a chromatic modulation for the end of the Kyrie of Obrecht's *Missa Libenter gloriabor*, leading to a cadence in F♭ major. It did not bother van Crevel that:

1) the singers of the Mass would have to accomplish the near miracle of ending the Kyrie on F♭ and beginning the Gloria on F;

2) there is no poetic, emotional, or iconographic conceit that would justify so extreme a departure from the traditional harmonic conception at so early a time;

3) there is no theoretical counterpart to such a modulation before 1505 (the year of Obrecht's death) that would conceptualize the use of C♭, F♭, and B♭♭, as I have shown to exist for the secret chromatic art, for Josquin's, and even for Willaert's chromatic compositions; and

4) the chromatic modulations in the repertory of the secret chromatic art that he later rejected are musically infinitely superior to his construction, and historically more plausible.

However, van Crevel, afraid of his own courage, while holding fast to the possibility of the F♭ ending, proposed—in order to appease "troubled singers and musicologists"—a compromise solution which is so unmusical, indeed anti-musical, that I hesitate to quote it: from G♭ major, arrived at by way of D♭$^{4-3}$ chord, van Crevel pushes without transition to C minor and, in the space of two measures, on to an F-major ending.

It is an ironic reflection on the state of musicology that of the critics of the secret chromatic art, who have over the years referred to van Crevel as their chief spokesman, not one has pointed to the anomaly between van Crevel's pro-chromatic stand in an Obrecht Mass and his anti-chromatic stand in motets of two generations later. None of them has remarked on the anti-musical results of his interpretation or its paradoxical implications discussed above. One reason for my long silence has been the melancholy realization that between a musician and a nonmusician there simply is no common ground.

(1) There must be a fluent, logical, and flawless modulation.

(2) That modulation must be artistically superior to the diatonic reading.

(3) It must coincide with a significant emotional or religious concept of the text.

(4) It must last no longer than this particular section of the text.

(5) At the point of text change, it must arrive at a cadence that does not leave the music stranded in some remote key but that leads it back to the diatonic mainstream.

(6) To render the transition from the chromatic to the diatonic zone frictionless, the cadence should preferably consist of an empty fifth or octave so as to establish a neutral zone between, say, the preceding F minor and the coming F major, and, if possible, pauses should be inserted to extend the neutral zone.

I repeat, the fortuitous coincidence of all or most of these procedures is highly improbable. This improbability has escaped the skeptics.

Let me illustrate in one last example what happens when the editor creates something that the composer did not plan. One of the most extraordinary works of the Medici Codex is Andreas de Silva's *Omnis pulchritudo Domini*.[64] Its beginning has three C♯s, but not a single F♯ or G♯ (Ex. 16). If we read the text as the Medici Codex transmits it, we find two striking augmented fifths, intervals more strictly forbidden and more out of tune with ordinary sixteenth-century counterpoint than diminished fifths. But any attempt to impose a secret chromatic reading on this passage fails. In fact, if sung as notated, the work sounds marvelous. The augmented fifths are built into a sonority novel in the richness of its colors and its unaccustomed intervals. The beginning of de Silva's motet soars up from an A-major transposed Phrygian to a melodic-rhythmic-harmonic climax on F major, followed by a cadence on D Dorian, designed to celebrate the Resurrection of Christ.[65]

How conscious de Silva's choice of colors and coordination with the theme of the Resurrection is can be seen from the beginning of the *secunda pars* (Ex. 17, p. 122) in which a variation of the beginning of the *prima pars* appears, transposed a fifth higher to E major on the words *Ascendens Christus in altum*. The thrice-indicated G♯ in the soprano draws in its wake not only D♯s, F♯s, and G♯s in bass and alto, but also a G♯ instead of a G in the Gregorian *cantus firmus*. In this passage the D♯s and F♯s coexist with D♮s and F♮s; again, augmented fifths cannot be avoided. These intervals (and an inverted diminished fourth) lend their eerie floating sound to the depiction of the miracle of the Risen Christ. I

---

64. In Edward E. Lowinsky, *The Medici Codex of 1518: A Choirbook of Motets Dedicated to Lorenzo de' Medici, Duke of Urbino*, 3 vols., *Monuments of Renaissance Music*, III–V (Chicago, 1968), IV, 329–38.

65. For an extensive analysis of the work, see *ibid.*, III, 205–13.

Ex. 16 A. de Silva, *Omnis pulchritudo*, beginning of *prima pars*

Ex. 17 A. de Silva, *Omnis pulchritudo*, beginning of *secunda pars*

have compared the work with the fantastic iridescent colors of the contemporaneous Resurrection painted by Matthias Grünewald.

If de Silva's Ascension motet did not appear in the Medici Codex of
1518, no one would guess that this work, with its futuristic sounds, was
written in the early sixteenth century. Nothing can demonstrate more
convincingly how much we are still on the threshold of a full understanding of the immense harmonic imagination of the Renaissance musician.
Here we deal with a full-blown work of musical mannerism in which
unaccustomed, indeed forbidden, intervals are used with ingenuity and
brilliant effect for the representation of an extraordinary event of a mystical character. We dare not approach the music of any period, least of all
the Renaissance, with a firm notion as to what is possible and what is not

possible. We must remain ever open to the surprises of genius, the working of imagination, and last but not least, the creative response of the freest form of man, the artist, to a regime of religious or political repression.

We must do away with that peculiar myopia, the partial view of history. It makes no sense to admit secret modulatory technique in Josquin's *Fortuna*; to concede, by necessity, his bold use of written-out modulation in David's lament on Absalom; to accept the undeniable theoretical proof of a Listenius (and his predecessors Ornitoparchus, Rhau, and Martinez de Bizcargui); to acknowledge the irrefutable evidence of Willaert's chromatic experiment of 1519, Greiter's incredibly bold *Fortuna*, or Costeley's written-out chromaticism of 1558; and then turn to the works of secret chromatic art, which operate on precisely the same principles, and deny their validity—indeed, their very possibility.

That same partial view of history prevents an understanding of the common bond that ties the secret chromatic art to other cultural phenomena.[66] Gleefully my critics contended that only a man who confesses defeat in basing his argument on musical grounds would have gone to the trouble of exploring related extramusical phenomena of Renaissance culture. Against so small a view there is no salvation in controversy. This is why I have kept my peace on the subject for almost twenty-five years. The one answer that bears no contradiction is the intrepid continuation of search and research in the firm belief that truth, which knows no friends and minds no enemies, will prevail in the end.

DISCUSSION

LEAVITT: Was it primarily musical or extramusical ideas that led you to the hypothesis of the secret chromatic art?

LOWINSKY: I was led to the formulation of a theory of "secret chromatic art" primarily, indeed exclusively, by musical ideas. Only after having struggled for years with the source material and the musical technique did I pose the question of the "meaning" of the secret chromatic art

66. In his review of Reese's *Music in the Renaissance*, van den Borren had this to say about the problem: ". . . in a passage dealing with Clemens non Papa and his motet on the raising of Lazarus, Mr. Reese refers to those 'secret chromatic arts' to which Edward Lowinsky devoted a captivating book, rich in insights of all sorts. While Mr. Reese is inclined to accept this author's practical conclusions, he refuses at the same time to see any reasons other than purely musical ones for these audacious modulatory 'excursions' (p. 353, n. 78), political and religious considerations appearing to him to be entirely separate matters. The question is delicate. Granted the mentality of the Renaissance man (Rabelais, for example), we are tempted to be persuaded of the intrusion of that intellectual element into the cryptic technique that Mr. Lowinsky makes out in certain musicians on the borders of religious orthodoxy" (*Journal of the American Musicological Society*, VIII [1955], 128).

in a larger cultural context. Then I analyzed the texts and discovered how close they were to the world of ideas of the various reform movements, and I conceived the notion that we deal with an expression of crypto-Reform sentiment—a thesis developed in the chapter "Religious Background of the Secret Chromatic Art." Still later I began to search for parallel phenomena in sixteenth-century thought and art and wrote the chapter on "The Meaning of Double Meaning in the Sixteenth Century."

If you ask what prompted the discovery of the technique, it was the work by Clemens non Papa, *Fremuit spiritu Jesu*. As you know, I wrote my dissertation on Orlando di Lasso's first motet book, published in Antwerp in 1556. This motet print contains Lasso's setting of the same text. In studying the motet repertoire that had been published in the Netherlands before 1556, I discovered the earlier *Fremuit spiritu Jesu* by Clemens non Papa, and I saw that the ostinato that Lasso had used was taken from Clemens. The ostinato begins on C and on F. But in one passage of Clemens's motet it starts on B♭. I had no doubt from the beginning that it was to be sung with the same solmization, producing a transposition with E♭ and A♭, but I was overwhelmed to find how well the chromatic reading fitted, how beautiful it sounded, and how appropriate it was to the words "et lacrimatus est Jesus" (and Jesus wept). At that time I thought that this was a unique occurrence. But as I continued transcribing Netherlandish motets, I was astonished to find other passages with a diatonic aspect suggesting a chromatic reading by the logic of the musical context and the rules of *musica ficta*. I was fortunate in having the constant warm encouragement of Charles van den Borren, with whom I corresponded from 1937 to 1940, when our contact was interrupted by the war. He and I discussed every single example of secret chromaticism in complete detail. I had the satisfaction of seeing the great Belgian scholar agree with my interpretation of every single case of secret chromaticism.

BERLIN: The secret chromatic art raises the question of musical temperament. Would you give us the acoustical and technical background?

LOWINSKY: Throughout the Middle Ages, the Pythagorean tuning system reigned supreme. It regulated the measurement of intervals on the basis of a pure fifth with the proportion 2:3. One must try to imagine what the Pythagorean experiment meant to understand why the theory had such a tremendous hold on medieval thought. When Pythagoras found that musical intervals that strike the ear agreeably have proportions of great simplicity, and that the octave can be measured as 1:2, and the fifth 2:3, and the fourth 3:4, he had made an extraordinary discovery, something that Goethe called an "Urphänomen"—a phenomenon so fundamental as to be incapable of reduction or explanation. Sculpture and architecture, too, were known to have a mathematical basis. The same proportions governing the spatial relationships of the visual arts were found to govern musical intervals. Truth and beauty, far from being opposed forms of human experience, were thus revealed to be two different forms of one and the same concept. Beauty is truth become visible and audible.

Now something strange happened that occurs time and again in the history of ideas. The creator of the idea becomes its prisoner. Having started from the sensual experience of a consonance and then proceeded to the numbers, the numbers became so important to the Pythagorean thinker that he could not accept as consonance something that was not expressible in the simple mathematical proportion of the superparticular ratio, that is, the relationship of a number to its next higher (or lower) neighbor. The major third, for example, calculated in the Pythagorean manner of using the intervals of the fifth and octave (four fifths minus two octaves), results in the ratio 64:81. Likewise, if the pure fifth is made the basis of tuning, the octave that is reached after twelve fifths is about one eighth of a tone higher than the seventh octave. This "Pythagorean comma" is not noticed in diatonic music but becomes disturbing to the extent that chromatic intervals and modulation in the circle of fifths invade modal polyphony.

The most important developments in acoustical theory took place in opposition to Pythagorean theory; they tended toward recognition of thirds and sixths as consonances and their acceptance into the sacrosanct canon of superparticular ratios (major third, 4:5; minor third, 5:6). This development began around 1300 with Walter Odington, who, with the pragmatic sense of an Englishman—and the English loved thirds and sixths —pointed out that the difference between 64:81 and 64:80 was an imperceptible interval, nothing to worry about, and that 64:80 was equal to 4:5 and would thus continue the series of superparticular ratios. That Odington had a twelfth-century forerunner in the English monk Theinred of Dover, at least in the attempt to consider the thirds as consonances, if not in the mathematical reasoning, has been shown by Gilbert Reaney. Now, a mathematician cannot accept the equalization of 64:80 with 64:81. This is why Odington's reasoning was anathema to Pythagorean dogma and why it took so long for his approach to gain the ascendancy.

The fifteenth and sixteenth centuries produced men who moved toward a recognition of thirds and sixths as consonances as well as toward those changes in tuning that would accommodate chromatic intervals and modulation in the circle of fifths. One of the first pioneers was Bartolomé Ramos, who in his *Musica practica*, published in Bologna in 1482, dared to defy the Pythagorean tradition openly; he was chased out of Bologna. Ramos recognized thirds and sixths as consonances; he replaced the hexachord with the octave system, constructed a complete chromatic scale, and proposed the first steps toward temperament. The other, John Hothby, an English Carmelite monk teaching in Lucca, was more careful; he wrapped his astonishingly progressive theory of mutations (allowing hexachords with up to five flats and five sharps) in so enigmatic a form that it took a great effort to decipher its meaning.[67]

The enigmatic form of Hothby's radical theory of mutations—the very title of his treatise, *Calliopea legale*, hints at the obscure allegorical form —reminds one of the famous cryptogram that Galileo Galilei sent out to the great mathematicians of his time after he discovered the first three moons of Jupiter through his self-constructed telescope. The cryptogram contained the jumbled letters of the discovery.[68] Galilei, not willing as yet to publish his dangerously progressive discovery, wished to protect his authorship by wrapping it in the form of a cryptogram. Perhaps Hothby, a much more cautious man than Ramos and a monk to boot, possibly fore-warned by Ramos's fate, wished to do the same: to publish and yet to protect with the thorn fence of obscure allegory his ideas of radical muta-tion, but stopping short of enharmonic change, and thus basically holding on to the tenets of Pythagoras.

Now let us cast one look forward and one backward. The first man after Hothby to give a systematic theory of mutations, but now in simple, technical language, was Pietro Aron in the second edition of his treatise on the modes, *Il Toscanello in musica* (Venice, 1525).[69] If we assume Hothby's treatise to have been written about 1480—he died in 1487—then it took close to half a century for the system of mutations to be put into a generally understandable form and to be published.

But the prehistory of Hothby's system reaches back to the very founda-tions of the medieval tone system. The Guidonian scale contained one single chromatic note, the B♭, which from the beginning on was felt to be an intruder.[70] It was allowed to enter the scale to fight the devil, the tritone being regarded as *diabolus in musica*. The B♭ was the opening wedge in the gradual chromaticization of the scale. For where there is a B♭, an E♭ will follow in due course. Gustav Jacobsthal, in his book on *Die chromatische Alteration im liturgischen Gesang der abendländischen Kirche* (1898), showed that originally there were B♭ and E♭, F♯ and C♯ in the Gregorian chant, and that later certain transpositions were made to avoid these accidentals. Why were they first used and then elimi-nated? Because the period of 1100 to 1200 was a time of immense sys-tematization; it was the time when the eight church modes were being

67. See A. W. Schmidt, *Die "Calliopea legale" des Johannes Hothby* (Leipzig, 1897).

68. *Altissimum planetam tergeminum observavi*; see Zsolt von Harsányi, *Und sie bewegt sich doch* (Leipzig, 1937), pp. 458, 466.

69. See Willem Elders' beautiful reprint, published by *Musica revindicata* (Utrecht, 1966), Ch. XXVI–LXV.

70. *Minus est regulare*, and *quandam confusionem et transformationem videtur facere*, says Guido of the *b molle* in Chapter 8 of his *Micrologus*, defending its intro-duction—as it would be defended throughout the Middle Ages—by the need to avoid the tritone (see J. Smits van Waesberghe, *Guidonis Aretini Micrologus* [American Institute of Musicology, 1955], pp. 124–25).

systematized. It was the time of the Cistercian Reform, and with it the development of a systematic—indeed, dogmatic—theory. The Cistercians thought nothing of transposing whole parts of a melody so as to avoid the offending accidentals that spoiled the purity of the modal system. If that did violence to the melody—never mind, we must have order.

It is important to remember that without a sense of order, without intellectual ideology, there is no music. Music, like any other art, is as much an intellectual construct as it is an artistic creation. We have to understand and study the mental attitudes, the ideologies, the mental biases, and the prejudices of medieval musicians. The ideology of the early fathers of the church who opposed chromaticism as an expression of the pagan spirit, the sense of order that was so important to the theorists leading to the Cistercian movement, they account for the fact that medieval music and theory favored the diatonic system; but the musicians constantly worked around and against that order. There was unceasing tension between the mental order and the artistic impulse. The efforts of musicians were directed at expanding the tone system without destroying its foundation. This movement led to the theory of mutation in the advanced forms that Hothby and Aron gave it. Since they stopped short of enharmonic change, they could make do with the mean-tone temperament that Aron described for the use of keyboard instruments.[71] Yet the mean-tone temperament would not be adequate for the performance of works of the secret chromatic art going as far as Ab, Db, Gb, and in one case even Cb.

Here we must remember the epoch-making piece of Adrian Willaert, *Quid non ebrietas*, written as far back as 1519, in which the tenor goes through the whole circle of fifths, placing a flat even before C but then continuing without written accidentals to Fb, Bbb, and ending on Ebb, which meets with the D and A of the other three voices to prove the Aristoxenian proposition of equal temperament by equating D with Ebb. This piece demanded a theory of equal temperament that was not long in coming. Giovanni Lanfranco furnished it in his treatise *Scintille de musica* (Brescia, 1533).

BERLIN: Why do you feel that in vocal music, where the singer can adapt and adjust—unlike the situation in wind instruments or in keyboard instruments—we are really talking about equal temperament when we are dealing with advanced chromaticism?

LOWINSKY: That's a very sharp question, and it goes to the heart of the pragmatic attitude of the Renaissance musician. When he was dealing with fretted instruments such as those of the viol family and the lute, he had equal temperament right there. When he was dealing with keyboard instruments he had to be satisfied with mean-tone temperament. Now it is

71. *Il Toscanello in musica* (Venice, 1523), last chapter of Book II.

entirely true that the singers are not bound to fixed tunings; they can and do adjust by ear. But when you speak of vocal music of the Renaissance you must keep in mind that voices and instruments were often mixed in performance. Bottrigari, in his treatise *Il Desiderio ovvero de' concerti di vari stromenti musicali* (Venice, 1594), shows the despair of the Renaissance musician at the sounding together of instruments in all of these various tunings, when the fretted lutes and viols with their equal semitones are played together with keyboard instruments, with their minor and major semitones, with wind instruments having holes (such as flutes and cornetts) and others having no holes (such as trombones); when all of these instruments play together, he complains, a sensitive ear hears nothing but cacophony. Therefore, chromaticism and modulation in vocal music, in view of the particular performance practice of the Renaissance, were found to create difficulties in the tuning of instruments. These difficulties were overcome either by musical temperament or—for those whose ears could not suffer the impurities contained in any temperament—by creating instruments—keyboard instruments, that is—with split keys or with more than twelve keys per octave. In the sixteenth and seventeenth centuries a number of proposals for tuning and temperament were formulated; also numerous instruments with more than twelve keys per octave were constructed.

Here lies the reason why it is impossible to derive an adequate general theory of *musica ficta* from tablatures of instruments that are limited in their capacity to produce chromatic notes—an error compounded if the tablatures chosen are of German origin. For if the Spaniards are *musica-ficta*-happy and the Italians *musica-ficta*-drunk, then the Germans are *musica-ficta*-shy. German music of the fifteenth and sixteenth centuries, at least until 1550, has no history of chromaticism. Nor are the Germans in the fifteenth and early sixteenth centuries in the forefront of musical developments. Plain as these facts are, they have not succeeded in discrediting the notion that sixteenth-century German keyboard tablatures can teach us how *musica ficta* was used in the performance of sixteenth-century vocal music. Of course, this theory contains another erroneous premise, the belief that a piece of music was always done in the same way. But the Renaissance musician was above all an experimenter, and with various instruments, in various settings, he did various things. A study of Italian lute tablatures, that is, the tablatures of an instrument fretted so as to produce equal temperament, will lead to entirely different and to vastly more accurate results.

BUSHLER: What would you say are the research opportunities today for a student of the Renaissance? What are the things he ought to look for?

LOWINSKY: If I were to tell you what you should be looking for, I might block your very vision; you may come up with something that I cannot even dream of. But I can speak in general of how one goes about finding new things. It's a simple recipe. Study previously unexplored sources. Study theory and practical music together. The medievalists do it all the time, but in our field, a few hundred years later, few are the people who take music and theory together. Yet the sixteenth century is perhaps the only century in which theory completely keeps pace with the imaginative innovations of the musicians. Of course, many, if not most, theorists were composers: Tinctoris, Ramos, Gafurius, Aron, Vicentino, Zarlino—they all composed. There was here a most productive confluence between the creative and the intellectual effort for a new art. A lot of interesting theory has not yet been explored or interpreted or even edited. And few of the editions strike me as satisfactory. An edition, to answer the scholar's needs, should be critical in the establishment of the original text and include—preferably on facing pages—the translation. It should contain a glossary explaining in detail meaning and possibly history of technical musical terms.

When it comes to the edition of musical sources, I believe in studying a source as a whole, and that means also editing it as a whole. There are good musicologists who believe that only works of the great masters ought to be published and only the best works of smaller masters. Aside from the difficulty of finding agreement in matters of taste and value, such an approach leaves the historical and cultural-political context out of consideration. The minor composers illuminate the great masters; at times they also make highly interesting contributions to the social and political scene, particularly in the choice of texts they set to music. Also, minor masters can write major works, as you heard yesterday when the New York Pro Musica performed Andreas de Silva's *Omnis pulchritudo*. Matthaeus Greiter's *Fortuna* is a major work not only by dint of its amazing technical achievement but also by virtue of its musical quality.

MRS. JORGENS: I should like to ask whether the motet in the middle of the century moved out of the liturgy and into the home, as you seem to claim. I noticed that one of your critics took issue with this and said that, on the contrary, the motet was still being used in the liturgy.

LOWINSKY: I doubt that your recollection as to what I wrote is correct. But let us begin by asking how we know whether a motet was written for the liturgy.

MRS. JORGENS: If you find it in a cathedral archive or library then it should be liturgical.

LOWINSKY: There is a much simpler test than that.

MRS. JORGENS: If it has a Gregorian melody that comes from the liturgy.

LOWINSKY: True. But it does not have to use a Gregorian melody to be suitable for use in the liturgy.

Mrs. Jorgens: Perhaps it depends on the complexity of the music itself?

Lowinsky: No. Liturgical music can be both extremely simple and exceedingly complex. A motet is liturgical if you can find the text in the liturgy, and in particular if that text can be found in sources of Gregorian chant.

Mrs. Jorgens: Would you say that texts that are not based on chant texts are not liturgical?

Lowinsky: Yes; this is the only way in which we make a differentiation that is often lost sight of: church music and liturgical music. Not everything sung in the church is *eo ipso* liturgical music; this has always been true, and never more so than in the Renaissance, where we find increasing liberty in matters of church music. Few were those who cared whether it was liturgical or not.

This situation concerned the Council of Trent which moved decisively against the prevailing *laissez-faire* attitude in matters of church music and redefined it as music serving the liturgy and being anchored in the music and the texts of Gregorian chant. In the process it even weeded out centuries-old musical forms such as tropes and sequences.

Mrs. Jorgens: How can one establish a text as liturgical?

Lowinsky: First you search through modern chant books. Aside from the *Liber usualis* there are the more complete *Liber gradualis* and *Liber antiphonarius*—the latter with a valuable appendix of old hymn texts (the *Liber usualis* contains the hymns in the seventeenth-century literary reworking of Pope Urban VIII)—the *Liber responsorialis*, the *Variae preces* containing the old sequences, and the *Processionale*. Beyond this you have the books for special services, the *Vesperale*, the chant books for Easter, and the books for the monastic service. Finally, there are the special publications on hymns and on sequences, there is Bruno Stäblein's series *Monumenta monodica medii aevi*, there are the great catalogues, Chevalier's *Repertorium hymnologicum* and Julian's *Dictionary of Hymnology*. Of course, you can take short cuts by consulting such helpful works as Carl Marbach's *Carmina scripturarum*, or the recent *An Index of Gregorian Chant* by John R. Bryden and David G. Hughes (Cambridge, Mass., 1969). If you then still do not succeed—which is entirely possible, because none of the works mentioned is all-inclusive—you may have to search in the original chant manuscripts of the fifteenth and sixteenth centuries themselves, as did Jacquelyn Mattfeld with fine success in her dissertation on Josquin's motets.

Mrs. Jorgens: But don't you eventually get into difficulty trying to define liturgy on that basis? At what point do you pick up with assurance the definition of the liturgical body of music? Eventually chant disappears even further; later in the sixteenth century many free compositions on Latin texts were incorporated into the liturgy, into the service, at least.

LOWINSKY: This is the point: "service" and "liturgy" are not the same thing. They probably never were, because accretions to the liturgy go back to the early Middle Ages. For the purposes of the student of Renaissance music it is helpful to hold on to the definition of liturgy as comprising the body of prayers and texts contained in the various liturgical books of the early Middle Ages and to distinguish them from texts newly written in later centuries, particularly at the time of the composers themselves.

In the study of religious music we come to the following useful distinctions: liturgical music, church music—that is, music written to later texts not contained in the early medieval liturgy—and religious music for the home, such as the *Souterliedekens* or Coclico's collection of psalm settings specifically dedicated to the city fathers of Nuremberg as spiritual refreshment when they return from their labors to their homes. In the *Secret Chromatic Art* I have analyzed Clemens non Papa's motet *Jesus Nazarenus rex Judaeorum* as a "nonliturgical" work written for a private occasion. A frequent telltale of a specific contemporary destination is the construction of a text from a number of different sources, a text not to be found as such in the liturgy, although simulating such origin.

A very interesting development standing between the church and the home deserves much more study than it has received so far: the religious confraternities. I have studied their function in the archives of Antwerp. The most important religious confraternity in Antwerp had its own chapel in the Cathedral of Our Lady. It had the finest organs and the best singers. It even hired the town pipers on occasion and commissioned its own choir books. The confraternities concentrated on the celebration of daily Vesper services, and this reveals their function: after the close of business and the exchange in Antwerp, the brethren of the confraternity would come together, bringing their merchant friends from elsewhere and from abroad to enjoy the finest that Flemish art and taste created in sculpture, painting, and music. Many of the free texts set to music may have been written for confraternities, which were under no obligation to adhere to strict liturgical observance.

This brings me to a point that I omitted before. Among the research needs and opportunities of the student of Renaissance music is work at the archives. There is hardly a field of musicological research that is so little organized and yet so fertile. Not having had the privilege to hear François Lesure, who lectured on this very topic, I shall confine myself to the remark that in addition to the study of composers' lives, to which the archives make such indispensable contributions, we should lay greater emphasis on the study of musical institutions as they emerge from archival documents.

HARMS: I wonder whether you would be willing to talk about your reaction to reviews of the *Secret Chromatic Art*, specifically to that by Leo Schrade.

LOWINSKY: What I objected to—and I refer specifically to Schrade's review—was not that the critic did not agree with my views, but that I was not being criticized for what I wrote. Schrade distorted the text, the context, and the meaning of what I wrote. The second thing that I found objectionable was that Schrade refused to publish my reply to his review, although he was the coeditor of the magazine in which it appeared. My reply has remained unpublished to this day, and many writers have referred to Schrade's review not fully aware of the extent of its unreliability.

HARMS: How important is it for a scholar working in Renaissance music to subscribe to your hypothesis? Is it an isolated phenomenon, appearing only in a certain number of pieces, or is it something that affects the entire milieu of Renaissance music?

LOWINSKY: First of all, it is not important that anybody subscribe to any theory, particularly not to this theory. But it is important that he study the musical and theoretical evidence with great care not only for its application to works containing secret chromatic modulation, but also for its implications to the whole of Renaissance music. The importance of the theory of secret chromaticism lies precisely in the fact that it is not an isolated phenomenon. It is, after all, an outgrowth of *musica ficta*; it shows the liberalized uses of the age-old theory in one particular repertory; it opens our eyes to the existence of a much bolder concept of harmonic color and emotional intensity in the Netherlandish repertory (this, incidentally, may have been what provoked Schrade's ire, for he was just then writing his *Monteverdi*, in which he constructed a theory of absolute opposition between the cool, contrapuntal *Ars perfecta* (as he called it) of the Netherlanders and the new, colorful, emotional world of Monteverdi's music, a theoretical construct that distorts the true evolution of music from Josquin to Monteverdi); it marks the meeting point between North and South, the Netherlands and Italy, Clemens non Papa and Orlando di Lasso; it is a historical phenomenon that points both backward and forward, without which works like Josquin's *Fortuna* and Willaert's chromatic experiment would have seemed to remain without effect on the next generation, and without which such contemporaneous phenomena as Greiter's *Fortuna* and the astonishingly advanced theoretical testimonies of "chain reaction," in which one accidental leads to a whole sequence of others in the circle of fifths, would remain inexplicable—that is, without their counterparts in musical practice.

MRS. FRIEDLAND: I wonder if it would be appropriate to move a few centuries ahead and ask a question concerning your article on "Taste, Style, and Ideology in Eighteenth-Century Music."[72] The role of Rous-

---

72. Edward E. Lowinsky, "Taste, Style, and Ideology in Eighteenth-Century Music," in *Aspects of the Eighteenth Century*, ed. Earl R. Wasserman (Baltimore, 1965).

seau as ideologue of the Enlightenment is certainly significant, but the musical worth of *Le Devin du village* could be argued. I cannot believe that it could have had a serious impact.

LOWINSKY: As a philosopher of music and a writer on music Rousseau had an immense impact—more so than is realized in most histories of music. I also agree that *Le Devin du village* is not a great work of art. Our difference, then, boils down to this question: Can a small work of art have a big impact? To this my answer is: Yes, if the circumstances are right. The France of Louis XV was not the France of Louis XIV. Politics, personalities, society, taste, and manners had changed. That change was mirrored in painting, which replaced sculpture as the dominating art, it was manifested in interior decoration, which took the place of architecture as the innovative art, and it was reflected in philosophy and literature. But in music Louis XIV's Lullian opera held on with unbelievable tenacity. Even Rameau did not change the basic outlook of opera as a form of royal entertainment involving mythological plots, elaborate stage settings, formal ballets, and brilliant choruses. In such a situation a work of small artistic merit can have a great impact, provided it expresses a real need. Rousseau's *Le Devin du village* had such an impact simply because it broke so radically with a tradition that was out of step with the present: it was novel, it was natural, it was utterly unpretentious, it had tunes the people could sing. Even the court was delighted with it, because nothing was more popular at court than to impersonate the shepherds and shepherdesses and the simple people as they liked to think of them. This is why this piece had a success out of proportion to its artistic significance; we must remember that it was played from 1752 till 1828, and that is quite a remarkable career. It was surely in Mozart's mind when he wrote *Bastien und Bastienne*, and you can still see its effect in *The Marriage of Figaro*—that is, in the idea of the libretto, at any rate.

MRS. FRIEDLAND: I think its influence wasn't so much musical as it was philosophical.

LOWINSKY: Certainly, but I do not belong to those who deny its musical worth completely.

BROOK: Some years ago, a Swiss scholar and musician, Samuel Baud-Bovy, director of the Geneva Conservatory, revived a very little-known opera of Rousseau, *Les Muses galantes* (1745).[73] It had the same kind of simple music, even simplistic, as *Le Devin du village*, but it had a very successful production and recording in Geneva. It worked; it worked by its very simplicity, its folklike quality, its naïveté. The same is true of *The Beggar's Opera*.

LOWINSKY: Quite so. But Rousseau is superior to Pepusch, who merely

73. See also André Brugère, "Les Muses galantes, musique de Jean-Jacques Rousseau," *La Revue musicale*, CCXVIII (1952), 5–31.

furnished the bass to English folk tunes; Rousseau wrote his own melodies.

MRS. FRIEDLAND: Are we not ignoring the comic style, the association of Lully and Molière in music, the music at court, for ballets—*Le Bourgeois Gentilhomme*, for example?

LOWINSKY: There is a world of difference between the comic element in a ceremonial court atmosphere such as Lully's comédie-ballet offers and the naïve popular realism of *La Serva padrona* or *Le Devin du village*. The comic is not identical with popular music, nor can it be equated with the new realism. Here the middle class finally comes into its own. That, of course, is something that Molière had already been doing in the theater. But certainly Lully's music to the comédie-ballets has nothing to do with the naïve popularity that pushes through in *The Beggar's Opera*, in *La Serva padrona*, in *Le Devin du village*.

BROOK: I agree completely. The comédie-ballets of Lully were musically very sumptuous, they were magnificently costumed, and they involved elaborate dance forces; they are not to be compared with musical playlets in which two or three people dressed in shepherd's robes sing simple folk tunes. Furthermore, the music for *Le Bourgeois Gentilhomme* is twice as long as all of *Le Devin du village*.

VAN SOLKEMA: Do you agree with the philosophical position of the ethnomusicologist who believes that all music is performed and heard in a certain social context and that it is the task of the musicologist to study the social context as carefully as the music itself?

LOWINSKY: This has always been my position. But for the historical musicologist to be able to study the social, cultural, and political scene in which the music of any age lives, he has to be a humanist. To the extent that we allow our students to lose the languages and the related fields, our study of music will become merely technical; it will lose its relationship to the whole of human experience. Once this happens, the young people will then ask, What is the relevance of all this technical study? This is what we ought to remind them of when they demand an end to the study of languages, history, and the like. There is no relevance to any undertaking except in terms of the whole human condition.

BROOK: Thank you, Mr. Van Solkema, for your question, and Mr. Lowinsky, for your answer. I think they are a fitting epigraph for this entire series of lectures.

READING LIST

Einstein, Alfred, *The Italian Madrigal*, 3 vols. (Princeton, N.J., 1949), I, 384–423 (Cipriano de Rore).

Kaufmann, Henry, "Vicentino and the Greek Genera," *Journal of the American Musicological Society*, XVI (1963), 325–46.

——— "A 'Diatonic' and a 'Chromatic' Madrigal by Giulio Fiesco," in *Aspects of Medieval and Renaissance Music: A Birthday Offering to Gustave Reese*, ed. Jan LaRue *et al.* (New York, 1966), pp. 474–88.

Levy, Kenneth, "Costeley's Chromatic Chanson," *Annales musicologiques*, III (1955), 213–63.

Lowinsky, Edward E., *Secret Chromatic Art in the Netherlands Motet*, Columbia University Studies in Musicology, 6 (New York, 1946; repr. New York: Russell & Russell, 1967).

——— "The Goddess Fortuna in Music, with a Special Study of Josquin's *Fortuna dun gran tempo*," *Musical Quarterly*, XXIX (1943), 45–77.

——— "Matthaeus Greiter's *Fortuna:* An Experiment in Chromaticism and in Musical Iconography," *Musical Quarterly*, XLII (1956), 500–19; XLIII (1957), 68–85.

——— "Adrian Willaert's Chromatic 'Duo' Re-examined," *Tijdschrift voor Muziekwetenschap*, XVIII (1956), 1–36.

——— *Tonality and Atonality in Sixteenth-Century Music*, 2nd rev. printing (Berkeley-Los Angeles, 1962), pp. 38–50.

——— Foreword to *Musica nova*, ed. H. Colin Slim, *Monuments of Renaissance Music*, 1 (Chicago, 1964), pp. viii–xxi.

——— Introduction to *Ottaviano Petrucci, Canti B*, ed. Helen Hewitt, *Monuments of Renaissance Music*, 2 (Chicago, 1967), pp. ix–xiv.

——— *The Medici Codex of 1518: A Choirbook of Motets Dedicated to Lorenzo de' Medici, Duke of Urbino*, 3 vols., *Monuments of Renaissance Music*, III–V (Chicago, 1968), III, 205–13; IV, 329–38.

——— "The Musical Avant-Garde of the Renaissance or: The Peril and Profit of Foresight," in *Art, Science, and History in the Renaissance*, ed. Charles S. Singleton (Baltimore, 1968), pp. 111–62.

——— "Echoes of Adrian Willaert's Chromatic 'Duo' in Sixteenth- and Seventeenth-Century Compositions," in *Studies in Music History: Essays for Oliver Strunk*, ed. Harold Powers (Princeton, N.J., 1968), pp. 183–238.

Schrade, Leo, "A Secret Chromatic Art," *Journal of Renaissance and Baroque Music*, I (1946), 159–67.

van den Borren, Charles, "Y avait-il une pratique musicale ésotérique au temps de Roland de Lassus?" *Revue belge de musicologie*, II (1948), 38–43.

Two Research Lacunae in
Music of the Classic Period

H. C. ROBBINS LANDON

I.   Music in Eastern Europe after the Czech Crisis (1968)

IT MIGHT be thought that with the steady progress of RISM
there would be little likelihood today of unearthing new and important
manuscripts, much less undiscovered works, by great composers. But a
recent *New York Times* (February 2, 1969) reminded us that even at this
late stage in the collection of musical sources, it is still possible to discover
a lost and apparently genuine piano fantasy by Franz Schubert.

It is possibly significant that this lost Schubert composition turned up in
a trunk stored in an attic of a small provincial town called Knittelfeld, in
the Austrian province of Styria. It is unlikely that one would find lost
masterpieces of Schubert or Mozart or Beethoven nowadays in Vienna,
where the holdings of the principal libraries are well known and where
many scholars have long been on the lookout for such lost treasures. But
the provinces have many secrets to reveal. This is particularly true of
provinces in the socialist countries, where music scholarship has not perhaps been able to proceed with the same speed or the same international
affiliations as has been the case in Western capitals. Events in the summer
of 1968 in Czechoslovakia focused attention on political events in that

136

tragic country. I believe that Czechoslovakia is potentially the most rewarding of all the little-explored socialist countries as far as musicological discoveries are concerned, and that a reassessment of lacunae in musicological research there (and in other socialist countries as well) has become particularly pressing.

It has been known for some years following World War II that the manuscript and published music holdings of the Prague National Museum have grown to enormous proportions. Since the circumstances regarding this important enlargement of Prague's collections are perhaps not well known to everyone, a few words of explanation may not be unwelcome. During the height of Austro-Hungarian prosperity, when the monarchy was still flourishing, many of the nobility had summer castles in Bohemia or, indeed, had their family seats in that beautiful province. In the course of the years, many of these castles came to house not only important libraries but also collections of music manuscripts. And while the libraries were often well known to literary scholars, many music collections were never catalogued and, indeed, their existence was hardly remembered by their owners.

In 1947, after Czechoslovakia became a communist country, many of these libraries and musical archives were deposited in Prague or in other centers such as Brno (Brünn). The amount of music contained in these confiscated collections is so enormous that it will be many years before the scholarly world knows the holdings of the Prague Library in their entirety. In the process of this vast collectivization, many precious manuscripts perished. We have hair-raising accounts of Haydn manuscripts lying in the streets of Bratislava (formerly Pressburg) and large piles of eighteenth-century music moldering in the rain in the courtyards of obscure provincial castles. What perished in the process can only be imagined.

But, on the credit side, this collectivization brought to light many hitherto unknown music collections, some of them of enormous importance. Such a library as that of the Clam-Gallas family, housed in Frýdlant (Friedland), is certainly one of the most important in Central Europe for music of the second half of the eighteenth century. In it I was able some years ago to find in two days half a dozen lost Haydn works.[1] The catalogue of the library formerly at the Wallenstein Castle of Dorsy (Hirschberg) requires two large printed volumes and includes among other things one of two known copies of the earliest libretto of Haydn's lost opera *Der neue krumme Teufel*. It was in this collection that Czechoslovak scholars discovered, some nine years ago, the only known copy of Haydn's Cello Concerto in C major, which has since entered the international repertoire with such extraordinary swiftness.

1. The March in G "Regimento de Marschall" (Hob. *deest*), a *Cassatio for Four Horns and Strings in D* (Hob. *deest*), and several *divertimenti* for wind band.

While the authorities have removed many of the aristocratic collections to Prague and other centers, some collections, not burdened with the dubious political associations of the Austro-Hungarian aristocracy, have been allowed to remain where they were. In several trips to the Czech provinces I was soon aware that the situation outside the large cities was quite chaotic. In 1959 scholars at the Prague Library estimated that it would take them fifteen years to finish cataloguing the holdings at Prague. If this is a realistic estimate (and I believe it to be that), then we may safely state that it will take thirty years, or a whole generation, before the music-manuscript holdings of the Czech provinces are catalogued and made known to the world. Such a provincial collection is that in the town archives of Cheb (Eger), where I was able to find manuscript copies of Mozart piano concertos written by Johann Radnitzky, who often served Haydn as a copyist. Many of the parish-church archives in Czechoslovakia remain to be studied. The charming Symphony in D major by one of the Miča (Mitscha) family that was published in 1946 by Jan Raček and which came from an obscure Bohemian parish church has proved thus far to be the only copy of that particular work in existence.

To return to the importance of the Prague holdings: since the collection has been available to Western scholars, nearly fifteen lost Haydn works have been discovered there, including the afore-mentioned Cello Concerto in C, the *Aria pro adventu* in D major, and various other pieces of church music and instrumental works such as those referred to earlier. These holdings are not only important for Haydn; they are absolutely essential for any study of the music preferred and cultivated by aristocratic circles and local musical institutions in Bohemia during the second half of the eighteenth century. For example, Prague owns one of the most complete collections of symphonies by Vanhal, Dittersdorf, and Ordonez known to us.

Within the confines of this paper we can do no more than mention the important holdings of some other Czech libraries. Another center for confiscated manuscripts—and these include the holdings of many monasteries —is in Brno. Here, cataloguing has proceeded more quickly than in Prague; the cards themselves are models of accuracy, and also include incipits. In Brno, the Haydn holdings alone include the only known copies of two piano sonatas missing in the Hoboken catalogue—the String Quintet in A major (Hob. II:A/1),[2] and one of the three known copies of the Organ Concerto No. 3 in C, which was until recently believed to be lost. Near Brno is the small town of Kroměříž (Kremsier), with the library of the archbishops of Olomuce (Olmutz). Kroměříž is perhaps best known for its holdings of Renaissance and Baroque wind music, but is also vital

2. The piano sonatas are published by Georg Feder in his edition for G. Henle Verlag, also in the collected editions of Haydn's sonatas edited by Christa Landon and published by the Universal Edition in the *Wiener Urtext Ausgabe*. The String Quartet is published by Doblinger Verlag, Vienna.

for its Haydn holdings. There are at least ten unique Haydn works in Kroměříž, which is particularly rich in its holdings of the early Haydn keyboard trios.[3]

Czechoslovakia is important for other aspects of music history. The Prague Museum contains a highly important collection of musical instruments, many of them unique. Czechoslovakia is also particularly rich in its iconographic holdings dealing with musicians, their patrons, and so forth, of the second half of the eighteenth century. Anyone who studies the illustrations of music magazines will know the appalling standard of musical iconography in most countries today. We seem content to see Beethoven in romanticized etchings of 1850 and Mozart in pictures that look nothing like Mozart. The voice of the late Otto Erich Deutsch remains, iconographically speaking, that of a prophet crying in the wilderness. In the collections of Czech castles you can find the only known portrait of the Baroness Dorothea von Ertmann (the renowned interpreter of Beethoven's sonatas) and a wide variety of handsome oil portraits, most of them never photographed in color, ranging from Beethoven's patron, the Prince Carl Lichnowsky, to an unknown portrait of Sir William Hamilton. These represent an important neglected field of our discipline.

II. The Problem of Saving Old Keyboard Instruments

The second part of this brief survey will deal with the question of newly discovered keyboard instruments in Europe. Harpsichords, fortepianos, and organs have been chosen because I believe that in these neglected areas we have a great deal to learn, or at least to transform into practical terms. Also, the question of falsifications does not really arise as far as harpsichords, fortepianos, or organs are concerned, or at least not with the same monotonous regularity that we have in the case of falsified violins with faked inscriptions of Stradivarius or Guarnerius. Moreover, while there has long been an acute demand for great seventeenth- and eighteenth-century violins, old keyboard instruments have been curiously neglected until recently.

In a short survey it is hardly possible to do more than touch on the problems involved. To preface this brief sketch, it is necessary to emphasize that the average modern harpsichord hardly represents the typical eighteenth-century harpsichord, if, indeed, there be such a thing. There were, and (so far as the instruments have been accurately preserved and restored) still are, enormous differences among Italian, German, French, Flemish, and English harpsichords. It cannot be the purpose of this paper to enter into discussion of these differences. But if we must generalize it is fair to say that the average Neupert harpsichord is a far cry from almost any eighteenth-century harpsichord whatever, both as to the general,

---

3. A new edition of all of Haydn's keyboard trios, edited by the writer of this article, is about to be published by Doblinger Verlag.

over-all sound and to the disposition of the various registers. Of course there were complicated two-manual harpsichords, particularly northern European instruments, with as many as four or five registers, but these were not the typical harpsichords for which much of the literature (and particularly that of Italian composers) was written. Similarly, there is a vast difference between the harpsichord that Handel used in, let us say, 1720, and the harpsichord Haydn may have used in London in 1795.

Almost all present-day harpsichord players, particularly in America, use far too much 16-foot in their playing and recording. I have never seen a single Italian harpsichord with a 16-foot register; nor has Michael Thomas, who has restored some fifty Italian harpsichords since World War II and inspected several dozen others. It is very unlikely that Handel ever wrote a single harpsichord work with a 16-foot in mind. Most of his early harpsichord music was written for an Italian-type instrument with one manual and two 8-foot stops, which incidentally were almost always coupled and were separated only for tuning. Italian harpsichords having these two 8-foot registers plus a 4-foot are rarer, but by no means uncommon. The Metropolitan Museum of Art here in New York owns a handsome Roman harpsichord which is at present on display; it contains three registers, one of which was presumably a 4-foot. Mechanically speaking, these Italian harpsichords are far more primitive than their northern counterparts, but they generally have a warm and at the same time brilliant tone which makes them very endearing to the ear.

As a result of the French Revolution, the supply of old French harpsichords is so limited that hardly any come on the market. German or Austrian instruments are even more scarce. Nowadays the two principal sources for old harpsichords are either Italian or English, with an occasional Ruckers or other Flemish instrument coming to light. Two questions now arise: What can we do about saving such instruments as appear in the auction houses, and how do they increase, or change, our understanding of the harpsichord repertoire? The first question can be answered only by eternal vigilance and a great deal of luck.

The second can perhaps be grasped if one compares the enormous sound and wide variety of registration of the typical big Pleyel harpsichord with the subtleties of, say, the four harpsichords recently restored by Michael Thomas.[4] The first is an instrument signed by Franciscus de Paulinus, who was the parish priest of Rimini. Dated 1726, it was discovered in Florence a few years ago in the cellars of an antiquarian on the Via Maggio. It has a handsome painted case of very simple construction, and both case and soundboard are made of very fine pinewood. The interior is almost completely devoid of struts or other supports, and there is

4. The recordings cited in footnotes 5 and 7 were played as illustrations: Frescobaldi, *Partita Sopr La Folia* (Franciscus de Paulinus harpsichord, 1726); Zipoli, Suite in G minor (Alessandro Cresci Pilano, Levano, 1760); Couperin, Ordre No. 26 (Ruckers, 1623); Handel, Suite No. 15 (Crang, 1745).

only one small bar on the soundboard to keep it flat. The instrument has that typical Italian combination of a bright bass and a rather fluty treble, and there is one manual with two 8-foot stops.

The second instrument is a later Italian harpsichord, signed and dated Alessandro Cresci Pilano, made in Levano in 1760. It consists of two 8-foot and one 4-foot. Mr. Thomas has described the instrument as follows:

> Every part of the instrument runs at a peculiar angle: this harpsichord represents the last phase of Italian building where much of the old shape was kept but everything is slightly turned on different angles. The strings are turned so that they pass over the bridge nearer the centre of the instrument in the bass to give a fuller and rounder fundamental tone. The brightness in the tone is given by an extra soundboard above the keys which adds bright upper harmonics to every part of the instrument. This extra soundboard is sometimes found in very early Italian harpsichords, often only in the treble. Instruments with this second soundboard are very brittle in tone and do not sustain well. That the maker was interested in the attack rather than in a clear sustaining tone, is shown by the fact that it is not possible for the 4′ to have dampers on it. The 4′ plectra can be heard plucking the string a second time when the note goes back, or at the end of a section. Nowadays it would be possible to make a harpsichord with all this vitality, but we would do it by altering the vibrating areas without the complexity of strings running diagonally, or keys that form an "S" bend.
>
> The bass of these Italian instruments is full of harmonics, forceful and driving. Emphasis on melody and bass accompaniment is impossible. Instead, the bass must lead and give the percussive accent. It must also, on occasion, suggest the phrasing for the right hand as it sustains and slurs better than the treble.
>
> The right hand melody must not be much slower than a third of a second for each beat as it does not sustain well. If it is slower, then the Italian ornamentation of changing notes must be used to fill the gaps. There is an enormous difference between this kind of ornamentation and the harmonic emphasis given by French ornamentation.[5]

In extreme contrast to these Italian instruments is the unbelievably sophisticated sound of, say, a great double-manual Ruckers harpsichord of 1623.

Our final example is a beautifully constructed English harpsichord made by Crang in 1745, about which Mr. Thomas writes:

> The Crang has a perfectly preserved sound board and for its time, is comparatively large. Crang was considered to be the leading maker of his day. Not only is the workmanship of this harpsichord splendid but also it is large with an organ-like tone and very full bass. A lute stop gives a nasalized effect which contrasts with the eight foot and four foot chorus on the lower manual.

5. The technical descriptions of these instruments are taken from Michael Thomas's excellent notes to the recording *Historic Harpsichords/Clavichords* (Oryx 725).

Each note of this instrument needs a strong pluck from a powerful quill to develop the tone. This is its limitation. It is not more expressive than an Italian and lacks the vitality and the brilliance of the high harmonics. It is ideally suitable for the long flowing pieces of Handel. Each note is a positive statement. The staccato quavers in the Jig at the end of the meter can be made to sound slightly soft, but they have enough power, even so, to give a forward drive. The instrument is best for positive, extroverted music.[6]

Each one of these four eighteenth-century harpsichords has its own distinctive sound and construction, but if we may take the liberty, at more than two hundred years' interval, of suggesting that all four have a certain characteristic sound, it must be admitted that this collective sound is a far cry indeed from the average twentieth-century instrument. Theoretically speaking, Handel's early harpsichord music should ideally be performed using two coupled 8-foot registers. Much harpsichord music of the first part of the eighteenth century was designed for these simple instruments; even if it were written for more complicated harpsichords, they were so rare that the composer could hardly expect most of his unknown audiences, who would buy his music and know it only from the printed page, to own anything else but a simple instrument of one manual and two 8-foot registers.

Undoubtedly there are many lovers of the harpsichord in this country who have hardly heard an old instrument that has been accurately restored. Yet we are still, in this day and age, in a position to find such instruments in auction houses and antique shops. The other day, during the antique fair here in New York, I noticed a beautiful late-seventeenth-century spinet with the characteristic short octave made in York, which had never been restored and which could, at the hands of an expert, be made to recapture the sounds appropriate to Blow or Handel. As examples of the kinds of instruments that keep turning up in Italy, may I cite two harpsichords, both found in antiquarian shops in Italy during the past five years. The first (see Pl. 14a) is a one-manual harpsichord with two 8-foot registers, made about 1700, with the short octave in the bass. It bears the coat of arms of Cardinal Pietro Ottoboni, that famous patron of the arts in Rome at the end of the seventeenth and first half of the eighteenth centuries. Cardinal Ottoboni was a friend of Handel's and it was at the Palazzo della Cancelleria, where Ottoboni lived, that the famous contest between Handel and Domenico Scarlatti took place. Ottoboni's *maestro di capella* was none other than Arcangelo Corelli, and his painter in residence, in the early years of the eighteenth century, was Francesco Trevisani, who painted the handsome *Flight from Egypt* that may be seen on the inside lid of the harpsichord. This instrument, which has meanwhile been restored by Josef Mertin and Michael Thomas, was found in an antique shop in Montecatini Terme.

6. *Ibid.*

The second (see Pl. 14b) is a far more elaborate-looking instrument, a handsome one-manual harpsichord with two 8-foot registers, painted by a North Italian master, Faustino Bocchi, whose dates are roughly contemporary with those of Johann Sebastian Bach. The extraordinary subject of the painting is typical of Bocchi's work, as is his predilection for the rather sinister dwarfs you see on it. This harpsichord came from a Florence antiquarian in 1968; it, too, has been restored by Michael Thomas and is in completely playable condition. By restoration we mean, in this case, no more than putting in order, because the soundboard of the Bocchi instrument is intact as are all except a dozen of the original jacks; and of course the entire keyboard is the instrument's own.

Not only do harpsichords still turn up with considerable frequency, but they are very often threatened with a treatment hardly envisaged by their makers: nowadays many of these instruments are gutted and turned into bars for rich Milanese industrialists. Small organs are similarly threatened. It has been estimated that since World War II one thousand old organs have been destroyed in Italy. Their cases, after the pipes have been removed, are used for television sets or as bookcases. Some seven or eight years ago, the author arrived one day too late at an antiquarian shop in Prato, to find a perfectly preserved 1705 chamber organ gutted, its delicately painted pipes twisted double and thrown into a heap in the corner. Twenty-four hours earlier the organ had been in perfect playing condition.

Of all the keyboard instruments, however, none has suffered more neglect than the early piano, known in German as *Hammerklavier* and nowadays as the *fortepiano*, to distinguish it from our modern instrument. Indeed, eighteenth-century pianos have been destroyed so rapidly that hardly any are left in Austria, for example, where, toward the end of the eighteenth century, the grand piano achieved its first and brilliant flowering. In the last ten years only one such grand piano, a Viennese instrument of about 1795, turned up in a Salzburg antiquarian shop. Unfortunately the piano was in a very damaged condition and its restoration would have been a major undertaking, the results of which might or might not have warranted the trouble. Yet a study of these eighteenth-century pianos will show that the difference in sound between a Viennese piano by, say, Anton Walter and our modern nine-foot concert grand is even more astonishing than the difference in sound between an old and a modern harpsichord. Anton Walter was the principal piano manufacturer in Vienna from about 1780 to the end of the century, and Mozart owned, and much loved, a Walter piano which, dubiously restored, is now in Mozart's birthplace in Salzburg. Hardly anyone, apart from the experts, realizes that the whole of Beethoven's early piano music was written for an instrument very similar to that for which Mozart and Haydn composed, and which bears only a nodding acquaintance with our modern Steinway and Bechstein.

Recently an important instrument by Anton Walter, made about 1780, was discovered in the tiny town of Raiding in Burgenland, where Franz Liszt was born. The instrument was restored by Professor Josef Mertin in Vienna, and is now in Haydn's house in Eisenstadt.

The man who has done the most toward saving these priceless instruments is Dr. Victor Luithlen, the former custodian of the old instrument collection of the Vienna Museum. Thanks to him we have in that collection two beautiful Walter instruments dating from about 1785 and 1795 respectively. Recently Dr. Luithlen arranged to have a recording made that includes Mozart's Sonata for Two Pianos in D major, K. 448, played by Jörg Demus and Norman Shetler, on these two Walter instruments.[7] The difference in sound, particularly in treble sustaining power, between the 1780 instrument of Eisenstadt and these two more technically perfect instruments will readily be heard. It must be also borne in mind that this is the kind of instrument on which Beethoven played his first three piano concertos, his early sonatas, and his early chamber music such as the Op. 1 trios. Beethoven himself preferred Walter's pianos when he first came to Vienna, and we have several contemporary eyewitness reports of Beethoven playing Walter instruments. It is believed that he actually owned one[8] for the first ten or fifteen years of his stay in Vienna, or from 1792 on.

Instruments of this kind are rarer than harpsichords, but they do turn up—not in Austria and Germany (ravaged by recent wars), but rather in Italy, where the Austrian influence in Lombardy, Tuscany, Reggio Emilia, and even Naples (Queen Maria Carolina was the daughter of Empress Maria Theresa) was responsible for the introduction of Austrian pianos at the end of the eighteenth and early nineteenth centuries. Until quite recently, big Viennese grand pianos of the early nineteenth century turned up at extraordinarily small prices in Italy; for whereas Italian harpsichords are usually painted, and thus have a certain decorative appeal, Viennese pianos were not, and are therefore considered less attractive from the antiquarian point of view (and thus far less expensive if and when they are discovered). Last year a beautiful Viennese piano made about 1795 by Giovanni Heichele was discovered in an abandoned villa in Bagni di Lucca, and is now being restored.

For obvious reasons, the supply of these harpsichords, organs, and pianos is not unlimited; but there is still, I believe, a reasonable opportunity for American museums, libraries, and universities to acquire examples of these important historic instruments and thus fill one of the major lacunae in our musicological holdings in this country.

7. RCA Victrola VICS-1495.

8. Carl Czerny went to meet Beethoven about 1801 and later reported the composer living in a sparsely furnished room with a "Walter fortepiano (then the best ones)." F. Kerst, *Die Erinnerungen an Beethoven* (Stuttgart, 1914), I, 42.

DISCUSSION

BROOK: There has been talk for many years about the absence of a comprehensive book on the Classic period. I wonder if, as a result of the many dissertations on the period in recent years and the extensive investigations that you yourself and other established scholars have been making, it is not now time to put an over-all picture of the Classic period into book form. Obviously, the final word will not be said right away—the final word can never be said; nonetheless, it should by now be possible to put the period into some perspective.

LANDON: The trouble with that book is that even if it is just a survey, it is going to be hopelessly large. And unless it is in three volumes of, let's say, 600 to 700 pages each, it is going to be so superficial as to be useless. It will have to cover some 15,000 symphonies written between 1740 and 1800, to say nothing of other forms. And even *such* a book would tend to be too much of a survey.

BROOK: But is it not a fact that when Bukofzer wrote his book on the Baroque, the same difficulties existed; there were hundreds of composers, some of whom have since turned out to be quite significant, who had hardly been looked at. Yet his book has been of incalculable value in the education of American college students *and* teachers.

VAN SOLKEMA: Your first interest is eighteenth-century music, of course, but have you, in the course of your travels, uncovered places, particularly in Eastern Europe, where there are treasures of earlier music?

LANDON: Yes. Indeed, I have. Kroměříž (Kremsier) is one of the biggest. Some experts worked there before I did, but it is enormous. It would be a very rewarding center for research in the fields of Baroque and Renaissance Czech music. In fact, nobody really thinks of this as a collection of eighteenth-century music at all. I do, because I'm interested in all the keyboard music of Haydn they own. But if you mention Kroměříž to any knowledgeable musicologist, his first reaction would be: "Wind band and brass music of the late Renaissance and the early Baroque." There are many similar collections throughout Eastern Europe. There is a very big center now at Graz, where they have gathered together music from the entire Austrian province of Styria, including a lot of Renaissance music that has hardly been investigated at all.

Prague now has quite a sizable collection of little-known Renaissance and Baroque documents, from all the outlying castles. Poland is rich in the same periods, because it was so extremely isolated from the rest of Europe —unlike places in Austria where they kept throwing out their older church music to make room for the new.

VAN SOLKEMA: You have said that Czechoslovakia appears to be the most important country of Eastern Europe from the point of view of its unexploited sources. Could you sketch a broader picture of the potential musicological source material in Eastern Europe as a whole?

LANDON: If we assume that Eastern Europe includes Hungary, Albania, Yugoslavia, Austria, Bulgaria, Romania, and the whole Danube basin, then it is easy to explain why there is so much in Czechoslovakia, why there always *was* so much in Czechoslovakia, and why there was less in the other countries. For example, while looking for Haydn materials, I went to Goldfadein in Romania, where Michael Haydn was *Kapellmeister* in the early 1760s. Now, Romania is not an industrial country; it has always been a food-producing, agrarian land; and towns like Goldfadein are few and far between. There was no thickly settled, aristocratic land tenure system as there was in Czechoslovakia, where there were a great many nobles closely connected with the Austro-Hungarian establishment. We drove to Goldfadein with high hopes and found nothing. Refugees from the war ended up in the archbishop's palace and simply burned the manuscripts to keep themselves from freezing to death in the winter. They are gone—nothing!

As one drives through Romania and Bulgaria, or even Yugoslavia, one begins to understand why, under the old Austro-Hungarian monarchy, these areas were really the never-never provinces. To a lesser degree the same is true of Hungary, which even today is a backward country, measured by its degree of industrialization. In Hungary, since there was practically no middle class, sophisticated culture existed only in the châteaux of such nobles as the Esterházys or the Wals. This is one of the reasons why you find few major collections of books, manuscripts, or anything else.

Yet in many ways Hungary is a special case. Hungarian musicologists have recently found some extremely important collections in the provinces. One of these was taken back to Budapest, where it proved to be the most valuable single collection of early Haydn symphonies ever discovered! The parts contained corrections in Haydn's hand, and were perhaps even used by him for performance.

In Czechoslovakia, to add just a word to what I said in my lecture, the riches are not confined to aristocratic chateaux. You can dip into any province and find something. I have done this. Once, when we had driven into the little town of Lainck, I went to the local archive and asked: "Do you have a music archive?" "Yes," I was told, "there is not much there, but you can look at it." There was not a lot, but all of it was most interesting: local manuscripts from about 1740, 1750, 1760, mainly church music by local Czech composers.

In the eighteenth century, Poland was in much the same situation as Romania and Hungary. Have you ever read that fantastic description of the Polish travels of Maria Carolina, the wife of King Ferdinando IV of

Naples? She was a daughter of the Empress Maria Theresa. For a time, starting in 1799, as a dethroned queen, she spent her life in fantastic castles, mostly medieval, with myriads of servants, and in between, as she saw it, nothing but mud, mud, mud, and rain. She wrote that there was hardly any difference between the dogs and the people who used to shuffle along beside her coach. Then her party would arrive at another unbelievably beautiful château, with marvelous eighteenth-century French furniture and beautiful imported pianos from Vienna on which they made music in the evenings. This seems to have been very typical of the situation in Poland. The music that has been found in such oases of culture, including the great churches and monastery archives, is now being systematically explored by the Poles themselves.

BROOK: Have you encountered any kind of restrictions on research by foreigners in Eastern European countries, or restrictions on publication such as exist in some Western European countries for certain library holdings?

LANDON: The Eastern Europeans have always been extremely nice to me. The dealings that I have with libraries and with individuals connected with libraries have always been charming, with no publication restrictions at all. I don't think, unless the political situation over there grows much worse, that scholars need anticipate any difficulty. Now, of course, if you were to rush over there and try to publish, under the noses of Polish scholars, the beautiful Requiem Mass in E♭ by Mateusz Zwierchowski that they just discovered in their own Cathedral of Gniezno, I don't think they would appreciate that.

MRS. FRIEDLAND: I would like to bring up another question, which is relevant to all of Haydn's music and, indeed, to that of many of his contemporaries. That is the controversy over the use of the term *Sturm und Drang*. Some scholars deny its existence as a period in Haydn's development. Others have serious reservations about any facile take-over of terms from other disciplines, for example, from the visual arts—Impressionism, Baroque, mannerism—or from literary history—*Sturm und Drang*.

LANDON: I think this is largely a battle of words. I think nobody can ignore the fact that in the middle of the 1760s, mostly in Austria, there came a great self-examination, and a deepening of styles by means of various devices including a return to fugues, which cannot be accidental. It did happen, and it happened to many composers. There is also a new significance attached to the minor mode—a significance it was far from having in the seventeenth century or among the late Baroque masters. For example, if you were to take the hundreds of Vivaldi concertos and were to compare those in the major mode with those in the minor, it would be very difficult to show any great change of emotions between the C-major and C-minor concertos, between the G-major and the G-minor concertos.

By contrast, when this new movement of the 1760s—whatever we choose
to call it—started, there was quite suddenly an enormous distinction between work written in the minor keys and those in major. Take a work
we all know: Haydn's Quartet in F minor, Opus 20, No. 5, did not sound
like any quartet that was ever written before. The same applies to the
G-minor Quartet. His Symphony No. 26 in G minor does not sound like
any earlier symphony we know—and this is 1768. Similarly, the F-minor
Symphony (No. 49) really is a very somber work, any way you choose to
look at it. This new attitude toward music occurs frequently in Haydn's
other works of this period—for example, the G-minor *Stabat Mater* of
1767, which is entirely different from his earlier church music, or the
C-minor Piano Sonata, which sounds like no piano sonata before. I don't
care what we call it, but there is an easily discernible change that makes
this period entirely different from the period the preceded it.

BROOK: I think a valid case can be made for using the term *Sturm und
Drang*. I believe it effectively sums up a widespread European malaise at
the time—although I agree that the phenomenon, not the label, is what
counts. It is a fact that, prior to about 1767 in instrumental music of the
Classic period, virtually no *Sturm and Drang* music—or literature or art
—can be found. From the late 1760s many composers, authors, and artists
all over Europe began composing, writing, and painting—in certain works,
at least—in a more somber and more impassioned fashion than before.
These include, for example, in literature, Goethe, Schiller, and Klinger; in
art, Fuseli, Piranesi, and Mortimer; in music, Martin Kraus, Simon Leduc,
Gaetano Brunetti, Vanhal, Dittersdorf, Haydn, and Mozart.

This movement was at its peak for only about a decade. Whatever the
reasons for its birth and decline, whatever its antecedents and later incar-
nations, its existence as a period of the history of the arts cannot be denied. To my mind, *Sturm und Drang* is as good a name as any.

LANDON: I agree with Professor Brook that in many countries, and in
many arts—literature, painting, drama, etc.—people began to question the
status quo. In painting, about the same date, one finds demons and
macabre effects—obviously not new in art, but relatively new and more
numerous around 1770.

MISS COHEN: We have been speaking largely of *Sturm und Drang* in
instrumental music. How about operatic music? How about the contemporaries of Haydn?

LANDON: There is some *Sturm und Drang* in Mozart's *Lucio Silla*, which
I find absolutely marvelous; to me it is astounding that people can ignore
music like this. Even among Mozart scholars, few have really studied it.
There are pages upon pages of that extraordinary work, written at the age
of sixteen, that have the same kind of driving unrest that I believe is part

of *Sturm und Drang*. How far apart *Lucio Silla* may be from other works of this period, I am not in a position to judge.

BROOK: I believe you will find *Sturm und Drang* characteristics in opera earlier than in instrumental music. Daniel Heartz is investigating this question.

MRS. FRIEDLAND: Something that has always puzzled me is the long neglect of the Haydn operas, which are only now, thanks in part to your efforts, becoming better known. How is it possible, even after Pohl pointed out some thirty-five operas, that such an important body of work by so important a composer could be overlooked until so recently, even by musicologists?

LANDON: You are certainly right about the importance of opera in Haydn's career—especially after 1773. He wrote a few operas before that, but as time went on they became less and less sporadic. After 1776 opera became a regular, and soon an all-encompassing, feature of Esterházy. Whatever else he wrote had to be squeezed in on the side. In 1786, a characteristic year, Haydn conducted 125 events of opera at Esterházy castle, staged fourteen new operas, and resuscitated twelve others.

Part of the answer to your question is that it was not possible, as late as 1932, to write about Haydn's operas because the scores were unavailable. It had something to do with the attitude of the Esterházy family. They always regarded Haydn as their house *Kapellmeister*, and have always been mildly surprised that so many people were trying to get into their palaces and get hold of Haydn's music. To the most recent times, the reigning Esterházy prince never quite understood it, and he simply refused even well-known scholars any access to his archives. The only persons allowed to enter the Esterházy archives before the present regime took it over, to my knowledge, were Pohl, followed by Larsen, and, of course, the archivist himself. That was it. And since even Haydn's own copyist had described the precious material in the archives at Esterházy as moldering away, you can imagine the state it was in when Pohl got at it. Fortunately—and rather ironically—the Hungarian government today has made the Esterházy archives, with their unbelievably rich materials, widely available to scholars.

READING LIST

Brook, Barry S., *The Breitkopf Thematic Catalogue* (New York, 1966).
Haydn Yearbooks (Philadelphia, 1962 *et seq.*).
Haydn-Studien, Veröffentlichungen des Joseph Haydn Institutes (Cologne, 1965 *et seq.*).

Landon, H. C. R., *The Symphonies of Joseph Haydn* (London, 1955).
Mozart Jahrbücher (Salzburg, 1950 *et seq.*).

   Some new scholarly editions:
Haydn, Joseph, *Werke* (Munich, 1958–).
———— *The Complete Symphonies in Pocket Score* (Vienna: Philharmonia).
———— *Sämtliche Klaviersonaten*, Wiener Urtextausgabe, Universal Ed. 13337–
   39.
Neue Bach-Ausgabe (Kassel: Bärenreiter).
Neue Mozart-Ausgabe (Kassel: Bärenreiter).

Contemporary Music Composition and Music Theory as Contemporary Intellectual History

MILTON BABBITT

*I*T WOULD be as unrealistic of me to disregard privately as it is probably indiscreet and superfluous of me to observe publicly that I, of all the contributors to this series, am—to the best of my knowledge—the lone composer, and—although my presence here is perhaps best excused as an instance of my moonlighting as a theorist—it is in my primary role of composer that I am obliged to inhabit the world, or more aptly, that approximately disjunct collection of communities which, if I may judge from the absence of distinguishably scholarly faces and ears from those professional occasions which occur under the negligible auspices of our tattered "tiny kingdom," is known to most of you—if not all—only in the form of knowledge by incomplete description, whereas to me, as a composer, it is known very much in the form of knowledge by old acquaintance. And however tenable or tenuous this distinction may be epistemologically, psychologically and vocationally its consequences and its implications scarcely can be exaggerated. Perhaps, then, I should begin by bringing you the latest tidings from our sector: serious musical composi-

151

tion is still alive and well, and living in a number of universities, including my own. Or, in the interests of historical subjectivity, I could with equivalent candor report that serious musical composition is fighting for its life, is well on its way to extinction, and is still breathing only in a number of well-heeled nursing homes for the musically self-indulgent, of which my university fortunately is one. But the practical conditions of contemporary musical activity, beyond those reflected in these reports of equivalent truth values, which simply threaten the very survival of serious composition, and which—for some—dwarf the problems and lacunae within our quasi-professions, are—I trust—familiar to you if only by description, even—perhaps—my description, and—I hasten to assure you—are not going explicitly to occupy me here; but what may well be closely related concomitants of these conditions, even contributors to and results of these conditions, are going to concern me. For, is the status and state of music composition in the world of public performance, commercial publication, and mass-minded journalism simply a dreadful thing in itself, or not independent of the status and state of this same music and its verbal representations in a presumably more apposite environment, that of the confessedly, even proudly academic, that of nonmusical scholarship, that of nonmusical intellectual undertakings; in sum, in the environment of that activity and achievement which would constitute much of the intellectual history of our time? I am not concerned to discuss contemporary music and music theory as music history, but as a component of, if at all, what probably will become the intellectual history of our time and our country.

If we begin by seeking facts which are in this respect as comparably apodictic as those which characterize the position of serious music in the public domain, they may first be sought in those singularly unformed, uninformed assertions about music which appear in what otherwise would seem to be regarded as respectable writings. In seeking to discover why music is particularly susceptible to such irresponsibility and unconcern, we may even discover what—if anything—music itself has done to induce or even deserve such a fate. So I begin by searching out symptoms in the hope of eventually identifying the malady.

I begin with the relatively mild manifestation, a sentence from *Weimar Culture*, a study in intellectual history:

> Alban Berg's opera *Wozzeck*, first performed in 1925, was doubly radical: it used Schönberg's twelve-tone system and *Sprechgesang* in combination with more conventional musical means, and it had as its hero—or antihero—one of Büchner's most moving characters, the poor ignorant soldier who is humiliated by his betters and betrayed by his girl, and who ends up committing murder and suicide.[1]

1. Peter Gay, *Weimar Culture* (New York, 1968), pp. 64–65.

This once prevalent and completely revealing error has been banished, if only recently, even from the pages of most newspapers. The author of *Weimar Culture* is a distinguished university professor. So has music made strange bedfellows. And, one is tempted to ask in the interest of the cosmic condition, what of poor *Wozzeck*, now that its radicalism is reduced by, at least, one fourth? Can one conceive of a cultural historian comparably asserting that Joyce's *Ulysses* was originally written in Gaelic? Or even that such allegations would or should require research, particularly research into what are obviously the wrong books—for one is shocked to discover not only the extent to which gross misinformation about music can escape authors, editors, and readers, but the sources which a professional historian must have consulted to yield a mistake so revealing of ignorance of music itself and of music history.

Now to an intellectual of another breed and to the transcendance of the merely factual and apparently safely descriptive, to what appears to be daringly evaluative. Professor John A. N. Lee, who has not earned anonymity, in his highly technical, specialized, and otherwise perhaps trustworthy book on the compiler aspect of computer languages, includes this gratuitous and, therefore, one must conclude, proud exhibition of musical erudition:

> In music, tonality controls the construction of a harmony. Though the key signature of a piece of music is evident on the manuscript, the listener needs to have the key established by dominant and tonic chords before other modulating or chromatic progressions are introduced. Thus the student of music is taught the construct rules for the development of satisfying pieces. Similarly, the principle of seriality (in a 12 tone scale and in which no note is repeated), of which Stravinsky is the greatest exponent, establishes the rules that are responsible for the production of more modern music. However, since our ears have become attuned to the principle of tonality, seriality is not always as satisfying to some listeners as tonal compositions.[2]

A mere computation of the factual, verbal, and methodological lapses in this passage would itself require the use of a capacious computer. But the absurdly ignorant references to "a 12 tone scale" in which "no note is repeated," the normative presumption regarding Stravinsky, and, therefore, Schoenberg and others, the apposition of a musical language or system ("seriality") with a collection of compositions ("tonal compositions"), and the manifest lack of even superficial familiarity with the concepts whose names are so gaily dropped, for instance (and, of course, only for instance), the identification of "seriality" with the twelve-tone system, the latter itself so grossly mischaracterized—how can this happen? How can this be permitted to happen? If one be inclined to dismiss this as

2. John A. Lee, *The Anatomy of a Compiler* (New York, 1967), pp. 23–24.

but another evidence of the lighthearted impudence of the scientist vis-à-vis music, which I have documented and discussed at greater length elsewhere, then proceed to the next exhibit, extracted from one of the most widely used introductory texts on philosophy (the more generous might even term it analytical philosophy) by a college professor one of whose special fields is widely regarded to be, by others and presumably by him, "esthetics," which—you should be reminded—includes, in some unclear sense, music, usually in an even unclearer sense. The following quotation is from a discussion of the first movement of Mozart's G-minor Symphony, No. 40:

I. Exposition	II. Development	III. Recapitulation
a 1, a 1	d 1	a 1, a 1
a 2	d 2	a 2 (extended)
bridge passage	d 3	bridge passage
b 1, b 1	returning passage	b 1, b 1
b 2		b 2
bridge passage		bridge passage
c 1, c 1		c 1, c 1
c 2		c 2
c 3		coda[3]

This is presented as a "formal" analysis to students of, presumably, some intellectual sophistication but—very likely—little musical experience or sophistication, and so can be expected to be taken to reflect professional discourse on music, when, beyond all its other simplistic horrors, it smacks of a favorite device of journalists, which is therefore no part of the intellectual history of this or any other time: that of attributing a preposterous position falsely and then disposing of its implied proponent by dismissing the position. Here there is a mythical formalist, since the eponym—which, as a professional characterization, signifies a perfectly respectable, complex, and defensible position—is employed equivocally here to signify "someone" who subscribes to a crude and dubious notion of musical "form" as a surface pattern of repetitions and "variations," and according to which, in this movement there is a "development" whose "themes" and/or "variations" apparently have nothing to do with anything else in the movement, for whatever the d's may be taken to signify, there are no other d's to be seen or—presumably—heard.

While you contemplate what knowledge of the musico-analytical literature this "analysis" must reflect, I continue onward and downward to my last specimen, by another university professor who modestly reveals the purview of his expertise in the very subtitle of his book from which I am about to quote; the subtitle is *Biology, Behavior and the Arts.* I quote:

3. John Hospers, *An Introduction to Philosophical Analysis* (Englewood Cliffs, N.J., 1953), p. 519. The second (1967) edition of this book omits the chapter including this quotation, but only, according to the author's preface, "with regret."

What Schoenberg's twelve-tone system amounts to is that each composition is written in its unique mode of twelve tones, which are, however, not presented in ascending sequence, but in expressive sequence, as a melody perceived against the background of the chromatic scale. . . . Like diatonic music, twelve-tone music also permits the use of accidentals. But generally, it is only after the music has gone on some time that accidentals are introduced. Otherwise they would not be felt as accidentals.[4]

This authoritative crescendo of howlers I shall leave ungilded as one—if by no means the only—appropriate commentary, but I do suggest as an exercise for the reader that he detect such a howler for each half dozen or so words of this excerpt or otherwise regard himself as unequipped to continue the reading of this paper.

Finally, it must be remarked that these four quotations—extracted from a professional historian, a professional computer scientist, a professional teacher of philosophy, and a professional Renaissance polymath—are not atypical; on the contrary, they were selected from an ever-growing pile of such items, and I have failed to discover one instance of writing by a musical nonspecialist which is even approximately as knowing and informed as these instances are unknowing and malformed.[5]

What have we done to deserve this? Or, what have we done not to avert this? We composers, scholars, and theorists seem almost equally uninfluential in our respective domains, and this may just reflect, among many, many other things, the condition within and among our professional domains. This is a delicate matter, particularly for me—here a member of a musical minority group, who has rather indelicately described the composer-scholar relationship within the university on another academic occasion. But the state of our own fields—their, shall we say, normative diversity, the confusing, perhaps even confused, appearances they seem to present to those outside them—can scarcely explain why those whose professional and, by now, even traditional role is that of mediating and resolving just such real or apparent confusions and contentions, and who have performed and are performing in such a therapeutic capacity in other disciplines, have not done so with regard to music, by way of its existent theory. I mean those professionally trained, professionally equipped thinkers, with respectably analytic pedigrees, and par-

4. Morse Peckham, *Man's Rage for Chaos: Biology, Behavior and the Arts* (Philadelphia, 1965), p. 234.

5. I have been able to restrain myself only to the extent of relegating to this footnote the undisputed winner in presumption in this category. Professor Daniel Bell, on p. 220 of the Winter, 1965, issue of *Daedalus*, a publication of the American Academy of Arts and Sciences (!), writes: "Modern music, taking Schoenberg as the turning point, denies the necessity of any structural harmonic background and becomes obsessed with sound alone." This issue, under its title of *Science and Culture* and under the editorship of Professor G. Holton, has been issued in book form (Houghton Mifflin, 1965).

ticularly those who permit themselves to be associated with the word "esthetics," which itself smacks of dubious reification, and particularly since there are those "estheticians" who come gratifyingly close to recognizing and exorcising this hypostatization, and who—at least—disavow and renounce the traditional practice of professing to construct "esthetic systems" while, instead, addressing themselves to what they term "specific problems." But these specific problems are not those of examining the theories of music theorists, of clarifying and exposing their structure, of reconciling and opposing their contents, or any of those tasks which are so desperately needed and might well begin to clarify and then resolve our apparent normative contraries. Instead, they are concerned, at their most substantive, with metatheoretical issues many removes from these: ontological issues, such as whether the relation between a Beethoven symphony and a performance of it is to be construed as a type-token relation which then would construe the symphony as a class of performances, to avoid which neo-Platonic formulation, Richard Rudner—for one—takes the occurrence of the name "Beethoven's 5th Symphony" in the statement "that was a poor performance of 'Beethoven's 5th Symphony'" to be syncategorematic.[6] This example, though perhaps atypical in its sophistication, is typical in its area of concern and in its ultimate lack of concern with the substance of a musical composition, for the interest here is with the issue of a nominalistic metalanguage. Emphatically, I do not wish to seem to be depreciating such discussions, not even in their value for the theory of music, not even when they are as amusingly and surprisingly remote as in the case when Gustave Bergmann postulates that someone (guess who?) has been able to "find," to locate, our national anthem in the *Eroica Symphony* by note-picking the anthem's note succession from different instrumental parts; this but to pose the question: "Would we then have to say that the *Eroica is* our national anthem, or even that the latter *is a part* of the former?"[7] And all of this as a portion of a discussion of the mind-body question, not—I regret to say—in order to dissect a not too unfamiliar way of posing "relatedness" and "derivation" in a kind of musical analysis. Surely, the language of music theory must involve, with explicit awareness or not,

6. Richard Rudner, "The Ontological Status of the Esthetic Object," *Philosophy and Phenomenological Research*, X/3 (1950), 380; *id.*, "What Do Symbols Symbolize?: Nominalism," in *Philosophy of Science: The Delaware Seminar, 1 (1961–2)*, ed. B. Baumrin (New York, 1963), pp. 167–70.

7. Gustav Bergmann, *The Metaphysics of Logical Positivism* (New York, 1954), p. 173. The same essay, "Remarks on Realism," provides another bit of documentation of my dismay; Bergmann says, with no further relevant comment: "Simultaneous sounding of the c-major tonic triad in the middle octave exemplifies another pattern . . . ," obviously assuming "tonic" to signify a structural property determined by the stipulated pitch (and, therefore, interval) structure of the triad itself, rather than a functional property, determined dispositionally, contextually.

nominalistic or platonistic commitments, physicalist or phenomenalistic formulations (and here even the familiar, realistic problem of the graphemic and the auditory representations of music is suggested), and comparable issues, but of much more immediate and more sequentially natural concern are those analytically derived theories of music which already exist, compete for influence, and—by determining the content and procedures of music instruction—affect eventually the total professional musical climate. One searches in vain for even the names of the creators of such theories in the volumes on esthetics. One is obliged to assume that either they are not known to these writers or do not warrant mention. If not, why not? And if it be suggested that the absence of every such name from the index of a characteristically extensive contemporary collection of writings, Levich's *Aesthetics and the Philosophy of Criticism*, is to be attributed to the minor role played by music in these and other writings of the sort, is this, too, not significant? Would only that it meant that music has been excused from the province of esthetics. But it has not; it is simply that music in the form in which it would appear pertinently in the documentation of the intellectual activity of our time, as discourse on music by competent professionals, has not been admitted to membership in that activity.

It could be further suggested that contemporary music and the contemporary theory of music are not properly a part of that activity as it is characterized by the most central, crucial, widely and deeply discussed issues of our intellectual time, and I have no wish to attempt to counter this statement by invoking the necessary involvement of the composer of electronic music not only with contemporary technology, not only with the hardware and software that suggest novel formulations of traditional and new analytical questions, the extensions to artificial intelligence and compositional simulation, but with complex questions at the frontiers of acoustics, psycho-acoustics, perception, memory, and learning theory. Nor would I invoke the possible, at least, suggestiveness for analytical theory of concepts arising in information theory, signal detection, and pattern recognition, and in multidimensional scaling and statistical correlation theory for the characterization of that most multidimensional of concreta: the musical event. For however the glamor of the new intellectual era is intimated by computers, cybernetics, and the theory of automata, the contemporaneity of technological awareness is rarely matched by contemporaneity of methodological awareness, and these fields are surely not yet broadly central or pervasively crucial in the intellectual climate or the musical thought of our time, certainly not as manifestly so as are such issues as explanation theory, the relation of formal and interpreted theory, of metalanguage and object language, whose vital importance, whose intellectual vitality, whose unresolved questions and implications continue to generate a literature by the most sophisticated thinkers of our time; and

although I am not unconcerned to observe that some of the most flagrant
and constant instances of the misrepresentation and misunderstanding of
the achievements and aspirations of contemporary music and musical
thought are exposed instantly and disposed of as arrant violations of
rational intellectual behavior in the light of the most immediate and une-
quivocal distinctions and applications of theory construction and explanation theory, I am far more concerned to demonstrate that, while beginning with the simple musical instance, and while remaining deliberately
and even selfishly insistent upon musical matters, one finds oneself proceeding directly from the most habitual and seemingly innocent of musical inquiries to unavoidable confrontation by intricate and puzzling methodological issues.

So, with what must not now appear as a disconcerting discontinuity, I
offer one of the most familiar, most examined passages in contemporary
music: the opening measures of Webern's Concerto for Nine Instruments.[8] I wish merely to remind you that the first compositional
representation of what emerges most reasonably as the twelve-tone set of
the work (Ex. 1a) is presented instrumentally in a manner which reveals

Ex. 1(a) m. 1

explicitly its internal, "derived" structure; the set can be regarded as
deriving from the successive applications of the operations of the twelve-
tone system not to a total set so as to induce a permutation of pitch-
classes, but to a trichord so as to generate a set of four disjunct trichords.
(Only incidentally to this moment of discussion, but more than incidental
to the concern of this whole discussion, this characteristic manifestation of
nonpermutational serialism in Webern seemingly so contrasts with
Schoenberg's procedure of introducing "redundancy" into his set structure by combinational, order-independent content relations between discrete hexachords as to make all the more astonishing the extensive and
ramified relations between the results of these two procedures in their
extended and generalized applications.) The piano then presents the set in
a form (RIt₁S) that preserves pitch content within trichords. Then four
instruments present, in the trichord articulated form of the opening, RIt₂S
(Ex. 1b). How should one "explain" this choice of transposition of the
set, the first of which alters the pitch content within the trichords? Why
this transposition rather than any one of the ten others available? It would
be and has been regarded as acceptable to offer the "explanation" that this
particular transposition has the result of holding at least one note in

8. Anton Webern, *Konzert*, Op. 24 (Vienna, 1948).

(b) m. 6

common between each of the trichords in this set form and of the preceding set form (and necessarily of the initial set form). Obviously, this "explanatory sketch" includes the crucial suppressed assumption that pitch-class identification can function as a significant basis of musical relatedness, as it does in those notions of hierarchization associated with the "circle of fifths." Whether this is an acceptable assumption or not is immaterial to the present argument, as is the issue of the twelve-tone system or the value of this particular composition, but now allow me to live dangerously, and to plunge in and come up with a simple statement in a mildly abstract form, a modest theorem which asserts: if a collection of $n=pq$, elements is partitioned into p classes of q elements each in any two ways, then there is at least one collection of p elements (termed a system of common representatives) such that in both partitions each of the p classes contains one of the p elements.[9] Relative to any musical theory, this is a formal theory, since the descriptive terms are musically uninterpreted; no rule of correspondence has been established between these uninterpreted terms and the names of musical entities. But if we interpret "elements" as "pitch-classes," and "partitioned" as "partitioned instrumentally or timbrally" (as any twelve-tone set or aggregate necessarily is in a compositional presentation), then it follows that with $n=12$, and $p=4$, and, therefore, $q=3$, any such instrumental presentation of *any* transposition of the set (and, of course, any form of the set) would have the property of maintaining at least one pitch-class in common between trichords. Could one be said to have explained a particular occurrence, a particular choice, by citing a property necessarily associated with a class of occurrences, of choices? We could have discovered this property of all transpositions, or all set forms, or even all sets, by writing them out and checking the presence of this property, but a relevant formal theorem asserts the total and—very likely—startling extension of this property, so that it is known immediately that pitch-class identity between trichords cannot be offered to "explain" uniquely even the fact that any form of the set would have provided the property, for the formal theorem assures this property for any assignment of three notes to each of the four partitioning instruments. The resulting trichords need not be related to each other or to the trichords of the initial set statement through any musically familiar operation; only the number of partition classes, each with the same number of

9. See, for instance, Hadwiger, Debrunner, and Klee, *Combinatorial Geometry in the Plane* (New York, 1964), pp. 31, 85.

elements, need be the same between the two statements of the set. And, of course and again, the partition needn't be upon twelve-tone sets, but can be applied to any number of elements. So it would seem that it is necessary to assert that not only are the compositional facts of a set, and of a set derived from a trichord, compositional assumptions of the Concerto, but so too is the fact of this third set statement as the indicated transpositional level; further developments in the composition must be awaited to discover, if at all, the "justification" for the transpositional relation determined by the two set forms under discussion, in its integration into and reflection by other aspects of the movement.

So, for all of the justified warnings that the formally valid is not necessarily empirically true, or even empirically meaningful, the pertinent formal theorem obliges one to change drastically the scope of what is generally taken to be a germane statement of "explanation," and the basis for the change could not imaginably have been arrived at by any but formal means, since it involved showing that any trichordal partition would possess that attribute which had been assumed to be uniquely possessed by the set form presented. But if uniqueness is, as is more than tacitly implied here, a necessary condition for satisfactory "explanation," it is surely not a sufficient condition. For if it were, any characteristic of the set whose transpositional level was to be "explained" which differentiates it from the preceding set would function as such a condition. This provides another boundary (a lower bound, if you will) of *ad hoc* to oppose to the upper bound provided by the theorem in this application. For example, one would need but assert simply that the transpositional level was chosen "because," in the resultant set, the ninth pitch-class is the same as the fifth pitch-class of the initial set. For each such statement there is a corresponding such statement that can be made for any other transposition, each of them a genuine *ad hoc*, and a conjunction of statements of such unique properties, or of such properties with a "class property," is exactly as insufficient. This inability to discover a sufficient condition is equivalent to observing that any other transposition would have been as musically "coherent" (or "satisfactory" or "——") and that, again, the transpositional choice must be regarded as assumptive. The alternative is a normative hierarchy of attributes which would preassign greater consequence to certain of the available unique attributes. One might assert, with such a normative presumption latent, that the transposition was selected to identify the first dyad, stated in the clarinet, with the final dyad of the initial set, which also had been stated in the clarinet. But the explanatory force of this statement would derive from some more general principle involving pitch identification, proximity, etc., and that is one crux of our discussion. The familiar deductive form of explanation, in its simplest, least qualified representation can be presented as $(x) \ Px \supset Qx; \ Pa; \ Qa$. And whether the general law embodied in the $(x) \ Px \supset Qx$ be statistical or be only implicitly stated in a "sketch," and whether the explanation does or does not resolve someone's predicament or satisfy someone's psychological needs by a reduction to the familiar, this formal explication of the notion of explanation does suggest a cause of the informal uneasiness we have just experienced and the seemingly dead ends and infinite regresses we have just encountered. What has made musical explanation unsatisfactory is not the vagueness of the explanation, but the vagueness of the notion of the nature of a musical explanation. The formal theorem does partly satisfy the formal expression of the explanatory schematum, but it must now finally be said that—as in corresponding explanations in simple cases in the physical sciences—what the theorem explains is why the two different set forms possess a system of common representatives under the partitions in question (as an instance of a more general set of conditions subsuming this one), and our other attempts at explanation were simply not explanations in this sense, for whether we can expect to provide satisfactory musical explanations depends upon whether we can produce or discover "general laws" of a different theoretical category, at a different theoretical level, which poses questions closely and complexly related to those moot and tantalizing ones which arise in association with what is now so modestly termed "the derivation of 'ought' from 'is.' " A general normative principle was assumed from the outset of the discussion of the Concerto, involving the hierarchical primacy of pitch-class intersection between pitch collections, which I now reinvoke to revive and temporarily enter the discussion of formal and interpreted theories. The third-set occurrence in the Concerto (Ex. 1c) necessarily has a common system of representatives

(c) m. 7½

with each of the preceding two set occurrences, but—surprisingly—it has such a common system of representatives identical with a system defined by those two. Surprisingly, because not only can the formal system assert nothing about three such different partitions, but it easily can be shown (and the Concerto itself "shows" it later) that—in general—three partitions, even as limited in their structure as these, do not possess such a common system. Does the original "explanation" of the choice of the second set now legitimately apply to the choice of a third set, and perhaps even more so to the fourth set (Ex. 1d), which has such a common system with the first three? The injection of a "more so" might suggest a statistical, probabilistic "general law," and—assuming for the moment the symmetry of explanation and prediction—a predictive form in which the transpositional level of the fourth set is made not more probable by virtue

(d) m. 18¾

of some general law about successive set statement in terms of systems of common representatives, but in which the fact of the systems is a more probable explanation of the transpositional level of the fourth set.

These and a multitude of related issues are left dangling and unresolved, for I wished merely to indicate that apparently conventional and local questions about music cannot be even clearly formulated, and—therefore—certainly cannot be satisfactorily answered, and that the still larger question as to whether questions about musical composition are susceptible to resolution in the same form as questions in other fields, without involving genuinely theoretical issues whose scope is decidedly not confined to music. The formal-interpreted theory issue leads immediately to that of the distinction between metalanguage and object language, which arises as soon as a composition (object language) is referred to by a natural or formalized language (metalanguage), or when such a collection of references are themselves discussed in a meta-metalanguage. If this distinction between object language and metalanguage is maintained most vividly by the very difference between the act of composing and the act of talking about composing, the most vulgar and—therefore—most frequently encountered violation of this distinction is that in which a musical composition and—by faulty extension—a body of music are labeled "mathematical" because an expression containing mathematical terms (such as our previous theorem), under suitable interpretation, accurately characterizes some aspect of the musical composition. This is precisely equivalent to labeling a musical work "mathematical" because it employs two violins, or is 369 measures long, or to describing German word order as being in "English" because it is accurately describable in English, or—most absurdly and relevantly—to labeling someone a mathematician because he can be accurately characterized as being twenty-five years old or as having two children. Indeed, one must ask what could be described reasonably as "mathematical music"? This is not an impractical question, for there appears to be music which is so described, so dismissed, so admired, some of which is even so described and so admired by its composers. First, let's dispose of this latter intrusion of the intentional error, since—clearly—whether music can be justifiably described as mathematical is quite independent of who does the describing. And, if there is still a certain temptation to permit the adjective to be applied by a composer because he demonstrates how his composition was, might have been, and, therefore, can be considered as being generated by a polynomial function, or a time series, or a Goedel number, it need merely be remembered that any musical work, be it the B-minor Mass, *Melancholy Baby*, or *Topological Spaces* for antique cymbals, can be represented just as completely by a polynomial or a time series or a Goedel number, given the correspondence rules between these mathematical representations and the musical models. Then, in what sense can a work be termed mathematical in which the B-minor Mass is not? One sometimes suspects that the unexpressed but deeply believed answer is that there are certain mathematical representations which are "better evidence" that the work is "mathematical" than are other representations. Here there are two errors at play and work. One seems to be that "simpler" mathematical representations are "better evidence" that the composer employed mathematical methods in the creation of the work; this is a compounding of the intentional error with (what may or may not be an error) the assumption that composers know and can employ only simple arithmetic. But surely one cannot claim that one mathematical representation is more mathematical or makes the music more mathematical than any other, any more than one can claim that it makes the music more or less musical. Often, it would appear that there is at work an ignorance no less appalling than that which seems to assume that a sequence such as 1, 2, 3, 5, 8, 13, ... is "mathematical," but that 1, 2, 3, 5, 8, 7092, ... is not or is less so, when, of course, any sequence is representable by a generating expression—and I know of no inductively arrived-at basis for asserting that certain mathematical expressions are more likely to generate acceptable musical compositions than are others, and even if there were, this still would not serve to differentiate between "mathematical" and "non-mathematical" music. Such a differentiation is totally untenable. It might still be insisted that a composition could be justifiably or fruitfully described as "mathematical" if the "best explanation" or (now let us say) justification could be formulated in familiar mathematical terms, or if the only "explanation" were in such terms. But explanations are explanations within languages, and one cannot compare an explanation within an uninterpreted mathematical language with one within a musical theoretic language. For, if one despairs of "satisfactorily" justifying a work in terms of certain circumscribed musical concepts and, therefore, embraces a "mathematical" characterization of the same work, he can always be made to return and find a satisfactory characterization in terms of the most satisfactory with the minimum alteration of his musical concepts, and the crux of the satisfactoriness will ultimately, if only partially, hinge upon this alteration of the concepts. But who would wish to assert that any mathematical representation is more "satisfactory" than something like the following: suppose our musical concepts do not include those of "inversion" or "retrogression"; then, at the beginning of the Webern Concerto, there is no pitch-class reason for choosing the first three pitches as an assumptive unit to be regarded as transformed. Then, with only the concept of transposition, the work could be completely characterized in terms of the first pitch and this concept of transposition as applied to this first pitch. The more customary explanation, which assumes a trichord operated upon by the operations of inversion and retrogression, can assume an increase of the size of the assumptive unit by permitting this increase of the number of permissible operations. Only in passing, there is perhaps one suggestion of the level of generality and even the empirical source of what might approximate a "general law" in music theory if it be observed that the asumption of a single note transposed eleven times requires the recall of the order of eleven individual, independent (unless one assumes the structure of the twelve-tone set as an *a priori*) phenomena to remember the set to within total transposition, while the trichord assumption requires only the recall of the two intervals of the trichord and the order of application of three operations and their combinations; the latter suggests a psychologically more realistic recoding in terms of the "magic number seven, plus or minus two."

Without ever explicitly employing the term, we have been speaking throughout of what could have been termed "relations," an expression which, in musical theory, is so easily and dangerously transmuted into an apparent normative: "x is related to y" is taken itself to suggest something particularly, even uniquely, distinguished in associating the two elements x and y. But any two occurrences in a composition are "related," which is one of the bases for reminding the dogmatic that infinitely many true statements can be made about a musical composition. The relation between, say, two pitches twenty-nine pitches apart in a composition is an irreflexive, symmetric, and intransitive relation, exactly as is the relation of being "immediately adjacent to" or "next to," which is commonly, if only implicitly, invoked in the concept of "motive" or "theme" or "neighboring note," etc. So even the nature of a relation when so rigorously characterized can hardly be taken to determine its possible musical consequences.

Whereas in the Webern Concerto, the operations taken to apply to the first trichord to generate the total set preserve the usual contours under transformation in their first compositional realization so that the operation can be interpreted conventionally as transformations on pitches (as registral representatives of the pitch-classes) as well as on pitch-classes, at the opening of the Schoenberg Fourth Quartet[10] the set representation in the first violin cannot be reduced to an assumptive unit transformed by systematic operations in the domain of pitch-classes, but can in the domain of pitches, since the spatial deployment of the elements of the second hexachord produce an exact intervallic inversion of the elements of the first hexachord, explicitly revealing the inversional relation between the

10. Arnold Schoenberg, Fourth String Quartet (New York, 1939).

two hexachords as unordered pitch-class collections (Ex. 2). The privileged

Ex. 2

position granted the relations of inversion and transposition here, thus distinguishing this spatial disposition of the second hexachord from any of the other 719 possible dispositions, and which is conjoined with uniqueness for "justificatory" ends, further could be analyzed—as could retrogression—by reducing such operations to their dependence on the notion of interval, reminding one that those scales of measurement,[11] which are a central issue in contemporary psychophysics and its associated mathematics and statistics, are embodied, in their applicability to musical dimensions, in traditional musical notation itself. The instrumental or timbral equivalence class is signified by the use of the name of an instrument, thus suggesting merely a nominal scale. Customary dynamic indications, similarly, suggest an ordinal scale for loudness. The durational signification of rhythmic notation suggests the intervallic scale of protensity; and the "absolute" notation for pitch suggests the appropriateness of a ratio scale in this dimension. Incidentally, all of this could cause one to wonder how, under any reasonable application of the word "important," it could be suggested that pitch is not the most important of the musical dimensions, since its susceptibility to musical structuring includes and exceeds that of any other dimension. The Schoenberg example supplies but a modest reminder that unless we are prepared to produce some general principle relating—in this instance—inversionally derived complexes (or the class of operators of which inversion is one) and temporal position in a composition, we cannot "explain" the temporal succession of these related spatial distributions. Inversion is a symmetrical relation, and, therefore, the two hexachords could be reversed in order without affecting the derivational explanation; and so the ordering of hexachords must itself be regarded as primitive until explanatorily modified, for instance, by reference to the hexachordally independent tetrachordal structure of the set, whose identities under inversion are destroyed if the hexachords are reversed.

In the case of the Webern Concerto, a pre-existent formal theorem disclosed the generality of a property which otherwise might intuitively have been assumed to be unique; generality can be affirmed only by a production and examination of all possible cases (extensionally) or by a formal theorem (intensionally). The latter is usually more easily available and more useful in terms of practicality and the general insight and under-

11. S. S. Stevens, "Measurement, Psychophysics, and Utility," in O. W. Churchman and P. Ratoosh, *Measurement* (New York, 1951), pp. 18–63.

standing it can provide, and all assertions of uniqueness require such affirmation. After all, even the most trivial, apparently "tautological" such assertion is heavily theory-laden. The earlier, quickly dismissed statement of identity of the ninth pitch-class and the fifth pitch-class involves a statement of uniqueness which is itself founded on the formally provable property that under no transposition is the order number, pitch-class number-ordered pair preserved.

There is a familiar and musically important instance in the recent literature: Stravinsky's use of the twelve-tone set by employing discrete hexachords as compositionally explicit linear entities, and then arriving at what he terms "verticals" by "rotating" the pitch-classes with regard to order (that is, "transposing" the order numbers by 1) and transposing the pitch-classes of each successively so-arrived-at linear representation of the hexachord by the complements of the successive set intervals, so that the initial pitch-class of each of the hexachords is the same.[12] The emphasis on the employment of hexachordal transpositions as linear elements suggested the easy (and incorrect) conclusion that the "verticals"—the simultaneities produced by pitch-classes of the same order number in each of the six hexachords—were "arbitrary," which appeared to mean that they were both unrelated to one another through any familiar musical property and that their internal and relational structure (if any) were entirely dependent upon the structure of the specific hexachord in association with which they arose. When it is observed in a case such as that of the *Variations* (Ex. 3) that the verticals are related to one another inversionally—

Ex. 3

the second to the sixth, the third to the fifth and the fourth to itself (that is, it is internally inversionally symmetrical), with the first "vertical" trivially symmetrical—it may be assumed that this is "accidental," the result of

12. Milton Babbitt, "Remarks on the Recent Stravinsky," *Perspectives of New Music*, II/2 (1964), 53–54; Claudio Spies, "Notes on Stravinsky's Variations," *ibid.* IV/1 (1965), 66–70.

the particular constraints associated with this hexachord, which perhaps Stravinsky had constructed precisely to achieve these characteristics of the verticals. But, even though there appears to be no corresponding theorem in the formal literature, one need merely represent the operations on the hexachord formally easily to discover that these apparently surprising harmonic relations are entailed simply and completely by the "rotations" of the hexachords (Ex. 4). Once the generality of this result has been dem-

Ex. 4

	a	b	c	d	e
Φ	a	b	c	d	e
Φ	b - a	c - a	d - a	e - a	a
Φ	c - b	d - b	e - b	- b	a - b
Φ	d - c	e - c	- c	a - c	b - c
Φ	e - d	- d	a - d	b - d	c - d
Ψ	- e	a - e	b - e	c - e	d - e

onstrated, it seems less surprising, and predictable by one who has understood the similarity between retrograde and inversion operations, clearly revealed when they are themselves represented formally, as the complementation of, respectively, order numbers and pitch-class numbers, and immediately revealed in the fact that the interval defined by two ordered pitch-classes is replaced by its complement under both inversion and the reversal of this order (retrogression). And such distinctions between particularity and systematic generality, discoverable often only by formal techniques, are manifestly useful—perhaps essential—in defining the scope of a composer's "style," his compositional particularities in relation to a norm of generality.

Once the possible seductions and musical irrelevancies of results in the formal domain are understood and guarded against, their possible and not coincidental consequences and suggestions cannot be automatically dismissed. As a particularly practical but surely not superficial example, consider the compositional fact that in any twelve-tone work or serial composition the statements of the serial unit, set, or aggregate necessarily are partitioned instrumentally (as well as in many other ways). That there are seventy-seven partitions of the number 12 (to confine the example to the twelve-tone case) would seem to have no reasonable musical implications, and their embodiment in a composition to have no possible musical consequences. But when the necessary musical consequences are scrutinized, along with the realization that the formal notion of partition itself is simply a pre-existent concept faithfully modeled in an independently manifested musical property, the seventy-seven partitions are recognized to constitute a hierarchization of dependence of each of the partitions upon the ordering of the referential compositional set, ranging from the complete independence of the (1^{12}) partition, which need not convey any information about set order—since it can be contextually ordered to represent any set—to the complete dependence of the (12) partition, which can be only an explicit set form. This inter-aggregate dependency, a specific mode of inter-event dependency, is—quite literally by definition—an assurance of musical structure. Still further reaches of the structural implications of such partitioning can be intimated by the fact that the systematically most constrained partition (12) must and the systematically least constrained partition (1^{12}) contextually can compositionally represent a set form—indeed, exactly the same set—whereas most other partitions (depending on the structure of the set and the exact content of the parts of the partition, systematically less constrained than (12) and more constrained than (1^{12}), in general, cannot represent a set form.

But such theoretical and metatheoretical issues as have here occupied us are somber inquiries. Surely a jauntier manifestation of the mental climate of our time is the extent to which and the abandon with which such terms as "random," "chance," "indeterminacy," never forgetting "entropy," "aleatoric," and "stochastic," are bandied about by some musicians, providing but further sad evidence that some musicians rush in where wise men tread only with care and caution. But however sticky, ambiguous, intricate, and volatile these terms may be, they do involve certain incontrovertibles even when informally transferred to musical discourse. Randomness is, in any accuracy, a possible attribute only of an infinite sequence, and the finite subsequences to which our discussion, in all realism, must be limited also must be viewed always in the light of this crucial emendation; for randomness is a property of a collection or ensemble of events, not a description of how the collection was produced or generated, since it is fundamentally characteristic of a random sequence that it can contain any subsequence. And although, in an informal context, the term "random" is often taken to be defined and evidenced by some notion of unpredictability, associated with the absence of discernible inter-event influence, inter-event contingency and dependency, it is formally impossible to be justified in asserting that the *Eroica Symphony*, or any other piece of music, was not produced by random processes, that is, by having employed a so-called randomizer to produce as output a sequence of numerals, which were then correlated with musical notational symbols by a stable rule of correlation so that the resultant musical events were functions of the generated numerals. If the *Eroica Symphony* had been the final result—the "model"—of this formal procedure, the initial numerical sequence itself probably possessed characteristics which would not normally be regarded as probably random (long runs, repeated subsequences, biased frequency distribution), but this cannot be inferred as undesirable or as discrediting the randomizing abilities of the randomizer. Anecdotally, but pertinently, there should be recalled the tale of the randomizer which is constructed to produce 0's and 1's independently (that is, randomly), and proceeds to produce one thousand consecutive 0's. Does one reconstruct the randomizer so that it will not be able to produce so many consecutive 0's? Obviously, if one does, such a constraint, by introducing a basis of prediction, destroys the desired attribute of the randomizer. How many consecutive 0's should be permitted? And if the randomizer ran continuously for a year, would not the very absence of a run of a thousand consecutive 0's be equally suspect?[13] Translated into the musical domain, since any musical work could be produced by such methods, to concern oneself as to whether a work was or was not, and to assume that such a decision would, therefore, provide the best explanation or even an explanation of the work would be at least to be victimized by the genetic error. The familiar formulation of the property that an infinite random sequence "contains" any finite subsequence is the celebrated "monkey theorem," which asserts that if a monkey were let loose to pound a typewriter "randomly" and his progeny continued the activity, eventually they would produce all of the books in the British Museum. For our musical purposes, we are substituting trivially for the books in the British Museum the scores in the Library of Congress, and permitting our monkey and his progeny the use of a musical typewriter. Perhaps more importantly, to the listener who lacks a musical memory any musical work is, necessarily, "random"—that is, lacking predictability, structure, inter-event association. "Randomness," in music, is not only in the music but very much in the ear and in the mind of the beholder. The commonplace and common manifestation of this phenomenon is contained in the observation that "a child could write such a work" and, therefore, that its creation required no musically informed intelligence; that any event could follow any other and create at least as structured a composition as the present one; that, indeed, the work is "random." The degree to which the memorative capacities of different beholders vary in terms of what is memorable, susceptible to conceptual unitization, is strikingly and frighteningly instanced by a work such as Schoenberg's Op. 23, No. 3, which remains a succession of "arbitrary," musically unrelated occurrences to most listeners even after numerous hearings (which repetition, in principle, is exactly what makes the notion of finite randomness self-contradictory), but a work whose bases of succession and association are so explicit and determinative that it is easily, some might say too easily, responsive to retrodiction and—perhaps, therefore—prediction by a professionally trained listener.

Since every musical composition is, one hopefully assumes, finite, then

13. See, for example, G. S. Brown, *Probability and Scientific Inference* (London, 1957).

no matter how it be produced—by "randomizer" or by the most select and, therefore, selective composer—it is simply representable by a mathematical expression; this converse of the "monkey theorem" must be taken as a complete exposure and confutation of those who traffic in such "esthetic" imperatives as "the work of art must contain the element of surprise!"—presumably to banish thereby those "mathematical compositions" which, since they are "mathematically" specifiable, are therefore "predictable" and thus cannot be "surprising." Not only, as I have already shown, can no composition possibly be termed more "mathematical" than another and, therefore, in such terms "more or less surprising," but even without any references to mathematics, one might still ask if an occurrence is to be regarded as more surprising when it occurs in a musically unstructured (random) context, where every event is equally unexpected (or expected) or surprising (or unsurprising), or when it occurs in a structured context which, by definition and whether it be triadically tonal or twelve-tone or more contextual, inductively establishes inter-event dependencies which, in the same dubious terminology, make one event hierarchically more or less "expected" than another.

The absurd conceit—that unavailable to vulgar demonstration but instantly clear to the sensitive intuition is the "musical" similarity of that music which is allegedly arrived at by randomization and correlation, and that which is produced by the procedures of so-called "total organization" —is founded upon the apparent revelation that the two musics "sound equally random" even though they are produced by what is here represented as two virtually disjunct sets of musical procedures. The key to a simple demonstration simply is that they are not. For the methods of "total organization" that must be assumed to be under discussion in this context are usually based on a numerical sequence associated with rules of correlation which are independent of the scales of measurement appropriate to the individual musical dimensions and are thus as likely to produce musical "randomness," under the same criteria of randomness as those procedures which are presumed to insure randomness by initially employing a randomizer. For a rule of correlation which induces, say, intervallic structure in a dimension susceptible to intervallic scaling may well induce no distinguishable basis of structure in a dimension susceptible only to, say, ordinal structure. And even more generally and—by now, I trust—more familiarly, the initial series from which the "total organization" derives is no more inherently potentially "musically structural" than any subsequence of the numerical representation of any composition or of, say, a "random number" sequence. So, such procedures of "total organization," like the procedures of "randomization," necessarily can give rise to any composition so that—indeed—both can give rise to exactly the same composition. And it is this easily demonstrable that from so-called "total chance" to so-called "total organization" is not a giant step or even a random walk; it is no journey at all. The probability that a composition produced by these ultimately equivalent methods will be judged musically coherent rather than unstructured depends, in simple classical terms, upon the number of "favorable cases" (according to a specified basis of acceptability) within the totality of possible compositions, precisely as an explanation's adequacy is determined with respect to an acceptable basis.

Since predictability is a measure, if informal, of randomness, a second performance of a composition is random—as suggested above—only to without the memorative abilities of the listener, since any event in the work is predictable by having occurred when and where it did in the previous performance. The memorative capacity is itself dependent on recoding and unitizing, on inducing principles of inter-event dependency and regularity, and, as a result, structure breeds structure. But even a work that attempts to defeat structuring by admitting, even seeking, considerable differences between performances must still be predictable in those respects which are invariant among the performances, and such invariance must be present to the extent that there are any performance specifications which distinguish that composition from any other composition. The delegation of an unusually broad area of compositional choice to the performer, resulting in "improvisation," a term denoting a relative condition, far from necessarily securing randomness is more likely to produce a highly and conventionally constrained result, since the performer, composing with little time for circumspection and no opportunity for revision, is, first and above all, a constrained human who, as such, produces patterns of dependencies detectable as such by other humans, and he is likely to be a more constrained composer than the non-"real time" composer, who also is more likely to have at his command or to be able to invent from experience more and new modes of musical continuity and coherence.

The desire to achieve musical non-structure may have been suggested by the peripheral vogue of information theory (or, more accurately, of the words "information theory") where, the proponents of non-structure may have heard, equaprobability of events (the absence of inter-event influence) is associated with maximum information content of the ensemble. But this quantitative, not qualitative, measure in statistical communication theory is actually nothing other than a definition of independence of events within the theory, and in the normative musical domain such a maximum is by no means necessarily to be regarded or has ever in the past been regarded as desirable. Surely it is not in natural languages, where 50 per cent redundancy is not unusual and apparently helpful.

Characteristically, intimations of the virtue of non-structure hinge upon the equivocal use of terms from areas of greater prestige in the intellectual cosmos. The principle of "uncertainty" or "indeterminacy" has been appealed to as "justification," but one need just realize that this principle was not itself arrived at and formulated by "uncertain" or "indeterminate" principles and procedures to discover how, if one insists, to most assuredly create "music" which will pass any given test of randomness. Simply write it as deliberately and calculatingly to satisfy such a test as the test itself was constructed and is applied. Why take a chance with chance?

   This thin slice of the intellectual life of our time might have been augmented by extensions to the more practically urgent or even the more compositionally immediate. In the first category might come questions of normative discourse about music, and who among those who traffic for pleasure and profit in the dissemination of evaluative pronouncements, unexamined and analytically unfounded, could not profit from the informed and sophisticated literature addressed to these questions in other disciplines? Even such brief and nontechnical examinations as those of Ziff or Vendler of "good" and "goodness" might serve to inhibit beneficially those who presume to evaluate that which remains only vaguely identified and inaccurately characterized.
   Compositionally, that augmentation of the modes of structuring which may produce on the relatively undifferentiated surface the initial appearance of independence while providing dimensional confirmation of the contextually most locally defined pitch and temporal materials tends, in the more complex compositions, to that maximum of functional determinacy which admits no dimensional reduction. For example, the traditional conjunction of the temporally proximate and the instrumentally identical can be and often is expanded to the independent dimensions of temporal successiveness and compounds of instrumental classes, with like compounds by no means necessarily successive.
   The loosely scrutinized metaphor of music as a language and, almost unbelievably, as a universal language has reasserted itself in a new and demanding guise as structural linguistics, and most particularly, transformational grammars suggest tantalizingly the possibility of helpful analogies or, even, the means of sharply clarifying the probably deep distinctions between music and language. In the light of the apparent parallelism between the transformations of Schenkerian analysis and synthesis and those of transformational, generative grammars, the implied analogy between the semantic identities of deep structure transformed into syntactical individuals and musical background identities transformed into foreground individuals involves categorical identifications that may be profoundly enlightening or profoundly misleading. Surely music theory is not yet concerned with any notion of musical universals; it still seeks satisfactory grammars of individual musics and has probably made the mistake of seeking too simple grammars while, paradoxically, attempting to characterize too much. The apparent parallels between the internalization of rules in music and language, between competence and performance in the

two, in the creative function of the grammars of both, seem as suggestive as the lexical classifications in the two fields suggest fundamental dissimilarities. The one thing of which we can feel certain is that what Nelson Goodman has said of linguistics is applicable to music theory: "It is not so old a subject that one can predict what aspects of the theory (of structure) may eventually prove to be pertinent."[14]

What, indeed, may prove pertinent and helpful for music theory and, thus, music from our contemporary abundance of intellectual activities, I have only scantily suggested, without even so much as mentioning, among others, that field (structural graph theory) to which Goodman alluded. But very probably this will be regarded as the least of my lacunae. It may be objected that I have not represented the heterogeneity of contemporary music and musical thought, which would be the obligation of any history which presumed to mirror our time's musical temper. And particularly, that my examples have been drawn from the twelve-tone literature, which may be inferred to imply that this is the sole truly contemporary music. Clearly, I mean to suggest anything but this, and the diversity of serious musical creation, of which the twelve-tone system is one important option, is probably the most singularly significant factor of our musical condition. But I assume it is to be noted historically that the twelve-tone system prompted, even made possible, such diversity. By consolidating the techniques and resources of high contextuality into a fundamentally novel communality, while providing the very grammar of a widely practiced and evolved alternative, while directing concern and study to previously only slightly examined issues fundamental to all musical systems: octave equivalence, the empirical characterization of the separable musical dimensions, the status of such concepts as "register," and on and on. These may not be explicitly the stuff of intellectual history, but the formulations of these problems, and the modes and implications of their solutions, are intimately such stuff, for that neither the formulations nor the solutions of these questions had ever before even been attempted suggests not only that the means of formulation had not been provided from outside of music, but that the ways of resolving the problems, of responding to the questions, were inconceivable within music.

And we have been examining just such means and ways, in their direct application to just such questions. So, if we are the intellectual children of our time—and some of us are—and the vocational adults of our place— and some of us are—then let intellectual history record that in our time, in this place, music is being composed, music is being written about, which is becoming of that history.

14. Nelson Goodman, "Graphs for Linguistics," in *Structure of Language and Its Mathematical Aspects*, ed. R. Jakobson (Providence, 1961), p. 51.

DISCUSSION

BROOK: As musicologists, talking about music is one of our daily occupations; but talking about contemporary music is one of our greatest difficulties. Questions raised on this subject interest everyone here. In this connection I am sorry you suggested no items for advance reading.

BABBITT: So am I, but after considering the matter carefully, I decided not to. I could come up with no books or articles (such as the ones I now have included in the reading list accompanying this chapter) that I felt would help to prepare or motivate my talk as I hope my talk now has served to prepare and motivate them. Such a list could have appeared only precious or even perverse in its intricate variety, unified only by abstruseness and its apparent remoteness from anything explicitly musical. I trust that now even some of the unavoidable difficulties of these readings will have been slightly reduced, if only because their musical pertinence now should be considerably more evident. I am amused to observe that, after the fact, they all eventually will have to do with discourse about music, though—in their relation to any musical theory or metatheory—at different theoretical levels, at different distances from the musical data. I say "after the fact" for, until your opening remark, I did not regard my talk as primarily concerned with or addressed to the issues of discourse about music, perhaps because I was happily being informally reassured of the substantial contemporaneity of the most sophisticated contemporary music by the degree and extent of its intersections of suggestiveness with other domains of contemporary thought, and because I was concerned to attend to the specific data of my topic. But, of course, the relations of music to the intellectual world of its time, particularly in our time, are likely largely to depend upon verbal characterizations and understanding, while the grave misunderstandings of our music and about our music are likely to be resolved, if at all, largely—and certainly, initially—by appeals to the shared standards of rational discourse. And those of us who have been concerned to direct attention to the central importance and the complex difficulties of musical discourse are most distressed to find ourselves depicted as those who presume to know all the answers, when—on the contrary—we know how few answers we think we have, how difficult answers are to come by, particularly when the questions themselves are so murkily formulated as often to admit no answer, or only trivial answers, or to reveal themselves under analytical clarification as not being questions at all. We are more often obliged simply to indicate why what have passed or are still passing for answers are not and cannot be answers.

And, as you say, talking about music must be our daily concern, not only—though importantly—in our role as teachers, but even more importantly in our role as composers. For, as I so often have been obliged to say before, talk about music—particularly a brand of performative talk —largely determines what is performed and, therefore, what is heard and, therefore and necessarily, what is composed. Compositions are read about before they are listened to and, as a result, are often never listened to, for all that words about a composition can be evaluated only formally, logically apart from the composition, and only upon comparison with the composition itself can they be evaluated even for mere accuracy of representation. Almost all such current disquisition can be dismissed summarily as internally, formally faulty or as possessing no possible musical referent (thus, as being false or as being undefined with regard to any familiar language system).

But let me return to the question of the reading list and further attempt to explain my apprehensions. Suppose I had suggested an article which ostensibly has a musical subject, and which appeared in an ostensibly music periodical: Michael Kassler's "Toward a Theory that Is the Twelve-Note-Class System."[15] Even those who struggled beyond or even resolved their perplexities at the title probably would have assumed that I listed this demanding article because it was demanding (knowing my reputation), or because it appeared "mathematical" (knowing my reputation), or because it had to do—at least some of the music examples suggested this—with twelve-tone music (knowing my reputation), when, for the purposes of my subject, I would have chosen it as an example (in music, a rare example) of expert formalization to exhibit a technique of and the explicational virtues of such formalization in achieving clarificatory precision, the removal of vagueness, and—even—the exposing of necessary consequences which reveal new empirical possibilities. But I felt certain that few, if any, readers would penetrate and pursue the formalism in order to secure the therapeutic and—even—creative benefits available. Now, I hope, some will.

But if Kassler's work seems complex, even needlessly so, let me recall that I was trying to suggest yesterday that one of our problems has been that we have been seeking essentially simple solutions to immensely complicated problems. If we ask what is wrong with music theory, and we all admit that something is wrong and that we are dissatisfied with it as composers and teachers in one way or another, we are likely to seek the source of our discomfort in some such unanswered question as: "Should we teach counterpoint or harmony first?"—which, insofar as it is a primarily pedagogical question, is of no immediate theoretical import, and which, insofar as it is a question of musical theory (involving notions of musical structure), is already too theory-laden to admit consequential reconstruction at the implied stage (like trying to save what already is

15. "Toward a Theory that Is the Twelve-Note-Class System," *Perspectives of New Music*, V/2 (Spring-Summer, 1967), 1–80.

theoretically spent). The causes of our uneasiness, no matter how only
vaguely identified or only "intuitively" articulated, are likely to be
reflected in what would otherwise be regarded as the labyrinthine niceties
of theory construction. Remembering that our concern with more satisfactory theoretical formulation is not to the end of making music more
dependent upon theory but of making it independent of inadequate, inac-
curate theory, we should not allow ourselves to be dissuaded from entering the labyrinths. How far we should penetrate is a ticklish, only apparently tactical, matter; prudence and practicality suggest that we stop at
the points that suffice for our musical needs, but one so often can be, so
often has been, mistaken in proceeding only as far as seems to yield an
answer, an evanescent answer which is undermined by fundamental
difficulties which emerge at yet a further stage. In the light of this, I sym-
pathetically understand but cannot condone those who protest our theoretical enterprises initially by insisting that music is far too complex a phenomenon to yield any of its secrets to analysis; then—provisionally—defer
to our examples of refractory, non-musical phenomena which have
responded to such investigation; and then, when confronted by the procedures and considerations which seem to be required, though they are rudi-
mentary by the standards of other, analytically more successful fields,
finally cry, "Why should anything so direct and immediate in its effect as
music require so complex an exegesis?" So music begins by being too
complex, and ends by being too simple to demand a (relatively) complicated analysis.

But that considerable complication is unavoidable not only supports our
"intuitions" about music and about our interests in it, but immediately can
be inferred from a book which would have been on any preliminary book
list I might have ventured, no matter how sparsely selective: Nelson
Goodman's *The Structure of Appearance*. I am amused and gratified to
have seen, every couple of years during the almost twenty since its publication, a young composer and/or theorist discover this book for himself
and breathlessly or angrily or virtuously assert that he cannot imagine
how any of his fellow composers and/or theorists could fail to discern the
deep and expansive co-extension of the volume's concerns with those of
the music theorist. But—and, again, this is why there was no list—the
necessary obstacles which must be overcome, the processes which must be
mastered before this aptness can be discerned and the methods applied, are
formidable. But the book is concerned to use symbolic logic (at a not
very demanding level, incidentally) in the "analysis of phenomena," and
this—necessarily—includes musical phenomena, and its forbidding complexities should, but will not, still the voices of those who take exception
to the occasionally "difficult" articles which occasionally, all too occasionally, appear in, say, *Perspectives of New Music*. For, be it in the significance of a constructional definition, of the choice of bases, or of the ana-

lytical application of relations (in the familiar sense that I have invoked in my talk), not to mention a host of even more immediately and explicitly relevant topics ("qualia," "order," "properties"), the obligations of a usable and useful musical theory obtrude forcefully.

I realize that while I have blithely, unchallengedly, and repeatedly used the term "theory," the question of what the term should and could signify is itself a contestedly open question among our colleagues in other fields. The apparently, but only apparently, deviant use of the term in structural linguistics as synonymous with "grammar" finds its elaborate and formal realization in Michael Kassler's construction of a theory of tonal music in the explication of Schenker's informal theory of tonal music, which many of us feel to be the most satisfactory theory of that music, however incomplete, unclear, and ambiguous it undeniably is in certain respects. Kassler's formulation not only exposes the ambiguities and lacunae, but is in the process of casting Schenker's "analytical" theory in "synthetic" form (not in the sense of that allegedly untenable dualism), so that its musical productions can be tested. Schenker's analytical theory, in other words, will be testable by synthesis. Whereas current linguistic theory is struggling to construct a theory that will generate all those and only those sentences of the language under consideration, Schenker-Kassler—comparably and incomparably—aims to generate not just the (musical) sentences of tonal music, but all those and only those complete tonal compositions. This far greater scope only befits the theory of a man, Schenker, who—however unrigorously and unknowingly—formulated an elaborate and fruitful generative-transformational theory of music decades before its linguistic counterpart burst upon the intellectual scene. Essentially, only implementation of Schenker-Kassler is needed before that infinity of tonal works (if the theory is validated) which are the predictions of the theory start being produced into inundation. (Fear not. Mr. Kassler is involved otherwise, and men and money are not available. Structural linguistics has become the province of hundreds, or thousands; such musical theory is the province of very few. Here, again, words before music.)

At this point, I fear that I run the risk of appearing to be legislating the study of a great number of topics in a great number of non-musical fields. I am not. That is another reason why I offered no book list, and even now offer one with misgivings. The primary proper object of music theory is music, compositions, and the goal of the theory is the understanding of music, compositions; some of the readings may have only the "negative," defining function of revealing the inappropriateness of certain pursuits which have been fruitful in other fields, the inapplicability of otherwise reasonable notions, those singularities of musical structure that define its modes of comprehension and, therefore, analysis. Most of them will be of primarily meta-theoretical assistance, necessary but certainly not sufficient to assure acceptable musical theory. Here, again, mathematics may be the most puzzling, beguiling, or intimidating of domains. I'll extend what I said in my talk in a slightly different direction, to the same conclusion. If I term a certain simultaneous, ordered collection of notes a "six-five chord," it may be adjudged (if, indeed, it is) a correct name of the collection with regard to, at least, two familiar theories: one a "figured bass" theory, the other a Rameau-derived theory (in which it is only a partial name). "Six-five chord," then, is a heavily theory-laden term, a "fact" of music only relative to one of its subsuming theories, not an immutable, inexorable, incontrovertible "fact of music," or even a transcendental explanation and justification. But for all that 6 and 5 are numerals, signifying integral distance measures of unordered interval classes, defined within scale structure mod. 7, the music accurately so characterized never, to my knowledge, has been called "mathematical"; indeed, even its familiar, conventional theory is not usually—although it correctly could be—termed "mathematical." And so, too, with such commonplace notions as "neighboring" or "passing" notes, at any structural level (the theoretical bias here, I trust, is obvious), for they depend upon the more primitive notion of "betweenness," which is one of the most familiar and ubiquitous of "mathematical" concepts. Any statement of relatedness—therefore, of musical structure—can be expressed mathematically, and probably already has been. Just as "the degree of mathematicality" of a work cannot depend on the degree of mathematicality of its associated theory, there can be no "degrees of ultmate mathematicality" among competing theories. Again, all compositions are equally "mathematical" and, so, vacuously mathematical.

Mathematics, only incidentally and instantively, and theory construction, strategically and profoundly, conjoin in a simple and yet immensely practical and powerful music-theoretical example of the distinction between "observational" and "theoretical" terms, a distinction that has occupied a central position in theory construction, and, although at its most refined extensions it—characteristically—is susceptible to subtle adjustments and demurrers, it is a valuable distinction at our level just in that it provides a distinction, and further provides yet another example of a "recondite," specialized metatheoretical concept instantiated by a fundamental, familiar concept of music theory, or—more correctly—a wide variety of music theories. We begin with the customary concept of a musical interval, defining or deriving from a finite equal difference structure. No matter what the derivational position of "interval" in your theory, if I go to the piano and play a D followed by the next higher F, you would be prepared to call it a "minor third," or "augmented second," or any of its enharmonic equivalents, or—without ambiguity in this respect, and to reduce the theoretical load—a "three," in the customary semitonal metric. You, further, can name and aurally identify other "threes," and D-F remains a "three" no matter what pitch is chosen as origin (as zero), since the difference between D and F is invariably "three." An interval is a direct musical perceptible, "observable," formally representable by the subtraction of one pitch number (or pitch-class number) from another. We can "hear" and compute the intervals in a pitch collection, and "hear" and speak of two pitch collections that are different in pitch content but intervallically identical. Then, suppose we take the representation of interval as a difference of pitch numbers; $a - b$, and now define a term—call its interpretation "pitch number sum" if you wish $a + b$, where a and b still designate pitch (or pitch-class) numbers. But, unlike $a - b$, this expression is not even computable until a "zero" is chosen, for its value varies with the origin chosen. And, when an origin has been chosen (say, set $c = 0$), what can the sum (say $2 + 5 = 7$) possibly define? How can it be interpreted? The difference of pitch numbers is a distance, an interval, but what is the sum of pitch numbers? Surely, no more than the difference, can the sum be a pitch number. What would it mean for a d plus an f to equal a g (a "seven")? And, then, $a + b$ would also equal $d + f$. What can that mean? It does, indeed, mean something, but what it means has no direct ostensive correlate, no immediate aural or acoustical exemplification. For the sum of two pitch numbers is truly a "theoretical term"; accordingly, there is no name for it in the traditional literature, so I have christened it "index number" for many reasons, corresponding to its many theoretical appearances. In all respects, it is a concept equal in scope of application and consequence to that of "interval number." Just as interval provides a basis of hierarchization in that the multiplicity of occurrence of an interval in a pitch collection defines the number of pitches in common between the original collection and the collection transposed by the number equal to the multiplicity number (this simple, obvious property is most commonly reflected in the "circle of fifths" hierarchization), so the multiplicity of occurrence of an index number in a collection determines the number of pitches in common between the collection and the collection transposed by that index number and inverted. This property is as applicable, of course, to that body of musical literature which contains the *Art of Fugue* as it is to that which contains Schoenberg's Variations for Orchestra. But the position of pitch-class inversion in the twelve-tone system makes the applicational extent of the index-number concept more immediately and profoundly evident. It and the concept of interval can be regarded as the two fundamental notions from which a myriad of twelve-tone properties can be derived, and by which they can be discovered, including all of those which have been compositionally employed. Itself, the index number is the basis of Schoenbergian inversional combinationality, and of all properties related to intervallic inversion and, therefore, to retrogression.

Such are the theoretical consequences of the "theoretical term," involving the simplest of mathematical formulations; yet it is this kindergarten arithmetic that makes it possible quickly to determine the range of application, to answer specific questions of quantity and existence, and even to suggest formal analogues—which may turn out to be empirically fruitful or, for the moment, at least, inapplicable.

BUSHLER: Why do people feel the need of making explanations of this sort?

BABBITT: I'm not sure I know what you mean by "this sort." For the moment, but only for the moment, I shall assume you are not alluding to "explanations" of another sort. I shall further assume that you, at this point, do not mean "of this 'mathematical' sort," for I trust I have discussed that sufficiently, and you can further infer similar reasons for the invocation of slightly more sophisticated mathematical ideas in the literature, such as "groups," or results from combinatory theory, or the many others which have proven useful on occasion. But allow me to recall Michael Scriven's words: "If we want to know why things are as they are . . . , then the only sense in which there are alternatives to the methods of science is the sense in which we can if we wish abandon our interest in correct answers." As theorists, scholars, teachers, and informed humans, we do want "to know why things are as they are," and we are interested "in correct answers." And although I have no wish to confuse "knowing that" with "knowing how" or the "context of justification" with "the context of discovery," neither am I so timorous or conciliatory or presumptuous as to pronounce that such knowledge will not, cannot, or should not "feed back" into composition. But if there are still those who, self-protectively, denounce even this as "scientism," happily restricted to a tiny domain of music, would their worst prejudices not be finally confirmed by the appearance in, say, *Perspectives of New Music* of an article entitled "Picking a Piece to Pieces"? It has not (yet) appeared. But Sinclair's "Taking a Poem to Pieces" appeared some five years ago. Indeed, there has been enough publication in professional periodicals of literary analysis that is comparably "scientific" and related to structural linguistics that at least five anthologies of such writings are available.

As I indicated in my talk, the issue of explanation has spawned a vast and proliferating literature that reflects its crucial implications and unsettled problems, so I have no wish to be cavalier or dogmatic with respect to any aspect of explanation. But surely people seek explanation to dispel perplexities, reduce uncertainties, and provide structured knowledge. Do "people" ever ask "why" when you teach music?

BUSHLER: Yes.

BABBITT: Then they are seeking explanations. And, surely, you do not respond with "why 'why'?"—if only because that is the seeking of an explanation for the seeking of an explanation. Rather, the issue becomes that of the context of the explanation, for the high-minded generality that "there are some things which are, and must remain, inexplicable" is less defensible than the corresponding, if not very profitable, generality that anything is explicable, in an infinity of ways. But it is just the purpose of the various models of explanation in the current literature to expose and dispose of such singular and isolated explanations, not necessarily as invalid, but as relatively uninformative; one desires an explanation with regard to a certain context of synthetic primitives and formal modes of inference, both to avoid ontic inflation and to relate the explanadum in question to other components of the explanatory "network."

If a student of elementary theory—harmony, counterpoint, or harmony/counterpoint—asks, as he so often has, why parallel fifths are forbidden, how do you answer? Surely not that unenlightened old fogies didn't write them very often, but that music finally freed itself of such superstitions, for although—name calling aside—this, if true, is an explanation, whether true or untrue, it does not answer the question as to why parallel fifths are, for the creative or recreative activity in question, "forbidden." The explanation is as good or bad, though manifestly seriously incomplete, as most—and as irrelevant as any—in explaining "why they were not written." Alternatively, you might try to derive the prohibition from established, more general principles; this has often been alleged and attempted, but never—to my knowledge—acceptably. I hope, therefore, you do not hesitate—in the dark of such hallowed homilies as "rules are made to be broken" or "music is not written by rules"—to assure the student that the prohibition is a "rule." A rule of what? Surely not of "music," since there is a great deal of what one, for a number of other reasons, wishes to call "music" that luxuriates in parallel fifths. It is a rule of a large, chronologically defined, corpus of music, in the sense that it is sufficient to violate the rule to not be writing an instance of such music, in the same sense that to move a rook diagonally is to violate a rule that defines chess and, accordingly, is to not play chess. For a musical rule is just the prescriptive, legislative formulation of an expression of the musical theory, cast in such a form so as to produce a "prediction," rather than explanatory postdiction, of the theory: a new "composition," for all that it may be termed a harmony or counterpoint or harmony/counterpoint "exercise," just as the predictions of the grammar (that is, the theory) of a language are new sentences in the language, and one does not hesitate to speak of "rules of word order" or "phrase-structure rules" as defining a language.

A rational reconstruction of a work or works, which is a theory of the work or works, is, thereby, an explanation not, assuredly, of the "actual" processes of construction, but of how the work or works may be construed by a hearer, how the "given" may be "taken."

Just as the analytical literature of ethical theory concerns itself with the question of "rules"—stipulative and regulative, general rules, rules of practices, and more—so the literature of language structure and learning concerns itself with internalized rules (even unto innateness), particularly those which are internalized without "conscious" formulation or formal theory construction. These are the kinds of rules in accord with which an illiterate is able to speak intelligibly an intricately constrained language, without his possessing a notion of grammaticality or even an awareness of how difficult and elusive such a notion is. Unformalized internalization is, naturally, a primary feature of musical conditioning and learning. It must be used and can be used in collaboration and coordination with formally inferred rules, which can themselves be then internalized (such is the task of "ear training"); but never let it be forgotten or overlooked that such internalized constraints are just that, and that ignorance or unawareness of the fact and features of such constraints is not "freedom" from constraints. On the contrary, such ignorance can make one only an uninformed captive of the constraints rather than one who, by being able to examine the range of their legitimate authority, can knowingly alter, even flout, that range, even by substituting other productive constraints.

Finally, I return to the possibility that "of this sort" was in contradistinction to those sorts of explanations or belligerently non-explanations that invoke terms such as "taste," "emotional cogency," or even "beauty." The issues associated with such normatives or undefined descriptives are thoroughly treated in the literature under such topics as the illicit inference from extensional equivalence to intensional equivalence, referential opacity, and the like. But the self-indulgent insistence that "I like it" or one of its more euphuistic equivalents is all that need or can be said of a composition (or "a work of art," in the usually associated hypostatization) is still widely adhered to by a variety of tribes of Philistines. Indeed, it even appears to be strongly implied that the circumstance that one can or should say nothing other or more is what makes the object in question truly "a work of art." Whereas "I like it" (and will not or cannot tell why), since it is undiscussable, is indefensible (since rational defense requires discussion), those who will not or cannot give reasons I just dismiss as unreasonable; but those who assert that "X is a masterpiece" would probably not so self-classify themselves. The cognitive status of such a familiar form, most easily ascertained by opposing to it its negation, reduces to that of one's statement about a composition being necessarily a statement about someone else's incorrigible statement about a composition, a report of someone else's announcement of personal disposition. Or the statement is undefined—that is, meaningless—since its language system is not defined, or the statement and its negation may be differently relativized linguistically, so that conceivably they are not mutual negations, but intensional and extensional overlaps. Or, if enough warrant terms are provided to augment and linguistically locate the assertion, then "masterpiece" must be adjudged supervenient, for surely you would not wish to say that two compositions are identical except that one is a masterpiece and the other is not. And when the supervenience is atomized, you would wish the concept's extension to include cases other than the one at issue—that is, not to be *ad hoc*. This notion of supervenience is dealt with extensively in contemporary ethical theory, and merely the knowledge contained in one of the many contemporary critical surveys of this theory suffices to expose as preposterously nescient those public utterances on music, whether they originate with those descendants of Epimenides who proclaim that "you can't really talk about music," or those descendants of Beckmesser who do not.

Mrs. Friedland: Yesterday in your talk, I thought, and I'm glad mistakenly, that the main thrust of your remarks was against the people in fields other than ours who came up with simple-minded comments about our area. Now I see that your main thrust, or at least your equal thrust, is against those of us in our own field who remain blissfully ignorant or underinformed about what's going on.

Babbitt: Frankly, I did not regard my "main thrust" as against anyone, but rather toward a definition of our situation, its possible causes, its apparent effects, and its probably impossible fate.

If I appeared, at least initially, to emphasize the presumptions and absurdities of some of our nonmusical colleagues with respect to music (and I could have multiplied the examples in number and horror), it is just that one can determine that there are confusions about music and the nature of these confusions only by examining the confusions in the discourse about music. And, further, if you wish to discover a man's social status, the sources of his societal discomfort, the reasons for his being treated like a pariah, for being beleaguered in his own home, you might do worse than start by finding out what his neighbors are saying about him.

READING LIST

The following books are some of those which, in addition to the obviously appropriate items mentioned in the footnotes, were either mentioned in subsequent discussions or are suggested as relevant to the paper and the following discussion. I do not presume to "recommend" those outside of the field of music as superior to others in their field, but merely to note that they have either been helpful to me or may prove helpful to the reader who wishes to pursue certain of the issues merely raised here. They are all as "nontechnical" as possible, and those outside of music assume little or no previous training in the field in question. The grouping is merely a rough indication of the domain of the collective subject matter.

I.

Babbitt, Milton, "Twelve-Tone Rhythmic Structure and the Electronic Medium," *Perspectives of New Music*, I/1 (1962), 49–79.

———— "The Structure and Function of Musical Theory: I," *College Music Symposium*, V (1965), 49–60.

Boretz, Benjamin, "Meta-Variations," Ph.D. diss., Princeton University, 1969.

Cone, Edward T., "A Budding Grove," *Perspectives of New Music*, III/2 (1965), 38–46.

Kassler, Michael, "A Sketch of the Use of Formalized Languages for the Assertion of Music," *Perspectives of New Music*, I/2 (1963), 83–94.

———— "Toward a Theory that Is the Twelve-Note-Class System," *Perspectives of New Music*, V/2 (1967), 1–80.

II.

Bergmann, Gustav, "Undefined Descriptive Predicates," *Philosophy and Phenomenological Research*, VIII (1947), 55–82.

Goodman, Nelson, *The Structure of Appearance*, 2nd ed. (Indianapolis, 1966).

———— *Fact, Fiction, and Forecast* (Cambridge, 1955).

Hempel, Carl, *Aspects of Scientific Explanation* (New York, 1965).

Kyburg, Henry E., Jr., *Philosophy of Science* (New York, 1968).

Martin, R. M., *Truth and Denotation* (Chicago, 1956).

Przelecki, Marian, *The Logic of Empirical Theories* (London, 1969).

Scheffler, Israel, *The Anatomy of Inquiry* (New York, 1963).

III.

Cherry, Colin, *On Human Communication: A Review, a Survey and a Criticism* (New York, 1957; 2nd ed., 1968).

Galanter, Eugene, *Textbook of Elementary Psychology* (San Francisco, 1966).

Miller, G. A., "The Magical Number Seven, Plus or Minus Two," *Psychological Review*, LXIII (1956), 81–97. Also reprinted in a number of collections.

Pfanzagl, J., *Theory of Measurement* (New York, 1968).

IV.

Hook, Sidney, ed., *Language and Philosophy Proceedings: New York University Institute of Philosophy Symposium* (New York, 1969).

Taylor, P. W., *Normative Discourse* (Englewood Cliffs, N.J., 1961).

Vendler, Zeno, *Linguistics in Philosophy* (Ithaca, 1967).

Ziff, Paul, *Semantic Analysis* (Ithaca, 1960).

V.

Hockett, Charles F., *Language, Mathematics, and Linguistics* (The Hague, 1967).

Jacobs, Roderick A., and Peter S. Rosenbaum, *Readings in English Transformational Grammar* (Waltham, 1970).

Lyons, John, *Introduction to Theoretical Linguistics* (Cambridge, Mass., 1968).

Musicology and Related Disciplines

PAUL HENRY LANG

*I*T *SEEMS* to me that my topic differs somewhat from the more concrete subjects offered at this forum. I shall not even give a bibliography, and I cannot offer methods, only intentions and suggestions. I imagine that the planners of this series of lectures assigned my topic because during the spectacular growth of musicology in this country in the last thirty years, the distance between our discipline and the surrounding cultural milieu has increased until it has produced a veritable isolation. But the justification for the embarkation of an institution of learning upon an ambitious program of graduate studies in any discipline whatever is, first of all, to place this discipline in the cross section of culture of which it is part. The greatest danger that threatens this burgeoning musicology is that its relationship to the humanities will become more and more tenuous if students eager to acquire scholarly status are taught nothing but specialized knowledge, independent of further connections; they will learn to master only the materials that make possible the acquisition of knowledge, not knowledge itself.

Members of the university community naturally represent considerable variety in individuality, beliefs, and principles; these differences are fruitful when they are related to, when they have reference to, a mutual center. And although the disciplines taught under the heading of the liberal arts do separate us, we can see, even within the framework of the different themes, the kindred nature of our research and the shaping of this research into communicable wisdom.

185

Culture is the sum total of our heritage in its historical development: religion, science, the arts, the social order, the forms of life. Literature is not simply the sum total of writings, and art is not the aggregate of artistic objects, because culture is more than the piling up of individual objectivations—it is a spirit pervading and linking them together. A scholar who, like a Hindu ascetic immersed in self-contemplation, confines himself to his narrow field of specialization, loses the larger view. The first requirement for the musicologist is to realize that the choice of studying other disciplines is governed not by his tastes and desires alone, but by sheer necessity. Further, he must not only absorb the content of other disciplines, but—and this is much more difficult—put each to constructive use in his own field. This is equally true of the technical means as of the final visions. The technique of research can be carried to a point where it embarks upon an independent existence, almost without reference to the material under investigation. On the other hand, it may and should lead to the uncovering of the inner regions of the spirit that lie beyond technique.

The second requirement may be called that of continuity. Once more, one may proceed on parallel courses—that of technique and that of idea. It seems to be an undeviating law that the continuity of the idea slackens sooner than that of the handling of the material. Consequently, what was meaningful in the enthusiasm and élan of the initiators may become changed, even meaningless, under the hands of their successors, who develop the original idea by manipulating its materials. To mention an example, the Baroque started out as an expression of the *Ecclesia militans*, of the Counter Reformation, but as it spread from the Latin-Catholic south to the German-Protestant north the original motive gave way to a different set of ideas. Yet musicology persists in dealing with Baroque music in elaborate isolation, expecting to explain it by pure stylistic research and elucidation, but producing only a good picture of formal and technical developments without accounting for the underlying meaning. This is no longer the history of ideas; stylistic research has become independent of culture. The history of ideas needs this competent stylistic analysis, but the musico-technical research should not be a Golem. What happened in this case is just what I said a minute ago: the researchers busy with Baroque music picked up the original idea and explored all the possibilities, which at its inception had a palpable cultural meaning; but by restricting themselves to chronology, paleography, morphology, typology, and general *Fachlehre*, they lost sight of the idea and missed its mutation.

This leads us to the third point. We are capable of contemplating and enjoying such music even though we are far removed from its original cultural meaning and associations. It can give us esthetic experience even though it is the product of a culture distant and strange to us. But make no mistake, this is an inadequate viewing and an inadequate experience—

and I am afraid that much of our musicology is built upon a system of inadequate viewing. This situation is not altogether graceless, because with our techniques and stylistic analyses we provide invaluable contributions; it is only regrettable that the admirable ability of the researcher is cultivated so exclusively.

In every branch of culture the historical development reaches a point where an estrangement begins. This becomes perceptible to the individual when new experiences move him and he becomes aware of his alienation from the old content and old forms. There is then an attempt at reconstruction, and there enter the historians, the scholars. It is extremely important that these exegetes of changing events should see clearly the varying mentalities and purposes that predominate in the different periods. When humanity is concerned with primordial facts, when what occupies the creative artist is the inscrutable yet ever-present soul, we are dealing with a religious culture. Then there are periods that feel, though not consciously and not theoretically, the inner laws of form, and the creative artist's work is concentrated on the optimum shaping of the material. Such a time is one of marked artistic development. The third orientation or state of mind becomes actual when the feeling of alienation comes to the fore, and the discrepancy of form and content becomes increasingly evident. When this point is reached the laws underlying the shaping of the material, of form, which the previous generation created by obeying their pure creative instincts, become conscious; now it is theory that can grasp what to the creative artist has become more or less strange. In such a period critical research, logic, esthetics, and history thrive. It seems to me that we are living in such a period; the great accomplishments of musicology during the last thirty years or so clearly indicate it.

The practitioners of any of the disciplines constituting the history of ideas are charged with the task of bringing to the surface the specific facts and qualities of their respective cultural domain and of examining how its development is regulated by internal laws. It becomes evident to the attentive student that these domains show essential differences, and that while the several manifestations of culture cannot be segregated from one another, neither can they be simply compared. Whether philosophy, or poetry, or music, or physics, every manifestation of the objectivation of the spirit possesses a different construction, which is due to the medium through which it comes to expression. Thus the construction of each of the cultural objectivations, their respective yet mutual autonomy, is the proper subject of scholarship.

Today we know more about the technique of archival research than did our predecessors, and our command of the tools and means for the processing of the gathered material is impressive; but we lag behind in our ability to cast what we have gathered into interpretative syntheses. Knowledge of the métier and of the mechanics of music is essential to the understanding of the work of art, and the young student of musicology must acquire these tools and practice with them for long hours. It is essential, however, that he not stop there; he must look around him, for knowledge has a very sly way of accumulating in odd places where it is with difficulty perceived. Specialization is inevitable and necessary, for it is only the expert who can deal with the subtleties of any given subject, but specialization should not be encouraged at the start of a musicological career. It goes without saying that no single person can master more than a fraction of his own discipline, let alone the related disciplines essential for the exploitation of music in all its manifestations. We recall the bon mot coined by an historian, that the last twenty minutes of the Renaissance would be too vast a subject for any one man to know adequately. It used to be the fashion among musicians to smile indulgently upon those writers who expended a lifetime of assiduous work and anxious archeology compiling the musical history of one city or one monastery. But we have come to see the inestimable value of this humble spade work, and we cannot withhold admiration from these men who delve deeply into their own little corners of music history, uncovering the great along with the insignificant. This kind of research is indispensable, although it usually offers only raw materials for the use of others. Such studies are not the historiography which becomes part of culture, for that historiography is at once a record of civilization and a contribution to it, and becomes so by virtue of its imaginative penetration and interpretation. Those whom we may call musical philologists often are not really aware of the difference between what is dead and what is alive; they want knowledge as a means for establishing a comfortable order. Their measures are quantitative, and everything available to them is equally worthy of attention. Their implicit or explicit thesis is that everything can be researched, everything can become object, for before scholarship everything has equal rights. So to them this is the meaning of life. But overgrowth of material, be it factual or spiritual, and overgrowth of means, be they technical, scientific, or artistic, restrict the power of choice and lead to the impoverishment of the humane.

The Greeks already had two schools of musical thought: Aristoxenus was a pragmatist, interested in music as an art, whereas the Pythagoreans considered it a science, a department of mathematics. The Aristoxenian school relied on the musical ear, the Pythagorean on numbers. Neither the scientific nor the artistic mind is by any means homogeneous, however; under these generic names have been subsumed many distinct types throughout the centuries. Some of the greatest scientists have been men of a concrete imagination; abstraction was alien to them. Within the field of art, literary, or music scholarship a kindred variety apparently exists, and possibly there is some direct affinity between the various types of scientific and mathematical minds and those that reveal themselves in the appreciation of arts and letters. But there is also a weighty difference between the scientist and the humanist, a difference the musicologist who wants to make his discipline an exact science tends to overlook: the exact sciences are largely nonhistorical. In physics or chemistry the facts are pre-existent; it is only that we discover them one by one. Unlike the laws of invertible counterpoint, the laws of thermodynamics have always been here and always will be, and, therefore, a physicist or chemist can make quite precise predictions, whereas the historian of the arts cannot, not even imprecisely. A work of art is the result of a particular history and every one of the histories is original, individual, and nonduplicable. Nevertheless, we have qualities that we share with the scientists, which indeed are shared by all scholars, the most important being the organization of thinking, which in the scholar's world occupies the same place as does composition in art. Behind each there is a view which can be just as sensory as it is intellectual, whether in physics or the arts. Only we must beware of the eternal danger of immediately freezing it into a system.

I spoke of the specialist and of his important role, but before the physicist becomes a specialist he has acquired a scientific view, an over-all attitude and awareness of the extent and nature of physics as a science and a part of our cultural make-up. This awareness he carries over into his specialized studies. And of course the surgeon, too, begins his specialized career only after he has studied medicine in all its concepts, observed facts, and attitudes. In the sciences this indoctrination begins in the college in a serious scholarly fashion; in music, regrettably, our young students are often taught to be like the romantic tourists who, guidebook in hand, are always ready to pounce upon the celebrated place to make it yield the proper and prescribed sensations.

We are all agreed that musicology needs the assistance not only of the humanities but of the natural and social sciences as well, despite the fact that right now there is less than the usual agreement as to what can properly be regarded as essential, what subordinate. The finished composition is, of course, an entity in itself, which can be detached from its cultural environment and examined purely on its own terms of construction. But music is a man-made art despite its physical foundations, and in the end we must trace the work of art to its creator, who is subject to many other than musical stimuli and influences; if we stop with the music, therefore, we have investigated but half the story. (On the other hand, if we investigate only the man, as Ernest Newman did in his massive four-volume biography of Wagner, without one paragraph devoted to music, we tell even less than half the story, because we leave out the work of art which should have been our point of departure.) This belief, that we can examine the product of human imagination completely divorced from its creator, is not true even in the sciences.

Sir Josiah Stamp's view, that economic tendencies are altered by the very fact that we study them, is applicable to music. This paradox is, indeed, the core of the case against *laissez faire* both in economics and in scholarship in the arts; but before we can embark on our study of music we run up against some serious obstacles. We must acknowledge the incontrovertible fact that neither the composition nor the enjoyment of music presupposes any scientific knowledge. Mozart and Schubert did not know the first thing about the laws of acoustics, the physiology of hearing, or the psychology of perception. Nor did either of them know anything about the principles of the social organization of their world beyond the fact that it was cruel to them. Yet both Mozart and Schubert managed to manipulate the physical phenomena underlying the art of music into supreme masterpieces. So all is serene and pleasurable in the world of music until the musicologist appears and disturbs the peace of this innocent enjoyment by asking questions, challenging the performing artists' conceptions, and establishing entirely new sets of values as well as the historical outlook. Until fairly recently—and, in not a few places, still—musicians, the public, the press, even university administrations, considered the music scholar an unwelcome intruder, an anomaly that threatened the orderly pursuit and enjoyment of music. Yet the end not only for music but for literary and scientific investigations is so evident that it deserves the high rank of platitude. We cannot solve problems by ignoring them, and we must insist that art is structured by reason and not solely by the waywardness of feeling and inspiration. The concept that the universe is a rational system working by discoverable laws is the essential foundation for all the activities which a university comprises. Without the life of reason conditioned by that concept of the world there could be no university discipline in arts, letters, and sciences. And while the laws of the workings of the universe are stressed more by the exponents of the sciences, consciousness of these laws is no less implicit in the other departments of learning. In musicology we speak of the auxiliary or subsidiary disciplines that have relevance to our work; they may be subsidiary to art itself, but they are nevertheless the ones that mediate between the rational system of the world and the arts. Thus acoustics, psychology, and physiology are, or should be, part of a musicologist's equipment; but it is a great mistake to begin musicological studies with the associated and auxiliary disciplines. Regrettably, all introductory textbooks on musicology begin with acoustics and the physiology of hearing even before the student knows anything about his musical tasks. Musicology deals with an art, not with an exact science. The young scholar should be taught pride in the unique quality of the arts, he should learn that the poetic idea as an abstract formation of the power of the imagination is totally independent of all science and physically indestructible. Once it is planted in the world, it is its own value that preserves it. Nevertheless, a scholar wishing to gain a comprehensive view of his field simply must have at least a nodding acquaintance with these scientific underpinnings. Besides, they are interesting. The musicologist is not expected to match the acoustician, the psychologist, and the physiologist on their own ground, but he should have some knowledge of the important processes whereby the physical phenomenon called sound is produced, perceived, and converted. There are excellent summaries available, like Geldard's *The Human Senses*, but those prepared by musicologists for musicologists should be shunned. Anything beyond that becomes an interdisciplinary matter carried out by collaboration. The musicologist should not attempt basic research in these areas unless he is willing to go through the mill and make it his specialty, which, of course, is entirely legitimate but calls for full devotion to the task.

Goethe declared that the literature of a nation can be neither recognized nor appreciated unless at the same time the whole content of its existence is taken into account. Substitute "music" for "literature" and we have arrived at the group of disciplines which are not only closest to the musicologist but without which he cannot properly function as a respectable scholar: religion, philosophy, literature, history, sociology, and the other arts. Since it would be impossible to deal with all of them within a brief address, I shall single out history and sociology, two disciplines that are always present in our everyday work.

If we grant that the development of the several branches of culture is marked by a steady distancing from an original point of departure, then the retrospective view of posterity, that is, history, is of paramount importance to us. If we add that even within a generation this distancing may be apparent, if we realize that already to the Athens of Pericles the Homeric world appeared as a very distant mythus, it becomes clear what an immensely difficult undertaking it is to interpret the cultural accomplishments of past generations. Put in the simplest terms, when the musicologist ascertains that the composer he is investigating lived and worked in a particular place at a particular time, he accepts the implication that the events surrounding this musician to a considerable part constituted his experience. Thus the question of style is also a sociological question: What does life give to the creative artist and what does it withhold from him? This is not useful "background" stuff, as one critic who wanted to say at least a few kind words about a recent book on Handel saw it, but the essential point of departure for the historian, for in certain periods only certain concepts of life are possible and others are excluded. The external social determinant is the effect whose causes are the more social the deeper they are. But the history of this effect immediately involves cultural psychology too, because we must find out what was pleasing in a given age, what influences predominated, and what made certain genres more acceptable than others. New levels in creative consciousness are achieved and manifested in the various periods of civilization, each expressing a characteristic principle. The historian must always seek the determining political-social blueprint; the causes, influences, and effects need close attention if an understanding, even a superficial understanding, of the history of music is to be obtained. Indeed, we must enlarge our horizon by investigating why a manifestation of culture such as music does have social relations, why in many respects art is all but determined by the social order within which it is realized.

Learning is never more industrious nor less helpful than when it accumulates facts without affirming their true relevance, without probing into how the sequential events are related to one another. History is not mere chronicling, nor is it a digest of events. We must always strive for the critical referent, and we must check and judge even old and traditionally accepted labels and catchwords, because they may be the residue of a once living force and truth. We peel back the layers of events one by one, from the outermost to the innermost until we arrive at the beating heart. It is true of course that to the historian nothing is alien, not even the amorous vagaries of kings and composers, but a constant critical vigilance is imperative. It may happen to any man of genius that his most trivial compositions, notes, or letters are preserved along with his important papers. But it assuredly does not follow that all trivia are worth studying and printing, yet we see it happen almost every month in one or the other of the professional journals devoted to musicology. The discovery of a harmless little minuet by the young Mozart or Haydn can send certain musicologists into transports of scholarly passion; they have visions of upsetting the whole Köchel applecart, perhaps of documenting a hitherto unreported spelling of forte and piano, and the paper may bear a watermark linking this with another equally insignificant piece. The discovery, complete with a ten-page *Revisionsbericht*, is duly published—and where does it get us? This is hand-to-mouth musicology, which we must guard against lest it become a habit. The mere bones of history will not do, for our task is not the collection and cult of relics but to find out what is still living and thus part of the present. The real meaning of history to the music scholar is to see where the highest possibilities were realities once upon a time; all his other activities, including the lost and found minuets, are only necessary preambles.

So far so good. We learn the *modus operandi* of the historian and it helps us enormously, we know that the various manifestations of culture are connected, and that this connection is their vital force. Still, we must never forget that we are historians of an art, and despite all our scientific equipment, to us the work of art really has no past, only different degrees of eternity; to us the great ones are great because of their never-fading newness, not because of their age, not because hundreds of years ago they were, but because after hundreds of years they are. The musicologists of the nineteenth century were the great pioneers of our discipline and their merits were outstanding, but they made mistakes, and it is extremely difficult to sponge out a picture imprinted upon the mind. They sifted out and put together the composers of every country in "schools" and left us with our musical masterpieces neatly arranged, grouped, and pigeonholed. Each one of the schools had its exclusive heroes handed down, bright from incessant polishing, and one marvels how quickly the human image dissolves into the mythical image. The consequence of this classificatory zeal was that the nineteenth century bequeathed to us, together with its industriously amassed facts, many misleading deductions and prejudices, as well as a large dose of national bias, all of which it is our business fundamentally to reconsider. Before continuing, perhaps it would be useful to illustrate the traps the musicologist can fall into if he fails to examine the inherited facts and conclusions and proceeds without sufficient critical historical preparation. Let us take first a case in which the entire musical culture of great musical nations was affected by historical events; and second, a small but very annoying misconception of performance practice that persists because of insufficient acquaintance with contemporary economic history.

Our textbooks deal with the Reformation as a general movement that exerted a weighty influence on the history of music. This is true, but only half the truth. The Protestant Reformation was a revolt against papal theocracy, clerical privilege, and the hereditary "paganism" of the Mediterranean races. Our first great mistake is to regard the Reformation as one unified movement whereas, broadly speaking, the first of the reasons for the revolt moved Luther, the second Henry VIII, and the third Calvin. But Luther, with his formalized thought that found expression in the ninety-five theses, his boisterous tongue that rolled off phrases rich and elemental, managed to tame his romantic emotions to disciplined issue in music—he is the typical German. Similarly, Henry is English—so English that he summoned Parliament to assist him in his conflict with the Holy See; while Calvin's cool, methodical, and uncompromising mind is impregnated with logic of the French genius. As a consequence we find not one common manifestation of European Protestantism, but three separate and altogether different movements, one German, one English, and the third prevalent among peoples whose emotional make-up leaned toward that strict conduct which only French thought can devise.

Faced with these facts, how can a music historian continue to deal with the Reformation as a whole? Only one of the three movements produced great music, and, what is more, a great musical culture: the German. The others hampered, if they did not virtually destroy, musical creativity where they prevailed. Now what are the answers, what are the explanations? The scores themselves will not explain why it is that, as early as the beginning of the seventeenth century, a pamphleteer in England ruefully says that "more musicians are out of order than their instruments."

The other example I should like to cite shows in one small detail how deeply economic forces can influence musical style and practice itself; it concerns the large choral-orchestral works of the late Classic era. The conditions of public music-making changed after the Baroque, and so did the hierarchy of musical genres. The old professional church choir was too expensive to maintain; on the other hand, the gradual but positive displacement of vocal by instrumental music and the increasing practice of public concerts called into existence professional orchestras that could earn their keep. The oratorios and other similar works reflect the reality of the socio-economic conditions: instead of the professional chorus and the *ad hoc* orchestra of the previous era, Haydn wrote for a professional orchestra and an *ad hoc* chorus. A good deal of nonsense has been written about Haydn's last great choral works, especially the oratorios, with their highly developed symphonic orchestral parts and their relatively simple choruses, but the fundamental regrouping of the constituent musical forces, the socio-economic as well as the artistic reasons for them, are ignored. Because of this ignorance neither conductor nor musicologist can account for certain anomalies which they blithely perpetuate. Take Mozart's Requiem, every performance of which is blighted and falsified by the incessant *colla parte* playing of trombones. Why should they play with the voices? Is it not difficult enough to get clarity from a chorus, and why should the lovely choral sound be overlaid by these insistent brasses? Yes, the trombones are marked in the score, but it was not Mozart who put them there, nor did Süssmayr really want them blowing from beginning to end, but he was compelled to do so. It is the musicologist's duty to enlighten the conscientious conductor who cannot be expected to study church history in Vienna and go over the imperial household records; the documents are all there and they tell a story that cannot be gained from a purely musical study of the score. The empress, a shrew and thrifty housewife, decided that the three music establishments maintained by the court consumed too much money, so she summoned the imperial Kapellmeister, Gregorius Werner, and told him that henceforth he must operate within a fixed budget and it was up to him how to apportion this money. Werner could not very well make economies at the court opera, for that was the showcase, but at Saint Stephen's he could fall back on the practice followed by ordinary churches: first of all reduce the chorus. The employment of trombones as replacement choristers was the customary solution, since each one of the stentorian instruments was worth half a dozen human lungs. (Incidentally, things got so bad that at times Saint Stephen's did not even have an organist.) When Süssmayr completed the Requiem, he put in the trombones because Count Walsegg, for whom it was composed, had a musical establishment as modest as the usual church ensemble: an orchestra that was reasonably complete and a handful of singers. We are faced with an ancient emergency practice that does not apply to the contemporary scene, yet we let the trombones pointlessly trot along with the vocal parts all the time for want of a little knowledge of history.

Now let us turn to the youngest branch of our discipline, formerly known as comparative musicology but today labeled as ethnomusicology. It is rapidly growing—indeed, so rapidly that its devotees already manifest the symptoms of the movement colonial regimes end with: they want independence, independence from the parent country, musicology; they want a discipline of their very own. How they intend to use this independence I do not know, because the demand is being voiced just when it becomes ever clearer that ethnomusicology has an organic and generic connection with universal music history. (Incidentally, the so-called theorists are also clamoring for a republic of their own, complete with customs guards at the frontiers. But unless theory stands for figured-bass realization, which is *Fachlehre*, or for what you can read in *Die Reihe*, which is surrealist metaphysics, I do not see how theory can be removed from the very center of historical musicology.)

How far can ethnomusicology be said to have justification and meaning, what degree of scientific value? If we were to judge by the way it is practiced in many institutions of learning, it would seem no more than a pseudo-intellectual tool for that vague interracial brotherhood that any decent person would naturally espouse, and for the sake of which foundations are happy to support anyone with a tape recorder who is willing to go to Tibet or Kenya. Again, we are dealing with a nineteenth-century inheritance that was neither digested nor correctly interpreted. The problem of folk art was first discovered by the Romantic era, that is, at that stage of cultural development when the alienation from form first became a conscious experience. It is for this reason that there began to be an interest in foreign cultures; and folk art, even their own, appeared to the Romantics as such a foreign culture. Ever since, the sentimental attachment to folk art has remained strong and it has great appeal to the layman. But ethnomusicology is not for the dilettante, not for the musician who suddenly takes a liking to it; the subject is of great importance to all of us and requires vast training and expert knowledge. Primitive culture is our own contemporary, but there is a likelihood that this primitive culture may reflect certain aspects of earlier stages of the higher cultures so that in it we can read some of our own past where other documents fail, and it thus becomes a link in our general history. And yet non-Western musical styles are better understood by us with reference to the art of the West, as Wiora has so engagingly demonstrated. This is vaguely realized, yet the way the idea is put to work is altogether dilettantish. To transplant Japanese or Indonesian music wholesale and expect it to flourish in an alien culture is mere *chinoiserie* which ignores the first principles of mental cultivation. An example of the sad results is that the Hindu sitar, now mass-produced in this country, is used by noble savages in discotheques to play Western junk. It is precisely because the sociological background of folk and primitive music differs vastly from our own and represents an alien culture that we must proceed with the utmost care. The scrappy collection of random observations here and there throughout the world that usually makes up the content of college courses on non-Western music is worthless, misleading, and basically unscientific. Any structure based on surface observations of fleeting travelers, or on brief sojourns, often without the slightest linguistic and other preparation, is good only for a travelogue. Primitive cultures are necessarily self-centered and attached to an inherited body of customary practices and associated beliefs. The only approach to such groups is through a sympathetic acquaintance with all phases of their lore, which in turn calls for elaborate preparation and studies. There is, happily, an undeniable improvement in the quality of ethnomusicological work, for we now have a number of genuine scholars working in the field who realize that a thorough training in plain musicology, social and cultural anthropology, linguistics, history, and other related disciplines is indispensable to honest scholarly results.

The concerns of ethnomusicology are really identical with our own; they go to show that every culture has its own recognizable roots from which the complicated branches of its development have grown. Society as a growing organization, a quasi-biological organ, is differentiated into more and more homogeneous form, and art, being a social phenomenon, supplying society's esthetic needs, can similarly be considered a quasi-biological organism that grows from the unorganized to the organized. But even if we connect all loose ends and relate all individual factions, we still get only the contours of historical sequence unless we learn to view comprehensively. At this particular juncture there is a danger that we may overestimate the range of applicability of the scientific mind and underestimate the value of accumulated wisdom. The computer, which some hold will revolutionize not only our economic life but also our esthetics, our morals, and our arts, can be a trusted and invaluable helper. But permit it to become the master, and the scholar is reduced to mere spectator. Neither the height of the mountains nor the depth of the seas can be measured in millimeters—such precision is feasible only to the unpoetic. The musicologist should always remember that the true function of the scholar is the illumination of the particular in terms of the universal. And if he bogs down in his work and cannot seem to find his way out, he should be mindful of the paradox that, uniquely in the arts, ideas can transform facts.

DISCUSSION

WINTERNITZ: I have a comment involving pseudo-ethnomusicologists. Would anyone consider it practical to establish chairs in Tokyo, in Ceylon, in Sumatra, enabling Oriental scholars to teach, say, Gregorian chant within the framework of the history of *their* national art? I put this question to demonstrate the absurdity and the arrogance of attempting to apply the criteria of Occidental musicology to the musics of so-called "primitive" people.

MRS. KRADER: As an ethnomusicologist, I feel that ethnomusicology too frequently meets prejudice and derision from historical musicologists, even in this enlightened series of lectures. It is true that we have not yet achieved a very high level of scholarship. Ethnomusicology and anthropology try to look at the function of music in society, try to look at the other aspects of life in which music is a functioning part. And I am happy to note that the broader definition of musicology we have heard here today is very close to our way of thinking.

LANG: I agree with you. At Columbia I always wanted a center for research in European folk song—which is, after all, a part of our musical heritage. I admire Wiora's insistence that the music of primitive cultures must be treated as an integral part of universal music history. The musicologists don't accept this task; the ethnomusicologists want to do it all by themselves. That's where the problem lies. Yours is a new discipline, and you have just as many amateurs now as *we* had thirty years ago, and dilettantism is still rampant in conventional musicology.

BUSHLER: Professor Lang, in talking about ethnomusicology, it seemed that you were equating it with the study of folk or primitive art. But there are—especially in Asia—several old civilizations with sophisticated traditions of art and music.

LANG: Of course. The ancient high cultures—the Arabic, Hindu, and so on—have a tremendous body of art and literature. But how many of our "ethnos" are intersted in this? How many of them know Arabic? Bartók spent decades studying the central European folk heritage— he learned all the languages; it took him nearly a lifetime before something was produced.

BROOK: One point you made was that you can't do much in ethnomusicology without a fundamental musicological background. But on the other hand, in order to compare many different cultures you need to be able to study them in depth and from many aspects.

LANG: The fact is that most of us haven't accepted the interdisciplinary approach even within the confines of our own culture. We have some fine people, but very few. Howard Brown's *The French Chanson in the Contemporary Theatre* is one example and a remarkable achievement. We have to do much more of this kind of investigation before we are really equipped for Asia.

MISS SINGER: Professor Lang, you hold that "ethnomusicologists want to do it all by themselves." Wasn't it the musicologists themselves who dismissed ethnomusicology? Is that not why the Society for Ethnomusicology seceded from the American Musicological Society in the fifties?

LANG: I don't know who the persons would be who would dismiss ethnomusicology. Most musicologists are terribly uninformed about ethnomusicology and vice versa; they should get together.

MISS SINGER: There is no college in this country that requires a musicologist to know anything about ethnomusicology, but every ethnomusicologist must have a solid background in conventional musicology. This would indicate to me a contradiction on the part of many musicologists who say they wish to embrace ethnomusicology, but in fact do not, as the college curricula show.

LANG: Before a surgeon becomes a surgeon, he learns about medicine in general. In music, there is not even enough time for the general background. High-school graduates from good high schools can begin advanced college work in English or in history or in science without any difficulty. In music they usually know nothing. Therefore, in the undergraduate college we are obliged to teach them what they should have learned in high school. What kind of a college course is Elementary Musicianship? And in graduate school we have to teach them the elements of a scholarly approach to their subject. The biggest shortcoming that I find in our students today is not so much their lack of knowledge of the musicological discipline; it is the music itself that they don't know.

MRS. JORGENS: The topic for this series is "Perspectives and Lacunae in Musicological Research." I'm wondering if you have any ideas about neglected areas that might be open to fruitful research but have not been investigated because people don't have the background in other disciplines.

LANG: Areas? The whole of musicology viewed this way is in its infancy. Tke opera, for instance. There is the old question of Gluck's reforms; there is no work that really deals with it. Everybody attests that Gluck reformed the opera and it was never the same again. Now, I would like to see this "reform" in perspective. He threw out da capo aria? It came back again. The fact is that people have not studied where Calzabigi got his ideas. You can read any history of opera and come to conclusions that are not correct because extramusical factors are ignored.

SCHWARZ: In your lecture, you had some criticisms of so-called "introductions to musicology." Is it indiscreet to ask whether you are still thinking of writing a new one?

LANG: As soon as I retire I will, and it will be "revolutionary"—it will begin with music and end with music. It is unfortunate that we are content to be more scientists than artists. In my student days at the Sorbonne, one had to write very long papers. After a great deal of labor I submitted one to André Pirro: thirty pages of text and about fifty pages of mensural transcriptions. Pirro looked at it and said, "Pas beaucoup!" "But maître," I said, "there are fifty pages of transcriptions." He looked at me and said, "C'est du travail mécanique." I learned then and there that you cannot offer only the normal equipment that every scholar must have as evidence of scholarly achievement. But we very often do just that. That "travail mécanique"—I never forgot it.

WINTERNITZ. You said, justifiably, that we cannot forecast the future of music, because it is an art. Is it possible to forecast the future of musicology? Or can one hazard some prediction as to the direction it may take in the next few decades? Perhaps one can say that our rapidly growing scientific approach—dealing with all past theories, styles, technical structures, etc.—has created a sort of unbiased, unimpassioned catholicity. And can one say that this basically impersonal attitude, which is perhaps unique to our time and certainly did not exist in Ambros's day, has had an impact on the art itself, by fostering a sort of eclecticism and perhaps even a diminution of creative talent?

LANG: I agree with you that we are very prone to establish rigid categories and then stick to them; that's not good. What always amazes me is how Ambros, in his day, with so little original research material available, could have such a superbly comprehensive view. And you can still read Winterfeld's *Gabrieli und sein Zeitalter*, 150 years old and still a magnificent book! That breadth of thought is what is missing today. If you get too "scientific" you lose that, because musicology is not a science. Art history is not a science. It has only certain scientific aspects and methods. But when you come to the point of formulating esthetic opinions, it is an art. And this is what we are not teaching. That's the best answer I can give you.

MRS. FRIEDLAND: I have some reservations about your main thesis, although I thoroughly agree with it in principle. I have never seen a scholar of another discipline pick up a central idea and convincingly relate it to our field, or vice versa. This often happens when we try to relate our discipline to art history. I find myself in disagreement with what I feel are contrived parallels between say, architecture and music of the Baroque. The only connection that I myself experience—and can, therefore, teach —is between Impressionist visual art at the end of the nineteenth century and Impressionist music of that period; and, to some extent, a connection between the music and visual art of German Expressionism in the early twentieth century.

LANG: Yes, it's important not to try to make one-to-one comparisons; the Baroque church and the Baroque fugue are not directly comparable. On the other hand, look at a Bach score, at the handwriting—these wavy lines of his—and you know it's pure Baroque. Fine arts, music, literature, they are all related, but you cannot take them out separately and establish simplistic connections.

BROOK: In talking about musicology and related disciplines, I think we could all agree that it would be advantageous to have musicologists who are also specialists in sociology, in Javanese culture, in acoustics, in archeology, and so on. Given the expansion of knowledge in our day, is it not perhaps advisable for some students to spend a portion of their limited time studying a related discipline rather than a third or fourth foreign language? To put it another way, would not musicology be better served if *some* of its practitioners studied more acoustics, say, and less—or no— Latin?

LANG: Well, I don't see how you can do without Latin—one might translate Coussemaker all right, but then what do you do with the other 999 Latin treatises? It's just impossible to do medieval musicology without Latin. And I am not in favor of specializing before obtaining at least a nodding acquaintance with the whole field and being able to find your way anywhere in it.

SCHOTT: We seem to have great difficulty in measuring accomplishment that is not achieved in a prescribed, formalistic way. I think that this is regrettable particularly in humanistic studies. I wonder if it is essential for all future musicologists to take a course in medieval notation?

LANG: One often hears a student say something like this: "I'll never work in medieval music. Why should I take mensural notation? My field is Baroque opera." But you can't afford to limit yourself to your planned field of specialization. You cannot be sure how your own research interests may develop and you cannot anticipate what you may be called upon to teach.

BROOK: What do you think about the establishment of research institutes in musicology, with research teams that would not have to teach but could concentrate on scholarship?

LANG: Well, as yet musicology does not have such institutions here. Some fine arts departments do, and have produced art historians respected everywhere. In general, musicology in this country is individual, not institutional. In the *Musical Quarterly*, for example, one reads excellent articles by people who work in unheard-of state teachers' colleges—it's most surprising. I think that there is more talent for musicology in this country than anywhere else in the world. In the last thirty years we have accomplished what in Europe took well over a century. The musicological talent is remarkable, and I wish that this could be organized so that it had a more institutional and a more interdisciplinary basis.

American Musicology
and the Social Sciences

GILBERT CHASE

> Since music is created by people, the social sciences will probably
> give us the orientation necessary for a proper study of music.
>
> Norma McLeod[1]

*F*IRST, what are the social sciences? Edwin R. A. Selig-
man, editor-in-chief of the *Encyclopedia of the Social Sciences* (1930),[2]
described them as "those mental or cultural sciences which deal with the
activities of the individual as a member of a group." He listed them in a
hierarchy of three orders: (1) the social sciences proper (politics, economics, jurisprudence, history, anthropology, penology, sociology, and
social work); (2) the "semi-social sciences" (ethics, education, philosophy, and psychology); (3) "sciences with social implications" (biology,
geography, medicine, linguistics, and art). The inclusion of art in the
third category is justified on the grounds that "Artistic creation is dominated by values and these are, at least in part, of social origin."

Is history a social science? For enlightenment on this question we may
turn to the *International Encyclopedia of the Social Sciences*, published in
1968 and "designed to complement, not to supplant, its predecessor."[3] In

---

1. Norma McLeod, in *Yearbook (Anuario) of the Inter-American Institute for
Musical Research*, Tulane University, I (1965), 127.

2. *Encyclopedia of the Social Sciences*, ed. Edwin R. A. Seligman and Alvin John-
son (New York, 1930). Under the topical heading "Music," this includes an article on
Music and Musicology by Charles Seeger, and articles on Primitive, Oriental, and
Occidental Music written, respectively, by Helen H. Roberts, Henry Cowell, and
Seeger (II, 143–65).

3. *International Encyclopedia of the Social Sciences*, ed. David L. Sills (New York,
1968). This includes, under "Music," articles on Ethnomusicology by Alan P. Mer-

his Foreword, the editor, David L. Sills, observes that the social sciences differ in their scope from generation to generation," and furthermore, that "there are also within-generation differences: witness the continuing controversy over whether history should be considered as one of the social sciences or as a humanistic discipline." He goes on to say, "These controversies will not soon be stilled, nor need they be. In fact, it can be argued that a certain amount of controversy and diversity is beneficial." With this view I entirely concur.

It is no part of my purpose to attempt to decide whether history "belongs" to the humanities or to the social sciences—as though this were a territorial dispute between two rival powers. Such, indeed, it may very well be; but that is not our primary concern as musicologists. We should rather be concerned with the relationship of history to the social sciences,[4] and with the relationship of both to our own discipline. This is precisely the area that I propose to explore.

In view of Professor Sills' remark about the differing scope of the social sciences from generation to generation, we may ask if there are any important differences in scope between the two authoritative encyclopedias published, respectively, in 1930 and 1968. In the latter work, the editor does not offer any new classification of the social sciences, but simply makes the factual statement that, "The majority of the topical articles are devoted to the concepts, theories and methods of the following disciplines: Anthropology, Economics, Geography, History, Law, Political Science, Psychiatry, Psychology, Sociology, Statistics." The importance given to "History" will be perceived by the enumeration of the various sections (each by a different author) included under this topic: I, "The Philosophy of History"; II, "History and the Social Sciences"; III, "Ethnohistory"; IV, "Culture History"; V, "Social History"; VI, "Intellectual History"; VII, "Economic History"; VIII, "Business History." The first five are directly pertinent to our subject; and of these, I shall refer particularly to III, Ethnohistory, as being of special significance to American musicology.

The 1968 *Encyclopedia* also includes an important article on historiography—"an analysis of what historians do when they write history and discussions of traditions of history writing in different parts of the world..."—which I believe all students of historical musicology should read. I particularly recommend the section on "The Rhetoric of History," by J. H. Hexter, for the sake of such trenchant statements as this: "Many

---

riam and on Music and Society by Hans Engel (X, 562–75). The latter contains the rather astonishing statement: "Another musical profession is that of the musicologist who does his work in the quiet of the university." In an ivory tower?

4. In this connection, see also *The Social Sciences in Historical Studies*, Social Science Research Council, Bulletin 64, which includes "The Social Sciences and the Problem of Historical Synthesis," by T. C. Cochran (reprinted in *The Varieties of History*, ed. Fritz Stern [New York, 1957], pp. 347–59).

historians receive the doctoral degree, which is supposed to certify their competence in their craft, without ever being compelled to rewrite anything they have written after having it subjected to rigorous and systematic criticism." Would this not also apply to many musicologists? And, on a broader plane, the following: ". . . historians must subject historiography, the process of writing history, to an investigation far more intense than any that they have hitherto conducted." I believe that the social sciences can help the musicologist, as well as the general historian, to achieve this kind of intense scrutiny. What is needed is a diminuendo of rhetoric and a crescendo of insight.

There are indeed many fields and disciplines that can be fruitfully examined from the point of view of the social sciences. One of these is esthetics, the subject of an extensive article in the *International Encyclopedia of the Social Sciences*, covering the following aspects: the creation of art, the artist's personality, meaning and understanding in art, empirical studies of inherent meaning, universality or cultural relativity?, perception of art, effects of art on viewer or audience, research on likes and dislikes, and esthetic evaluation. These aspects bear on both the psychology and the sociology of music—long recognized as important subdivisions of musicology.

The association of musicology with the social sciences is by no means new, especially as regards psychology and sociology. A pioneer work in the latter field was written around 1911 by Max Weber, one of the most influential sociologists of the twentieth century. First published in 1921 as *Die rationalen und soziologischen Grundlagen der Musik*, this short but important work belatedly appeared in an English translation in 1958, with an excellent introductory essay on "Max Weber's Sociology of Music" by Don Martindale and Johannes Riedel. As they explain:

> Weber attempted to trace the influence of social factors on the very creative core and technical basis of music. In its broadest sense, Weber's thesis was that Western music has peculiar rational properties produced by social factors in Occidental development. Right or wrong, Weber's thesis assumes a relevance for the deepest levels of musical theory. It also forms a test case as to the values of sociological and musicological sciences for each other.[5]

Weber's treatise differs from many other sociological approaches to music in that it deals not only with the social context of music but also with its basic elements—harmony, melody, scale systems, tonality, polyvocality, temperament, instruments—in relation to the total cultural context, including technical, economic, and social interrelationships (for example, in his discussion of modern music and its instruments). In the words of Alphons Silbermann, Weber "showed sociological thinkers that even so

5. Max Weber, *The Rational and Social Foundations of Music* (Carbondale, Ill., 1958), p. xii.

apparently inward and subjective a realm of experience as that of music could be treated sociologically, i.e. according to his concept of rationality."[6]

Silbermann is the author of a comprehensive theoretical work on the sociology of music, published in 1957 as *Wovon lebt die Musik* (English translation, 1963), in which he discusses, among other topics, "Music and Social Science." His basic premise is briefly explained as follows:

> We may say that music is chiefly a social phenomenon: social because it is a human product, and because it is a form of communication between composer, interpreter and listener. If music can be said to have an effect upon the individual in his social life, then this very relationship makes it a social phenomenon, and that in many ways particularly noticeable in our own time. Firstly as a result of its mission: music is no longer restricted to a small circle of cultivated listeners, but has cast off intimacy and reserve in order to become popular. Secondly as a result of its constitution: the essence of music has become more and more social. While music was once the preserve of the individual, it now belong to the masses, a fact which Taine, following Spinoza, was one of the first to recognize.[7]

Silbermann sums up the sociology of music in terms of five functions:

> (1) General characterization of the structure and function of the socio-musical organization as a phenomenon which, for the satisfaction of its needs, stems from the interaction of the individual with the group.
> (2) The determination of the relationship of socio-musical organization to socio-cultural changes.
> (3) Structural analysis of socio-musical groups, from the view points of: the functional interdependence of their members, the behavior of the groups, the constitution and the effects of roles and norms established within the groups, and the exercise of controls.
> (4) A typology of groups, based upon their functions.
> (5) Practical foresight and planning of necessary alterations in the life of music.[8]

Among the social sciences, two great multi-disciplines vie for the attention and the allegiance of musicologists: sociology and anthropology. I shall now present the case for the latter. Professor Glen Haydon, in his standard *Introduction to Musicology* (1941), included anthropology among "the various auxiliary sciences which contribute to our knowledge and understanding of music." He characterized it as the science "which deals with music as an element in the sociocultural makeup of the various

6. Alphons Silbermann, *The Sociology of Music*, trans. Corbet Stewart (London, 1963), p. 57.

7. *Ibid.*, p. 38.

8. *Ibid.*, p. 62.

peoples of the world."[9] These statements appear in the section summarizing "The Systematic Orientation" in musicology. The other "auxiliary sciences" mentioned therein are (1) acoustics, (2) psychophysiology, (3) esthetics, and (4) pedagogy. Now, if we turn to the main body of the book, we will find chapters devoted to each of these "subdivisions of systematic musicology," under their previously designated names. Consequently, following the chapter on "Musical Pedagogy" one would naturally expect the next chapter to be entitled "Musical Anthropology." Instead, the "auxiliary science" listed as anthropology in the Introduction is transformed in Chapter VII into: "Comparative Musicology: Folk Music and Non-European Musical Systems." This semantic metamorphosis represents a retrogression to the terminology and the concept of Guido Adler, who in 1885 recognized *vergleichende Musikwissenschaft* as a division of musicology and defined its task as "the comparison of the musical works—especially the folk songs—of the various peoples of the earth for ethnographical purposes, and the classification of them according to their various forms."[10]

It is not at all strange that Haydon, who received his Ph.D. in Musicology at Vienna,[11] should have adhered to the terminology and the concepts established by Adler and his immediate followers—a terminology which, moreover, was still current when he wrote his *Introduction to Musicology*.[12] What is surprising is that he came to the brink of being possibly the first musicologist to propose the term "Musical Anthropology" as a branch of musicology. He actually did this, tentatively, in his introductory listing of "auxiliary sciences," and had he remained completely consistent in his chapter headings, Chapter VII of his book might have been titled somewhat as follows: "Musical Anthropology: the Sociocultural Study of the Music of the Various Peoples of the World." Had he been thus happily inspired, Haydon might have given American musicological studies a great forward impulse, anticipating by nearly a quarter

9. Glen Haydon, *Introduction to Musicology* (New York, 1941), p. 9.

10. Guido Adler, "Umfang, Methode und Ziel der Musikwissenschaft," *Vierteljahrsschrift für Musikwissenschaft*, I (1885), 14. (Cf. Haydon, *op. cit.*, p. 217.)

11. University of Vienna, 1932; but it should be remembered that long before this, in 1917–18, Haydon was a member of the class in musicology (an introduction) that Charles Seeger taught at the University of California in Berkeley—the first formal course on the subject given at an American university. Seeger says that Haydon was "the outstanding member" of the class (see Charles Seeger, Foreword, *Studies in Musicology: Essays in the History, Style, and Bibliography of Music in Memory of Glen Haydon*, ed. James Pruett [Chapel Hill, 1969], p. vii).

12. Jaap Kunst's pioneer work on ethnomusicology originally appeared under the title, *Musicologica* (Amsterdam, 1950). The second edition, revised and enlarged, was published as *Ethno-Musicology* (The Hague, 1955); a third edition appeared in 1959. See also Bruno Nettl, *Theory and Method in Ethnomusicology* (New York, 1964), with extensive bibliography.

PLATE 1

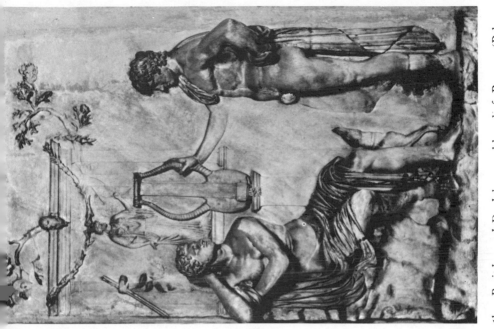

1b. *Pasiphæ and Dædalus*, marble relief, Roman (Palazzo Spada, Rome).

1a. *Apollo and Marsyas*, relief, ca. 1480.

PLATE 2

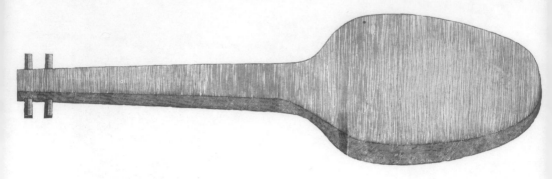

2a. "Egyptian lute," engraving from Burney, *General History of Music*.

2b. Detail from Utrecht Psalter, Psalm 108, ca. 800.

2c. Double-pipe instruments, tenth and eleventh centuries (left, Staatsbibliothek, Bamberg; middle and right, Bibliothèque Nationale, Paris).

PLATE 3

3a. Musicians playing double-reed pipes; illumination from the *Cantigas de Santa Maria*, thirteenth century.

3b. Simone Martini, frescoes in Assisi, ca. 1330, detail.

PLATE 4

4a.   Antonio del Pollaiuolo, bronze monument to Sixtus IV, St. Peter's, Rome: detail of Musica.

4b.   Giulio Romano, *Sacrifice of a Bull* (Palazzo del Tè, Mantua).

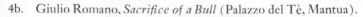

PLATE 5

5a. Peter Paul Rubens, Triumph of Silenus (National Gallery, Brussels).

b. Musicians playing hurdy-gurdies; illumination from the *Cantigas de Santa Maria*, thirteenth century.

PLATE 6

6a. Musician playing bagpipes; illumination from the *Cantigas de Santa Maria*, thirteenth century.

6b. Musicians playing a bagpipe and a hurdy-gurdy; marginal illustration from the Luttrell Psalter, ca. 1340. Lulworth Castle, Dorset (British Museum).

PLATE 7

7a. School of Giotto, *Glorification of St. Francis:* detail of fresco in Church of San Francesco al Prato, Pistoia.

7b. Antoine Watteau, *L'Accordée de village:* detail, showing musette and vielle played for dancing, ca. 1735.

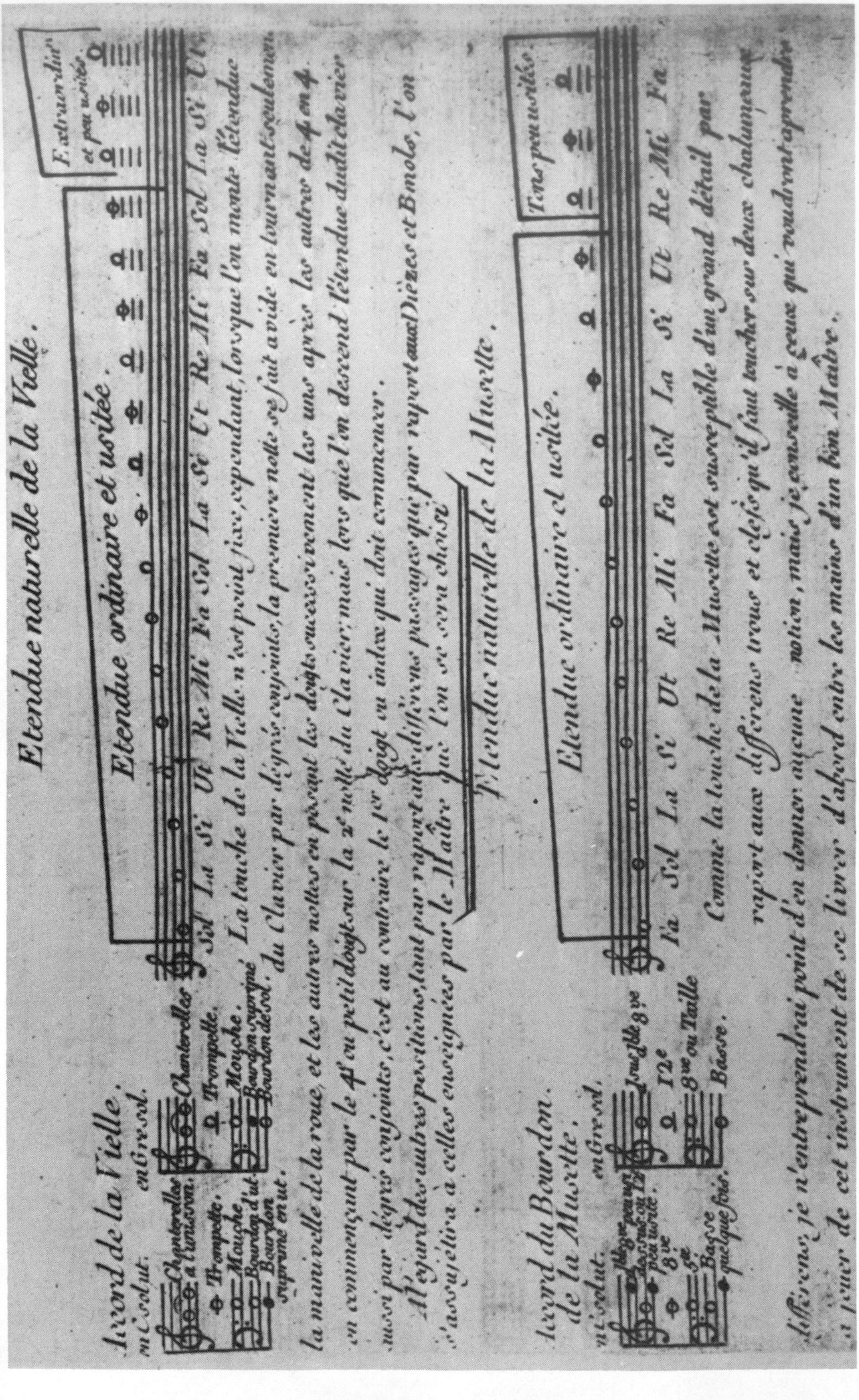

PLATE 8

8. Page from Bordet's *Méthode raisonnée*, Paris, ca. 1755.

PLATE 9

9a. Portal tympanum, Saint Pierre, Moissac, ca. 1120.

9b. Detail of Plate 9a.

PLATE 10

10a. Miniature from th
Saint-Sever MS (Biblio
thèque Nationale, Paris).

10b. Apocalyptic elde
holding a vielle; deta
from fresco in Saint-Ma
tin de Fenollar, Roussillo

PLATE 11

11b. Detail of Plate 11a.

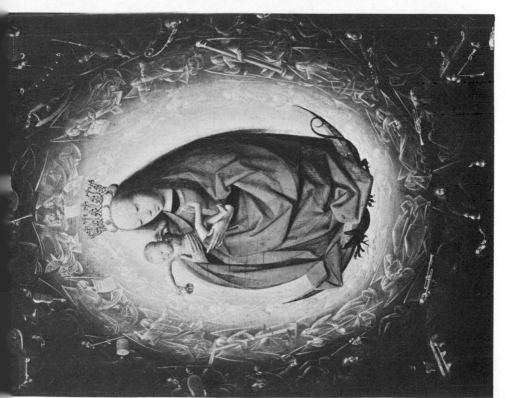

11a. Geertgen tot Sint Jans, *Virgin and Child* (Van Beuningen Museum, Rotterdam).

PLATE 12

12a. Illustration from a Florentine choirbook, ca. 1350 (Cleveland Museum of Art, J. H. Wade Collection).

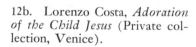

12b. Lorenzo Costa, *Adoration of the Child Jesus* (Private collection, Venice).

PLATE 13

13a. Euterpe, detail from Raphael, *Parnassus* (Stanza della Segnatura, Vatican).

13b. Sarcophagus of the Muses, detail (Museo Nazionale delle Terme, Rome).

PLATE 14

14a. · Harpsichord, Italian, ca. 1700.

14b. Harpsichord, Italian.

PLATE 15

15a. Reading from left to right: Wajang golèk figures from West Java (Ardjuna), Central Java (Amir Hamgah or Menak Djajengrana), and East Java (unidentified rough character).

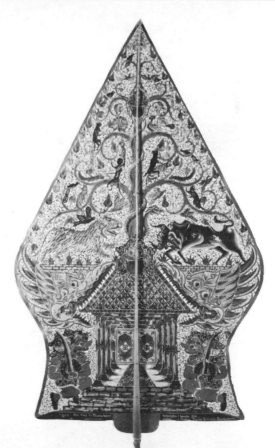

15b. The gunungan (literally, "mountain") used for opening the Javanese wajang kulit and for changes of scene.

PLATE 16

16a. The famous hero Bima. Balinese representation on the left, Javanese on the right.

16b. Performance of Javanese wajang kulit.

of a century the point of view so beautifully presented in Alan P. Merriam's recent book, *The Anthropology of Music*.

My purpose here is to establish at least a thread of continuity—and it is only a thread—between the thought of a highly respected traditional musicologist of the older generation and an influential spokesman for the anthropological approach in musicology. No one who knew Glen Haydon can doubt that he was genuinely interested in anthropology as one of the fundamental "sciences of man." In a footnote at the beginning of his chapter on "Comparative Musicology," he made the recommendation: "As a general background for this chapter read A. L. Kroeber, *Anthropology*, chapter I, 'Scope and Character of Anthropology,' Chapter IX, 'Parallels,' and chapters XIV and XVI, 'The Growth of Civilization.' " One suspects, sadly, that very few readers or students followed his advice.

If we accept the view formulated by another traditional musicologist of (approximately) Haydon's generation—namely, Jacques Hanschin's statement that the proper study of musicology is not music as an object in itself, but rather man insofar as he expresses himself musically[13]—then anthropology becomes by definition the social science that has the most relevance for musicology. To quote from the article on anthropology in the *International Encyclopedia of the Social Sciences*:

> Anthropology, in consonance with the etymology of its name, "study of man," is the most comprehensive of the academic disciplines dealing with mankind. This completeness is displayed in its concern with the full geographical and chronological sweep of human societies, the breadth of its topical interest, which embraces such diverse areas as language, social structure, aesthetic expression, and belief systems, and in the fact that it alone among the sciences of man treats him both in his physical and sociocultural aspects. [This point is particularly important for musicology, since music consists of both physical and sociocultural components.] In addition to these fundamental biological and social scientific components, anthropology has a significant humanistic aspect, as shown, for example, in its empathetic search for the bases of aesthetic valuation in the arts of alien people.[14]

13. *Report of the Fourth Congress of the International Musicological Society* (Basle, 1949), p. 10. The citation is from Handschin's paper on "Musicologie et musique," in which he begins by objecting to the notion that the aim of musicology "serait d'étudier les lois selon lesquelles la musique est formée." He bases his objection on the premise that ". . . la musique, telle qu'elle se présente dans la réalité, n'est pas un produit de la nature, mais une œuvre de l'homme; ce n'est pas un objet donné, mais . . . une chose faite et se faisant par l'homme." Hence, "La conclusion s'impose que le véritable objet de la musicologie n'est pas la musique en tant qu'un fait donné par lui-même, mais l'homme, pour autant qu'il s'exprime musicalement, ou alors c'est la musique considérée dans ses rapports avec l'homme."

14. *International Encyclopedia of the Social Sciences*, I, 305.

Anthropology, of course, has many branches. These embrace cultural, economic, physical, social, and applied anthropology, as well as archeology, ethnography, ethnology, and linguistics. All have some bearing on musicology, and several—notably cultural anthropology, archeology, ethnology, and linguistics—are of fundamental importance to our discipline. At least two—archeology and ethnology—are of particular significance to American musicology, i.e. for the sociocultural study of music in the New World. American musicology, indeed, may be said to have begun in the 1880s with the work of musical ethnologists such as J. Walter Fewkes, John C. Fillmore,[15] Benjamin Ives Gilman, and Theodore Baker, whose doctoral dissertation, *Über die Musik der nordamerikanischen Wilden* (Leipzig, 1882), was the first strictly musicological monograph published by an American.[16] Fewkes was the first to employ the phonograph for recording Indian tribal melodies, among the Pasamaquoddy of Maine[17] and the Pueblo Indians of the Southwest (the latter transcribed and analyzed by Gilman).[18]

David G. Mandelbaum, the author of the section on cultural anthropology in the *International Encyclopedia of the Social Sciences*, also emphasizes that:

> There is a fundamentally humanistic component in much of cultural anthropology. It is not only that the arts of a people are studied, and these at the humblest levels as well as at the pinnacles of aesthetic achievements. It is also ... that an anthropologist tries to see a culture from the inside as well as from the outside. As a participant observer, he experiences some part of the life he observes, and his personal experience finds expression in his studies, so that they entail humanistic insight as well as scientific objectivity.[19]

The basic task of cultural anthropology is "to study the similarities and differences in behavior among human groups, to depict the character of the various cultures and the processes of stability, change, and development that are characteristic to them...." Inject music into this cultural framework and you will have defined the task of the musicologist in its broadest aspect. The basic methods of cultural anthropology involve field study, comparative analysis, generation of theory, and an holistic view of cultural analysis. "This view assumes that one is free to study any kind of human behavior relevant to the problem being examined." In musicology, for example, it would be desirable to study not only the behavior of those who make music—as composers or performers—but also the behavior of

15. John C. Fillmore, *The Harmonic Structure of Indian Music* (New York, 1899).
16. Deplorably, this has never been reprinted or published in an English translation.
17. J. Walter Fewkes, "Contribution to Pasamaquoddy Folklore," *Journal of American Folklore*, III (Oct.-Dec., 1890).
18. *A Journal of American Archaeology and Ethnology*, I (1891).
19. *International Encyclopedia of the Social Sciences*, I, 315.

those who influence or control the makers of music, which in turn may cover the whole spectrum from political and economic to social and religious factors.

The cultural-anthropological approach to musicology is developed in a masterly fashion by Alan P. Merriam in his book, *The Anthropology of Music* (Evanston, Ill., 1964). The title of this work was well chosen, for had it been presented simply as another book on ethnomusicology it would have at once set up a mental barrier for those historical musicologists who believe that a solid line should be drawn between ethnomusicology and their own discipline. Merriam's title situates the subject in the comprehensive terrain of the study of mankind, that vast meeting ground of interrelated disciplines for sociocultural and humanistic studies which surely offers the firmest foundation for the intellectual concourse of history, musicology, and the social sciences.

In his Preface, Merriam states that his purpose is "to provide a theoretical framework for the study of music as human behavior; and to clarify the kinds of processes which derive from the anthropological, contribute to the musicological, and increase our knowledge of both conceived within the broad rubric of behavioral studies." Part One consists of three introductory chapters: "The Study of Ethnomusicology", "Toward a Theory of Ethnomusicology"; "Method and Technique." Part Two deals with "Concepts and Behavior"; Part Three with "Problems and Results." The last four chapters are especially pertinent to our topic: "Music as Symbolic Behavior"; "Aesthetics and the Interrelationship of the Arts"; "Music and Cultural History"; "Music and Culture Dynamics." It is in these chapters that the correlation of anthropological and humanistic interests stands out most clearly. The following paragraph from the chapter on "Music as Symbolic Behavior" further illuminates the holistic approach:

> Anthropologists have long stressed the concept of the integration of culture, for it is clear that no body of learned behavior can exist as a whole if its parts exist as separate entities. Thus there are interrelationships among the elements of culture, and it is usually assumed that changes in one element produce changes in other elements as well, that is, that culture is itself a system. Further, various psychological approaches to the problem of the integration of culture have indicated basic themes, configurations, sanctions, or patterns which tend to run through an entire culture bringing holistic unity to it. . . . We would expect, therefore, that any aspect of any given culture would reflect other parts of it, and this is certainly the case with music.[20]

The chapter on "Music and Culture History" makes passing reference to an historical technique that has particular relevance to our topic:

20. Alan P. Merriam, *The Anthropology of Music* (Evanston, Ill., 1964), p. 247.

Although our focus is not primarily on historic documentation from written records, this source of understanding cannot be overlooked. Nketia has made an ethnohistorical study of West African music, using written materials to assess the "factors which appear to have influenced the main lines of change in musical organisation." These he lists as the following: "political factors, such as those which governed or facilitated the creation and administration of states and empires, ... the pursuit of trade, and ... religion." Kirby has used historic documents to trace the xylophone in East Africa back to 1586. ...[21]

In the chapter on "Music and Cultural Dynamics," Merriam deals with the complex and challenging problem of culture change, observing that, "Change in music is barely understood, either as concerns music sound as a thing in itself or the conceptual behavioral activities which underlie that sound."[22] And he adds: "The study of the dynamics of music change is among the most potentially rewarding activities in ethnomusicology"—to which I would add: and of historical musicology as well, and of the two together.

Cultural anthropology generally considers change from two main points of view: that of internal change, originating within a culture (innovation); and that of external change, coming from outside the culture. The term usually applied to the latter process is acculturation, which was thus defined by a Committee of the Social Science Research Council: "Acculturation comprehends those phenomena which result when groups of individuals having different cultures come into continuous first-hand contact, with subsequent changes in the original cultural patterns of either or both groups."[23]

A particular type of acculturation, known as *syncretism*, has been particularly important in the Afro-American musical synthesis. According to Merriam, "... syncretism is specifically that process through which elements of two or more cultures are blended together; this involves both changes of value and of form."[24] Merriam also formulated the following hypothesis concerning the operative factors in syncretism: "When two human groups which are in sustained contact have a number of characteristics in common in a particular aspect of culture, exchange of ideas therein will be much more frequent than if the characteristics of those aspects differ markedly from one another."[25] This hypothesis would account for greater effectiveness of syncretism between African and European-American musical elements, as compared with syncretism involving Amerindian tribal music. A paradigmatic study of musical syn-

21. *Ibid.*, p. 279.
22. *Ibid.*, p. 319.
23. *American Anthropologist*, XXXVIII/1 (Jan.-March, 1936).
24. Merriam, *op. cit.*, p. 314.
25. *Ibid.*

cretism involving African and European musical traits is Richard A. Waterman's "African Influence on the Music of the Americas" (1952), which postulates "the presence of similar concepts of harmony and basic scale construction."[26]

The first major impetus for the systematic study of Afro-American music came from Melville J. Herskovits, a cultural anthropologist with a keen interest in music. In a paper on "Problem, Method and Theory in Afroamerican Studies" (1945), Herskovits not only defined the field in a masterly fashion but also related it to the concept of *ethnohistorical method*—the "combined ethnological and historical approach." What he has to say on the background, the development, and the potentialities of this method is highly pertinent to our subject:

> Strangely enough, the resources of ethnology and history have only recently been welded into a usable tool. Despite the fact that there are historical schools of ethnology and social historians, there has been but little contact across these disciplines. The "history" of these ethnological schools has been based on the reconstruction of events rather than on documentation; while the social historian, despite the illumination his writings have thrown on the development of the institutions with which he has dealt, has worked primarily as an historian and only rarely and recently has had recourse to the methods of the social sciences. . . . Experience is teaching us that the methods of these two disciplines, more than any other two, must be jointly called on if the varying situations that are to be studied comparatively in the Afroamerican field are to be analyzed with comprehension.[27]

The gist of my thesis is that the ethnohistorical method in musicology is equally valid—and, indeed, necessary—for the comprehensive study, not only of the Afro-American field, but of American music as a whole. The unique value of Afro-American musical studies is that this field, in the words of Herskovits, "derives its greatest significance from the fact that it so superbly documents the problems of cultural dynamics." Yet, despite this paradigmatic situation, nearly twenty-five years after Herskovits' paper was published, we still do not have a comprehensive history of Afro-American music.[28] If such a work is ever to be undertaken, either on a national, regional, or hemispheric basis, it can only result, in my

26. Richard Alan Waterman, *African Influence on the Music of the Americas*, in Sol Tax, ed., *Proceedings of the 29th International Congress of Americanists* (Chicago, 1952), II, 207–18.

27. Melville J. Herskovits, "Problem, Method and Theory in Afroamerican Studies," *Afroamerica*, I (1945), 10–11. This also contains an admirable explanation of the ethnohistorical method. Reprinted in Melville J. Herskovits, *The New World Negro: Selected Papers on Afroamerican Studies*, ed. Frances Herskovits (New York, 1969), pp. 43–61.

28. One segment of the field has been excellently covered by Charles Keil in *Urban Blues* (Chicago, 1966). [Since this paper was written, Eileen Southern's *The Music of Black Americans* (New York, 1971), has appeared—Eds.]

judgment, from application of the ethnohistorical method. Needless to say, such a comprehensive history would cut across all strata of musical expression, from the so-called primitive to the most highly developed art forms, embracing the entire spectrum in between, from traditional folk-song to the folk-pop-rock-soul-gospel-jazz synthesis of the 1960s.

Probably the vastness and formidable complexity of the field have deterred such an undertaking. But the basic deterrent to this or any other project of comparable scope is the underdeveloped state of American musical studies—undoubtedly the neglected orphan in the growing family of American studies. As far as the graduate schools are concerned, little or no encouragement is being given to the emergence of an American emphasis in musicology. This negative situation may be changing some-what, though very slowly, for the better. But the major breakthrough, I believe, will occur only through the fusion of the two disciplines—histori-cal musicology and ethnomusicology—under the more impelling impact of the social sciences, to which we must necessarily look for an under-standing of the forces that are even now changing the shape of society in the postindustrial era.

In the words of Charles Seeger:

> In comparison with the most admired scholarly disciplines of the twen-tieth century Western World, musicology has only tardily formed concepts of its total field, or universe, and of its lowest common denominator. And these concepts, such as they are, have not yet made a dent upon the "exces-sive historicism" still entrenched in academic fortresses. Meanwhile, the nat-ural and social sciences have advanced from positions of main reliance upon analytical techniques to bold syntheses of universal proportions, while in musicology, even mention of synthesis is not quite respectable.[29]

The social sciences have a major role in resolving the problem of histor-ical synthesis, without which we cannot advance beyond the compilation of facts, the editing of texts, or the production of self-contained mono-graphs. As E. H. Carr reminds us, ". . . what distinguishes the historian from the collector of historical facts is generalization"[30]—and generaliza-tion is par excellence the method of the social sciences. The historian Richard Hofstadter, discussing history and the social sciences, states that ". . . the historian's contact with the social sciences is clearly of more importance to the present generation of historians than it has been at any time in the past."[31] I believe the same could be said of the musicologist. In

29. Charles Seeger, "Factorial Analysis of the Song as an Approach to the Forma-tion of a Unitary Field Theory for Musicology," *Journal of the International Folk Music Council*, XX (1966), 33–39.

30. Edward Hallett Carr, *What Is History?* (New York, 1962), p. 82.

31. Richard Hofstadter, "History of the Social Sciences," in *The Varieties of His-tory*, ed. Fritz Stern (New York, 1957), p. 360.

support of this opinion I would cite the Princeton volume on musicology in the United States (1963),[32] which, although presented as a survey of humanistic scholarship, is nevertheless strongly oriented toward an anthropological approach to musicology. One of the three essays that make up the volume, "Music, the Unknown," by Mantle Hood, develops with great force and cogency the viewpoint of ethnomusicology. As Hood points out: "Art history and criticism are based on the assumption of a world of art. Music history and criticism have remained insular in their promulgation of Western theories and tradition. Any kind of insularity is hardly compatible with the demands of the last half of the twentieth century."[33] He sums up the three basic and interdependent objectives of musicological study as follows:

(1) the function of music as an aspect of the behavior of man in his society;

(2) characteristic musical style identified in its own terms and viewed in relation to society; and

(3) the intrinsic value of individual pieces of music viewed in relation to the world of music.[34]

Frank Ll. Harrison, in his essay on "American Musicology and the European Tradition," endorses Handschin's view that the aim of musicology is the study of men in society insofar as they express themselves through the medium of music. Harrison then develops the implications of this approach:

> One corollary of this shift in aim would be a widening of the range of musicological interest. For example, it has been considered "respectable" for a musicologist to be interested in the jongleurs and minstrels of the Middle Ages but not in modern music-hall and popular music. Similarly, he can properly take notice of the musical devotions of the sixteenth century Italian layman as expressed in the simple *laude* written especially for him, but not of the evangelical hymns of the nineteenth century churchgoer. . . . If the subject of musical history is the history of musical man in society, then its province must include the musician and his audience at all levels of the social order. . . . With the further emphasis on the history of music as an aspect of the history of man in society, the traditional enterprises of musicology can no longer be pursued *in vacuo*. For their ultimate meaning and value rest on their contribution to restoring silent music to the state of being once more a medium of human communication. . . . Looked at in this way, it is the function of all musicology to be in fact ethnomusicology, that is, to take its range of research to include material that is termed "sociological." This view would still assume the basic importance of analytical and

32. Frank Ll. Harrison, Mantle Hood, Claude V. Palisca, *Musicology*, Princeton Studies in Humanistic Scholarship in America (Englewood Cliffs, N.J., 1963).
33. *Ibid.*, p. 282.
34. *Ibid.*, p. 264.

stylistic studies, but would look further than has been customary in investigating the various aspects of music as an expression of an individual in his social context.[35]

The third contributor to the Princeton volume, Claude V. Palisca, discussing "The Scope of American Musicology," states that, "The musicologist is concerned with music that exists, whether as an oral or a written tradition, and with everything that can shed light on its human context."[36] As a corollary, "the musicologist must scrutinize poor works as well as masterpieces, for the process of history is revealed in the humble as well as in the great."[37] When it comes to American musical studies, Palisca has this to say:

> Very few American musicologists can have an easy conscience about the subject of American music, for not many of them have even a passing acquaintance with the personalities and facts of our national musical history. This is a subject that has only a negligible role in graduate study and is treated as a serious research specialty by only a handful of American scholars, few of them in teaching positions.[38]

An unhappy situation, indeed. But, says Palisca, "A healthy trend has been observable recently toward closing the gap between American music studies and the academic world." I wish that I myself could be more optimistic about this allegedly "healthy" trend. It looks to me more like the shackling of American musical studies in the grip of academic historicism, bent on piling up dissertations and monographs without any adequate conceptual or theoretical framework. Graduate students and research scholars are supposed to hustle up new facts; yet, as Hofstadter observes, "many a monograph . . . leaves its readers, and perhaps even its author, with misgivings as to whether that part of it which is new is truly significant."[39] And he sums up the weakness of the monographic method in these words: "Monographs are useful, but when put together they do not yield comprehensive answers to the comprehensive questions. No synthesis—at least no 'scientific' and commonly acceptable synthesis—can be reached through sheer addition."[40] That is well and truly said.

Genuine history depends not on the accumulation of facts per se, but on seeking "comprehensive answers to the comprehensive questions." It is my contention that the social sciences offer the best material for formulating such questions and for finding the answers.

35. *Ibid.*, pp. 79–80.
36. *Ibid.*, p. 116.
37. *Ibid.*, p. 120.
38. *Ibid.*, p. 210.
39. Hofstadter, *op. cit.*, p. 359.
40. *Ibid.*, p. 369.

Specifically, in the confluence of anthropology, history, and musicology I see the most propitious conditions for further advances in the study of man as music maker and music user.[41] To quote Sol Tax, "General anthropology today not only unites scholars of all the disciplines which converge to study mankind; it also is the most world-wide of sciences, uniting scholars of mankind wherever they are. . . . The first attraction of anthropology is the very breadth of our subject—the study of mankind as a whole—which brings and holds us together, and gives us the special character which we then pass on. . . . It is not surprising that anthropology should characteristically form a society of scholars open to new techniques, tools, ideas, and men. . . . We have freely adopted, reinforced, and made our own whatever has appeared useful to our varied problems."[42]

This is precisely the sort of open-mindedness and universality that I am advocating for musicology. A further analogy may be made with respect to history and the social sciences, as expressed by Robert F. Berkhofer, Jr., in the Preface to his recent book, *A Behavioral Approach to Historical Analysis*:

> The fundamental assumptions of my essay are that the subject of the historian concerns the past of man, that man individually and collectively is complex; that to study man in sufficient complexity requires social science concepts and theory; that man can only be studied as an analytical entity through some conceptual framework; and that once a knowledge of human behavior is gained, then other aspects of historiography fall into their proper sphere. History is its own discipline, but it needs to be enriched by borrowing from other disciplines for its own purpose.[43]

Substitute "musicology" for "history" in the foregoing quotation and you will have a succinct restatement of my main thesis.

As early as the 1930s, the American Historical Association sponsored a series of meetings and discussions to explore "The Cultural Approach to History." The immediate result was a pioneer volume of that title, edited by Caroline F. Ware (New York, 1940), which remains a basic work for anyone interested in this subject. Particularly pertinent is Part Six:

41. This phrase is borrowed from Charles Seeger, "Preface to the Description of a Music," in *Report of the Fifth Congress of the International Society of Musical Research, Utrecht, 1952* (The Hague, 1953), p. 366.

42. Sol Tax, ed., *Horizons of Anthropology* (Chicago, 1964), pp. 248, 251, 252.

43. Robert F. Berkhofer, Jr., *A Behavorial Approach to Historical Analysis* (New York, 1969). See also Max Gluckman, ed., *Closed Systems and Open Minds: The Limits of Naivety in Social Anthropology* (Chicago, 1964), which deals with the problems of isolating a field of study. The authors deal, both theoretically and empirically, with "some of the problems which the anthropologist may meet in trying to isolate one aspect of reality for his own analysis from the aspects of reality studied by other disciplines, or in trying to close off his own field of analysis from the rest of reality."

"Sources and Materials for the Study of Cultural History," including "Folklore as a Neglected Source of Social History," by B. A. Botkin, and "Folk Music as a Source of History," by Charles Seeger. Botkin makes a plea for ". . . history as produced by the collaboration of the folklorist and the historian with each other and with the folk; a history of the whole people, in which the folk are seen as people and as human beings, and people are seen in their folk relationships, among others; a history, also, in which the people are the historians as well as the history, telling their own story in their own words. . . ."[44] If such a "collective history" of American music were ever to be written, it would be a truly living document, not merely an accumulation of facts in print between two covers. It would, in effect, be a "Musical History of the American People."

Charles Seeger, in his paper, calls for acceptance by musicologists of the following concepts: (1) a concept of the field of music as a whole; (2) a concept of music as a social and cultural function; (3) utilization by musicologists of current concepts of total culture; (4) understanding of the relationships between written and unwritten, and between verbal and non-verbal source material.[45] This four-point program is as valid today as it was thirty years ago.

As regards the fourth point, there was a very stimulating and highly relevant discussion in connection with the session on "The Contribution of Ethnomusicology to Historical Musicology," at the Eighth Congress of the International Musicological Society (New York, 1961), of which Paul Collaer was chairman, with papers by André Schaeffner and Nils Schiorring. The former makes this challenging statement: "The principal contribution of ethnomusicology is to place in doubt that the evolution of our own [Western] music really occurred as described by historians relying on the testimony of theoreticians or on the support solely of written documents. Apart from the considerable gap that may always exist between the formulated principles and the practice (a situation confirmed by the ethnologist in the field), many phenomena have not been mentioned, either because they appeared only in popular usage, or, on the contrary, because they were so commonplace that they were not noticed."[46]

Schaeffner also observes that "the task of the ethnologist is not so very different from that of the historian."[47] This is so because "A society is never without a past, any more than it presents itself to the observer as a uniform mass." This relates to the statement by Bernard S. Cohn, "In his use of written documents, the ethnohistorian initially has the same prob-

44. Caroline F. Ware, ed., *The Cultural Approach to History* (New York, 1940), p. 308.
45. *Ibid.*, p. 318.
46. *Report of the Eighth Congress of the International Musicological Society, New York, 1961* (Kassel, 1961), I, 379.
47. *Ibid.*, p. 378.

lem and uses the same techniques as conventional historians."[48] The main difficulty appears to be that, "The ethnohistorian who has been trained as an anthropologist and has carried out field work is often highly frustrated when he has to depend on documents."[49] Here the tables are neatly turned, for with the historian or historical musicologist the situation is reversed: he deplores the lack or scarcity of documents in field work. As Dr. Otto Kinkeldey remarked in the above-mentioned session of the IMS Congress, "Help for the musicologist may indeed come from the ethnomusicologist; but the historical musicologist cannot but be aware that in entering the ethnomusicological field he advances toward fields where there are no documents and no monuments."[50]

Both of these views reflect an oversimplification and an incomplete statement of the problem. What needs to be corrected is the assumption, on the one hand, that written documentation is the only valid source for historical research; and on the other hand, that ethnology, being concerned with the description of human groups in a field situation, does not need to rely on written documentation. Both of these assumptions have been challenged—and I think we may say, refuted—by recent trends in the social sciences and in historiography. There is general recognition that:

> Even in the most rigid synchronic ethnographic study, the ethnographer must deal with the dimension of time. . . . Invariably the field ethnographer asks questions about the past; he must confront the question of norms and changing norms, accidental social arrangements, and enduring aspects of the social structure. . . . Through historical study the anthropologist may identify changes within the system which are the result of flux, accident, or cyclical sequences and those which are due to structural realignments. . . . If we want to account for change, then historical methods for studying a society—primitive, peasant, or industrial—are the prerequisite for the development of adequate theories.[51]

Thus the historian and the cultural anthropologist have this fundamental point in common: they must both ask questions about the past; and in making these questions and the answers as comprehensive as possible, each needs to draw upon the methods and concepts of the other. The dimension of time is the common denominator.

The reader, I fear, must be asking himself why the qualifying term "American" was included in the title of this lecture, since I appear to be addressing myself almost entirely to general principles and theoretical

48. *International Encyclopedia of the Social Sciences*, VI, 443.
49. *Ibid.*
50. In *Report of the Eighth Congress of the International Musicological Society*, II, 154.
51. *International Encyclopedia of the Social Sciences*, VI, 445.

approaches applicable to any area of musicology. The fact is, I was originally invited to lecture on research opportunities in American music. It
seemed to me, however, that in a field so neglected by musicologists, so
little understood by the majority of music scholars, and so often deni-
grated or ignored in academic circles, I would be missing the most important opportunity of all if I did not take advantage of this occasion to present the subject within a theoretical and conceptual framework that
would not merely delineate the work to be done in American musical
studies, but that would also, and mainly, emphasize the broadening of
horizons, the grasp of fundamental problems, and the necessity for interdisciplinary approaches. Nevertheless, I allowed the term "American" to
stand in the title for various reasons. First, because I am, in the scholarly
sense, an "Americanist," concerned with both general principles and specific problems of music history in the Americas. Secondly, because I
believe that the concept of area studies can be very fruitful in the future
development of American musicology, particularly in stimulating the
interdisciplinary approach that forms the basis of all area studies. And
thirdly, because I believe that American musicology, emulating the universality of the social sciences, and of anthropology in particular, could
lead the way toward a new sociocultural-humanistic concept of musicology within the general context of the sciences of man.

Perhaps one aspect of this sociocultural-humanistic synthesis might be
described as "anthropological historicism"—a term borrowed from the
contemporary English historian Sir Isaiah Berlin. I think it worthwhile to
quote the passage, from *A Note on Vico's Concept of Knowledge*, in
which he used the term:

> His [Vico's] boldest contribution, the concept of "philology", anthropolog-
> ical historicism, the notion that there can be a science of mind which is the
> history of its development, the realization that ideas evolve, that knowledge
> is not a static network of eternal, universal, clear truths, either Platonic or
> Cartesian, *but a social process* [my emphasis], that this process is traceable
> through (indeed, is in a sense identical with) the evolution of symbols—
> words, gestures, pictures [music also], and their altering patterns, functions,
> structures and uses—this transforming vision [is] one of the greatest discov-
> eries in the history of thought. . . .[52]

Whether we work within or without the area of American studies,
whether primarily in historical, systematic, comparative, or ethnic musicology, it is this "transforming vision" that we need in order to make of
our discipline a true science of man. If we must have historicism in our
graduate schools, let it be "anthropological historicism," not bound by
"the narrowing educational influence of the Cartesian insistence on the
deductive method as the sole path to knowledge." Let us, in the words of

52. In *New York Review of Books*, XII/8 (April 24, 1969).

Isaiah Berlin again, give their due "to other faculties and methods of mental development, especially the imagination."

In our preoccupation with method we have neglected theory. Yet for any scientific study to progress and be fruitful, method should be subordinate to theory. As Gunnar Myrdal reminds us, "Facts come to mean something only as ascertained and organized in the framework of a theory."[53] And he adds, "A non-theoretical approach is, in strict logic, unthinkable." Yet how many graduate students have been permitted—perhaps even encouraged—to take this "unthinkable approach," to get on with their research in the empirical investigation of facts. The difficulty resides in the truth that "the formulation of theories always involves an imaginative leap and is never arrived at by a simple process of induction from the empirical data."[54] It is this "imaginative leap" that our graduate departments tend to regard with distrust. Making a distinction between theory and knowledge, they fail to recognize that, "Theory is knowledge organized so that facts are subsumed under general principles."[55]

The generation of theory is one of the strongest achievements of the social sciences.[56] Conversely, this is the weakest aspect of musicology. The most significant contributions in this area—at least during the past thirty years or so—have been those of Charles Seeger.[57] Because his theories are grounded in both historical and systematic musicology as well as in ethnomusicology, they provide a fertile terrain for the development of "a unified field theory" for musicology.

In conclusion, I maintain that the term musicology should have the same sort of breadth, scope, and depth that the term anthropology has in the social sciences. Historical, systematic, and comparative musicology should be major subdivisions without geographical, chronological, or cultural restrictions. I believe that the term "comparative musicology" is still useful and should be revived; not in the sense in which it was originally used—the study of non-European musical cultures—but as it is used in linguistics, referring to the study of changes in language. As stated by

53. Gunnar Myrdal, *Rich Lands and Poor Lands* (New York, 1957), p. 164.

54. Robert A. Manners and David Kaplan, eds., *Theory in Anthropology* (Chicago, 1968), p. 7.

55. *Ibid.*, p. 11.

56. This does not mean that all social-science theory is equally valid or well conceived (cf. Robert Brown, *Explanation in Social Science* [Chicago, 1963], Ch. XI, "Theories"). But a great deal of important work has been done in this area, and all social scientists recognize its fundamental necessity. In addition to Manners and Kaplan, *Theory in Anthropology* (see n. 54 above), consult Walter L. Wallace, ed., *Sociological Theory* (Chicago, 1969); and Walter Buckley, ed., *Modern Research Systems for the Behavioral Scientist* (Chicago, 1968). See also Patrick Gardner, ed., *Theories of History* (New York, 1959).

57. See the bibliography of Seeger's writings in *Yearbook of the Inter-American Institute for Musical Research*, II (1966), 37–41. Seeger's *Selected Papers* on theory of musicology are being published by the University of California Press.

Dwight Bolinger, "The job of the comparative linguist is to measure and codify change. This he does by comparing a language with its earlier stages and with other languages or dialects."[58] This is actually a diachronic or historical discipline, since all change occurs in time.

The term "ethnomusicology" seems rather restrictive in the context of its wide geographical, temporal, and cultural scope. It may be entirely appropriate, for example, to the musical study of an American Indian tribal culture. But why should it be applied to the study of Japanese court music or to the art music of India? I agree in principle with Seeger's statement that we should extend "the techniques of ethnomusicology to the music of the Occident—its fine, popular, and folk arts, regarded as one integrated unit."[59] I favor the *idea* of an "ethnomusicology" of Western music; but I do not favor the terminology: it is too narrow and inappropriate for the intended purpose (conversely, it is good and useful for other purposes). What we need is a term of larger scope that will contain the same idea—namely, the sociocultural approach to musicology. For this I propose the term "cultural musicology"—by analogy with "cultural anthropology."

Paraphrasing the previously quoted description of the task of cultural anthropology (*vide supra*, p. 208), we might describe the task of cultural musicology as being "to study the similarities and differences in musical behavior among human groups, to depict the character of the various musical cultures of the world and the processes of stability, change, and development that are characteristic to them."[60]

Whether or not this proposed terminology is adopted, I believe that the concept it represents is not only valid but essential if musicology is to take its rightful place among the sciences of man.

DISCUSSION

CHASE: Let us restrict the discussion to the specifically American aspect of our topic, and in a general way to the context of the social sciences—at least to what might be called a "socio-cultural" approach as distinct from the historical-systematic approach of traditional musicology. For example, the pioneer work of Oscar Sonneck in early American music is paradigmatic for the bio-bibliographic method that is standard practice in histori-

58. Dwight Bolinger, *Aspects of Language* (New York, 1968), p. 84.
59. In *Report of the Eighth Congress of the International Musicological Society*, II, 153.
60. In an ideal situation, this would simply be a description of the task of musicology *tout court—without any qualifier*. But we are far from an ideal situation; and as long as the term "musicology" has in practice been misappropriated to designate a very narrow range of study, we must in the interim have recourse to modifiers.

cal musicology, and his great contribution was to apply this method to a hitherto neglected area—doing this, moreover, with rigorous standards of scholarly research. At the same time, if one reads some of Sonneck's miscellaneous essays very carefully—for instance, "The History of Music in America"—one finds glimpses of a much broader vista.[61] He contested the narrow view of early American music taken by those writers who saw it all through "a New England church window." And he remarked that if the historian were limited to the esthetic factor, then the history of American music would be a sorry thing indeed. This is, for me, a very important statement. It is the historian's task to study and interpret what *was*—the values and events and cultural configurations of a given time and place —not what he regards as valuable or beautiful or edifying in terms of his own cultural time-space niche. Sonneck's commitment to the "raw data" of American music history, rather than to an *a priori* esthetic ideal, is what makes him a truly significant pioneer in American musicology and justifies our placing him within the context of a socio-cultural approach.

My own work in American music owes its initial impetus to the example of Oscar Sonneck in history and the influence of Charles Seeger in theory. The desideratum, as I saw it, was a synthesis between the bio-bibliographical and the socio-cultural approaches.

BROOK: Why was Sonneck's research not immediately followed up? Was it because early American music history was not regarded as an important topic in terms of the predominant norms of academic musicology?

CHASE: Yes. There was a considerable time lag before American music studies became really "respectable" in an academic context. That is why so much of the first "follow-up" work was done outside graduate departments or schools—for example, by H. Earle Johnson[62] and Irving Lowens.[63] Later, Sonneck's bibliographical work was extended chronologically by Richard J. Wolfe in his excellent three-volume work, *Secular Music in America, 1801–1825.*[64]

There were also people who were attracted to the study of American music from other fields of specialization. For instance, George Pullen Jackson, to whom I am much indebted for the shaping of *America's Music.* He was a southerner who became a professor of German at Vanderbilt University and who developed a life-long enthusiasm for the religious group-singing of the rural "shape-note" tradition. His research in the history, the morphology, and the socio-cultural context of the "spirit-

61. Oscar Sonneck, *Miscellaneous Studies in the History of Music* (New York, 1921), includes "The History of Music in America."
62. H. Earle Johnson, *Musical Interludes in Boston, 1795–1830* (New York, 1943).
63. Irving Lowens, *Music and Musicians in Early America* (New York, 1964).
64. Richard J. Wolfe, *Secular Music in America, 1801–1825,* 3 vols. (New York, 1964).

uals"—both white and Negro—is embodied in half-a-dozen books containing hundreds of tunes.[65] It is true that he was not entirely objective, but he gave another dimension to the historiography of American music.

The first serious study of Afro-American music was written by a music critic, H. E. Krehbiel: *Afro-American Folksongs: A Study in Racial and National Music*.[66] The first comprehensive history of jazz was written by a professor of English literature specializing in Chaucer: I refer to *The Story of Jazz* by Marshall Stearns.[67] The most recent and musically the most literate history of jazz was written by a composer: *Early Jazz, Its Roots and Musical Development*, by Gunther Schuller.[68]

BROOK: Would you say that topics such as jazz go by default into the hands of nonmusicologists?

CHASE: By and large, yes. Some musicologists have begun to take jazz seriously—perhaps too seriously. But generally within a rather narrow context; jazz really demands a broad and deep socio-cultural context—an application of the ethnohistorical method. Traditional musicologists simply do not have the necessary tools—conceptually, analytically, methodologically—to cope with the history of jazz.

I'd like to mention two other valuable contributions to American music studies made by nonspecialists—that is, eminent academic musicologists who momentarily turned aside from their main specializations in order to deal with a particular aspect of American music that attracted them. I refer to J. Murray Barbour, who wrote the first scholarly analytical study on the music of William Billings; and to Hans Nathan, author of a very important work, *Dan Emmett and the Rise of Early Negro Minstrelsy*[69] —an example of what I would call ethnohistorical musicology.

BROOK: Much of the documentation on Emmett had been known to other people before, but no one undertook to explore it systematically— apparently because it was not considered to be a significant field for musicology.

CHASE: That reminds me of my favorite definition of art: "Art is what-

65. George Pullen Jackson, *White Spirituals in the Southern Uplands: The Story of the Fasola Folk, Their Songs, Singing, & Buckwheat Notes* (Chapel Hill, N.C., 1933); *Spiritual Folk-Songs of Early America: Two Hundred & Fifty Tunes & Texts with an Introduction & Notes* (New York, 1937); *Down East Spirituals and Others* (New York, 1943); *White and Negro Spirituals* (New York, 1944); *The Story of the Sacred Harp* (Nashville, 1944); *Another Sheaf of White Spirituals* (Gainesville, Fla., 1952).

66. H. E. Krehbiel, *Afro-American Folksongs: A Study in Racial and National Music* (New York, 1914).

67. Marshall Stearns, *The Story of Jazz* (New York, 1956).

68. Gunther Schuller, *Early Jazz, Its Roots and Musical Development* (New York, 1968).

69. Hans Nathan, *Dan Emmett and the Rise of Early Negro Minstrelsy* (Norman, Okla., 1962).

ever artists do as art." And what the musicologist makes important by his work is *ipso facto* important as musicology. Musicology is not a value system but a *methodology*—like all the other sciences of man. Its aim is—or should be—to discover *relationships* through research and/or field work combined with analysis.

MRS. KIRK: What should be done to spur trained musicologists to work in American music studies? Would you suggest that university music departments introduce courses in ethnomusicology?

CHASE: I believe there *is* a trend toward offering more undergraduate courses with an ethnological slant, such as "Non-Western Music" or "Musics of the World." This is a step in the right direction. However, I think that young people in general are more open to various kinds of music than are their elders. Contemporary rock, for example is a *very* eclectic type of music. What other kind of music gives comparable importance to the guitar, the harpsichord, and the sitar? The danger, I think, lies in another direction: when the potential musicologist gets into a restrictive graduate program that prescribes rigid norms as to what is "acceptable."

Here I think the strongest pressures for change will come from ethnomusicology—from scholars with a background in anthropology who have done field work among "primitive" peoples or minority groups, and who have not been indoctrinated with the notion that scholarly prestige depends on doing research in early European art music in the libraries of Florence, Rome, Vienna, or Paris. A fruitful situation can be created, I believe, by really effective interdisciplinary work between musical anthropologists and historical musicologists. The desideratum is for every graduate student in historical musicology to have some training in ethnomusicology, and *vice versa*.

We do not need to "recruit" students for American music studies; we need only encourage them—i.e. the potentially interested ones—by offering first of all an example of personal dedication, and second of all a propitious intellectual and academic atmosphere in which these studies are regarded, not as marginal, but as central to the purpose and scope of contemporary musicology.

The number of doctoral dissertations and masters' theses in American music is steadily increasing. The main problem, as I see it, is not so much to "spur" the graduate student to undertake more theses and dissertations in American music, but rather to broaden the scope of such studies to include wider segments of American musical culture within the dynamic methodology of the social sciences, particularly cultural (or social) anthropology and ethnomusicology.

VAN SOLKEMA: Mr. Chase, in your lecture you announced that you were reserving the topic of art music for our seminar discussion, but you have said very little about this so far. In view of the fact that so many people here are involved (for the present, at least) almost exclusively with art music, I think this is one of the most important topics we could get to at this point.

CHASE: Very few of us really know what to do with art music in a socio-cultural context—which I take to be the conceptual framework of this seminar (in relation to my lecture). Charles Seeger has stated that he would like to see the techniques of ethnomusicology extended to include the art music as well as the folk and popular music of the West.[70] I agree with this in principle, but thus far—at least in the domain of art music—no one has shown us how this is to be done in actual practice. Alan P. Merriam offers some valuable guidelines in his book, *The Anthropology of Music.*[71] But Seeger postulates that his "extension" of ethnomusicology should be effected "under the guidance of European historical musicology," and as yet I can perceive only the dim outlines of any such "guidance." There is some encouragement to be found in the approach taken by the authors of the Princeton volume on *Musicology.*[72] I particularly like Claude Palisca's view that music should be studied *because it exists*, not because it is "good" or "bad."[73] None of man's cultural products needs to "justify" its existence in order to become "worthy" of scholarly attention. American art music of the nineteenth century may not be "great," but there is no doubt that it existed. If we ask ourselves, Why?—that is a perfectly legitimate historical question.

We are only on the threshold of a "total" musicology as a comprehensive science of man. Any further advance, I am convinced, will have to come through the concerted and integrated efforts of humanists and social scientists.

VAN SOLKEMA: Leaving aside the question of American art music of the nineteenth century, what about that of the twentieth century, which is a different matter. Surely we have had important American composers of our time. Are you interested, for example, in composers like Varèse and Carter?

CHASE: Yes, of course. But this is primarily an esthetic and critical interest. As a music historian, I see no reason why I should be any more interested in them than in Billings or Law or Fry or Gottschalk or Paine. As a matter of fact, if you look at a list of theses and dissertations in American music, I think you will find that many composers whom you—or Joseph Kerman—would regard as "unimportant" (for instance, James Hewitt,

70. Charles Seeger, in *Report of the Eighth Congress of the International Musicological Society, New York, 1961* (Kassel, 1961).

71. Alan P. Merriam, *The Anthropology of Music* (Evanston, Ill., 1964).

72. Harrison, Hood, and Palisca, *Musicology, op. cit.*

73. *Ibid.,* p. 116. "The musicologist is concerned with music that exists, whether as an oral or a written tradition, and with everything that can shed light on its human context." Also, "To the musicologist a good musical work is, to be sure, a work of art, but it is one in a stream of works, good and bad" (p. 120).

Jacob Kimball, Dudley Buck) have nevertheless received the full scholarly "treatment." According to Professor Kerman, "they're *dead*"—and maybe they are only being embalmed in dissertations. In any case, it is quite safe to predict, statistically, that in due course they will *all* get the full Ph.D. treatment—which is as it should be. I don't mean for a moment that this is *enough*—far from it. Rather, it's a beginning along limited lines: the uni-linear approach of the bio-bibliographical-analytic method. But at least it's not neglect or indifference; the basic job is being done, and thoroughly.

Whether we are dealing with American composers of the eighteenth century, or the nineteenth, or the twentieth, I do not see any *essential* dif-ference in methodology or in the conceptual framework within which the methodology can be developed. If we are aiming for a total, unified field of musicology—which is certainly what I am talking about—then it must be able to cope with *any* aspect of music with equal effectiveness. What we need to borrow particularly from the social sciences is the capacity to generate theory—not just facts—from our research; and second, to develop our techniques for generalization. We could undertake, for exam-ple, a typology of the American composer, or of groups of American composers in the context of a particular temporal-cultural situation, such as that of the "First New England School" (1770–1830) or the "Second New England School" (1870–1920).

Mrs. Hampton: Would you define typology?

Chase: Typology is a kind of generalization used in the social sciences for the purpose of classifying, comparing, and deducing relationships among various classes of cultural phenomena. For example, if we wanted to compare the first and second "New England Schools," it would be wasteful, clumsy, and unproductive to attempt to do this on the basis of individual, one-to-one comparisons. We would try to formulate the "typology" of each group in terms of characteristic traits, socio-cultural-economic backgrounds, esthetic and intellectual influences, formal and stylistic patterns, and so forth. Each typology could also be considered as a theoretical "model" for purposes of comparison or deduction.

Mrs. Hampton: So this typology has to do with more than style char-acteristics?

Chase: Yes, certainly. But it seems to me that if you have in mind only the "style characteristics" of the music itself, as an isolated object or prod-uct, you are taking a very narrow view. How did these "style character-istics" come to be what they are? Surely many external or contextual factors must be brought to bear on this question. What I am arguing for, I suppose, is a multidimensional or multifaceted approach to the study of any music composition—or for that matter, any kind of cultural expres-sion whatsoever.

Berlin: Do we have enough information to draw up a valid hypothesis for such a typology of American music?

CHASE: We don't have to do the whole job all at once, you know! But we certainly have enough data to start setting up some "models" immediately. The two New England groups I mentioned would make a good beginning; and there are others, too. For instance, the "innovators" of the Wa-Wan Press group in the first decade of our century, and those of the 1920s who are documented in Cowell's book, *American Composers on American Music*.[74] American musicology does not suffer so much from lack of data as from lack of a dynamic theory and an imaginative methodology.

I do not claim that the social sciences offer a solution to all our problems. In fact, I strongly recommend that they be used with caution. But I do suggest that they can help us to know what the problems are, and perhaps how to understand their significance. Even if the social sciences have only a diagnostic function at this stage, that in itself would be worth the price of consultation.

READING LIST

Harrison, Frank Ll., Mantle Hood, and Claude V. Palisca, *Musicology*, Princeton Studies in Humanistic Scholarship in America (Englewood Cliffs, N.J., 1963).

Haydon, Glen, *Introduction to Musicology: A Survey of the Fields, Systematic and Historical, of Musical Knowledge and Research* (New York, 1946).

Herskovits, Melville J., *The New World Negro: Selected Papers in Afroamerican Studies*, ed. Frances S. Herskovits (Bloomington, Ind., 1966; New York, 1969, paperback ed.)

Keil, Charles, *Urban Blues* (Chicago, 1966).

Kunst, Jaap, *Ethno-Musicology, a Study of Its Nature, Its Problems, Methods and Representative Personalities to Which Is Added a Bibliography* (The Hague, 1955).

Merriam, Alan P., *The Anthropology of Music* (Evanston, Ill., 1964).

Nettl, Bruno, *Theory and Method in Ethnomusicology* (New York, 1964).

Seeger, Charles, "Music and Musicology in the New World," *Hinrichsen's Musical Yearbook*, VI (1949–50), 36–56.

———— "Tradition and the (North) American Composer: A Contribution to the Ethnomusicology of the Western World," in *Music in the Americas*, ed. George List and Juan Orrego-Salas, Indiana University Publications: Interamerican Monograph Series, 1 (The Hague, 1967).

Silbermann, Alphons, *The Sociology of Music*, trans. Corbet Stewart (London, 1963).

Weber, Max, *The Rational and Social Foundations of Music*, trans. and ed. Don Martindale, Johannes Riedel, and Gertrude Neuwirth (Carbondale, Ill., 1958).

74. Henry Cowell, *American Composers on American Music: A Symposium* (Stanford, 1933; new ed., New York, 1962).

Music Historiography
in Eastern Europe

GEORGE KNEPLER

WHAT we call Eastern Europe is composed of some ten countries in which a score of languages is spoken, ranging from branches of the Slavonic family to Hungarian, Romanian, and German. In some of these countries, after World War II, musicology had to begin practically from the start and did so with the impetus characteristic of new starts. In other countries, such as the Soviet Union, the Polish and the Czechoslovak People's Republics and the German Democratic Republic, there already existed a tradition of musicology upon which scholars could, and did, build and enlarge. Thus the material for my lecture this afternoon is taken from a great number of books, periodical articles, music editions, and discs in more than a dozen languages. It will, therefore, be clear that I cannot possibly aim at completeness. Instead, I propose to concentrate on the methods of music historiography employed in Eastern Europe. In doing so I will refer to certain works that seem noteworthy to me, with the understanding that I may have omitted others of equal importance.

Turning to methods of historical research used in Eastern Europe, I should first point out that they are not uniform. The Marxist method, about which I will have more to say in a moment, is not accepted by several musicologists, some of them of high repute. Let me name Max Schneider, Heinrich Besseler, and Walther Vetter in the German Democratic Republic, similarly Bence Szabolcsi in Hungary, Hieronim Feicht in Poland, and so on. A few of these scholars have expressed interest in, and respect for, the Marxist approach, and said that they owe something to it; but they come from different schools of thought and traditions and cannot accept it as a whole—some not at all. Others, among them some young scholars, feel that they have to reject the philosophically materialistic approach of Marxism although they find its methodology indispensable. This is, in my view, inconsistent, yet it must be recorded as a fact.

Marxist philosophy is taught in schools and universities in most socialist countries. Its application to the method of various branches of knowledge, including historiography, has produced arguments, hypotheses, and working methods which, while continuously being developed, have grown into a system. I will try to expound some of its implications for the writing of music history.

Discussing the scholar's motives for investigating the history of music, Professor Arthur Mendel has said that we should, according to a common explanation, "maintain that we study music history in order to understand history in general, which, in turn, we study in order to learn from the past what to do about the future." He added: "But in actual fact those who inquire into the past are in general not those who do a great deal about the future." And he came to the conclusion: "No—our primary reason for studying history is not utilitarian."[1] Without fear of being contradicted by most of my colleagues in Eastern Europe I can say that our aim is utilitarian. Our aim is the improvement of our musical culture.

As soon as one has made such a statement one finds oneself involved, I know, in a number of philosophical problems. Can one apply standards of value to musical culture? Even if one can, is it possible to influence the course of music history, or general history? And if the answer be in the affirmative, what is the relation between one's activity and the laws of development? Obviously, if one cannot design a model for a better musical culture because there is no way of deciding whether one is better than another; if there are no laws discernible in the development of music; if music history moves in cycles, the course of which we cannot influence any more than the ebb and flow of oceans; if it develops according to laws the depths of which we cannot ever hope to fathom or else according to no laws at all—what use would there be in a "utilitarian" history of music, to quote Professor Mendel's expression once more?

I will not try to answer all these questions fully, but rather outline the way in which we think answers can be found. Marxist music historians regard their subject as part of general history. One could say, to formulate it in a radical way, that there is no such thing as "music history." When we deal with our subject we are, whether we know it or not, concerned with the history of man. Our subject, though of special interest to us, is but one of several aspects of mankind's history. While one cannot and

---

1. Arthur Mendel, "Evidence and Explanation," *Report of the Eighth Congress of the International Musicological Society, New York, 1961*, II (Kassel, 1962).

should not necessarily inflict the economic, juridical, cultural, and other ramifications of history on a person interested in, say, the history of the sonata, one should keep in mind that all these ramifications are, to a lesser or greater degree, relevant to the sonata. This thesis is probably not controversial in itself. But how are the links between general history and music to be viewed? Curt Sachs must have thought about this a great deal. In his *Commonwealth of Art*, he makes short shrift of those who, "in establishing a self-sufficient, autonomous music history in which some symphony stems from some other symphony in virgin birth . . . lead the catastrophic way to severing music from man and music history from the evolution of the human mind. This should not happen."[2] Sachs himself gives examples of the way in which he sees music tethered to society. "It has almost become a truism," he says, for instance, "to connect the political currents in later Greece with her subjective art; medieval universalism with Gothic art; the new society in the cities of the Renaissance with their vocal chamber music; the enlightenment of the eighteenth century with its *style bourgeois*. Such connections are perfectly legitimate and even indispensable. . . ." But at this point, as if he had gone too far, Sachs qualifies his statement and warns that no "priority of politics," as he puts it, must be implied. And a few pages earlier he gives examples of how "art is able to ignore the trends of outer life." Philip II of Spain had "plunged his country into misery and moral disintegration; whole quarters were deserted, crafts died out and the treasurer's collecting box rattled from house to house. . . . And this was the Spain of Cervantes and Lope de Vega, of Greco and Victoria. . . ." Another one of Sachs's examples refers to Beethoven: ". . . Napoleon won a crushing victory over Austrians at Austerlitz, not too far from the gates of Vienna, where the master was busy with *Fidelio* and the three Leonoras, with the gay Fourth Symphony, the Concerto for Violin," and so on. "Was this," asks Sachs, "his anguish, dejection, defeat?"

I should perhaps make it clear, before I go on, that we think of Curt Sachs and his work with great respect. I single out this, to my mind, less successful book of his because it is typical of a certain tradition in music historiography. This tradition goes back to a group of German philosophers of the late nineteenth century, of whom Wilhelm Dilthey was the most influential in the historiography of the arts. The tradition of this philosophy lives on in countless publications on music history and general history to this very day. It is characterized by the attempt to sever the laws of nature from those of society, and to draw a dividing line between man's artistic and philosophical production on the one hand, and his economic, social, and political activities on the other. This is of particular interest in our connection because ideas of this sort developed in more or less conscious opposition to Marxist philosophy, which began to influence

2. Curt Sachs, *The Commonwealth of Art* (New York, 1946), p. 21.

thinking as early as the forties of the last century. Nobody would wish to overlook the differences between a natural law and a social law. Nature works without consciousness, while in society human beings, each with his or her own psychology, are at work. Nevertheless, as Marxist philosophers point out, laws of an objective, general, essential nature are detectable in society, no less than in nature. We spend a great deal of thought on the difficult interrelationships between subjective human activity and objective social forces. The term "dialectical determinism" has been coined to denote this relationship. Take the musical style of a given period. Obviously, it is the work of a great number of individual musicians. But one would not speak of style if the products of these countless individuals had not a certain minimum of characteristics in common. Now how does this come about? Certainly not only through learning from and imitating one another. One is forced to conclude that, while general trends are carried along by individuals, in a certain manner individuals are carried along by general trends. There must be detectable laws which link general trends and individual effort.

To come back to Curt Sachs's problem, one may assume that he had come across writings, perhaps professed Marxist writings, which postulated a "priority of politics" over the production of art or drew what we would call mechanical parallels between social events and artistic production. Not so Marx and Engels: not so the more recent Marxist philosophy and theory of culture. Curt Sachs simply overlooked the fact that what goes on in the artist's mind—or in anybody else's, for that matter—is not directly dependent on what he experiences and cannot, therefore, be judged along the lines of behaviorism. Nobody is mechanically conditioned by his surroundings. He sifts, interprets, evaluates his experience. Sachs's alternative—either an impoverished Spain could not have produced great art and Beethoven had to write bellicose music in times of war, or else outer events can play no role in the production of music—cannot be accepted. A highly complex network of cultural and ideological phenomena has to be taken into account. And our insight into the mechanism of the human mind is as yet small, as we all know. But nothing prevents us from analyzing the class structure of the society in which a piece of music is produced and consumed, this society's sociological and cultural structure and the different sets of ideas at work in the various social layers of that society and in the artist's mind, in such detail as our knowledge of history, sociology, and psychology will permit.

We think that one must allow for a certain independence of the various branches of human knowledge. It would be just as wrong to claim that a man who philosophizes or writes a mathematical treatise or paints moves along paths that are outside society, as it would be to ignore the very specialized set of ideas, rules, and methods that he uses. These are not independent of general conditions of society either, but their relationships to society are of a complex nature. While this in no way deflects from the fact that, in the last analysis, the workings of economy determine the general laws that are responsible for social phenomena, including the production of music with all its rules and methods, one must take into account the ways in which the special ideas, rules, and methods work. Neither the common chord nor the prohibition of parallel fifths can be directly deduced from the social conditions of the society in which they originated; nor can they be separated from that society and reduced, say, to the workings of eternal laws of nature. To denote this general truth the term "relative autonomy" has been coined.

Relative autonomy—to turn toward music sociology is not the worst way of finding out how relative this autonomy is. In view of the abundant definitions of, and ideas about, music sociology, it will not be superfluous to explain what I understand the term to mean. In accordance with a recent book on the subject, I would say that music history concentrates on genetic and music sociology on structural matters. Music sociology has the task of presenting a cross section of a musical culture at a given historical moment, never forgetting that all the facts, relationships, and artifacts it reveals are the result of historical change and are subject to change again as soon as one's momentary picture is mapped and even while it is being mapped. History, on the other hand, while it is per se directed toward change, cannot but work on the assumption that it deals with quasi-stable configurations. In other words, music history and music sociology complement one another—only the stress is different. The use of empirical methods is not a necessary criterion of sociology; sociological methods can be used in the analysis of musical cultures of the past to whatever extent available material allows. And, as a rule, it allows for far more than the majority of music histories would lead one to assume.

Let us try to examine the emergence of composition from the sociological point of view. Unless one is aware of the fact that within one and the same society and at one and the same historical moment various social layers were engaged in very different ways of making music—music different in structure, in function, in effect—the emergence of composition from age-old traditions of making music by improvisation cannot be accounted for. For a start, composition may be defined by the fact that three phases must be detectable: conceptual thinking and working; notation in writing; performance in which the composer himself need not take part. A further definition of composition—the decisive definition, I think—can be gained from a description of the oldest pieces of music that can without any doubt be regarded as compositions. These seem to me to be the organa of the twelfth and thirteenth centuries; no criteria applicable to even the most highly developed forms of improvisation apply to these. When analyzing these pieces the term that springs to mind is "synthesis." Heinrich Besseler, for example, speaks of a turning point that was reached in the Notre Dame art and sees in this "the final separation of European musical language from the Gregorian. The force on which the historical effect of the Notre Dame organa rests does not stem from the church but from the region of song and dance. The organum emerges as a daring synthesis."[3] Heinrich Husmann also points out what was "completely new" about the compositions for Notre Dame and speaks in this connection of the "abandonment of Gregorian rhythm" and of the linking-up of the two opposed types of melody: "Gregorian church music and secular lyric."[4]

About 1,500 years earlier the great conservative, Plato, had raised a warning voice in his *Laws* against those people who, although gifted, had placed themselves above all law. "They mingled elegies with hymns, paeans with dithyrambs, imitated aulos music with string instruments, mixed everything with everything," and had also committed the irregularity of judging music by the pleasure and happiness that it gave. Does it not appear that what Plato meant was an activity that approaches composition? Is not in fact the linking together of musical elements stemming from different social spheres an important characteristic of composition? So the sociological point of view has produced a thesis which could not have come to life had one regarded the musical culture of a given period as a monolithic block. The compositional synthesis of various elements emerges clearly when compared with ancient types of improvisation. Nothing is synthesized there. Before the improviser has opened his mouth or enticed the first sound from his instrument, one knows—so long as one knows his traditions—within what bounds the expected music will lie. This is not so in the case of the composer. The worst composer is that much ahead of the best improviser in that he has far greater possibilities to surprise. Where the musical traditions of a social sphere were unbroken, no composition occurred; where they were questioned, codifications were laid down to which the improvisers were bound; where social traditions became unstable and people with other ways of life, thought, and music making could no longer be banned from the orbit of the learned music makers, composition was born.

Let us turn to the problem of value criteria in music. When it comes to comparing musical cultures of various epochs or countries, accepted artistic standards are not helpful. In every single culture you can expect to find many men of talent and a few of genius. But such attention to individuals does not help us either to discern trends in the development of music or to find a yardstick by which to measure one music culture

3. Heinrich Besseler, "Ars Antiqua," *Die Musik in Geschichte und Gegenwart*, I, col. 682.

4. Heinrich Husmann, ed., *Die drei- und vierstimmigen Notre-Dame organa. Kritische Gesamtausgabe (mit Einleitung)* (Leipzig, 1940).

against another. Yet this, certainly, is a prerequisite for improving musical culture. The picture changes when one examines not only the individual composer and his work, but the listener as well; not only those of whom we know, or have reason to assume, listen to masterpieces, but also those who, for whatever reason, do not listen to masterpieces at all. We use the terms objective and subjective culture to denote what is, at any given historical moment, objectively available and to what an extent a social class, a group, an individual makes use of this availability. All known cultures, from the time when social classes originated in primeval society, show a gap between objective and subjective culture. To narrow and finally overcome this gap is one of our aims in improving musical culture, and this provides a useful, although not the only, criterion for the value of a musical culture. In this way social progress comes into the picture, progress being measured by the degree to which the forces of material and intellectual production are released and the results made available.

But can working for progress be reconciled with objectivity? Professor Grout, in his essay "Current Historiography and Music History" enumerates what he calls "certain rough but generally satisfactory criteria of objectivity . . . : criteria such as respect for truth, no blinking at awkward facts, no gratuitous moralizing, no ulterior interest (as in propaganda)."[5] When I examine these four criteria I have no quarrel at all with the first three. If the historian has no respect for truth, if he hasn't learned to look facts in the face, including facts that do not seem to square with his ideas, if he engages in moralizing, gratuitous or otherwise, he had better give up writing history. Professor Mendel, in the address to which I previously referred, quotes Isaiah Berlin, who formulates the historian's wish to come as near the facts as possible " . . . seen from as many points of view and at as many levels as possible, including as many components, factors, aspects, as the widest and deepest knowledge, the greatest analytic power, insight, imagination, can present." One can subscribe fully to these words. It was, if I am not mistaken, Charles Darwin who said that he was equally interested in facts that seemed to contradict his theory as in those that seemed to bear it out—indeed, more interested in them.

But the Marxist historian would part company with Professor Grout on his fourth point: "no ulterior interest." In the Marxist view it is unavoidable for this historian to have an ulterior motive. I do not refer to personal interests, of course. The historian is a product of history himself, and of his situation. However hard he may try, he cannot escape the molding of his mind by his experience and his surroundings. Professor Grout also quotes E. H. Carr as saying that an historian "is the less likely to be at the mercy of his own particular situation the more he is aware of it." This is

5. Donald Grout, "Current Historiography and Music History," in *Studies in Music History: Essays for Oliver Strunk* (Princeton, 1968), p. 27.

very true. As soon as he becomes aware of his own particular situation, and as soon as he realizes that there is such a thing as progress in society, he will find it difficult to be persuaded that objectivity should prevent him from taking sides with progress. Nor can the philosophical arguments underlying this interdiction be easily defended. Progress, as we see it, is the course of history, although this course is anything but straightforward or secure. Our own individual ideology cannot be independent of the course of history; the freedom given to us is only the margin between seeing, accepting, and throwing in our lot with what we have recognized as the course of history on the one hand, and being indifferent to or working against it on the other. Nor does experience teach us that objectivity is the key to understanding history. The great advances of the French in the eighteenth century in writing the general history of mankind were inspired by the passionate desire to bring to an end the very conditions into whose history they had delved so assiduously. "Ulterior" means "lying beyond what is immediate or present." If you want a change for the better, you have to find out, and if you want to find out, you have to go beyond, both in the direction of the past and of the future.

It is in this light that historical research in the Eastern European countries must be seen. In the fall of 1966 a remarkable congress was held in the Polish town of Bydgoszcz. Several visitors from the United States were present. It was called Musica Antiqua Europae Orientalis. It lasted a full week and consisted of a congress proper, at which papers were read and discussed, and a festival of music, which offered performances of old music of some ten different countries, all in Eastern Europe. Professor Zofia Lissa, of the University of Warsaw, planned and organized it. In her opening address, she stated that its aim was to draw attention to the fact that, not only since the nineteenth century but all through the ages, Eastern Europe had played its part in the world history of music, and the time had come for this fact to be recognized. The Bydgoszcz congress came at the right historical moment. From several sides it had been recognized that the time when Western Europe was *considered* the center of music making, and *was*, actually, the center of thinking and writing about music had irrevocably come to an end. (Parenthetically, I have sometimes wondered why musicology in the United States, on the whole, was not quicker to see this.) As we now know, the modern musicologist must take into consideration the whole world, not as peripheral regions (*Randgebiete*, as the music cultures of several countries used to be called by German writers not so long ago), but as regions demanding, and gradually receiving, full attention.

In the socialist countries considerable research is devoted to the documentation of their individual musical pasts. A wealth of new material, part of which could be heard in performance at the Bydgoszcz congress, has come to light. Romania and Bulgaria had to begin their investigations virtually from the start; but colleagues from Poland, Czechoslovakia, Yugoslavia, and Hungary had already achieved much in the rewriting of their history. The list of publications is growing fast.

But the main significance of our work lies in the interpenetration of historical and theoretical research. We see many unsolved problems. But the question of whether or not objective laws of history can be uncovered is not one of them. This problem was solved by Marx and subsequent philosophers. What is on our research agenda is a further development of these laws and their application to the special problems of our field. It is impossible for us to accept a skeptical philosophy of history that tends to reduce theory to a matter of personal opinion, which can neither be proved wrong or right. The various aspects of Marxist historiography—those I have mentioned and others I have not—have been worked out to such a degree that they tend to form a system in the cybernetic sense of the term. This is well in keeping with Marxist tradition.

More than a hundred years ago Marx spoke of society as an "organic system." Marxist philosophy and theory of history have applied the findings of cybernetics and have thus broken many a traditional pattern of historiography. One has to imagine society as a hierarchical system. The class structure of a given society, which, in turn, rests on its economic structure, determines its workings in the last analysis. But, as I have pointed out before, we see the action of men not as mechanically tied to the system of society to which they belong, but as relatively autonomous, dialectically determined. This theory has been specially worked out by philosophers, theoreticians of historiography, and general historians. While I am better informed about what has been done in this field in the German Democratic Republic, particularly in the pages of the *Deutsche Zeitschrift für Philosophie*, I know that writers in the Soviet Union, in Poland, and in Czechoslovakia have made contributions to this philosophy of history. Moreover a comparatively large number of musicologists are well grounded in a modern approach to music history. In the universities of the German Democratic Republic, groups have been formed to bring into closer contact historians of fields related to historiography of the arts. There is also a growing tendency toward integrating various branches of the sciences, both within and without the compass of traditional musicology. Important spade work has been done in the field of music sociology, first, by Czechoslovak colleagues, later also in the DDR. Professor Antonín Sychra[6] of Prague has worked on problems of phonetics, psychology, semantics, and theory of information to deepen the understanding of Marxist esthetics. Professor Zofia Lissa must be mentioned again as having contributed to various theoretical areas of esthetics and music his-

6. Antonín Sychra, *Hudba a Skutečnost* [Music and Reality], in preparation.

toriography. Professor Harry Goldschmidt of the DDR is working on a new theory which sees vocal and instrumental music as an esthetic entity. Young scholars in the DDR have worked in sociology and analysis of music with the help of a computer.

In short, the stage is set for writing of music history that incorporates not only the results of other branches of musicology, especially of esthetics, analysis, psychology, and sociology, but the knowledge, the hypotheses, the methods of our philosophers and theoreticians as well. So far, it is true, the most significant contributions of Marxists to music historiography have been monographs and biographies. One of the best is still E. H. Meyer's *English Chamber Music*.[7] It was, as far as I know, the first Marxist essay to deal with a lengthy period of music history. I think that some Soviet authors have produced remarkable contributions in similar fields. János Maróthy's books[8] should be mentioned—and the list could be prolonged.

It seems to me that the way of further progress lies in the direction of tackling ever more complex and comprehensive tasks, such as a world history of music into which all available knowledge can be integrated. Many lacunae will become apparent in the progress of such work. It is obvious, for instance, how little we know about the effect of music on people. But without such knowledge how can a history of music be complete? No single discipline can hope to find the missing links by itself. But history and sociology could do a great deal more in providing us with detailed charts of the respective historical fields in which man makes, and listens to, music. Experimental psychology, while it cannot answer all questions of music esthetics, could certainly help to pose and answer some of them more precisely. Music analysis, if presented with results of music psychology, would find it easier to escape the ruts of traditional analysis. In short, if history, sociology, psychology, analysis, esthetics of music (and other disciplines) were made to ask one another more exact questions, the resulting cross-fertilization could contribute a good deal toward filling many lacunae.

Finally, I would suggest that the manner of presenting music history is undergoing revision. It is traditional to write music histories as narratives and somehow to smuggle in the unavoidable explanations. But if it is true that so many factors must be integrated into music history this will have to be reflected in the presentation. In my opinion the subject should be looked at from various angles, one at a time, and the various findings be presented in such a way that jointly they form the whole story. Hard and

7. Ernst H. Meyer, *English Chamber Music, the History of a Great Art from the Middle Ages to Purcell* (London, 1946).

8. János Maróthy, *Az európai népdal születése* [The Birth of European Folksong] (Budapest, 1960); and *Zene és polgár—zene és proletár* [Music and Bourgeois—Music and Proletarian] (Budapest, 1966).

fast rules cannot be laid down—I can only say that I have found it advantageous to use four such avenues of approach.

The first consideration would be general, including economic and social history, history of philosophy, literature, and the other arts. Generally speaking, the music historian will not, at this point, be concerned with formulating matters for himself. He will not, as a rule, develop his own theories of history, but will be content to point out relationships that are important to investigate further. For example, it would be superfluous in a presentation of the music history of the First World War and the twenties to discuss military events. But it would be important to show how, with the crumbling of states at the end of the war, old traditions also crumbled and events like the revolution in Russia and other countries opened up new ways of looking at things.

The second consideration is the first of the specifically musical approaches. Among these we give precedence to the most general, to the genetic before the structural, to the historical before the sociological. Here the broad trends of musical development within the given period should be outlined. The emphasis should be on music making in its historical development. The more clearly each approach is worked out in its separateness, the better the chance of making its interaction with the others clear. Furthermore, trends in compositional methods must also be dealt with. They must be reviewed in their relation to newly emerging subject matters and tasks, and to the changing demands and needs of the potential audience. Musical theories and their consequences should be viewed in relation to objective needs and possibilities. *The achievements of individual artists and thinkers*, however, can be only incompletely shown by this approach. We are more concerned here with general trends. At best only a minor composer may be completely characterized by a general tendency. But the greater the composer, the more he will elude such classification. With our approach one would examine trends and schools of composition and thought, and exemplify them by what seems to represent them most clearly. In this way one would do justice to the trends without pretending to have dealt adequately with the individual artists.

A third approach would be more specific than the above, more structural than genetic, more sociological than historical. It would be devoted more to the musical genres than to the predilection for this or that type of music. Especially when confronted with the social spheres of music making, the genres allow one an insight into the fabric of music life. It is highly significant that opera is completely missing in peasant and bourgeois strata of the seventeenth century, while in the nineteenth century it penetrates various spheres of many European countries. To take another example, in seventeenth-century Germany the song can be found practically everywhere, but in very different types and qualities. These are facts which tend to be overlooked unless dealt with specifically.

Finally, when we have adequately examined the general conditions under which a composer works and a "noncomposer" listens, we may concentrate, in our last approach, on what all too often used to be the only subject matter for music historians: the creative achievement of the individual. Carried by trends and schools, participating in them, helping to create, modifying and overcoming, renewing and learning, integrating what seems irreconcilable, the composer can now be viewed as a creative individual in a network of social conditions. His life and work will be better understood, the more clearly the fabric of social relationships is spread out and examined from the several points of view outlined above. Musicologists in the United States have expressed concern that research in their country is "too positivistic, too preoccupied with the collection of data and the determination of detail."[9] It is my impression that music research in Eastern Europe, while not neglecting data and detail, is well equipped to escape their snares. It is the cornerstone of our views that mankind today possesses all the prerequisites for overcoming our age's fundamental ill—privilege—and, thereby, for bringing out creative potentialities in all human beings. This belief determines the climate in which we work. Thus it is no accident that our quest for the understanding of the past focuses on points of view, concentrates on connections that have never been fully investigated. Nor is it accidental that in so doing we synthesize findings of various branches of knowledge. The Marxist method of music historical research, emerging from dogmatic deformation of the recent past, demands such a synthesis. Since we aim at guiding historical change, we have to understand the past, for our own guidance, as thoroughly as advanced methods will allow.

Eastern European music history offers several points of great interest. Wide stretches of that part of Europe, over long periods of its history, offered very limited opportunities for the emergence of rich musical cultures. It is, therefore, all the more illuminating to investigate conditions in those eminent musical cultures of Eastern Europe that did emerge. Also, the origins of composition, after age-old traditions of music making without notation, can be observed in certain parts of Eastern Europe even today; it is everywhere in this part of the world a more recent phenomenon than in Western Europe. But perhaps the most important claim to universal interest lies in the fact that Eastern Europe offers one of the rare chances of observing something like a gigantic social experiment. The social and political conditions have been created for the development of a socialist music culture. I believe that it is worthwhile to study our experiences and achievements in the theoretical and practical fields, our plans for the future, as well as our shortcomings and what we do to overcome them.

9. Edward A. Lippman, "What Should Musicology Be?," *Current Musicology* (Spring, 1965), p. 58.

DISCUSSION

MRS. HAMPTON: Professor Knepler, in your lecture you said that the goal of the music historiographer should be the improvement of musical culture. To improve musical culture, one must determine a set of values. How would you define improvement?

KNEPLER: The perfection of individual pieces of music cannot be the criterion of progress. Perotin is, in history, as "good" as Ravel. But when we consider an individual piece from the point of view of its role in a given society, then our picture changes a little. In modern society, we can expect music to do more for people than it did hundreds of years ago. We can *imagine* a musical culture in which music has new tasks to fulfill. From this point of view, perhaps, with a concern not for the perfection of an individual piece but for its function in society, one might come to a notion of progress.

Perhaps this would constitute a standard of values: if we can agree that a certain piece of music does something for us which we consider important, then we would obviously wish that as many people as possible should be able to partake of it. Here, obviously, is where a lot can be done to improve musical culture. I need not tell you of the potentials of technology and science, which are practically unlimited. For the first time we have a chance to use these potentials for really developing people and eradicating the vestiges of the elite culture we have always had.

SCHOTT: I wish I could believe that one can really bring Mozart, or Goethe, or Shakespeare to a broad mass of people.

KNEPLER: But why not? Why should we believe that we, who can appreciate Mozart or Shakespeare, are so much better qualified than anybody else, if not through better opportunity and better education?

SCHOTT: This is just the point. Your question rejects the individual variable: the fact that some people have motor and sensory nervous systems that equip them to hear or perform Mozart in a way that other people cannot.

KNEPLER: This is not a process that can be expected to produce immediate results. It is a trend of social development lasting a generation or two. How much time have we had? Fifty years in the Soviet Union, twenty years in the German Democratic Republic. And there were all sorts of events that hampered this progress. Perhaps we should recess this discussion for 200 or 250 years! To *enable* people to have the kind of nerves to appreciate Mozart would be something worthwhile. It *is* possible to educate people, not only for music, but for a fuller life. We few

Mozart lovers today are not so much better than anybody else, we only had better chances.

Mrs. Jorgens: What kind of music education do people in East Germany receive? You speak of an improvement of musical culture. From your lecture, I could not see how you were putting what you as a musicologist are learning back into society. What do the people get from it?

Knepler: First of all, we have music in the elementary schools. Children attend elementary school when they are six and leave, as a rule, when they are sixteen, unless they go to a university, in which case their preliminary schooling is extended two years until they are about eighteen. During these ten years, they have one hour a week of music education. During the additional two years, the eleventh and twelfth classes, they have either music or drawing for one hour a week.

Mrs. Jorgens: Is this music history?

Knepler: No, this is singing, reading music, general music, with a little music history, depending on the teacher. Then there are the music schools proper, several hundred of them, some in the villages. Here, talented children can have instrumental classes in addition to their regular school work. Then we have Hochschulen for music, which would correspond to your conservatories.

Brook: At what age do students go to the Hochschule?

Knepler: At eighteen, for the Hochschule proper. The Hochschulen now also have children's classes. In the university we train music teachers for the elementary schools. Teachers for the music schools are trained at the Hochschulen. Both the Hochschulen and the universities take students when they are eighteen to twenty-two.

Brook: Could a student attend the two simultaneously?

Knepler: It is possible, but these would be isolated cases. We do have applied music at the universities. Suppose somebody who has attended elementary school for twelve years wants to study musicology. He comes to us at the university at eighteen; he is examined and we find him suitable. We usually expect him to have certain training as a pianist, but we do make exceptions. He would then come to study musicology for five years. For two years out of the five, he would take piano lessons, ear training, harmony, counterpoint, and such subjects, in addition to lectures on history, esthetics, and so on.

Brook: But would he also study mathematics, history, sociology, languages? In other words, could he receive a liberal-arts education with musical specialization in the university? This would be close to our curriculum.

Knepler: I have not seen your universities in New York, but in Pittsburgh and in Lexington, Kentucky, there was not such a broad educational emphasis. The emphasis was much more on applied music. We think that the musicologists should get a bit of everything, so we would not give anyone a diploma who has not had history of music, esthetics, some sociology, psychology, and ethnology, apart from practical music. Also, he would normally have to have a *Nebenfach*, a minor subject. This could be anything; for instance, a second language. (One foreign language is obligatory.) In this way we try to give the student a wider range of interest. He would know what the elements of music ethnology are, even though his field of concentration may be the nineteenth century.

Right now, a reform of higher education is taking place in the German Democratic Republic. One of its aims is to make it possible for one scholar to talk to another who has a different specialization or even a different field. This consists, among other things, in organizing what used to be *Institute* into *Sektionen*. A *Sektion* comprises several former *Institute*. For instance, the *Sektion für Aesthetik und Kunstwissenschaft* would have historians of music, art, theater, film, television, and so on, as well as philosophers who specialize in esthetics and in theories of culture. Another part of the reform is that all students, regardless of their subject, whether they study theology or economics, will have elementary courses in mathematics, statistics, *Leitungswissenschaft* (management science), and a few subjects of this sort. This should help us to communicate with one another, to introduce mathematical methods into subjects which have not used them before.

WERNER: You mentioned Sir Isaiah Berlin. He was the man who, I think, first brought the problem of dialectical determinism into sharp contour. Do you believe that the methods and priorities of dialectical determinism, as left over from nineteenth-century natural science, may be applied to social science? Modern natural science has for the most part abandoned deterministic reasoning, but is this antinomy fundamental to Marxism, based on certain theological concepts of the socialistic philosophy?

KNEPLER: No, it is not. I am not a philosopher, and least of all a philosopher of natural science. But if I understand the Marxist philosophers of science, they tell us that even in natural science we have come to see that the law of cause and effect is not the only law. But that doesn't mean there are no laws. There are also statistical laws, laws of structure, laws of probability. And these would apply both to nature and to society, according to philosophers whom I am inclined to believe. We certainly cannot say that the conditions in the given society are a, b, c, up to n, and, therefore, the composer will have to write F♯ in the second bar of his symphony. Perhaps we even could say that the conditions create a certain field of possibilities in which he will probably do such and such. And if we take into consideration his psychological make-up as well, then we will be able to come very much nearer to what he is likely to do or not to do.

WERNER: If you replace a strictly deterministic law by a law of probability, we are perfectly in accord.

KNEPLER: Good.

WERNER: Second, you made a very interesting remark about Beethov-
en's martial side. You remember, of course, the famous passage in the
Missa solemnis, in the *Dona nobis*, where suddenly martial trumpets
sound. I think this cannot be easily explained on rational grounds. You
have to go into the question of genius, for no deterministic law will provide us with an explanation.

KNEPLER: You will remember that I brought in Beethoven on a completely different level. I didn't discuss Beethoven; I discussed Curt Sachs's
view. Sachs's opinion on Beethoven is that outer events cannot be made
responsible for his music, because Beethoven wrote peaceful music while
Napoleon fought the Battle of Austerlitz near Vienna. If one wanted to
go into this, of course, one would say Beethoven's mind worked in a much
more complicated manner than Sachs would allow for in this case. His
parallels are much too simple. Beethoven had a very ambiguous attitude
toward Napoleon; at the time of the Battle of Austerlitz he was no longer
a blind admirer, but was very critical of him. So the fact that he did not
reflect Napoleon's wars in his music doesn't prove a thing. It doesn't prove
Sachs's point at all. That is all I wanted to say. Whether the trumpets in
the *Missa solemnis* can be accounted for in a rational way, I would not
like to debate. I think they can, especially when one knows Beethoven's
abhorrence of war and, at the same time, his feeling that war had to be.
He wanted Napoleon conquered so he had a very ambiguous attitude
toward war as well. And I don't see why this should be outside explanation, except that we know very little about human psychology.

MRS. FRIEDLAND: Your reply to Professor Werner's question about
determinism indicates that laws of probability, field theory, and similar
new approaches—including systems analysis, I would imagine—are engaging the interest of scientists and philosophers in your society just as in the
Western countries. But the application of these concepts to social and
artistic phenomena seems to be fraught with as many difficulties and dangers as the older attempts at mechanical, cause-and-effect explanations. It
is my understanding that systems theory aims at evaluation and quantifica-
tion of all interrelating variables in a field, reducing error to as close to
zero as possible. Bypassing for the moment the knotty problem of the creative process itself, do you think it feasible to "mathematicize" all the elements in the web of music and society? Can you tell us of some starts at
providing mathematical models for the various factors operative in the
development of musical culture?

KNEPLER: No, we haven't done anything of this sort, and I think it will be some time before we are able to do it. I think the way to achieve it is to analyze the individual elements which could constitute the system. To examine a given musical culture, don't regard it as a unified block of, say, Baroque culture, and then try to find out what Baroque is. I don't think this leads very far. We should examine the various social stratifications; this is why I made the point about sociological and historical methods as applied to a given period. Before we can think of "mathematicizing" the creative process, a great deal of research work will need to be done in a number of fields. We should agree what these fields are and what their interrelationships are. I think, for instance, that there is a great lacuna in experimental psychology, applied to the effect which music has on man. Which factors in music do whatever music does? How much can we take away or distort in a given piece of music without changing its effect? I know a little of your psychological literature, but certainly not enough. When I use the phrase, "if music psychology and music analysis could ask one another more precise questions," this is what I mean.

Our methods of music analysis are very traditional. We analyze according to harmony, melody, rhythm, form, and a few more such criteria. But whether these are the relevant ones, as far as the effect of music goes, we can't tell. I think that if music psychologists would say, "We assume that a certain piece of music has certain effects—say, it makes people happy," then the analyst should say, "A piece of music that makes people happy looks like this," and proceed to analyze it as fully as he can. The psychologist would query the analyst and the analyst would put more pertinent questions to the psychologist. In this way we could come a little closer to *one* of the problems: what music does to man. This question would have to be applied to several other strata. Obviously, what music does to various kinds of people in modern societies, say in New York, or in the United States today, is most diverse.

Mrs. FRIEDLAND: Your answer suggests an approach to musical experience which differs markedly from the starting premise of most contemporary estheticians in the Western world. Music, or art in general, is viewed not for what it does but by what it *is*; in other words, seemingly excluding the element of *function* from the esthetic experience.

KNEPLER: I don't think I would overlook this factor: not only what music does but what it is. But would you divorce the two things? Obviously music is created in order to *do* something. You would know more about what music *is* if you knew more about what it *does*. Since this is a most neglected point of view, I think this could be an important key to our understanding of what music is. Certainly we don't create it only for its own sake. We want to achieve something with it.

WINTERNITZ: With reference to your admirably clear formulation of the sociological aspects of the history of music or any other art, I wonder to what extent, in Eastern European publications, the concepts of Max Weber and his theory of *Idealtypus* have been utilized. Has there been any attempt to write a comparative history of the arts—the history of the visual arts and of music go together in many ways—a comparison of theoretical, methodical speculations in both the streams of art?

KNEPLER: No, unfortunately. I cannot say that we think a great deal of Alfred and Max Weber's *Idealtypus*, because it underrates the fact that man is an historical phenomenon. If there were such a thing as an *Idealtypus*, it existed before history began. How could we, then, account for the various epochs of history? Max Weber wrote the first essay on music sociology, although if you look very closely, you find that it is unfinished work and does not really contain very much music sociology. By and large, I do not think Max Weber's approach can be profitably used as a basis for further sociological work, although one would have to be aware of his ideas. He was, after all, an important thinker and had great influence.

SCHOTT: Could you tell us to what extent the new music of the Western countries is being heard and studied in the German Democratic Republic?

KNEPLER: I would say that all of our young composers and music historians try to keep abreast of the developments in the West. Unfortunately, we don't receive all Western publications. This is not a question of censorship but of money.

VAN SOLKEMA: Americans have been giving considerable attention to the direction of their musicology in recent years. I wonder if you would offer a comment on American musicology as it appears to you—its direction, its goals? Also to what extent do your students read, say, the *Journal of the American Musicological Society*, the *Musical Quarterly*, the books of American musicologists?

KNEPLER: I'm amazed to see how great the influence of German musicology (especially that of the late nineteenth century and the early twentieth) still is in this country—at least, on the authors whose books I know. I admire much of what is produced here, but as a visitor, I would rather not offer a critique even if I were competent to do so. On your second question, our students would certainly know Paul Henry Lang's *Music in Western Civilization*. The more advanced ones would certainly know Gustave Reese's two books, Grout's two books, and Strunk's *Source Readings in Music History*. Those who specialize would know, say, William Newman's work on the sonata and Barry Brook's book on the French symphony. As to the periodicals: the *Musical Quarterly* and the *Journal of the American Musicological Society* are read, but not widely enough; we do not have enough copies to go around.

BROOK: It must be said that *our* knowledge of East German and Eastern European scholarly literature has been all too limited. Two hopeful developments are the increase in music-literature-exchange arrangements made by American and Eastern European libraries and, of course, RILM.

MRS. FRIEDLAND: RILM receives abstracts from all over the world. Having worked on the RILM staff, may I say this? There are a number of pieces from the DDR that seem far more political than scholarly. One instance is a review by Dieter Zechlin of a recent record of the Swingle Singers. The abstract, as translated in RILM I/3, 2079, reads:

> Whatever the capitalistic entertainment industry takes up loses forthwith its harmlessness and takes on a new and frightening dimension. One recent instance: the capitalistic entertainment and phonograph-record industry is busy organizing—by utilizing Mr. Swingle and his singers as marketable merchandise—a world-wide Bach parody that is tantamount to a permanent carnival. What might be acceptable as a one-time incident of a daring Bach adaptation leads—when channeled into the workaday world of millions of people—to aesthetic disorientation, to musical brain poisoning.

Now, being a person of social conscience, I cannot entirely dismiss your appeal for musicology to place itself "squarely on the side of progress"; on the other hand, this article epitomizes, for me, the kind of heavy handed, humorless music criticism that comes out of rejecting Grout's *caveat* on ulterior interest. I find the Swingle Singers great for introducing Bach and contrapuntal music in general to beginners; and, truthfully, I also enjoy the music! I'm afraid I remain unconvinced about this particular application of Marxist thinking. Even Ernst Meyer's fine volume on English chamber music is diminished somewhat by a certain insistence on linking musical trends with social developments; he often resorts to rather fanciful explanations to establish the connection.

KNEPLER: Articles coming out of the DDR are not always our best advertisement. Some of our periodicals may overemphasize politics and use a few standard phrases all too often. But you know, when an abstract is written, the more detailed, more original, more relevant parts, which would have been of greater interest, often have to be dropped. As to the article in question, I disagree with any criticism of the Swingle Singers. I love them. On the other hand, the article is much more interesting and enlightening, has more substance than you could gather from the abstract.

MRS. JORGENS: Is there any emphasis in East Germany on bringing out editions of lesser-known composers?

KNEPLER: No, we do not do much of this; personally I would not direct my students to editing still another composer. I don't say this should not be done, but I think too much emphasis has been laid on it. We know a great number of composers already. While every additonal *Gesamtausgabe* is of value, we have a store of knowledge and don't know what to do with it. The *theory* of historiography and the *theory* of musicology are much less developed than the accumulation of ever more knowledge. We have so many catalogues and complete editions.

BROOK: I agree that we need to be far more concerned than we are with the *theory* of musicology and historiography. Still, the number of musicologists is so great and the field of musicology so broad that there is room for many approaches to our discipline. We desperately need the paleographers, the bibliographers, the estheticians, the ethnologists, the Marxist historiographers, the devotees of the "higher criticism," the Schenkerians (be they Salzerites, Jonaserians, or Osterizers); we need those who collect data and verify detail, and, indeed, those who edit. I disagree with the view that we have enough music in print. Although the Josquin edition is nearly complete, the works of Isaac and Haydn are still not all available. And I don't believe that secondary figures, significant for the understanding of the musical life of the time, can be neglected. Musicology is richer and stronger when a variety of approaches is available.

KNEPLER: This is, of course, also my view. All I want to say is that even today the emphasis on mere editing is very marked, particularly in West Germany, and many make a philosophy of it. I wish only to emphasize how important it is to take a more universal view of all facets of our discipline.

READING LIST

Czechoslovakia

Generální katalog hudebnín a knih o hudbě [Catalogue of music and music literature of the State Publishing House] (Prague, 1963).

Ormisová-Záhumenská, Božena, *Súpis hudobnín z bývalého . . .* [Catalogue of music autographs at Jasov Monastery] (Martin, 1967).

Patnact' let života ČSR . . . [Catalogue of literature and discs on music, literature, film, 1945–1960] (Prague, 1960).

Potúček, Juraj, *Súpis slovenských hudobnín a literatúry o hudobnikoch* [Catalogue of Slovak music and literature on musicians] (Bratislava, 1952).

Súpis slovenských hudobnoteortických prac [Catalogue of Slovak writings on music theory] (Bratislava, 1955).

Telec, Vladimír, *Soupis hudebních informativních a bibliografických publikacíve . . .* [Catalogue of reference and bibliographical literature on music in the University Library, Brno] (Brno, 1962).

German Democratic Republic

Bericht über die musikwissenschaftlichen Arbeiten in der Deutschen Demokratischen Republik, 1966 (Berlin, 1967).

"Bibliographie der Schriften über Musik aus der Deutschen Demokratischen Republik, 1949–1959," *Beiträge zur Musikwissenschaft*, I/3 (1959), 51–75; II/1 (1960), 50–68; II/2 (1960), 64–78.

Bibliographie der Schriften über Musik aus der Deutschen Demokratischen Republik, 1945–1968 (Berlin, 1970).
Deutsche Musik-Bibliographie, herausgegeben und bearbeitet von der Deutschen Bücherei (Leipzig—monthly).

Hungary

Csomor, T., *A muzsika világában* . . . [Selected bibliography of books, essays, articles on music] (Budapest, 1964).
Stoll, B., *A magyar kéziratos énekeskönyvek* . . . [Bibliography of song-book and poetry-book autographs, 1565–1840] (Budapest, 1964).

Poland

Katalog polskich druków muzycznych 1800–1863 [Catalogue of Polish printed musical works, 1800–1863] (Kraków, 1968).
Materiały do bibliografii muzyki polskiej [Material for a bibliography of Polish music] (Kraków, 1954 ff.)
"Musikwissenschaftliche Literatur sozialistischer Länder, 2: Volksrepublik Polen, 1945–1965," in *Beiträge zur Musikwissenschaft, Sonderreihe Bibliographien* (Berlin, 1966).
Zambrzycki, Z., *Popularna literatura wokalna z lat 1945–1954* [Popular song, 1945–1954: bibliographical notes] (Kraków, 1956).

Romania

Initiere Muzicală: Indice bibliogr. de recomandare [Musical instruction: bibliography of recommended literature] (Bucharest, 1962).
"Musikwissenschaftliche Literatur sozialistischer Länder, 1: Sozialistische Republik Rumänien, 1945–1965," in *Beiträge zur Musikwissenschaft, Sonderreihe Bibliographien* (Berlin, 1966).

Soviet Union

Antipova, E. K., *K. Glazunova v fondach Gosudarstvennogo centralnogo Muzeja musikalnoj kultury imeni M. I. Glinki* [Catalogue of Glazunov autographs in the Glinka Museum] (Moscow, 1968).
Fischman, Natan L., *Avtografy L. Betchovena v chraniliščach SSSR* [Catalogue of Beethoven autographs in public libraries of the Soviet Union] (Moscow, 1959).
Kisesev, V. A., *Avtografy M. A. Balakireva i materialy* [Catalogue of Balakirev autographs and other sources in the Glinka Museum] (Moscow, 1959).
Koltypina, G. B., *Bibliografija muskalnoj bibliografii* [Bibliography of music bibliographies] (Moscow, 1963).
——— *Spravočnajo literatura po muzyke* [Catalogue of reference literature on music in the Russian language, 1773–1962] (Moscow, 1964).
Letopis musikalnoj literatury [Chronicle of music literature] (Moscow, 1931 ff.).
Literatura o muzyke [Literature on music bibliographies] (Moscow, 1955).
Livanova, Tamara N., *Muzykalnaja bibliografija russkoj periodičeskoj pečati XIX veka* [Bibliography of Russian musical periodicals of the nineteenth century] (Moscow, 1960).

Muzična literatura Ukrainskoi Radjanskoi Socialističnoi Respubliki, 1917–1965 [Bibliographical guide to music literature of the Ukranian Socialist Soviet Republic, 1917–1965] (Kharkov, 1966).

Petermann, Kurt, and Heinz Legler, *Sowjetische Tanzliteratur. Ein annotiertes Bücherverzeichnis der in der Deutschen Staatsbibliothek zu Berlin . . . gesammelten Schriften sowjetischer Autoren. Mit einem Anhang: Sowjetische Tanzliteratur in deutscher Übersetzung* (Leipzig, 1968).

Sidelnikov, V. M., *Russkaja narodnaja pesnia* [The Russian folksong: biblographical catalogue, 1735–1945] (Moscow, 1962).

Sovjetskaja litertura o muzyke [Soviet literature on music], I: 1918–1947, ed. I. Starcev (Moscow, 1963); II: 1948–1953, ed. S.-L. Uspenskaja (Moscow, 1955); III: 1954–1956, ed. S.-L. Uspenskaja (Moscow, 1958); IV: 1957, ed. S.-L. Uspenskaja (Moscow, 1957); V: 1958–1959, ed. S.-L. Uspenskaja (Moscow, 1963); VI: 1960–1962, ed. A. Kolbanovskaja (Moscow, 1967).

Zosimovskij, V. A., *Bibliografičeskij spravočnik po choreografii* [Annotated bibliography on choreography] (Moscow, 1959).

The Present State and
Potential of Music Research
in Latin America

LUIZ HEITOR CORRÊA
DE AZEVEDO

*T*O *UNDERSTAND* the present state of music research in Latin America, our first step must be to see how such research started and progressed, and to consider what basis it offers for further serious work.

In the history of music as a whole, Latin America was long considered terra incognita. As recently as thirty years ago—that is to say, before the Second World War—Latin America was still virtually excluded from the picture presented by European music encyclopedias, dictionaries, and histories of music. In the more sophisticated of these works, of course, one could find occasional references to the indigenous music of Latin America or to the music of a few composers who had acquired a certain European reputation. But Riemann or Grove would say, for instance, that those composers were born "of European parents." And sometimes grotesque misinformation was provided in those books. Thus the 1944 edition of Willi Apel's *Harvard Dictionary of Music* defined *saudade* as a "Portuguese term for longing, nostalgia; hence, denomination for Brazilian dances of such character." But who ever danced a saudade in Brazil? If the term appears, as it does, in the titles of many compositions by Brazilian or by foreign composers who spent some time in Brazil (as did Darius Milhaud, the composer of the well-known piano series, *Saudades do Brasil*), it does mean longing, nostalgia; so much is correct. It often appears with this meaning in Portuguese and Brazilian poetry and consequently in songs based on these poems. But there is no Brazilian dance called saudade.

This pitiful state of affairs no longer exists, at least generally speaking. Today the publication of an encyclopedia history of music of nearly 2,000 pages, like the *Histoire de la Musique* issued by Pléiade in Paris in 1963 under the editorship of Roland-Manuel—a history for whose authors Latin America just does not exist—represents a musicological scandal. In the alphabetical index you may look in vain for the names of Villa-Lobos, Chávez, or Ginastera. Such a work is now an exception, but before World War II the available documentation on the music of Latin America, especially on its historical development, was very scarce. Archival research was almost nonexistent. Musicologists in Latin America seemed to believe that only primitive and folk music were worthy of their efforts—an attitude which may be interpreted as a late reflection of a colonial mentality. For how could such "new" countries be expected to have produced any art music of value? Why undertake difficult research, most of it under particularly arduous conditions, to exhume from dusty manuscript files or register books a lot of second-rate compositions and data on third- or fourth-rate composers? The fact is that ethnomusicological research preceded historical musicology, all over Latin America.

When, in 1942, Juan Bautista Plaza started publication of the *Archivo de música colonial venezolana*, unveiling names and scores of eighteenth-century composers born in Venezuela and resident in Caracas, he opened the way to a larger picture of the Latin American musical past. It became clear that to understand the cultural history of Latin America, we would need to know how, and to what extent, music was a part of its development. And from that date, historical research acquired a new importance and attracted people who, forty years ago, would have preferred field work, hunting the native music of the people.

Does this mean that the present situation is good enough and that musicological research in both ethnic and art music is making satisfactory progress in Latin America? The answer is no! Positively not! What has been done is only a beginning. It is my responsibility in this lecture to trace the present state and potential research in these fields: what has been done and what could be done in the near future. And since in order to understand the present situation it is necessary to know what kind of job was performed by the pioneers, I propose to start by examining the past, discussing the roots of Latin American musicology. This means bibliography. Let us embark, then, on a brief critical survey of Latin American musicological literature.

As is logical and natural, we must start with ethnomusicology.

As far back as the early sixteenth century, we find books published in Europe, and occasionally in this hemisphere, with references to the songs, musical instruments, and dances of the American Indians, as well as engravings and even music notated on the staff. Just as Claude Levi-Strauss considers Montaigne the father of modern anthropology, we must see in men like Motolinía, Sahagún, López de Gomara, Mendieta, Martín de Morúa, Garcilaso de la Vega, Huamán Poma de Ayala, Hans Staden, or Jean de Léry the very first specialists in American studies, men who sometimes pioneered in ethnomusicology. Their works are among the standard sources for our knowledge of pre-Columbian cultures. They have been often quoted and the Tupynambá melodies revealed by Jean de Léry have been used by Brazilian composers, as they were by Heitor Villa-Lobos in his *Three Indian Poems*.[1]

After the contribution of those writers, with their freshness, charm, and authenticity, we have, in the nineteenth and early twentieth centuries, a series of well-intentioned amateurs writing on music and folklore of a very different society: that of the colonial melting-pot. In almost all of those books, some of them written with naïve candor, there is something to be explored. Their information, of course, has to be carefully checked against the material offered by their contemporaries or by writers of a later period and, when possible, against the personal field experience of the researcher. Let us review the most representative of these picturesque pioneers of Latin American ethnomusicology.

A typical example is General Ramón de la Plaza's book, *Ensayos sobre el arte en Venezuela*, published in Caracas as early as 1883. Here we find a certain amount of useful information on the music and musical instruments of the Venezuelan aborigines, followed by transcriptions of "44 Aires nacionales de la República."

For Cuba, the pioneering work was Serafín Ramírez's *La Habana artística*, published in 1891, in Havana. Here we find notes on nineteenth-century Cuban dances and art music plus a kind of alphabetical dictionary of composers.

Guilherme de Melo's history of music in Brazil was published in 1908.[2] Melo, a modest provincial musician, was born in Bahia, where he industriously assembled quite an important music library. This led to his deci-

---

1. The authenticity of those melodies is discussed in my article "Tupynambá Melodies in Jean de Léry's *Histoire d'un voyage faict en la terre du Brésil*," *Papers of the American Musicological Society: Annual Meeting, 1941* (Richmond, 1946), p. 85.

2. Guilherme de Melo, *A música no Brasil* (Bahia, 1908; reprinted 1947 by the School of Music of the Federal University of Rio de Janeiro).

sion to write his own book on the music of his country. It was a difficult enterprise, since he had no historical materials at his disposal except occasional references to music in books and essays devoted to other subjects. He searched through such references as were available to him, but without doing any first-hand research of his own. In this way he assembled the information that forms the second, historical part of his book. This is the less interesting half, totally lacking in scholarship, and including discussions of the contemporary musical life of Bahia that have no meaning for us today. But the first part of the book, dealing with folk music, remains a valuable source book. Guilherme de Melo speaks from personal experience, tells what he himself saw, notates the melodies he heard.

To this same kind of literature belongs the work of Rubén Campos, *El folklore y la música mexicana* (1928). Despite its title, the book discusses serious music as well as so-called light music, which sometimes incorporates authentic traditional music. Songs and dances, in piano arrangements, are to be found at the end of the book.

Much more serious is the essay by the distinguished amateur and diplomat Narciso Garay, on *Tradiciones y cantares de Panamá*, printed in Brussels in 1930. Some two hundred pages long, this book offers numerous music examples and includes descriptions of the fiestas and other settings in which these melodies were performed.

About 1930, a new phase of ethnomusicological studies started in Latin America. They were undertaken in scholarly spirit, by such men as Mário de Andrade in Brazil, Vincente Mendoza in Mexico, and Carlos Vega in Argentina. The last representatives of this generation were active until recently.

Mário de Andrade (1893–1945), a very attractive personality, exercised a tremendous influence on the generation of artists and writers who were young in the 1920s. Andrade was not a musicologist, but he received a good musical training at the São Paulo Conservatory of Music. A poet, novelist, and art critic as well, he devoted much of his writing to music. His *Ensaio sôbre a música brasileira*, which first appeared in 1928, served as a guide to more than one generation of Brazilian composers. This is a didactic work, based on an analysis of the elements of Brazilian folk music. On the basis of Andrade's theories in this essay, young Brazilian composers evolved the firm national orientation that characterized their music and enabled them to surmount the world-wide crisis that later discredited so much of this type of music. The ethnomusicological writings of Mário de Andrade, collected and revised by his former pupil Oneyda Alvarenga, are included in his complete works; they comprise several volumes, among them three devoted to what the author called "dramatic dances," that is to say, folk theater and related rituals of the Brazilian people.[3]

3. *Obras completas de Mário de Andrade* (São Paulo): VI, *Ensaio sôbre a música*

Vincente Mendoza (1894–1964), a research scholar at the Institute of Esthetic Research of the National Autonomous University of Mexico, was deeply versed in the many areas related to music in his country. A prolific and indefatigable author, he included a large number of folksong transcriptions in his many important books. Probably the most valuable of these is his study in comparative folklore, *El Romance español y el corrido mexicano*.[4]

Carlos Vega (1898–1966) was one of the great personalities of Latin American musicology. Like many of his contemporaries, he explored not only primitive and folk music, but music history as well. His ethnomusicological research was not confined to his native country. He was aware that Argentinian ethnomusicology could not be studied as an isolated phenomenon, separate from musical phenomena in the neighboring regions of La Plata and the Cordillera. Thus what Vega discusses in his various books is the music of an area of South America extending from Uruguay to Ecuador. He was deeply concerned with theory and methodology; in the two volumes of his *Fraseología*[5] he laid down the principles that were to guide him in his analysis and notation of traditional music. In several other books he speculated on the origins of the folk music, which was his speciality, and explained how it should be classified.[6]

Oneyda Alvarenga, already mentioned as one of Mário de Andrade's students and the editor of his musical writings, was for many years the director of the Record Library of the City of São Paulo. She must be considered one of the leading Latin American ethnomusicologists of her generation. Her book, *Brazilian Folk Music*, is comprehensive and rigorous in its critical evaluations.[7]

The Argentine scholar, Isabel Aretz, who married the Venezuelan ethnomusicologist Luis Felipe Ramón y Rivera and now lives in Caracas, is another pre-eminent figure in this field of Latin American research. Among her teachers was Carlos Vega. She has published a book on

brasileira (1962); VII, *Música, doce música* (1963); XI, *Aspectos da música brasileira* (1965); XIII, *Música de feitiçaria no Brasil* (1963); XVIII, *Danças dramáticas do Brasil* (1959); XIX, *Modinhas imperiais* (1964).

4. Vincente Mendoza, *El Romance español y el corrido mexicano* (Mexico City, 1939). See also *La Décima en México* (Buenos Aires, 1947); *Panorama de la música tradicional de México* (Mexico City, 1956); *Lírica narrativa de México: el Corrido* (Mexico City, 1964).

5. Carlos Vega, *Fraseología, proposición de un nuevo método para la escritura y análisis de las ideas musicales y su aplicación al canto popular*, 2 vols. (Buenos Aires, 1941).

6. Carlos Vega, *Danzas y canciones argentinas* (Buenos Aires, 1936); *Panorama de la música popular Argentina* (Buenos Aires, 1944); *Los Instrumentos musicales aborígenes y criollos de la Argentina* (Buenos Aires, 1946); *Las danzas populares argentinas* (Buenos Aires, 1952).

7. Oneyda Alvarenga, *Música popular brasileña* (Mexico City, 1947; also published in Portuguese and Italian).

Argentinian folk music, and also an important volume on the musical instruments of Venezuela.[8] Isabel Aretz works with her husband at the Folklore Institute of Venezuela, which was founded in 1947 under the guidance of Stith Thompson. It is impossible today to evaluate Latin American literature in ethnomusicology without taking into consideration the numerous essays on Venezuelan folk music published by that Institute. They all have been edited by Isabel and Luis Felipe Ramón y Rivera.[9]

In Latin American ethnomusicology many avenues of research are open to the scholar and student. The three largest areas are: aboriginal music, European musical traditions, and Afro-American acculturation. Most of the authors just mentioned have explored all three areas simultaneously, if not with equal energy.

Study of the aboriginal music can lead to the well-established field of Inca and Aztec archaeology. I will return to this field. The relevant European traditions are primarily Hispanic (including the Portuguese), but there are also French traditions (and not only in Haiti). Starting with the nineteenth century, the newly independent Latin American countries were particularly hospitable to everything that came from countries other than Spain and Portugal. This tendency was strengthened by immigration from other European countries and by growing communication facilities. Non-Hispanic traditions grew in importance. The contredanse, the waltz, the polka, the schottische developed peculiar Latin American hybrids, which absorbed local melodic or rhythmic formulas and really became Latin American folk music. These non-Hispanic traditions in the folk music of Latin America have not yet been sufficiently investigated. Carlos Vega, however, focused attention on these influences and one must read his books to appreciate their importance and to understand how they were integrated into the American Hispanic cultures.

Afro-American music is better understood. Many distinguished North American scholars have joined eminent colleagues of the areas concerned, to improve our knowledge of this important field. Harold Courlander, Melville Herskovits, Alan P. Merriam, and Mieczyslas Kolinsky, to mention only a few, have contributed especially fruitful studies. Fernando Ortiz of Cuba, with his monumental *Los instrumentos de la música afrocubana*,[10] is one of the most respected specialists in the field. Today, Argeliers León, head of the Music Department of the José Martí National Library in Havana is following in the footsteps of the great man. His report on African contributions to the culture of Latin America and the

8. Isabel Aretz, *El folklore musical argentino* (Buenos Aires, 1952); *Instrumentos musicales de Venezuela* (Cumaná, 1967).

9. Most of them appeared in the *Boletín del Instituto de Folklore*, which was started in 1953.

10. Fernando Ortiz, *Los instrumentos de la música afro-cubana*, 5 vols. (Havana, 1952–55).

Caribbean, prepared for the Havana Colloquium organized by UNESCO last December, is an excellent introduction to the subject.[11] For the same colloquium Roger Bastide, of the Paris *École Pratique des Hautes Études*, prepared an extremely useful list of institutions and individuals having done or presently doing research on African influences in Latin America.[12] In almost every great country touched by African culture, there is a scholar who has devoted part of his activity to this subject.

Primitive music of the aboriginal populations of Latin America has been explored primarily by anthropologists who notated and even recorded the music, photographed and described the musical instruments and dances. Ethnomusicologists of the first generation (who at that time were not yet called ethnomusicologists) subsequently transcribed and analyzed the collected material. Hornbostel did so for the native populations of Tierra del Fuego, northwestern Brazil and, the region between Sierra Roraima and the Orinoco (Brazil and Venezuela).[13] H. H. Manizer, a Russian anthropologist whose work is not widely known, made an interesting study of the music and musical instruments of some indigenous tribes in Brazil.[14] The Swedish Karl Gustav Izikowitz deserves particular mention for his very comprehensive book *Musical and Other Sound Instruments of the South American Indians* (Göteborg, 1935).

In the field of what may properly be called folk music, besides the names previously mentioned (Andrade, Mendoza, Vega, Alvarenga, Aretz, Ramón y Rivera), we must list some additional distinguished researchers who furnish a vital impulse to those studies in several countries today. In Colombia, for example, Andrés Pardo Tovar is prominent; George List, of Indiana University, has also been very active, and is presently assembling important material to be published in the near future. Manuel Dannemann in Chile and Charles Boilés (a United States citizen) in Mexico should also be mentioned.

Samuel Marti, Mexican himself, is associated with the study of pre-Columbian music. His books on the musical instruments and dances of that period are indispensable to the student of the musical world of the

11. Argeliers León, "Música popular de origen africana en América Latina," *Colloquium on the African Contribution to the Culture of Latin America and the Caribbean*, 4 (Havana, Dec. 16–20, 1968).

12. Roger Bastide, "Répertoire contenant une liste des instituts de recherche et des spécialistes afro-latino-américans avec leurs adresses actuelles et un bref énoncé sur leurs recherches actuelles," *ibid.*, 9.

13. Erich M. von Hornbostel, "Über einige Panpfeifen aus Nordwest Brasilien," in Theodor Koch-Grunberg, *Zwei Jahre unter den Indianer*, II (Berlin, 1910); "Musik der Makushi, Taulipang und Yekuana," in Theodor Koch-Grunberg, *Von Roroima zum Orenoco*, III (Stuttgart, 1923), 307; "Fuegian Songs," *American Anthropologist*, XXXVIII (1936), 357.

14. H. H. Manizer, "Música e instrumentos de música de Algumas tribos do Brasil," *Revista brasileira de música*, I (1934), 303.

Maya, Aztec, and other ancient civilizations.[15] The great pioneering work on musical instruments of ancient Mexico is by Daniel Castañeda and Vincente Mendoza: *Instrumental precortesiano* (Mexico City, 1933).

To appreciate the importance today of the literature on the musical culture of the pre-Columbian nations, it is useful to survey the thirty-page bibliography of Robert Stevenson's recent *Music in Aztec and Inca Territory* (Berkeley, 1968). Yet that bibliography is not complete; as the author himself declares, it is only "a convenient list of the titles cited in the present volume."

The basic works for the study of the music of the Incas and other peoples who lived in the Cordillera are those of Raoul and Marguerite d'Harcourt, two French anthropologists who were in Peru early in this century and worked close to Paul Rivet when that eminent authority in American studies was exploring the same region.[16] Their theories concerning the structure of that music have proved to be highly controversial, and such native authors as Carlos Vega (Argentina) and Segundo Luis Moreno (Ecuador) have shown some resistance to them.[17]

This fascinating subdivision of musicological research in Latin America remains closely connected to archeology and paleography. It is mainly through the extremely delicate analysis of museum instruments and the interpretation of sculptures and paintings from monuments or codices that hypotheses can be proposed and eventually verified. But students of Inca music have not neglected the evidence offered by the present-day descendants of the Incas, on the assumption that they have preserved certain elements of the ancient traditions. So, Inca music can be observed from living evidence instead of being deduced entirely from iconography.

As we come to historical musicology, the best way to evaluate the situation is to proceed by country. Let us start with Argentina and go from south to north.

Argentina, the country where Carlos Vega developed a new and scholarly concept of Latin American music research, was late in producing a serious history of its national music. A few essays, such as those of the Jesuit fathers Pedro Grenón[18] and Guillermo Furlong,[19] cover certain

15. Samuel Marti, *Instrumentos musicales precortesianos* (Mexico City, 1955); *Canto, danza y música precortesianos* (Mexico City, 1961).

16. Raoul and Marguerite d'Harcourt, *La Musique des Incas et ses survivances*, 2 vols. (Paris, 1925).

17. See Carlos Vega, *Escalas con semitonos en la música de los antiguos peruanos* (Buenos Aires, 1934); Segundo Luis Moreno, *La música de los Incas* (Quito, 1957).

18. Pedro Grenón, *Una vida de artista: H. Luis Berger, S.J. (1588–1641)* (Cordoba, 1927); "Nuestra primera música instrumental," *Revista de estudios musicales*, V–VI (1950–51), 11, VII (1954), 173.

19. Guillermo Furlong, *Los Jesuitas y la cultura rio-platense* (Montevideo, 1933); *Músicos argentinos durante la dominación hispánica* (Buenos Aires, 1945); "Domenico

aspects of the past; opera history was particularly fortunate in the books of Mariano Bosch,[20] Alfredo Taullard,[21] Alfredo Fiorda Kelly,[22] Oscar Beltrán,[23] J. Luis Trenti Rocamora,[24] and others. But the first comprehensive survey of Argentinian musical activities of the past century was Vicente Gesualdo's two-volume history of the period 1836–51, published in 1961.[25]

In Uruguay the first volume of a similar survey, by Lauro Ayestarán, with 818 pages, many illustrations, and musical examples, was published in 1953.[26] The author, who stands with Andrade, Vega, Mendoza, Isabel Aretz, and others as one of the great figures of Latin American musicology, died in 1966. Among his many contributions to the history of music, not only of his own country but of an extended area of South America, his research on the last days of the Italian composer Domenico Zipoli must be emphasized. Before Ayestarán, no one had known that that famous organist of the Jesuit church in Rome had gone as a missionary to Argentina, where he died in 1726.

Renato Almeida is the standard historian of Brazilian music: a distinguished writer and essayist, albeit without professional training in music. His very important *História da música brasileira* (2nd ed., Rio de Janeiro, 1942) offers sound information and well-balanced judgments of men, institutions, and musical works. Before Almeida, a pioneer work had been published in Italian in Milan by Vincenzo Cernicchiaro, a violinist who had spent his life in Brazil.[27] This is a book to read with caution, since accuracy is not its major virtue, and the author, who as a professional musician took an active part in many of the events he describes, was unable to avoid a subjective point of view.

As in the case of Almeida in Brazil, it is an historian rather than a musicologist who has given us the fundamental books on the history of music in Chile. Eugenio Pereira Salas's two volumes are a convenient introduc-

Zipoli, músico eximio en Europa y América, 1688–1726," *Archivum historicum Societatis Jesu*, 1955/XXIV (Rome).

20. Mariano Bosch, *Historia de la ópera en Buenos Aires* (Buenos Aires, 1905); *Historia del teatro en Buenos Aires* (Buenos Aires, 1905).

21. Alfredo Taullard, *Historia de nuestros viejos teatros* (Buenos Aires, 1932).

22. Alfredo Fiorda Kelly, *Cronología de las óperas, dramas líricos, oratorios, himnos, etc. cantados en Buenos Aires* (Buenos Aires, 1934).

23. Oscar Beltrán, *Los orígenes del teatro argentino, desde el virreinato hasta el estreno de "Juan Moreira" (1884)* (Buenos Aires, 1941).

24. J. Luis Trenti Rocamora, *El teatro en la América colonial* (Buenos Aires, 1947); see also "La música en el teatro porteño anterior a 1810," *Revista de estudios musicales*, I (1949), 37.

25. Vicente Gesualdo, *Historia de la música en la Argentina, 1836–51*, 2 vols. (Buenos Aires, 1961).

26. Lauro Ayestarán, *La musica en el Uruguay* (Montevideo, 1953).

27. Vincenzo Cernicchiaro, *Storia della musica nel Brasile* (Milan, 1926).

tion to that particular area of Latin American historical musicology.[28] For the twentieth century, the book to consult is that of Eugenio Salas Viu.[29]

Coming to Peru, Bolivia, Ecuador, and Colombia, we must again refer to that prolific North American scholar, Robert Stevenson, and to his already mentioned *Music in Aztec and Inca Territory*. In various articles and papers presented to musicological meetings, he has also discussed the music of Ecuador and Colombia; that of colonial Bolivia is the subject of the last chapter of his book on *The Music of Peru*. Stevenson is a scholar to be trusted: everything he states is precise and backed by careful investigation.[30]

Perdomo-Escobar's *Historia de la música en Colombia*, enlarged in successive editions (3rd ed., Bogotá, 1963), provides a good background for further researches in that country. Aristocratic Bogotá of the past is portrayed in these pages in a candid yet very appealing way.

For Venezuela there is a similar book: José Antonio Calcaño's *La ciudad y su música* (Caracas, 1958). The articles of Juan Bautista Plaza, published in Spanish and in English in various periodicals, throw very helpful light on the important period of Venezuelan musical life immediately before the trying Wars of Independence.[31]

Alejo Carpentier is one of the major novelists of present-day Cuba, both before and since the Revolution. His *La música en Cuba* (Mexico City, 1947) was written for the Mexican Fondo de Cultura Económica collection, *Tierra Firme*, an ambitious project for the issue of a large series of books on many aspects of the Latin American countries. Informative and pleasant to read, Carpentier's book was the first to focus attention on the attractive figure of the eighteenth-century Cuban composer Esteban Salas. In recent years Pablo Hernández Balaguer, of the University of Oriente, in Santiago, has investigated the life and works of Salas and published some of his works. Balaguer's work was interrupted by his premature death.

We come now to Mexico, where the writings on music are important

28. Eugenio Pereira Salas, *Los orígenes del arte musical en Chile* (Santiago, 1941); *Historia de la música en Chile (1850–1900)* (Santiago, 1957).

29. Eugenio Salas Viu, *La creación musical en Chile (1900–1951)* (Santiago, n.d. [1951]).

30. Robert Stevenson, *Music in Mexico* (New York, 1952); *The Music of Peru* (Washington, D.C., 1960); *Spanish Music in the Age of Columbus* (The Hague, 1960); *Spanish Cathedral Music in the Golden Age* (Berkeley-Los Angeles, 1961); *Music in Aztec and Inca Territory* (Berkeley, 1968).

31. Juan Bautista Plaza, "Music in Caracas during the Colonial Period (1770–1811)," *Musical Quarterly*, XXIX (1943), 198; "Juan Manuel Olivares, el mas antiguo compositor venezolano," *Revista nacional de cultura*, LXIII (1947), 105; "José Angel Lamas," *ibid.*, C (1953), 21; "El Padre Sojo," *ibid.*, CXXIV (1957), 9; "Música colonial venezolona," *Boletín de programas de la Radio Nacional Colombiana*, CLXX-XVII (1960), 71.

for quality as well as quantity. The fundamental work is the *Historia de la música en México*, by Gabriel Saldívar and Elisa Osorio Bolio (Mexico City, 1934), now extremely difficult to obtain. Modern developments from Independence to the present are discussed with authority in Otto Mayer-Serra's *Panorama de la música mexicana* (Mexico City, 1941).

Some Latin American music historians, as we saw, have compiled archival documents. This was the case with Gabriel Saldívar in the book on Mexican music just mentioned. More recently, however, the dimensions of the Latin American musical past, particularly in the colonial period, have been greatly extended by the discovery of previously unknown musicians and a musical life the existence of which no one had suspected. This discovery has been due primarily to men like Juan Bautista Plaza in Venezuela, Francisco Curt Lange in Brazil, Steven Barwick and others in Mexico. The publication of the *Archivo de música colonial venezolana* in the early 1940s revealed a series of works by composers who had lived in Caracas at the end of the eighteenth century and who received constantly fresh stimuli from their European contemporaries; they studied and even performed works of the Classical composers then living in Vienna. In Brazil, also during the 1940s, another group of late eighteenth-century composers were laboriously rescued from the oblivion where they had remained since their death. This was the achievement of the German-born citizen of Uruguay, Francisco Curt Lange, who received financial assistance from the Brazilian authorities and from UNESCO to conduct his research in the state of Minas Gerais. Lange thought, with good reason, that if a rich (and now world-famous) Baroque religious architecture had developed in that region, the conditions which produced such architecture must have exercized a similar influence on the musical life. And he was proved right. More perishable than stonework, the music of that time had disappeared. Lange unearthed the surviving music, scored the works, edited them, traced the records of their composers, who had previously been mere names. Thus he was able to present in printed form, in recordings, and in public performances samples of this music, which for so many years had been reduced to silence.

Two United States citizens, Steven Barwick and Lota M. Spell, have concentrated their investigations in Mexico on what is currently called "cathedral music." Barwick's doctoral dissertation (Harvard, 1947) was on *Sacred Vocal Polyphony in Early Colonial Mexico*. In 1965 Barwick published the Franco Codex, containing works by Hernando Franco, the sixteenth-century Spanish-born chapelmaster of the Cathedral of Mexico.[32] Starting in the 1920s, Lota M. Spell, a veteran of Latin American research, published a number of interesting periodical articles, most of which have

32. Steven Barwick, *The Franco Codex of the Cathedral of Mexico* (Carbondale, Ill., 1965).

been translated into Spanish.[33] The Spanish composer Jesús Bal y Gay has also contributed to the diffusion of music composed in early Mexico, publishing the important first volume of the *Tesoro de la música polifónica en México* (Mexico City, 1952), which is devoted to the *Codice del Convento del Carmen*.

Music of Latin American colonial composers is now being published in a number of countries. Brazil offers a good example, with the work done by Cleofe Person de Matos on José Mauricio Nunez Garcia; by Regis Duprat on André da Silva Gomes; and by Jayme Diniz on Luis Alves Pinto, a Pernambuco composer of the early eighteenth century. All of the above editors belong to a generation of real musicologists, each specializing in one or more fields of music history. Their research is based on original documents, compiled at the sources, and not, as was the case with many pioneers, based on existing bibliography and collections of old newspapers (which, however, can yield very valuable information). When he died in 1966, Lauro Ayestarán was preparing for publication the score of one of the first operas composed in the western hemisphere: *La púrpura de la rosa*, based on Calderón de la Barca's play, composed by Don Tomás de Torrejón y Velasco and performed in Lima in 1701.

There is reason to hope that the next few years will see the publication of many more works by these early Latin American musicians and perhaps by others whose names are still unknown.

Since the study of Latin American music involves the use of some general reference works, let me indicate briefly several that are available.

Nicolas Slonimsky's *Music of Latin America* (New York, 1945), is still the only reference work that covers the entire region, country by country. I know that it may seem inappropriate to mention such a "light" book in such a scholarly context, but there is good reason why the book remains unique, and I believe this should be pointed out.

For quick reference, the two-volume encyclopedia dictionary by Otto Mayer-Serra, *Música y músicos de Latino América* (Mexico City, 1947), can be very useful. But this is now to a large extent outdated. For as we have seen, musicological research has made great strides in Latin America during the years since 1947, not to mention the intensive developments in contemporary music: new values, new trends and personalities, as well as the development of men who were but young composers when Mayer-Serra's dictionary appeared (the article on Alberto Ginastera is a good example).

An indispensable tool in Latin American musicology is Gilbert Chase's

33. Lota M. Spell, "The First Teacher of European Music in America," *Catholic Historical Review*, II (1922), 372; "The First Musical Books Printed in America," *Musical Quarterly*, XV (1929), 50; "Sixteenth Century Music in the Mexican Cathedral," *Hispanic American Historical Review*, XXVI (1946), 293.

bibliography, *A Guide to the Music of Latin America* (Washington, 1945; revised in 1962). Robert Stevenson, in his *Music in Aztec and Inca Territory*, pays a deserved tribute to Gilbert Chase when he says: "He has consistently remained a foremost figure in Latin American musicological and bibliographical disciplines." And he adds: "It goes without saying that any investigator bent on further research in our fields should make Chase's bibliographies his daily companions."[34]

Today, recorded music is tremendously important to the researcher, above all in the fields of ethnomusicology and contemporary art music. As to primitive and folk music, the record collections issued in the United States by the Library of Congress, by Folkways Records, and by the Columbia World Library of Folk and Primitive Music, and in France by the Musée de l'Homme and by l'OCORA, must be mentioned, along with scattered items in the catalogues of various phonograph companies and, above all, some very good records issued by national institutions of the countries concerned. At the moment, Argentina is publishing one such valuable collection of traditional music.

In a series sponsored by UNESCO, the International Folk Music Council published in 1954 an *International Catalogue of Recorded Folk Music.* Some supplements to that catalogue, prepared by Dr. Klaus Wachsmann, have since been published.

Much of the literature listed by Gilbert Chase in his bibliography was published not in book form, but in periodicals. So it is important to review briefly the Latin American journals devoted to music. Many have existed; few have published regularly. The most representative is certainly the *Revista musical chilena*, which has appeared regularly for more than twenty years. It is a well-presented quarterly, easy to find in any good library. Among many Mexican periodicals (*Orientación musical, Revista musical mexicana,* etc.), *Nuestra música,* one of the handsomest of Latin American music periodicals, offering very good material, was published for seven happy years, 1945 to 1952, under the editorship of Adolfo Salazar, Jesús Bal y Gay, and Rodolfo Halffter. In Brazil, from 1934 to 1944, the School of Music of the University of Rio de Janeiro published the *Revista brasileira de música,* a quarterly magazine similar to the just-mentioned Chilean and Mexican periodicals. I pass over the many current journals devoted to present-day music life in Latin America. *Buenos Aires musical* represents this kind of journal at its best, but for what concerns us here they have but slight interest.

Not a regular periodical, but an irregular publication of great importance, is Francisco Curt Lange's *Boletín latino americano de música,* of

34. Stevenson, *Music in Aztec and Inca Territory, op. cit.,* p. 335.

which six monumental volumes appeared between 1935 and 1946. It is difficult today to undertake the study of any aspect of music in Latin America without consulting that repertory of writings by the best-known specialists of that part of the world. Ethnomusicology, historical musicology, essays on contemporary composers—everything is discussed in the *Boletín*, and illustrated with copious pictures and musical examples. At the National University of Cuyo, in Mendoza, Argentina, where he was teaching musicology, Lange published a sort of continuation of the *Boletín*, less ambitious and more normal in size, called *Revista de estudios musicales*; seven numbers of the latter appeared. Among other valuable material to be found there, Lange's study on the last days of Louis Moreau Gottschalk in Rio de Janeiro deserves special mention.[35]

It would not be fitting to close this roll of periodicals without mentioning the *Boletín interamericano de música*, regularly issued since 1957 by the Pan American Union, Washington, D.C., with a parallel edition, basically different in content, especially edited for English-speaking readers: the *Inter-American Music Bulletin*. Besides useful information on current musical life in Latin America found in the Spanish edition, there are good articles, particularly in the English edition, which deserve bibliographical reference.

Both the music division of the Pan American Union and its own creation, the Inter-American Music Council (CIDEM), are among the agencies that assist people engaged in Latin American research. The musical publications of Pan American Union are not limited to the *Bulletin* just mentioned. A valuable series of catalogues of works by contemporary composers appears regularly;[36] and a series of monographs was published between 1941 and 1949.

A word must be said also about the Instituto Interamericano de Musicología, created by Francisco Curt Lange. With headquarters in Montevideo, the institute was active between 1940 and 1947, being responsible for the publication of the *Boletín latino americano de música* as well as scores by contemporary and colonial composers. Theoretically at least, the institute is still in existence.

Today, in the United States, such institutions as the Inter-American Institute for Music Research of Tulane University, New Orleans, and the Latin American Music Center of Indiana University, Bloomington, are repositories of important bibliographical and other information well worth exploration by scholars in the field.

In the field of ethnomusicology, almost every country of Latin America

35. Francisco Curt Lange, "Vida y muerte de Louis Moreau Gottschalk en Rio de Janeiro (1869)," *Revista de estudios musicales*, IV (1950), 43, V–VI (1950–57), 97.

36. *Compositores de America, datos biográficos y catálogos de sus obras* (Washington, D.C., I–XII [1950–66]); also published in English: *Composers of the Americas*.

has an institute prepared to help the investigator with publications, archival material, and experienced advice on local matters. The most important of these is the Instituto de Folklore in Caracas, organized in 1947, which continues its excellent work under the supervision of Luis Felipe Ramón y Rivera. The modest *Bulletin* of the institute contains an important quantity of scholarly material. In Brazil the government-sponsored Campanha de Defesa do Folclore Nacional publishes a very good *Revista brasileira de folclore*, assists those engaged in well-planned field work, and very diplomatically supports various organizations representing authentic folk traditions. Renato Almeida has been the moving spirit and is presently the director of this activity. The Instituto de Musicología of Buenos Aires, inspired by Carlos Vega, keeps alive the illustrious tradition of the many activities he carried on. In Colombia there is a Centro de Estudios Folklóricos y Musicales of the Universidad Nacional, in which Andrés Pardo Tovar has been very active. And in Mexico the Institute de Investigaciones Estéticas has made possible the important work accomplished by Vincente Mendoza.

The sources for historical musicology can be located in national libraries, national archives, cathedral and monastery archives. Conservatory libraries may also offer good opportunities for research. Everything depends on local conditions, which must be carefully examined. For his discoveries in Minas Gerais, Brazil, for instance, Francisco Curt Lange made no use (as far as the music was concerned) of ecclesiastical archives. Practically all the material he collected was in private possession and represented an inheritance handed down through many generations: it was the treasure of modest church musicians, who owned these musical materials as private tools for performing their jobs.

One must also bear in mind that information is to be found not only on this side of the ocean, but in European institutions as well. Colonial music, for instance, cannot be explored fully without methodical searches in Spanish and Portuguese collections. Connections between the American territories and the homeland were too close. Indeed, experience has shown that the study of western-hemisphere sources can also provide means to a better knowledge of music in the home countries of Spain and Portugal.

Much remains to be done. What has been accomplished is only a start. But we may hope that it is the start toward a bright future. Since 1949, when Steven Barwick's doctoral dissertation dealing with Latin American music was submitted to Harvard University, several others have been submitted to various American universities, and still more are in progress. This is not to say that Latin America is entirely dependent on the efficiency of scholars exported by the United States. Much basic research remains to be done, and must be done, by Latin Americans. In countries struggling to overcome underdevelopment, musicology has not been a field of academic priority. But the situation is improving, and I know some young people who have been able to obtain assistance to attend foreign universities for musicological training. On the other hand, at Latin American universities that do not offer specific facilities in this field, the departments of history and literature are increasingly sympathetic and offer more and more encouragement to musicological research. I am convinced that this new attitude will bear fruit during the next few years and that much will be accomplished. Meanwhile, researchers from the United States will be welcome and their cooperation will be very helpful. For the field is large and partially unexplored, and the number of those engaged in the arduous task of this difficult terrain is still small.

DISCUSSION

MISS ELLIS: Is musicological activity in Latin America today focused primarily on the collection of material, or on the organization and analysis of material already available?

AZEVEDO: A considerable amount of collecting has been done, but the gathering of source material still remains the principal task. Many tapes and records are to be found in the Musicological Institute of Buenos Aires, and the pioneering work of Carlos Vega in Argentina has been extended in Chile, in Ecuador, and in Bolivia. And in any major Brazilian university today, one may expect to find a center for folklore research. The most important job being done by such centers is collecting, rather than analyzing materials.

MRS. HAMPTON: Bibliographies I have seen suggest that most of the research that has been published deals with music of colonial or precolonial times. There seems to be very little written on the present state of music in Latin America. Is my impression an accurate one?

AZEVEDO: I would have some difficulty citing references for you, if you are speaking of music by young composers now in their twenties and thirties—although articles are just now beginning to appear in the music journals. Of the generations of Villa-Lobos and Ginastera, of course, very much has been written.

VAN SOLKEMA: Would you clarify what you mean by ethnomusicology as applied to Latin American music? Perhaps you might do this by indicating what, in nineteenth-century music, you would *not* think of as ethnomusicological?

AZEVEDO: In the nineteenth century, the division between ethnomusicology and historical musicology, even in Latin America, is very clear. From colonial times art music was written by trained composers in the European tradition. We can trace a very strong tradition of classical church music at least back to the eighteenth century in many countries, and in Mexico and Peru back to the sixteenth century. There is also a kind of dramatic music that was presented in church but was not exactly religious music.

What I would call the ethnomusicological panorama of Latin America is very complex. On one hand, there is the primitive music of the Indians —some of it from tribes that are very primitive indeed, such as some of the tribes of Brazil and southern Argentina. Their music may be built from scales with only two or three tones. On the other hand, there is a much more advanced Indian music—for example, music of the region of the Cordillera, which, in a certain way, I think, might represent the Inca music of the past. As soon as traditions were established, the picture becomes complicated. The social situation was such that the two principal avenues toward improving one's position were to become a priest or a musician. Those with musical talent could rise rapidly, regardless of race, in the predominantly white colonial society. For a priest, too, all doors were open. Even today in Brazil the masters of popular music—the men who compose the sambas of Carnival—are highly respected men throughout society.

On the side of historical musicology, we find in many countries libraries containing seventeenth- and eighteenth-century music. When Humboldt passed through Venezuela, for example, he met a cousin of Bolívar, Father Sojo, who had about him at his country house near Caracas some ten or twelve composers well-versed in the European traditions. On his return to Europe, Humboldt sent back to Caracas a quantity of Viennese music, including works by Mozart and Beethoven. Nunez Garcia's library shows that he, too, regularly received music from Europe.

BROOK: Does anything remain of that library? It is possible that things which no longer exist in Europe might survive there, as have some sixteenth-century Mass compositions in Mexico?

AZEVEDO: Yes. National libraries can be extremely important in this regard. When the king fled Portugal in 1808, as Napoleon's troops advanced, he went to Rio de Janeiro, with all the treasures of the court and the library. The library stayed in Rio de Janeiro, and its many important music manuscripts and printed editions are today the foundation of the music section of the National Library there. There are also first editions of Mozart in the library of the Conservatory of Music of São Paulo. Other manuscripts and editions can be found in Minas Gerais, in the interior.

BROOK: It is unfortunate that these holdings have not been adequately reported to RISM. Do you know of any efforts being made to improve this situation?

AZEVEDO: I believe that matters are improving somewhat. With regard to printed editions, there is really not a lot more to report. Despite what I have been saying, Brazil, Venezuela, and Cuba were poor colonies. They do not have the rich archives of Mexico or Peru. However, when the manuscript division of RISM begins, Brazil and South America generally will be able to contribute much more.

MRS. HAMPTON: In your *Brief History of Music in Brazil*[37] you note that until 1850 the music of Brazil was predominantly religious. Was all of this music in the European "composed" tradition?

AZEVEDO: Yes, this music was composed for the church. But in Brazil there is a very curious organization of church life, one that may be responsible for the lack of ecclesiastical music archives. Many of the churches in Brazil are the private property of cooperative groups—brotherhoods, which were in complete control of their churches. They paid the priests to celebrate mass. They seemed to have preferred to engage musicians for specific ceremonies, rather than to maintain elaborate musical establishments. Musicians brought in would depart without leaving anything in the church.

DITTMER: What dangers are present to Indian folk music today? How much time do we have to record, catalogue, and investigate such music before it disappears?

AZEVEDO: The answer to this question depends very much on the region. There are populations still living a Stone Age life in parts of Brazil and Venezuela. Work here has to be done very quickly; these populations are disappearing. The Indian population of Brazil, which was half a million thirty years ago, is less than 100,000 today. Many Indians who have come to the cities and have become involved in urban life cannot be considered Indians. There are tribes now composed of only fifteen or twenty people; they are very near extinction, and work with their cultures is urgent.

Outside the cities, the Indians conserve traditions and individuality, although they may dress as we dress, live in towns, and send their children to school. Some of their traditions will be preserved for a time, although we cannot know for how long. I believe the case is the same for all folk traditions today that are affected by mass communication. I am sometimes surprised to see how much they have resisted to date.

VAN SOLKEMA: We have not yet spoken of the African contribution to South American cultures. Of the African peoples who were brought to North America, most came from West Africa and the Gold Coast area. I believe this is not true for South America, at least not in Brazil. Can you tell us where the black populations of South America have come from?

AZEVEDO: They are to a large extent Bantu peoples from Equatorial

37. Luiz Heitor Corrêa de Azevedo, *Brief History of Music in Brazil* (Washington, D.C., 1948).

Africa, and in a small part an elite group of Sudanese. But in Brazil, at least, the Portuguese policy soon became one of avoiding the Sudanese because they were too organized, too intelligent, and all Negro rebellions in Brazil were organized and led by them. Nevertheless, because the Sudanese were highly cultured, their culture influenced or provided religious forms and order. Though few in number—and they are very few—they predominated culturally.

MRS. JORGENS: Is material available for the study of emerging national styles in Latin American music in the nineteenth century?

AZEVEDO: Yes, the music is available. The separation between the European models and the national styles can be seen very early in the nineteenth century. The same phenomenon can be seen in native literature. Before the trained composer enters the picture, the popular composers had developed vernacular traditions. By 1840–60, a national style was established in Cuba, and in Brazil above all, and this style gave birth to all of the many forms of popular music in those countries.

LINCOLN: I have noted in Mexico that very many churches contain organs that are of great interest—most of them Spanish, early eighteenth century, and in very bad state, but fascinating. I wonder if such organs are to be found farther down in South America and whether anything is being done to catalogue and preserve them.

AZEVEDO: I know of no systematic work. One does find magnificent archives and instruments from the rich colonies of colonial times—Mexico and Peru. When the gold and diamond mines were discovered in Brazil, late in the seventeenth century, a rich society began to develop there also. There are locally built organs in the baroque churches of Minas Gerais. Bahia and Recife possess many beautiful churches, although not as spectacular as the cathedrals of Mexico or Lima. In some of those churches everything was imported, from the stones to the organs. In the poorer colonies—in Equador and Paraguay, for example—organs were sometimes built by the Jesuit fathers, sometimes with the most primitive materials. We know that in Colombia there was an organ made of bamboo. But, as I said before, for the most part real organs imported from Europe will be found in the cathedrals of the wealthy cities. And in the seventeenth century a few organ makers came to Brazil and built organs for the very small but beautiful churches in the state of Minas Gerais.

READING LIST

The following writings are suggested by the lecturer:

Azevedo, Luiz Heitor Corrêa de, *Brief History of Music in Brazil* (Washington, 1948).

────── *150 anos de música no Brasil* (Rio de Janeiro, 1956).

Carpentier, Alejo, "Music in Cuba (1523–1900)," *Musical Quarterly*, XXXIII/3 (1947).

Chase, Gilbert, "An Approach to Latin American Music (Notes towards a Theory of Values)," *Studies in Ethnomusicology*, I (1961).

────── "Creative Trends in Latin American Music," *Tempo*, XLVIII (1958), L (1959).

────── "A Dialectical Approach to Music History," *Ethnomusicology*, II/1 (1958).

────── *Music of the New World* (New York, 1942–43).

────── *The Music of Spain* (New York, 1959).

Courlander, Harold, *The Drum and the Hoe* (Berkeley-Los Angeles, 1960).

Espinosa, Guillermo, "Colombian Music and Musicians in Contemporary Culture," *Inter-American Music Bulletin*, XXVII (1962).

Gallop, Rodney, "The Music of Indian Mexico," *Musical Quarterly*, XXV/2 (1939).

González Pérez, Alberto, "Discovery in Minas Gerais—On the Trail of Eighteenth Century Musical Scores," *Inter-American Music Bulletin*, XXXIV (1963).

Hill, Lawrence, *Brazil* (Berkeley-Los Angeles, 1947).

Jong, Gerrit de, "Music in Brazil," *Inter-American Music Bulletin*, XXXI (1962).

León, Argeliers, *Música folklórica cubana* (Havana, 1964).

Livermore, H. V., *Portugal and Brazil, an Introduction* (Oxford, 1953).

Marti, Samuel, and G. Probosch Kurath, *Dances of Anahuac—The Choreography and Music of Precortesian Dances* (Chicago, 1964).

Mayer-Serra, Otto, *Música y músicos de Latino-América* (Mexico, 1947).

────── *The Present State of Music in Mexico* (Washington, 1946).

Orrego Salas, Juan, "The Young Generation of Latin American Composers," *Inter-American Music Bulletin*, XXXVIII (1963).

Perdono Escobar, José Ignacio, *Historia de la música en Colombia* (Bogotá, 1945).

Pereira Salas, Eugenio, *Historia de la música en Chile* (Santiago, 1957).

──── *Los orígines del arte musical en Chile* (Santiago, 1941).

Plaza, Juan Bautista, "Music in Caracas during the Colonial Period," *Musical Quarterly*, XXIX/2 (1943).

Ramón y Rivera, Luis Felipe, "Negro Music of Venezuela," *Journal of the International Folk Music Council*, XIV (1962).

Seeger, Charles, "The Cultivation of Various European Traditions in the Americas," *Report of the Eighth Congress of the International Musicological Society, New York, 1961*, I (Kassel, 1961).

Stevenson, Robert, "The Bogotá Music Archives," *Journal of the American Musicological Society*, XV/3 (1962).

────── "Colonial Music in Bogotá," *Inter-American Music Bulletin*, XXVII (1962).

────── "Early Peruvian Folk Music," *Journal of American Folklore*, CCLXXXVIII (1960).

———— "European Music in Sixteenth Century Guatemala," *Music Quarterly*, L/3 (1964).

———— "Latin American Archives," *Fontes Artis Musicae*, 1962/I.

———— "Music Research in South American Libraries," *Inter-American Music Bulletin*, XVIII (1960).

———— "Sixteenth and Seventeenth Century Resources in Mexico," *Fontes Artis Musicae*, 1954/II, 1955/I.

Veliz, Claudio, *Latin America and the Caribbean, a Handbook* (London, 1968).

The Present State and Potential of Music Research in Africa

J. H. KWABENA NKETIA

M*USIC* research currently being undertaken in Africa is focused on the expressions of the indigenous populations of the continent, for the importance attached to these has assumed a new dimension in postcolonial Africa. Country-wide festivals of music and dancing have become a feature of cultural life, and are organized both for entertainment and as an outlet for mass expression of feeling at political rallies or in connection with events of national importance. No African country has so far rejoiced over her freedom from colonial rule without a program of traditional music and dancing.

The introduction of mass communications media has similarly brought a new dimension into African musical practice, since music that had been formerly confined to the "tribal" area[1] is now being relayed to entire nations through radio and television. These and recordings now make it possible to listen to music outside its usual social context. In this way a new habit of listening is being fostered, while the practice of recording music groups both within their community and in studios is generating new performance attitudes.

1. The word *tribe*, when applied to African peoples, refers to a wide diversity of population groups, ranging from stateless societies and village states to large centralized states of several million people occupying a large expanse of territory.

National theater movements are carrying all these further by drawing on traditional resources, at least as a starting point for a new African theater based on indigenous traditions. Not only are musical types and dances being performed outside their regular social and cultural contexts, but new modes of presentation are being introduced to meet the requirements of the new theater as well. There are national dance companies in Ghana, Sierra Leone, Senegal, Guinea, Mali, Uganda, and Tanzania.

There is, thus, a growing feeling that the arts must not remain forever as "tribal arts," governed only by traditions of the past and reflecting the creative efforts of an old changing era. There should be scope for creative innovations that might offer new lines for the development of common or "national" forms in addition to the purely local forms. Accordingly, new modes of making music, some of which reflect acculturative influences of Islamic and European periods of African history, are emerging alongside traditional forms, and new problems of musical values now have to be faced.

These developments are being encouraged not only by politicians, but also by those searching for an African cultural identity in the modern world, or those rediscovering and reassessing the relevance of traditional African values to contemporary Africa. Even the Christian church, which has been hostile in many ways to African music and which is largely responsible for the acculturative influences of Western music in many parts of Africa, now seems eager to reinstate African music and to encourage the creation of music in the African idiom for worship. *Missa Luba, Missa Bantu*, and similar recordings are examples of expressions of this new orientation.

If these new trends are to blossom into forms comparable in integrity to those of traditional music, they must be guided, it is felt, not just by enthusiasm or by a negative spirit of revolt against acculturative influences of the West associated with colonialism and Christian evangelism, but by creative imagination stimulated by a knowledge of the best in African traditions. It is no wonder, therefore, that at this period of cultural awakening active consideration is being given in some national development programs to the promotion of culture and, alongside this, to research into traditional African music, dance, and drama in African universities and national institutes. African musical resources and artistic values must be more clearly defined and documented for creative artists and performers as well as for music educators who have to plan new courses and develop curriculum materials in African music for African schools.[2] The African child cannot go on forever singing *Baa, Baa, Black Sheep* and *Here We Go Round the Mulberry Bush*.

Although African governments are concerned with the immediate

2. See J. H. Kwabena Nketia, "Music Education in African Schools," in *International Seminar on Teacher Education in Music* (Ann Arbor, 1966).

problems of nation-building in their respective countries, they have also been interested in interterritorial problems, in regional grouping, and in African unity. African artists—writers, painters, musicians, and dramatists —are responding to the demands of this new outlook, to the challenge of drawing on the creative resources of their own countries as well as those of the rest of Africa with which they are familiar.

The aims and scope of music research in present-day Africa, therefore, have of necessity to be broader and directed more to immediate, Africa-centered problems than was the case in the heyday of comparative musicology or of the colonial era. While research may be undertaken as before in pursuit of questions of theoretical interest, postcolonial Africa demands not only fundamental research of general interest to scholars, but also research geared to the solution of problems facing the development and practice of the arts in contemporary Africa.

Hence, the listing of priorities in national research may be different from what a research scholar interested in fundamental research might draw up. An Israeli musicologist studying African music in Israel may do so for reasons not relevant to the kinds of questions to which Africans are now seeking answers. A British musicologist may devote his time and energy to the solution of an historical problem raised by other musicologists on the probable Indonesian origin of African xylophones,[3] while the African may at present find it more urgent to devote his time to the study of the actual music of the African xylophone and its performance techniques. An American ethnomusicologist of the behavioral school may study African music as an aspect of behavior and not primarily as an art form,[4] just as a British social anthropologist has in fact examined the Kalela dance of southern Rhodesia in terms of social organization rather than the art of the dance.[5]

National institutes and research centers in Africa have to provide answers to certain basic questions that educated Africans, cut off culturally from their own society, might ask about the music of their country or of the ethnic group to which they belong. They must be concerned with the total musical heritage of their respective countries. Thus, a Tanzanian institute would be concerned with the Tanzanian heritage—that is, the aggregate of forms associated with the Wasukuma, Wanyamwezi, Wahehe, Wachagga, and, indeed, the one-hundred-and-thirteen-odd groups welded into a nation by a new political consciousness. Similarly the heritage of Ghana, Nigeria, Uganda, Kenya, and other African coun-

3. Arthur M. Jones, "Indonesia and Africa: The Xylophone as a Culture Indicator," *African Music*, II/3 (1960), 36–47; *id.*, *Africa and Indonesia, the Evidence of the Xylophone and Other Musical and Cultural Factors* (Leiden, 1964).
4. Alan P. Merriam, *The Anthropology of Music* (Evanston, Ill., 1965).
5. J. Clyde Mitchel, *Kalela Dance* (Manchester, 1956), p. 52.

tries may be defined in terms of the specializations within these territories.

Music research carried on in this manner may result in a number of territorial surveys, and one may look forward to publications parallel to *African Music in Ghana*[6] on African music in Uganda (an expansion of *African Music from the Source of the Nile*),[7] in Tanzania, in Kenya, in Nigeria, and so on. There is bound to be duplication of information in such surveys, information that may be of no special interest to those concerned with new discoveries. In some cases the same instrumental types may be listed, the same kind of statements may be made about the "use" of music. But this duplication should ultimately enable us to get a better picture of the continental or regional characteristics of the music of Africa and their distribution than we have at present.

The basis for selecting tribal groups for intensive study in a national program may also be different from the order of priority that other scholars might follow. For example, in Ghana one may begin, as we have done, with the Akan because, in the first place, they form the largest single group in the country and their language is much more widely spoken throughout the country than any other Ghanaian language, and, in the second place, by reason of historical interaction in the past, elements of Akan culture form an important part of the cultures of many areas of Ghana. Many Ghanaians share a common pattern of chieftaincy with the Akan. The talking drums of the Akan are played in Akan by the Ga of southern Ghana, the Ewe of the Volta region, the Dagbani, the Mampursi, and the Wala of northern Ghana. The songs of Akan warrior organizations (*asafo*) are sung in many of these areas. From a national point of view, therefore, ethnomusicological studies of the Akan may be given priority over studies of the Tallensi, despite the academic importance the latter have assumed because of the analysis of their society by an eminent anthropologist.[8] From the same point of view, we would put the music of the Adangme further down in our scale of research priorities, in favor of the Ewe, with their complex drum rhythms, or the xylophone cultures of northwestern Ghana, or the aerophone ensembles of the Kassena-Nankani and the Builsa.

Similarly, in Tanzania one would probably not begin, for example, with an assiduous search for the Watindinga (Bushmen) and their music, which would be of particular historical interest, but with, say, the Wasukuma and the Wanyamwezi, who make up about one tenth of the entire population of Tanzania and who have certain musical traditions that are drawn upon in the new national context; or one may study the Wazaramo, who

---

6. J. H. Kwabena Nketia, *African Music in Ghana* (Evanston, 1962).
7. Joseph Kygambiddwa, *African Music from the Source of the Nile* (London, 1955).
8. Meyer Fortes, *The Dynamics of Kinship among the Tallensi* (London, 1945).

because of their geographical location contribute to national activities in the capital more than any group, or the Wagogo, whose singing style has something to offer to the development of choral music in Tanzania.

Of course, every group must be looked at eventually, and a sampling of the resources of each one might indicate where fruitful studies relevant to creative and performance problems might be done.

It will be evident from the foregoing that music research in Africa must now be tackled on at least four different fronts:

First, there is the tribal context, the primary source of the arts of modern Africa, which must continue to be studied and documented. In spite of the far-reaching social, political, and cultural changes that have taken place in Africa, the tribe is still a basic cultural unit and its music must be studied in any cultural research program that seeks to discover the heritage of the past or to understand the present. However, it is important that tribal musical cultures should not be studied as isolated units but rather as integral parts of national cultures.

Second, there is the national context, which (as a product and an agent of change or the primary stimulus for new creative forms) seeks to give a new orientation to tradition by providing new opportunities for the enjoyment of tribal music outside the tribal enclave or by bringing together the musical traditions of the past within the framework of new cultural activities while giving a sense of direction to new forms. In this connection it is not only the phenomenon of political songs that must be studied, but also the dynamics of musical change in the national framework or the role that music is playing in the process of nation-building.

Third, there is the regional or interterritorial context, in which problems of interterritorial interest, particularly those of "splintered" groups, nomads, and migrant settlers, have to be considered. Splintered groups are tribal groups now found in different territories as a result of migrations of the past or the political divisions of the colonial era. The Ewe are in both Ghana and Togo. The Wanyakusa and the Wanyasa are found in both Malawi and Tanzania. There are also the Waluo in Kenya and Tanzania and the Watwa in Congo and Tanzania, while the Wasandawe in Tanzania are believed to be an offshoot of the "click-speaking peoples" of South Africa.

Fourth, there is the continental context, in which national, interterritorial, or regional specializations are investigated so that common forms and the aggregate of area specializations can be seen on a broad continent-wide canvas.

For some time to come, music research in Africa itself will be so engrossed in national problems that it may lose sight of the third and fourth areas. It is here that research carried on by individuals and institutions outside Africa can play a valuable complementary role in the urgent task of systematizing our knowledge of African music. This role would be greatly facilitated if research carried out both inside and outside Africa is guided by (a) a common conceptual framework derived from a common discipline, and (b) a new attitude toward Africa and its music that makes understanding the African heritage in its own terms its primary objective.[9]

In stressing the need for a new era of collaboration between scholars inside and outside Africa, a need created by the present African situation, I am not underrating what has already been achieved by scholars in this field, which provides a basis for further investigation. My main concern is for new directions that might increase the relevance of African music research to Africa itself. However, no one familiar with the present state of research or the sources now available for investigation will deny that there is little cause for complacency. A cursory glance at Gaskin's recent bibliography of African music[10] does give the impression that fruitful research in almost all fronts outlined above has been accomplished. There are general items as well as items listed by regions, countries, and tribes, and items listed according to subjects of special interest. Indeed, if the number of entries were anything to go by, one would be justified in assuming that African music research has made monumental strides since the publication of Wallaschek's *Primitive Music* (1893),[11] which includes some observations on African music based on information collated from travelogues.

However, anyone who has to rely on these publications for source material or for significant contributions related to the four areas of research will soon find that the situation is far from satisfactory. One has only to select a particular subject or area of study to find that there are gaps that need to be filled before it can be adequately studied in terms of current ethnomusicological theories and methods. If one were interested in doing a study of the music of Tanzania, for example, one would find only bits and pieces in periodicals—an isolated account of a Wapogoro flute, a brief description of Wanyaturu festival dance, a set of texts from Sukumaland, an account of the musical instruments of the Wasandawe considered from an ethnographic and historical point of view, and references in anthropological works that give good descriptions of contexts but hardly any illuminating information on style. For the latter, one must turn to what Rose Brandel was able to include in her work on the music of

9. See J. H. Kwabena Nketia, "Musicology and African Music," in *Africa in the Wider World*, ed. Brokensha and Crowder (Elmsford, N.Y., 1968), pp. 12–33.

10. Lionel John Palmer Gaskin, *Select Bibliography of the Music of Africa* (London, 1965).

11. Richard Wallaschek, *Primitive Music* (London, 1893).

central Africa,[12] which was based largely on the analysis of the few recordings she could lay hands on.

When we turn to the rather extensive recordings of the music of Africa that are now available, the situation is better, but by no means wholly satisfactory. For the study of limited stylistic problems on a regional or continent-wide basis, recordings are valuable, and it is in this way that Rose Brandel's study makes a contribution. The International Library of African Music (based in Roodepoort, near Johannesburg) offers a large sample of music across Bantu Africa, while the recordings of Ocora (a recording company in Paris) cover large parts of French-speaking Africa. These recordings give us a good idea of the range of sounds that could be subsumed under the general term "African music." However, for depth studies of countries and single tribes, the gaps become immediately apparent, for the collections are generally not guided by the need for depth studies but by the need for survey material, and more especially by the need for providing a range of new musical experience from Africa. Indeed, some field collectors also keep the needs of radio stations very much in mind, since the intention of their published collection is, first and foremost, to provide listening experience for the general public rather than documentation for specialists.

There are other problems raised by existing recordings, the solution of which the research scholar may have no clear guide. For example, he can never be sure of the cultural norms that the recordings in a particular album represent. The basis for the selection of the material may not always be apparent. Quite often, he has no means of telling whether the material represents what the particular society in question would regard as the best example of the selected items of music.

Coupled with this is the fact that a recording is only an abstraction. Athough it gives the total sound of a performance, it tells one very little about the actual organization of the performance, unless one has experienced live musical performances in the field. A motion picture gives much more of the context and is infinitely better as a research tool, but it can not, of course, be a complete substitute for what a trained observer can see in the total performance situation, since it also has to be selective.

Closely allied to the foregoing is the problem that recordings pose for the transcriber. Some recorded materials can be transcribed fairly accurately because of the simplicity or clarity of the underlying performance organization. Others, however, represent the sum total of a number of independent parts, which cannot be properly isolated in the absence of previous knowledge of the organization of the music. In some cases, a transcription accurately reflecting the underlying performance concept

12. Rose Brandel, *The Music of Central Africa* (The Hague, 1961; 2nd printing, 1969).

can only be made from a practical knowledge of the performance techniques—as the studies of Kiganda xylophones by both Gerhard Kubik[13]
and Lois Anderson[14] have amply demonstrated.

The upshot of all this is that research which contributes significantly to
our present knowledge of African music cannot always be done wholly
on the basis of published documentary sources now available. This is not
only because of obvious gaps, but also because we are dealing with music
practiced and perpetuated by oral tradition; it thus requires closer observation and more elaborate documentation than most field collectors not
engaged in scholarly research can afford to give it.

It is possible that this state of affairs will improve as time goes on, for
the question of detailed documentation is beginning to receive serious
attention not only in archives outside Africa (which are well ahead in this
matter) but also inside Africa. For the present, however, either some contact with the primary source in the field or with a carrier of the tradition
is necessary. Archival and library studies of some sort can be carried out
by those who are interested in transcriptions and structural analysis and
who do not mind working entirely from secondary sources. But it is as
well for even such people to bear in mind that verbal descriptions of transcriptions—which is what one frequently gets from many of those who
set out to describe African music analytically—are not the same as descriptions of performance or of musical structure arising out of the performance.

It is the continuing need for field work that has slowed down the progress of research into African music, for the area is vast and the magnitude
of the work involved in the study of the music of even a single tribe is
enormous. It is no wonder, therefore, that very few comprehensive or
depth studies of the total musical heritage of single tribal groups have
appeared, let alone large-scale studies, based on primary sources, of territories and regions. Scholars have had to concentrate on partial studies and
limited surveys—such as studies of the musical instruments of particular
tribes or regions,[15] or of the techniques or repertory of selected instruments in a few areas,[16] limited studies of songs and song texts,[17] or of the
social context of music in selected areas.[18]

13. Gerhard Kubik, "The Structure of Kiganda Xylophone Music,"   *African
Music*, II/3 (1960), 6–30.

14. Lois Anderson, "The Miko Modal Transposition System of Kiganda Xylophone Music," Ph.D. diss., U. of Cal., 1968.

15. Percival R. Kirby, *Musical Instruments of the Native Races of South Africa*
(London, 1934).

16. See Gerhard Kubik, *op. cit.*, also Alan P. Merriam, "Musical Instruments and
Techniques of Performance among the Bashi," *Zaire*, IX/2 (1955), 122–23.

17. See, for example, Alan P. Merriam, "Song Texts of the Bashi," *Zaire*, VIII
(1954), 27–43; also, J. H. Kwabena Nketia, *Akan Folksongs* (London, 1963).

18. See J. H. Kwabena Nketia, *Funeral Dirges of the Akan People* (Achimota,

However, taken together, these partial studies and surveys give us a good insight into the major theoretical problems with which music research in Africa must concern itself, and it is to these problems that I would now like to turn.

A major difficulty raised by the wide gaps in our knowledge of the music of Africa is the difficulty of generalizing for the continent as a whole or even for large areas of it. This is a problem that will remain with us for many years to come. Thus, it would even seem premature to talk about the music of Africa as a whole, in view of the insistence of some scholars that we can properly talk only about the *musics* of Africa. However, this position merely states the problem without offering an approach to its solution. In fact, the picture that we have is not one of completely isolated musical cultures but of unity and diversity.[19]

On the basis of the gross characteristics of these diverse forms evident in existing studies, the music of Africa can be described as the aggregate of musical expressions belonging exclusively to the African continent and sharing common features of internal patterns, basic procedures, and similar contextual relations.[20] This definition, which sets Africa apart as a major stylistic area in the world of music, excludes

(a) The music of Arab north Africa—the Arab music of Egypt, Tunisia, Morocco, Algeria—which belongs more to the Middle Eastern musical genre than to the African continent itself;

(b) The music of settler populations in Africa—in particular the music of white South Africa, which belongs to the mainstream of Western music, and the music of settler populations in Kenya and Rhodesia;

(c) Western music composed and performed on the African continent by Africans, since it does not share the features of internal patterning characteristic of the music that belongs to the continent of Africa.

On the other hand, it includes hybrids characteristic of the African continent, such as new art music composed by Africans that incorporates the essential features of internal patterning, as well as popular music in a new African idiom, such as the Highlife.[21]

1955), and *Drumming in Akan Communities of Ghana* (Edinburgh, 1963); Hugh Tracey, "Short Survey of Southern African Folk Music," *African Music Society Newsletter*, I/6 (1953); and Klaus P. Wachsmann, "Folk Musicians of Uganda," Uganda Museum, Occasional Papers, 2 (1956), p. 2.

19. See J. H. Kwabena Nketia, "Unity and Diversity in African Music: A Problem of Synthesis," in *Proceedings of the First International Congress of Africanists* (New York, 1964), pp. 256–63.

20. See Alan P. Merriam, "Characteristics of African Music," *Journal of the International Folk Music Council*, XI (1959), 13–19.

21. See J. A. Kwabena Nketia, "Modern Trends in Ghana Music," *African Music*, I/4 (1957), 13–17.

Thus, within the general term "African music" we can distinguish between traditional and nontraditional idioms of music. Within each idiom we can distinguish between different varieties. There are varieties of nontraditional music distinguished on a stylistic basis and associated with modern, nontribal institutions and wider national contexts. We can similarly distinguish between varieties of traditional music on the basis of styles identified with tribal groups. Thus, we may refer to the Akan variety of African music, the Yoruba variety, the Ewe variety, the Wanyamwezi variety, the Wagogo variety, and so on.

A comparison of the different varieties of African music shows that some of them bear very close resemblance to each other in certain respects. The similarity between the singing style of the Warufiji of Tanzania and the Baule of the Ivory Coast or the Akan of Ghana and the Ijaw of Nigeria is very striking. It should be possible, therefore, to group different varieties of African music into style types on the basis of selected musical criteria. This is one of the major tasks facing African music research.

The varieties that constitute a style type may cluster in a single area or they may be widely scattered, for style types do not necessarily coincide with linguistic boundaries or, indeed, with culture clusters or culture areas. There are instances of linguistic groups that are separated musically and thus might be placed in different style clusters. The Ewe of the Volta region of Ghana, for example, belong to two separate style groups; those in the hinterland belong more to the same style type as the Akan, their eastern neighbors; while those along the coast belong to the style type of the Fon of Dahomey.

The challenge which these facts present to us is one of discovery and exploration. We must discover the variety of musical expressions found in Africa. We must listen to as much of this variety as possible, in order to enlarge our knowledge and experience of the music of Africa, so that we can appreciate each type of African musical expression, in its own right, as music. In this way we can enlarge out concept of what is musically valid in the cultures of Africa, and avoid getting into a state of mind that prejudges this on the basis of familiarity with a limited geographical area.

The second task that follows from this is the systematic comparison of the music of African cultures in order to delimit the identical or common elements as well as the differences. Our examination of the latter must be concerned with the extent, distribution, and function of differences. We must seek to discover what are mutually exclusive or totally unrelated elements, or what are similar and could be regarded as variants. In other words, our study of African music should lead to the identification of style types within which similarities and divergent forms operate.

This presupposes a basic knowledge of the music of single cultures and a close analysis of the differentiations that each one contains within itself, as well as the functional values they represent. The musical types of each culture, with their component items and their interrelationships, would be analyzed on at least three levels: *sound, structure,* and *context.*

Investigation of sound would concern itself with all the variety of vocal and instrumental sounds used in the given society. It would deal with the attributes of sounds, including features of pitch, timbre, amplitude, and duration, as well as with tuning and scale systems related to these. The correlations between the phonetic features of speech and the sound attributes of vocal style would be dealt with on this level.

A few promising studies on this level of analysis have already begun. Measurements of the tunings of xylophones (some of them, unfortunately, museum specimens)[22] and hand pianos[23] have been made, and a rough idea of the variety of scale patterns commonly found in Africa has emerged from a number of such studies. Some work on the correlations of speech and song features is also being done in a few cultures.[24] However, the most difficult aspect of pitch, the vocal intonation in different African societies, is practically an untouched field. Since much of African music is vocal, we shall continue to be baffled by the musical intonation of African singing until this has been thoroughly investigated.

Studies of tonal contrasts in instrumental music and the function of these in structure have begun to be emphasized. Attention is being given more and more to performance techniques and the insights they give into the concept of the sound material. In drumming, for example, an effort is being made to understand the subtleties of tonal contrasts that are used, and to face the problems of notation they raise.[25]

Analysis of sound must be related to structure—the second level of analysis on which the organization of this material is studied. Here, units of structure and the elements that operate in these structures are considered, as well as the basic procedures governing this organization. The structure of melodies, problems of modes, rhythm, multipart organization, and so on, are dealt with on this level, as well as correlations between metrical structure of song texts and melodic organization.

Some studies in this area related to specific musical cultures have also

22. Olga Boone, "Les Xylophones du Congo Belge," in *Annales du Musée du Congo Belge*, Ethnographie Série III, Notes analytiques sur les collections du Musée du Congo Belge (Tervueren, 1936), III, fasc. 2.

23. Hugh Tracey, "Towards an Assessment of African Scales," *African Music*, II/1 (1958), pp. 15–20.

24. David Rycroft, "Zulu and Xhosa Praise Poetry and Song," *African Music*, III/1 (1962), 79–85; *id.*, "Melodic Features of Zulu Logistic Recitation" *African Language Studies* (London, 1960).

25. Hewitt Pantaleoni and Moses Serwadda, "A Possible Notation for African Dance Drumming," *African Music*, IV/2 (1968), 47–52.

emerged. The analysis of rhythmic organization—particularly in drum-ming[26] and in xylophone music[27]—the incidence of polyphony,[28] and the use of techniques such as hocket[29] have begun. However, there are many important geographical areas for which such studies have not yet been done, and we are still far behind in our knowledge of the details of melodic organization.

Context, the third level of analysis, is equally important and must go hand in hand with the analysis of sound and structure. Contextual analysis relates elements of music, song texts, musical items, and musical types to the context of society or the general context of culture, viewed synchron-ically or diachronically. It is on this level that we seek to understand the body of traditions in terms of which music is practiced and perpetuated. It is here that we look at the complex of values associated with the music and the cultural and historical dimensions needed for the understanding of these traditions and values.[30] In this connection, oral traditions about the origins of musical types and dances in a given society, the traditions asso-ciating a particular chief with a particular orchestra, instrument, musical type or even musical style, may be relevant.

For the music of some societies, existing publications in the fields of his-tory and anthropology provide valuable sources of cultural and historical information. In the local histories of Ashanti divisions given by Rattray in his work on *Ashanti Law and Constitution*, for example, one finds refer-ences to the capture of drums, the introduction of a new orchestra into a particular state, and so forth. In Reindorf's *History of the Gold Coast and Ashanti* and Sakyi Dzan's *Sunlight Magazine of History*, there are refer-ences to Boa Amponsem, king of Dankyira, who introduced the gourd drum into his state. The same king is said to have ordered the noses of three hundred slave girls to be amputated so that they could sing "sweet dirges" to him. This reference to pronounced nasal timbre ties up with the mention of the gourd drum, both of them suggestive of a period of stylistic innovation, most probably stimulated by new encounters with music of non-Akan origin.

Interest in such oral traditions, and in historical studies generally, has been shown by some scholars in the African field. Clement da Cruz's work on the musical instruments of Dahomey[31] makes several references to these traditions, which, in some regions of Dahomey, are very precise

26. Arthur M. Jones, *Studies in African Music* (London, 1959).
27. Kubik, *op. cit.*; and Anderson, *op. cit.*
28. See articles in *Journal of the International Folk Music Council*, XIX (1967).
29. J. H. Kwabena Nketia, "The Hocket Technique in African Music," *Journal of the International Folk Music Council*, XIV (1962), 44–52.
30. For a fuller discussion, see Nketia, "Musicology and African Music," *op. cit.*
31. In *Études Dahomeens*, XII (1954).

about the origin of particular orchestras. The migration of musical instruments in Uganda has been of particular interest to Wachsmann,[32] while Kirby[33] gives us some information about the historical interaction between the peoples of South Africa, resulting in the borrowing of musical instruments from one another.

Contextual analysis must always go hand in hand with the study of sound and structure, for the three levels are interrelated and not discrete. In the study of sound, it may be necessary to establish correlations of pitch features and tessitura with categories of performers, or to consider culturally defined qualities and those that have specific functions, such as the purposeful use of nasality, yodeling, and sound symbolism. It may be necessary to examine the interaction of vocal and instrumental qualities.

Similarly, musical structure must be related to performers and performance organizations, especially to the apportioning of roles such as those of solo and chorus, master drummer, secondary drummer, and so on, and to dance and drama, while the piece must be related to the occasion, the setting, the social or cultural function.

It follows from the foregoing that contextual analysis, if it is to contribute to our understanding of musical style, cannot be considered in isolation—that is, without reference to the analysis of sound and structure or to the musical piece.

When the analysis of the music of at least one society has been done, one could proceed to look at the range of contrasts that other subsequently analyzed cultures provide on each of these three levels. This must be done systematically. It is not sufficient to draw analogies between isolated features selected at random—such as intervals, range or melodic level, or tempo. The incidence of a common bell pattern may not in itself be a sufficient criterion for lumping together tribal groups in which it occurs, for when other features are examined one may easily find that there are more features separating them than uniting them.

It will be necessary, too, for African music studies to develop an adequate critical and descriptive terminology for handling the analysis of comparative data. Musicians have sometimes allowed themselves the liberty of resorting to random analogies, even with Western music, as a basis for some of their descriptions and statements. It is difficult to resist the temptation to cast one's mind back to usages in specific periods of Western music history when hocket, polyrhythm, and stratification are discussed, or to refrain from drawing an analogy between some forms of Yoruba singing and plainchant. However, the dangers inherent in such analogies become apparent when they inspire the publication of an histori-

32. Klaus P. Wachsmann, "A Century of Change in the Music of an African Tribe," *Journal of the International Folk Music Council*, X (1958), 52–56.
33. See Kirby, *op. cit.*

cal exposition in which a "missing link" in the history of the plainchant is seen in Yoruba music.[34]

There is, of course, a place for considering Africa and the wider world, and the process of contextualization should bring us to grips with problems arising from the interaction of African societies, both among themselves and with the outside world. Africa has long stood at the confluence of cultures and has, therefore, not been free from external influences or varying forms of acculturation. The invasion of the Arabs and the subsequent penetration of Islam left its traces on the music of vast areas of the continent, and stylistic analysis cannot ignore the implications of this. Similar problems are posed in Madagascar, where there has been a long period of interaction with southeast Asia, with the peoples of Malaya and Indonesia. Indeed, Jones[35] has suggested that musically this interaction was far-reaching, more so than is generally supposed, and that it extended beyond Madagascar and the east coast to the interior and the region of west Africa, although this hypothesis has not yet been proved beyond reasonable doubt.

The European era of African history has similarly left its mark on the musical practice of the continent, and the study of acculturation in music is of particular theoretical and practical interest. There is also the problem of African music and African-derived music in the New World, which offers a fruitful field for comparative studies.

It is such problems that should be of immediate concern in African music research, and not speculative history that tries to fill in gaps in Western music history by searching for "missing links" in Africa.

It is obvious from the foregoing discussion that the sheer enormity of the work involved in detailed descriptive and comparative studies of individual musical cultures will continue to make partial studies the most practical for research scholars. There should be no difficulty in bringing such studies together if they are guided by a common conceptual framework, such as I have outlined in this paper. While scholars may follow their own interests as before in the choice of subjects of investigation, the relevance of their studies to Africa itself would be greatly increased if they remember that people in Africa are as interested in their work as are their colleagues in Europe and America and, indeed, in other parts of the world.

For some time, scholars in Africa may have to concentrate on territorial research and on immediate problems which require the application of knowledge of traditional music. Their research must be related to music education on all levels, to the theater as well as to the needs of the com-

34. Thomas King Etundayo Phillips, *Yoruba Music* (Johannesburg, 1953).
35. Arthur M. Jones, *Studies in African Music* (London, 1959).

munity as a whole. If it is guided by a common conceptual framework, there should be no difficulty in reconciling this with scholarly research in music that will be of interest to ethnomusicologists. Moreover, such territorial research should contribute to our knowledge of the music of the continent as a whole if it keeps problems of the wider continental context constantly in view, for while one cannot safely generalize for the continent as a whole on the basis of our present knowledge, one can at least indicate what features are not unique to the given territory by drawing attention to the incidence of similar things elsewhere, where available data permits this to be done. Assembling comparative data would be greatly facilitated if the analytical procedures are well defined and directed toward a comprehensive statement of musical features on all levels of analysis.

In a survey of this nature, one naturally tends to put a spotlight on the weak spots and gaps and to pass quickly over the bright spots. There is no doubt that, comparatively speaking, considerably more progress has been made in African music research in the last two decades than before. But our strength lies more in seeing the task ahead and planning for it than in going over ground already covered for finer details. There is certainly much more to be accomplished than we have been able to undertake.

In conclusion, I would like to stress once again the need for collaboration between insiders and outsiders, between those involved in national research and uncommitted scholars who can devote all their time to continent-wide problems. There is certainly a need for joint research projects that will involve people on the spot and others interested in the analysis and study of the material. It is only through such collaboration that we can hasten the pace of research on so enormous an area, and realize the potential that African music research has for making a significant contribution to musicological knowledge.

DISCUSSION

BERLIN: African music is a relatively new area of interest to musicologists. Do the pre-twentieth-century European writings and transcriptions of African music play an important part in your studies?

NKETIA: To some extent. In Bowdich's *Mission from Cape Coast Castle to Ashantee*,[36] for example, there is a chapter on music that is remarkably interesting for the period. This work is useful in many ways, but the transcriptions are not good. It would appear that Bowdich had a fairly good ear for interval, but great difficulties in transcribing the rhythms. Never-

36. Thomas Edward Bowdich, *Mission from Cape Coast Castle to Ashantee* (London, 1819; reprint 3rd rev. ed., New York, 1966).

theless, there are sections that are still relevant. He was the first, for example, to write about the use of thirds; in 1819 one couldn't possibly imagine any kind of Western influence. He also talks quite accurately about a few musical instruments, and about Ashanti culture and oral tradition; historians turn to Bowdich quite often. And there are a few other similar publications that provide valuable pre-twentieth-century source material in African musicology.

BROOK: Are there not also collections of discs and cylinders made many years ago that are valuable as source material?

NKETIA: There is the Hornbostel collection of discs in Berlin, to which everyone refers. But in most African countries, our sound recordings go back only twenty or thirty years, when radio stations started.

BROOK: Are you suggesting that the older archives are not valid? And how about present-day efforts—for example, Daniélou's institute in Berlin, the collections of the Radiodiffusion-Television Française and the Musée de l'Homme in Paris.

NKETIA: Many of the older recordings are not properly catalogued, and it is difficult to identify the materials exactly. On the other hand, the recordings made by Herskovits in the 1920s are quite useful. As for the more recent activity you mention, I would say that the greatest achievement in African music research today lies in the accumulation of recorded material, which is mounting at an astonishing rate. It has been suggested that perhaps we should stop recording and start studying the material.

Regarding present-day efforts: unfortunately, recent recordings are not always as useful to the scholar as he might wish. You will often find that the accompanying notes have little depth. What is the instrument? Who is the performer? What is his background? Is he a musician full time? The musicologist wants to know a little more about the relationship between the organization of the music and the phases of the ceremony. Such recordings provide at least a sample of the music and some background; they can be used as limited data for examining certain problems.

Other organizations are more scientific, with field workers all over the world, and elaborate and efficient systems of classification. This kind of research is rare, however.

In comparing old and new material, you look for changes. A fellow at my institute is now studying recordings I made seventeen years ago and has rerecorded some of the same groups. We are interested in finding out just how a society transmits its musical tradition in the absence of written notation. And we are interested in discovering the processes by which certain songs become changed in different regions of the same cultural area. I think the results will be valuable.

MRS. HAYDEN: The work of the English scholar A. M. Jones has been cited rather often in recent studies—for example, in Gunther Schuller's discussion of the relationship between speech and melody in the first chapter of his *Early Jazz*.[37] I wonder if you would comment on Jones's analysis of speech elements in African melody, which have sometimes been criticized.

NKETIA: Personally, I don't like the way Jones has handled the problem. For example, he talks about melodic anticipation, which to me doesn't mean anything. One can too easily explain any inconsistencies in terms of melodic anticipation. I don't think that either Jones or Marius Schneider has looked at the linguistic analysis of tones and intonation in the languages about which they are writing. If they had, perhaps their explanations would have been quite different.

I am more in sympathy with Schneider's explanation,[38] although he offers some internal explanations that I cannot accept. This question of the elements of speech that are transferred into melody is a very important one. The situation seems to differ from place to place. I have written an article on the linguistic aspects of style—scheduled to appear in *Current Trends in Linguistics*—that you might like to look at.

I have a question that I would like to ask you. Do you think it is possible to study African music through available sources, without going into the field?

MRS. HAMPTON: I should think it would be almost impossible to do a thorough job without some field experience. You yourself have emphasized the important connection between music and its social context.

NKETIA: There are linguists in the United States who know something about African languages yet have not had field experience. They have worked here with people who know the languages as well as from recordings. I am interested in the possibility of applying to ethnomusicology the technique developed by linguists who work directly with a person who is a carrier of tradition.

MRS. ROWEN: In view of the bulk of recordings now accumulating, would it not be possible for research teams here to work in cooperation with scholars who have a good deal of field experience, at least to make transcriptions?

NKETIA: There are so many problems in transcribing from recordings. It has been demonstrated that some music can be well transcribed if the material is simple. But if you have a drum ensemble, things become very complex.

One solution I have found is to make analytic field recordings designed

37. Gunther Schuller, *Early Jazz, Its Roots and Musical Development* (New Jersey, 1968).

38. Marius Schneider, "Tone and Tune in West African Music," *Ethnomusicology*, V/3 (Sept., 1961), 204–15.

for study purposes—recordings that isolate elements and thus make analysis easier. For example, in working with Adowa music, I would record not only the full drum ensemble but also the individual parts separately, and in small combinations in which their essential contrasts can be studied. I usually begin with the bell pattern, since the bell is essentially the "time keeper," and then record this pattern with each drum, taking the drums in the order in which they generally appear in the music played by the full ensemble.

HARMS: I thought I noticed in one or two recordings a speeding-up of the tempo, which rather surprised me. Does the tempo speed up?

NKETIA: Sometimes, when the music gets exciting there is a speeding-up. This may be done by the gong player. But the gong is ordinarily supposed to be as steady as a metronome. There are not many people who can play it well. The rhythm is very simple, but keeping time is a discipline in itself.

HARMS: Is there much dynamic contrast?

NKETIA: Not intentionally. It is not a structural element or an expressive element.

VAN SOLKEMA: To what extent do public performances in Africa today approach the character of art music in the European tradition—that is, music that is listened to for its own sake?

NKETIA: As you know, African music is a part of social life. The musician performs when there is an event. He goes to a funeral because he has a ready audience there.

BYRD: Then there aren't any musicians who just sit around all day and practice?

NKETIA: One can, of course, but certain instruments are rarely heard outside a regular performance. Most people learn drumming, for example, while actually performing. Master drummers, while they are being trained, will drum somewhere alone during certain hours, and you may hear a musician playing the hand piano on his own. But "performance" takes place on public occasions.

People often come together in the evening for recreation. Other people may come to be entertained, but it is not the primary aim of the musicians to entertain others. They form clubs, which are usually associated with dancers. This is the normal kind of recreation, but there are other contexts: harvest festivals, sewing festivals, festivals for remembering ancestors, and other rituals. These are the occasions at which you would hear organized performances of music. I don't know if you would call this art music. The performer never advertises himself as a musician, hires a room, and invites people to listen. He goes to his audience. This presents a problem now, for example, when we are trying to establish a new theater in Accra. People sometimes come out of curiosity, but it's a new thing altogether and the theater is finding it difficult to live on this basis.

VAN SOLKEMA: The new theater, then, presents traditional music in a concert-hall setting?

NKETIA: Yes, but there are problems. How can traditional music be presented in a new context without destroying its essential character? We have met this problem in the dance. You may have seen the Ghana Dance Ensemble, a professional group associated with my institute. The group is trained to perform traditional dances; but in the presentation, certain modifications have to be made—not in the dance, but in the use of space. For example, in the village it is customary for the dancer to dance facing the drummers. If you do this in a theater, the audience would never see them. So the dancers now face the audience. This in turn creates a problem because the dancer is accustomed to getting cues by looking at the drummer. Now he must rely on the ear and listen for changes of rhythm pattern.

HARMS: Regarding heptatonic scales used in African music: are there different seven-tone scales?

NKETIA: You will find slight differences in the intervals, slightly larger or smaller according to the area.

HARMS: Do they correspond roughly to our major scale?

NKETIA: Very roughly. This is, in fact, a problem with the heptatonic people. They are more prone to cultural influences from the West than the pentatonic people.

MRS. HAMPTON: You mentioned earlier that the Hugh Tracey recordings were mainly of Bantu music. If such recordings from other parts of Africa are being broadcast now, has there been any noticeable acculturation process as a result?

NKETIA: We have broadcast Bantu music in Ghana, but I have not noticed any group trying to sing in this style. Traditional people are very conservative. They will adopt only those things that can fit into their pattern. It is a different matter in the area of popular music. Popular music from South Africa has followers in Ghana, just as popular music from the United States has.

BYRD: You stated in your lecture that exposure to Western music was not harming the appreciation for native music. I mention this because I recall a recent article in the *New York Times* reporting that a foundation was making quite a large grant for research for the reason that, with everyone walking around with transistors in the next twenty or thirty years, African traditional music would be strongly affected by Western music.

NKETIA: Yes. You will find similar statements made over thirty years ago in Hugh Tracey's *Newsletter*. If you look at the writings of anthropologists of the same period you will find a similar concern for change in Africa. They feared that everything would disappear, but this has not happened. There is still a lot of traditional music in Africa. There will be change, but I do not think it will be very radical. I can't see it dying out in the next twenty or thirty years.

Nationalism, too, has become an important force in preserving tradition. In the past, educated Africans were not keen about preserving the music. Now many feel it is important, even though they do not understand it. They feel that they have missed something and are now providing the opportunity for younger people to become imbued with their own culture.

Some of our people do not believe in tape recorders because they do not believe that you save our music by putting it in a museum. In the lecture I spoke of the dual problem in Africa of fundamental research and applied research. We are interested in learning how to play the xylophone as well as in talking about it. Music must be a part of the culture, and the way to preserve it is to promote it.

The Consensus Makers
of Asian Music

MANTLE HOOD

*T*O *SPEAK* of perspectives and lacunae in the study of European art music connotes a kind of scholarly mopping-up operation. It suggests that the major campaigns have been fought and won, that the enemies of scientific methods have been routed. It implies that the ultimate defeat of stragglers and elimination of pockets of resistance can be assured by tactical thoroughness. Total victory would seem to lie just beyond the next few hills. For all practical purposes, unconditional surrender is a *fait accompli.*

Before I become the target of a scholarly sniper, let me add quickly that I am speaking in a relative sense. The campaigns of European art music have been waged for a good many years. In fact, the very concept of musical campaigns, fought under the aegis of musicology, originated as part of the European tradition of music. And in the course of many battles there has developed and been tested a reasonably successful theory of strategy and tactics. Persistent problems and remnant lacunae, considered in this context, represent little more than stragglers and pockets of resistance in the European theater of operations, especially if comparison may be allowed to the relatively new campaigns of Asian music, African music, and others found in the non-Western world.

One can hardly stretch the meaning of the word "lacunae" in considering the musical traditions of China or Southeast Asia or Oceania. Here we are confronted not with lacunae but with gaping voids in our knowledge.

290

In terms of music scholarship this condition obtains in all musical cultures of the non-Western world. The young man or woman looking for a substantial dissertation topic need only spin a desk globe of the world and stop it at random with one finger. However, before charging off to the field in a fervor of excitement at the prospect of filling in some of these voids, the doctoral candidate will need some briefing. In considering perspectives in the study of a particular Asian or African music, he must temper his crusading spirit with an awareness that even the nature of the problems he will encounter has yet to be clearly identified.

In a field of inquiry that has almost as many approaches as there are established scholars, that encompasses many different objectives and, potentially, very diverse applications of knowledge gained, there is still a lack of generally recognized theories, not to mention a theory of theories. Therefore, we may point to some excellent models of scholarly research, but not to a common prescription for the training of scholars; to copious collections of field recordings, but not to any uniformity in their documentation; to an impressive array of technological instrumentation in the laboratory, but not to agreement nor even to an understanding of the question, What has musical significance?; to an uneasy truce between musicology and anthropology, but to no assurance that either of them, or both in combination, may represent an adequate approach to the study of non-Western music.

An understanding of the musical cultures of Africa or Asia—or any other part of the world, in my opinion—must take into account what Charles Seeger has often referred to as the "consensus." The consensus makers of music, I believe, represent three different but interdependent aspects of society: 1) the musical consensus; 2) the cultural consensus; and 3) the social consensus. The *musical consensus* includes the interaction of performers and/or composers with teachers, theoreticians, critics, users or audiences, patrons, and others involved in the processes of music making. The musical consensus is affected by, and also affects, the *cultural consensus* made up of the consensus of dancers, puppeteers, story tellers, native speakers of the language involved, literati, religious devotees—of any group involved in the processes of cultural expression outside music making *per se*. Both the musical and the cultural consensuses are affected by, and to some extent also affect, the *social consensus*, consisting of special interest groups and institutions, such as economic segments of society, the organized church, the military, the local and national governments, political elites, the hierarchy of social status, and so forth. These musical, cultural, and social entities, to a greater or lesser degree, are also subject to the forces of external alliance such as SEATO, NATO, the Warsaw Pact, international communism, capitalism, Islam, Buddhism, Christianity, and so forth.

These three—the musical consensus, the cultural consensus, the social consensus—are in constant interaction and together represent what I am calling the consensus makers of music. The voids in our present knowledge can some day be reduced to mere lacunae and the nature of persistent problems understood *if*—and only if—the musical campaigns of the non-Western world are based on intelligence operations in the camp of the consensus makers. We might also note in passing that in the here-and-now of the Western world of music, in researching the products of various coteries of the avant garde, jazz, rock music, folk music, country music, hillbilly and citybilly and rockabilly and all the other billies—in researching any kind of Western music viable in the contemporary scene, an awareness of the consensus makers, in my judgment, is equally important.

What approach is required to gain access to this world of the consensus makers? Musicology? Anthropology? Some combination of the two? Or still some other approach?

Sometimes anthropologists refer to musicology as the science of counting notes. Some musicologists believe anthropology is the science of ferreting out who-sleeps-with-whom-and-in-what-kinds-of-houses. To be more accurate, but not more enlightening, we might refer to the former as the science of music and the latter as the science of man. Or we could spend the rest of the time available in this presentation trying to reach a fair description of the two disciplines. Instead, let us proceed more directly. Let us stop our spinning desk globe at two different spots and seek to identify the discipline or disciplines needed to understand the interaction of the musical consensus, the cultural consensus, and the social consensus—the total of consensus makers responsible for the traditions.[1] First let us consider an illustration to which most Americans have had some kind of exposure—a development that began in the United States with the importation of Beatle music from Great Britain.

Almost from the beginning, this importation and subsequent emulations had certain characteristics, both musical and nonmusical, that established an immediate audience, initially limited to a certain age group. Points of appeal seemed to be: a characteristic instrumental ensemble, a characteristic "beat," a characteristic dynamic level, tempo, lyrics, hair style and costume, body motions of musicians and listener-dancers, lighting effects, and a defiantly carefree attitude. These features readily established communication with teen-agers in the United States, who at this stage of the life cycle in this particular society are quite naturally in revolt against the mores of their elders. Distinctive hair style, dress, and abandon in body movements gave the teen-ager an identity that set him apart from older age groups. Homespun, candid lyrics, special lighting, and an exaggerated go-to-hell attitude made the identity more expansive. A simple instrumen-

1. The two examples given in this paper have been extracted from *The Ethnomusicologist* (New York, 1971).

tation distinct from various kinds of jazz ensembles, a "beat" that teen-agers have described to me as being like "the heart beat or the drive of an orgasm," a high dynamic level, a monotonous tempo—this musical config-uration was an exclusive world of sound for the teen-ager that expressed his spirit of revolt in its diametrical contrast to the taste and habits of his elders.

The immense teen-age audience was quickly exploited by every con-ceivable entrepreneur and with such success that in a relatively short time Beatle music began to affect other segments of society as well. Soon, danc-ing in Beatle style was the "in" thing to do. The carefree movements of the teen-agers sometimes became clumsy, jerky, and desperately sugges-tive when the matrons and sexagenarians tried to imitate their youngsters. This idiom of music making invaded the singing commercials of radio and television, modified the style of commercial dance bands, raised the women's hemline well above the knee, altered the clothing fashions of both sexes, and in many other ways provided a field day for numerous commercial enterprises.

What had begun as an exclusive realm of identity for the teen-ager, a symbolic cry of protest in the revolt against his elders, became lost in the absorbing processes of commercial exploitation. So, he sought other ways of assuring his identity. The image deepened to include the use of halluci-natory drugs, love-ins, public nudity, light shows, the Indian sitar, beards and dirty bodies, communal sex orgies, the extreme fringes of the hippie world that were indicative of losing touch with reality.

In retrospect, who would ever think that the amplified guitar—backed and manipulated by clever management—could generate such a social nightmare!

Thus far we have touched superficially several kinds of users and exploiters of Beatle music. By now it should be apparent that we need the help of the psychologist, sociologist, psychiatrist, physiologist, the medical profession, the brain-research institute, experts in commercial marketing, and a host of others, if we want to understand the conditions and motiva-tions responsible for the attitudes of these several segments of society toward this kind of music. The *subject* of study, which we have not yet examined, is music. But the *approaches* needed to comprehend the subject in its socio-cultural context are legion. The *objectives* of such a study could provide invaluable information about the psychology of the teen-ager in the United States, about familial inadequacy and the shortcomings of educational institutions; and, in connection with the older generation, about the strong desire for social approval and the compulsive quest for eternal youth that plagues a number of Americans in their middle and declining years. Beatle music has also been exported to Africa and Asia. On a comparative basis one of our objectives might be to learn the differ-ence in response to this music among American, African, and Asian youth and among older generations as well. The *applications* of what we learn might be vital to the tycoons of commercial marketing, to the branches of our State Department concerned with the image we project abroad, to the political scientist who maintains sensitive contact with the political elites of foreign countries being exploited by the commercial music factories, to the home-based sociologist combating juvenile delinquency, to the president of the United States and his advisors in their concern over increasing crime in the large cities.

Any of these approaches, objectives, and applications, most of which are directly involved with the cultural consensus and the social consensus, should be based on a knowledge of the subject itself, Beatle music. Its brief history and its effects on society mentioned above are only the gross aspects that show on the surface. So far as I am aware, no systematic study of the music is yet in progress. Answers to some of the burning questions that are extramusical must certainly depend on answers to questions that are purely musical. Only a thorough research of the musical consensus can answer such basic questions as: What musical factors account for the immediate appeal of Beatle music? To what extent is the appeal nonmusical?

Some time ago the complete recorded repertory of the Beatles was used for comparative purposes in the Institute of Ethnomusicology at UCLA in a study centered on the question: "How do different societies and groups within them treat the element of time in relation to music?" Two points of interest emerged, which can be compared with the teen-ager's own appraisal of the "beat." It was learned that the basic pulse of the music is slower than that of the average male heartbeat and of course even slower compared to that of the female. The measurement of tempo from beginning to end of a piece revealed that it consistently slows down—a feature not readily comparable to "the drive of an orgasm." However, perhaps the teen-ager's association of the "beat" with the heart pulse and sexual climax are suggested by additional musical factors: the heavy reinforcement of the beat by the ensemble of instruments, the relatively low pitch range, a particular quality of instrumental timbre, the monotony of the rhythm which, even in the course of a slight ritard, might induce a kind of hypnotic climax. It might be pertinent to study the harmonic rhythm, melodic formulas, melodic range, textual stereotypes and their relationship to different musical elements, instrumental tone quality including attack, decay, and release, the degree of technical articulation required of the performers, and so forth.

It would be important to have musical case histories for a number of the earlier successful performers to determine the extent to which a limited musical aptitude may be responsible for the simplicity of the style or whether limited requirements in musicianship are incidental. The same source of information might lead to other genres of music that have contributed to the Beatle style; and by comparison we might learn why the one has been so successful in communication and the degree to which its precursors were or were not successful with the same or different audiences.

Our evaluation of the attitude of the teen-ager would be more complete if we understood fully how he regards the performer. Is he merely accepted as a peer, regarded as a hero, or idolized as a mystical god? To gain perspective on this question we might want to compare the status of the Beatle musician among teen-agers with the status of performers in the symphony orchestra or chamber ensemble among concertgoers. Does the segment of society that subscribes to the concert series regard the oboist or cellist as socially equal, superior, or inferior? Is the concertgoer likely to imitate his haircut, his clothes, copy his manner of walking and talking, ask for his autograph, tear buttons off his coat as a treasured souvenir? How does the greater society award the two types of musicians? Does it give the Beatles more money than the string quartet? How do you compare the relative value of these two types of musicians to their respective segments of society? To other members of the professional class of musicians? To the society as a whole? In this reckoning of value, of course, we must take into account the percentage of society directly affected by the two types of music. Is the audience for each exclusive, or is there a mutual audience for both?

If the musical consensus can be likened to a wheel, we have been considering only the spokes. What about the hub—the consensus of performers and composers? To understand this hub of the musical consensus it is necessary to negotiate two modes of discourse: speech and music. The most accurate way to understand the verbal jargon of speech is to learn to speak it. By the same token, access to the music mode of discourse can be gained most directly by learning to perform the music—in this instance, Beatle music. Need a research scholar be prepared to go so far? Yes, if he is truly bent on research. Must a writer commit murder in order to write about it? Considering the quantity of sexy paperbacks that are continually being ground out to formula, we certainly hope not. But we know a great deal, perhaps too much, about physical violence and psychotic motivation. Given these facts, a formula, and some imagination, the pulp writer is ready to produce. By comparison we know very little about "musical facts" and their psychological implications, not to mention the far more difficult problem of attempting to relate musical facts to musical values as determined by the musical consensus. And, I contend, actual participation in the music mode of discourse, performing Beatle music, will yield far greater insight into these problems than merely listening to it or looking at transcriptions of it.

By way of summary, let me emphasize the fact that, viewed in relation to the consensus makers, 1) Beatle music represents a void in our present knowledge, and 2) it lacks perspective in our limited understanding of the question, What has musical significance? Notwithstanding the fact that this popular expression is part of our own musical tradition, we can only speculate on the nature of the problems to be faced in determining those musical factors which account for the appeal of this music. For some time this style of music has been merging with rock music, and, perhaps, like other fads, it will continue to change and be modified until one day it fades away. The likelihood of eventual dissolution, however, hardly excuses our present ignorance. This musical phenomenon has had an impact on many different aspects of society: mass media of communication, multiple segments of the economy, moral and esthetic standards, human behavior, a national stereotype projected abroad, scales of values. The pertinence of such a force in these times of social conflict can hardly be brushed aside with the argument that if it is ignored, some day it will fade away. The motivating spirit, the consensus makers, will not fade away. And perhaps we need to be reminded that the consensus, in one way or another, includes all of us as parents or teachers or students or consumers. Through a study of Beatle music we might begin to understand the generative force responsible for the phenomenon and be better prepared for the next onslaught from the consensus makers. But to do this, as scientists of music and man, we shall have to broaden our horizons considerably in order to reduce the present void to remnant lacunae.

I deliberately stopped our spinning desk globe with a finger on the United States in order to provide an illustration to which most of us have had some kind of exposure. Let us spin it again and put a finger on the opposite side of the globe.

If the study of a musical expression within our own familiar culture portends such complexity, we can be sure that the study of a particular Asian musical expression is no less complex. The form and style of the musical consensus, the cultural consensus, and the social consensus will be different; and the relative importance of each may vary with the tradition under consideration. But together, in some particular configuration, they represent the consensus makers of Asian music. Let us consider one example that would seem to be far removed from Beatle music, a classical tradition that has been viable for more than a thousand years. I am referring to the music of the puppet plays found in Java and Bali. In the course of the following brief overview, let us remember that proper perspective of the subject requires constant reference to various interrelated consensus makers.

Although historically the origin of the puppet play in Indonesia is subject to some difference of opinion, there is general agreement among scholars that it is at least a thousand years old. In addition to the autochthonous stories of the culture hero Pandji, poetic literature based on the Indian Mahabharata and Ramayana began to develop during the late tenth and early eleventh centuries in East Java and subsequently spread throughout Java and Bali. Sometime early in this development, it is probable that the religious literature and style of puppetry as well as musical instruments, tuning systems, scales, modes, performance practice, and so forth, were closely related among the Sundanese of West Java, the Javanese of Central and East Java, and the Balinese. Each of these three societies had adapted Indian Hinduism to regional beliefs in animism and ancestor worship. But over a span of centuries the norms of style surrounding the puppet play developed differences in response to the ever-changing cultural and social context of each society and in response to external forces as well.

Today a comparative perspective reveals that the style of the music, the style of the music ensemble, the style of the puppets, the style of the puppeteer's singing, the style of the language, the style of the empathic audience, the style of the environment—this bundle of traditions is remarkably different among the Sundanese, the Javanese, and the Balinese. The emotions are the same, the function and usage of the dramatic vehicle are quite similar. The sociologist would contend that in each of the three societies the puppet play has the same social meaning. But the fact remains that in each society the norms that regulate style are different. Each of the three societies has long since refashioned the Indian literature on which the puppet play (known as *wajang purwa* or *parwa*, the "old stories") is based, to reflect its own, its unique cultural image. This composite art form represents the purest distillation of cultural heritage. Comprehension of the norms of musical style in this context requires an understanding of the norms of style that govern the whole bundle of traditions. And each segment of the bundle, as it touches and affects other parts to which it is bound, offers unique insight into the whole of the tradition.

Such an approach to the subject carries the implication of social meaning far beyond the sociologist's interest in ritual, in mere function and usage. It includes definitive information relating to human behavior, human values, social interaction, codes of morality, standards of taste, and, in historical perspective, even a capsulated account of social evolution. These, too, of course, are of profound interest to the sociologist. But unless he is prepared to negotiate not only speech discourse but also music discourse and dance discourse—traditional dance styles are based on the movements of the puppets—unless he acquires expertise in modes of communication that are exclusive to the arts, he will have access to little beyond the superficial descriptoin of function and usage. And on this basis alone, as we have indicated, there is little apparent difference among the three quite different societies.

In comparative terms let us consider briefly some of these differences as they are reflected in the style of puppet theater. The most ancient form of the puppet play, probably originating in East Java, has been retained in

Bali. The music ensemble consists of a pair or quartet of ten-keyed metal-lophones tuned to five-tone *sléndro* and known as *gendèr wajang*. Al-though Jaap Kunst was persuaded on the basis of ethnological evidence that seven-tone *pélog* represents the older tuning system in Java,[2] there is recent evidence that five-tone sléndro predates the seven-tone system by as much as eight centuries.[3] The ten-keyed metallophone itself represents an ancient form of the gendèr, which in more recent times has fourteen or fifteen keys and is one of the principal improvising instruments in the large Javanese *gamelan*. It is also worth noting that in Balinese gendèr wajang there is no improvisation.

The Javanese and Balinese leather puppets are supported by a central rod; both arms articulate at the elbow and shoulder, and some of the Balinese humorous characters have articulated jaws. The Balinese style of the flat leather puppets is more realistic than that of the Javanese counter-part—evidence, according to some scholars, that the more abstract style of puppet developed in Java after the advent of Islam with its prohibition of making graven images.[4] Wajang figures found on the bas reliefs of tem-ples built in East Java prior to the encroachment of Islam support this theory; they are quite similar in style to the wajang puppets found in Bali today.[5] It is remarkable the extent to which under the skilled hands of the puppeteer all these puppets come to life, especially viewed from the shadow side of the screen where the flickering rays of the oil lamp add to the illusion of breathing and other subtle movement. The puppeteer is also skilled in handling several puppets, separate weapons, and possibly horses or a chariot in action-packed battles, which are very popular.

As a principal carrier of the religious literature of Balinese Hinduism, the shadow play is an important part of the ritual of temple festivals and rites of passage. For all three societies the puppet play is also a form of entertainment. It is filled with humor, wit, tragedy, topical satire, adven-ture, battles, philosophy, sex, morals, manners, ethics, history—the full gamut of human and godly experience. And, as we shall see, even though the Sundanese and the Javanese were converted to Islam more than three centuries ago, the deeper social meaning of the literature still derives from the socio-cultural configuration achieved during the period of the East Javanese empires from the tenth to the sixteenth centuries. In Bali, where the external force of Islam never gained a foothold, Balinese Hinduism has become a way of life. And the essence of religious devotion is expressed through music, dance, poetry, puppetry, carving, and decoration. In this society audience and performer, carver and beholder, priest and parish-

2. Jaap Kunst, *Music in Java* (2nd ed., The Hague, 1949), I, 18–24.
3. Mantle Hood, "The Effect of Medieval Technology on Musical Style in the Orient," *Selected Reports*, Institute of Ethnomusicology, UCLA I/3 (1969).
4. Frits A. Wagner, *Indonesia*, Art of the World Series, 2 (London, 1959), p. 127.
5. *Ibid.*, pp. 126–27.

ioner, composer and instrumentalist, temple offering and the shrine have a common identity. Each facet of this identity has something to tell us about human behavior; the style of communications, the style of political fervor, or individual and communal responsibilities, of loyalties, prejudices, discrimination.

In spite of its organic function as an expression of religious devotion—or more probably because of it—on some occasions the shadow play might seem to be rather casually regarded by the Balinese. Actually such an interpretation is quite misleading. It is difficult to find an analogy in Western societies. Perhaps to some degree it is like the difference between the relatively formal attitude of the Catholic in the United States toward the regular rituals of his church compared to the more matter-of-fact acceptance of trappings of church dogma characteristic of Catholic countries like Italy and Spain. Neither attitude indicates a greater or lesser religious devotion; but the governing norms of style, developed in response to their respective cultural contexts, are different. Sometimes in the context of a Balinese temple festival where several different types of gamelan orchestras, dance, incantations of the priests, women singing, are all going on at the same time, little attention may be paid to the concurrent performance of the shadow play. And yet, with attention directed to dance or some other activity, devotees of the temple are aware that the ritual includes the shadow play. On other occasions, however, a whole evening of the temple festivities may be devoted to *wajang kulit*, and no more rapt audience for theater could be found than the Balinese watching such a performance (see Plates 15–16).

In Central and East Java, also, the shadow play, wajang kulit, is performed in connection with rites of passage and is considered an indispensable panacea for pestilence and disease and the alleviation of calamity and disaster. The formal attitude of the Javanese toward the shadow play compared to the more casual acceptance of wajang by the Balinese may be slightly analogous to our earlier comparison of American and Italian Catholics. The restraints of Javanese etiquette and an idealized sense of refinement permit only the subtlest show of emotional response. For example, there is no raucous laughter when the clowns are engaged in ribald humor; but the smiles and polite giggles of the audience make clear the depth of emotion even though the norms of style require a markedly different response from that of the Balinese. Evidence of the high percentage of saturation of the tradition in Javanese society can be seen in the regular broadcasts of wajang kulit from the radio stations of Central Java. The listening audience is so familiar with the theatrical elements of the shadow play that it can visualize all of the dramatic action through the narration and singing of the puppeteer and the music of the supporting gamelan—a literal example of tele-vision.

The environment and, in some instances, the physical arrangement of the audience also tend to be more formal in Java than in Bali. In the towns and larger villages a performance of wajang kulit is usually staged in the *penḍopo*—the pavilion that is the entry to the house proper in a princely residence or the home of a wealthy businessman. It is here that the head of the household entertains male guests on the formal occasion of the celebration of a wedding or other rites of passage. Female guests are accommodated within the house proper. The screen is set up in the *pringgitan*, the entry bridging the pavilion and the house, with the puppeteer and the gamelan facing it from the penḍopo, so that the shadows of the puppets may be seen only from the house. Some scholars believe that in former times wajang kulit may have been a form of male initiation rite which allowed only the men and adolescent males to see the actual puppets and the puppeteer functioning in the role of priest, while the women and children, watching from the other side of the screen, saw only the shadows.[6] Although today in many places either sex of any age may sit on either side of the screen, in some regions the older tradition still obtains.[7] In Bali, where there apppear to be no prohibitions of this kind, the entire audience, except for a few youths who perhaps themselves aspire to be puppeteers one day, sits on the shadow side of the screen. In fact, in Bali the puppet play is physically staged so there is no room for an audience on the puppeteer's side of the screen.

Javanese wajang kulit may also be performed in a public building or even in a bamboo pavilion temporarily attached to a private house in connection with rites of passage. In the small village the environment may be extremely simple. However the puppet play may be staged, there is always an air of formality with the occasion.

The style of the production in Java is also quite formal. The musical accompaniment is provided by a large *gamelan sléndro* in contrast to the pair or quartet of gendèr wajang used in Bali. The Javanese performance begins about seven thirty in the evening with an overture by the orchestra that may last a half-hour or forty-five minutes. The play begins shortly after 8:00 P.M. and has a structure divided into three time periods: the first ending around midnight, the second about 3:00 A.M., and the third at six o'clock in the morning. It is a very long production, without intermission. In Bali, by comparison, the staring time of the overture by gendèr wajang is quite variable, and the total production lasts less than five hours.

An indication of the special regard of the Javanese for wajang kulit and the high value they place on it can be seen in their frequent philosophical and sociological interpretations of the shadow play.[8] Comparison is made

6. R. L. Mellema, *Wajang Puppets*, Department of Cultural and Physical Anthropology, 48 (Amsterdam, 1954), pp. 8–9.

7. According to a verbal communication from Max Harrell, who saw such a division of the audience in a performance held in Tjeribon, 1964.

8. Mangkunagara VII of Surakarta, KGPAA, *On the Wajang Kulit (Purwa) and*

betwcen the three time periods of the wajang night and the time periods of the life cycle: youth, maturity, and old age. Mystical interpretations of various passages in the poetic texts and symbolism ascribed to the many characterizations represented by the dramatis personae could, in themselves, comprise a sizable body of literature.

Above all, the Javanese, like the Balinese, accept the stories of wajang kulit as the story of their own ancestry. It does not matter that some of the principal characters and some of the story line derive from India; some of the characters and some of the story lines are purely Javanese. The technical terms of the puppet apparatus are Javanese, the style of the music, the instruments, the singing, the style of the puppeteer, the language are all Javanese. The poetic forms of the texts have long since been Javanese. The rich mixture of religious and superstitious beliefs and the complex fabric governing behavioral ideals, which stem from the ancient kingdoms of the East Javanese empires, are Javanese. Yes, it is true: this bundle of traditions, these cultural norms of style are indeed the story of Javanese ancestry.

In West Java, the Sundanese version of the Mahabharata is performed in a kind of puppet play known as *wajang golêk*. Unlike the stylized puppets of the Javanese, which are delicately carved from buffalo hide and meticulously painted, or the more realistic leather puppets of Bali, those found in Sunda are round wooden figures. These, of course, are not shadow puppets, so, although they perform within the boundaries of a frame, the screen is omitted.

The style of Sundanese audience behavior and typical environment are somewhere between those of the Balinese and the Javanese, more formal than the first and less formal than the second. Sometime during my residence in Central Java during 1957–58 I heard that there would be an evening performance of Sundanese wajang golêk in the large public building in the square south of the sultan's palace. I was genuinely surprised to learn that there was enough interest here in the heartland of Javanese culture to support a performance of Sundanese wajang golêk. That night in the middle of the performance I walked to the back of the room and joined several Javanese friends for coffee while we continued to watch the production. All evening long I had been amazed at the overt display of changing emotions in the audience. I turned to my Javanese companions and said that I had never heard a Javanese audience so boisterous in their laughter or so openly demonstrative in their enthusiasm for a female singer, a special feature of the Sundanese production. One of the Javanese sipping coffee put down his glass, looked at me rather stiffly, and said, "This is not a Javanese audience! These are Sundanese people living here in Djogja."

Its Symbolic and Mystic Elements, trans. Claire Holt, Southeast Asia Program, Data Paper No. 27 (Ithaca, 1957).

Sundanese wajang golêk is a younger form of puppetry than the Javanese and Balinese wajang kulit. It also has greater articulation. Not only do the arms of the round wooden puppets articulate but the head also turns from side to side and the trunk moves up and down and rotates partially. The figures are gowned in traditional Sundanese dress, often including a long scarf important in the dance. And one of the delights of wajang golêk is the realistic manner in which the puppets perform traditional dances. Realism reaches a marked credibility at the conclusion of a vigorous dance when the puppet's chest rises and falls in response to the exertion and gradually comes to a point of repose as he catches his breath once again.

The Sundanese gamelan that accompanies wajang golêk is much smaller than its Javanese equivalent used for wajang kulit. It is located behind the *dalang* or puppeteer, and the audience sees only the puppets in action, the puppeteer and musicians being relegated to the dim background. A female singer is a prominent and very popular feature in the ensemble. The function and usage of wajang golêk are similar to those of Javanese wajang kulit, but increasingly, especially in the larger towns, wajang golêk often functions purely as entertainment. There is no less concern among the Sundanese than among the Javanese for the mystical and symbolic interpretations of the literature.

This brief comparison of three related but distinctive traditions is intended to suggest the kind of perspective required to understand the music of the puppet play in Java and Bali. If it is apparent that mere description of function and usage yields only a superficial impression of the social meaning of the puppet play, it should be equally apparent that a consideration of musical style must include more than abstract description of musical practice. All three societies share a common tuning system, some type of modal practice, closely related musical instruments, certain structural relationships between the roles of the puppeteer and the musicians, a basic poetic literature, stereotyped musical forms corresponding to dramatic structure, and other similarities. But these gross features reveal little more about musical style than does a description of function and usage about social meaning. In each society within these abstract principles of musical practice the performer and composer are guided by *particular* norms of musical style that represent the interaction of the musical, cultural, and social consensus. It is in this realm of interaction, the realm of the consensus makers, that the distinctive differences among the three societies become apparent.

How does the researcher of music gain access to this world of the consensus makers? Through the speech mode of discourse he can rely on two forms of communication: scholarly publications by colleagues in other disciplines and first hand discussions with representatives of the consensus makers. Publications by the historian, the ethnologist, the linguist, the art historian, the anthropologist, the archeologist, the social geographer, the agriculturalist, the psychologist, and others will provide the necessary foundation for these discussions. In addition, he must also aspire to a modest capability as a performer of the music itself. Only the music mode of discourse can provide access to the nonverbal levels of music communication known to the consensus makers. These two modes of discourse, speech and music, together with representative recordings and motion pictures, will provide basic materials for the laboratory and the writing desk.

Let us assume that in a laboratory equipped with tape recorders, a Stroboconn, a Seeger Melograph or its equivalent, and other instrumentation he can finally produce a precise description of the musical details. How is he to judge which of them have musical significance? Let us approach the question by analogy. The sociologist tells us that the puppet play is an important ritual associated with various rites of passage in all three societies. But we have also observed that the deeper social meaning of the puppet play requires a recognition of the detailed *differences* among the three traditions. And the significance of these differences must be judged in relation to other aspects of the socio-cultural context of the puppet play in each society. By the same token the deeper musical meaning is not to be found among the similarities of musical practice but rather among the musical details *unique* to each society. And the significance of these differences must be established in relation to other aspects of the socio-cultural context. In other words, significant details are developed and retained by the musical consensus in response to the ever-changing scales of values fostered by the cultural consensus and the social consensus. Therefore, accurate musical perspective—that is, recognition of the musically significant—depends on the degree to which accurate communication can be established with representatives of *all* the consensus makers of music.

DISCUSSION

Miss Foster: Your lecture started me thinking about absolutes or generalizations that transcend the specifics of a culture—for example, literal meaning, symbolic or allegorical meaning, and specific function in the culture. I would be interested to hear your comments on this question of absolutes.

Hood: Sooner or later, preferably sooner, we have to get at such questions. There have been a lot of assumptions in the study of Western music and we have to get outside it to test whether these assumptions are really valid. We must increasingly take into account the fact that any cultural expression, and especially music, is bound to be in constant interaction with many other elements. Music persists as it is only to the extent that interlocking requirements allow it to. We can point to a number of traditions that are tottering on the edge of extinction right now, but I am not particularly interested in seeing them put on black velvet under glass—I think they are dead then, anyhow. When a culture has finished with any tradition, when it no longer communicates or ceases to fill whatever function it has filled esthetically or otherwise, then it will most certainly disappear, particularly in cultures where there is no form of written record of such things. In our own culture I think many traditions have not completely disappeared because we do have some kind of written record. I suspect that in many ways, however, their real identities are gone. I think we are looking at skeletons, without being sure what kind of flesh they ought to be clothed in.

Where we have the opportunity, I think we ought to try to understand how music is interacting with all the other cultural and social forces that really allow it to be, recognizing that at some point these forces in constantly shifting emphasis may lead it not to be. When we are lucky enough to be involved where it still exists—I speak of "exists" in terms of "being viable to the culture"—we have the chance of knowing a lot more about it than if we have to go at it when it no longer exists.

To offer just one example: the more I think about what I call the "short score" of Javanese music, which is a basis, just a skeleton, for generating group improvisation by forty or fifty musicians, the more I am reminded of some very early medieval manuscripts that were also a generating force, and one cannot help but wonder at the extent to which we have lost contact with the flesh.

Miss Foster: In such music could one say that, at least to some extent, the symbolism is readily apparent to the people who are participating. In other words, when people listen to the well-known music of a shadow play on the radio, they are able to visualize what goes on, and they have very intimate associations with it.

Hood: You would be surprised. There is quite a cast of characters in the Mahabharata and the Ramayana—which, by the way, any cultivated individual ought to know just as he is expected to know the *Iliad* and the *Odyssey*. But in Java and Bali these characters are well known as, say, Laurel and Hardy are here. You have an immediate image when I say "Laurel and Hardy"; in a similar but deeper way, the Javanese characters are used symbolically for characterization. It is not just something one discusses philosophically of an evening; it is an immediate frame of reference, a living thing.

Miss Foster: This may provide a valuable insight into medieval situations where Biblical characters permeate drama and art—one thinks of the vast narratives in the cathedrals and in paintings, although it is sometimes hard for us to realize that the people had such intimate ties to these narratives.

HOOD: I think it does give very definite insight into our Middle Ages. It was Nino Pirrotta, I believe, who years ago first used the term "stratification" in connection with medieval practice, and this term has been widely borrowed by ethnomusicologists. It has been applied to African and Asian music of all kinds, to refer to a principle of orchestration in which an instrument or voice has a predictable register or stratum, which in turn has a predictable density. The Romantic orchestra is also layered, to be sure, but with a much less predictable relative density for each layer. In the Middle Ages one could manipulate the basic elements of music in many ways and emphasize them in form. Western music started that way. Javanese music also started that way, at the same time or earlier (there is pretty good evidence that it was earlier). The direction continued in Java, and today the most highly stratified ensemble in the world is the central Javanese gamelan with its highly complicated process of group improvisation. I have often thought that we could have gone in the same direction in the West. But although we started that way, other factors—social and cultural consensus, and, to some extent, external forces—were at work, and we took a different route. Nevertheless, I think these cultures of the non-Western world could provide great insight into our Middle Ages.

MRS. HAMPTON: Are characters identified or recalled primarily through melodic association in the music which accompanies the puppet plays?

HOOD: No, it is not only melody; a character can be identified by a particular pattern, a characteristic rhythm. All of this music is modal. The degree to which modal practice is rigorous varies considerably, of course, from one tradition to another. In Java the traditional music is still completely realized by the improvising musicians. This can be said only of traditional music, however. Since World War II this part of the world has encountered Japanese occupation, the aftermath of the revolution in Indonesia—some fifteen years of tremendous upheaval—and along with it the declaration of independence and compulsory mass education, which meant that the master-disciple mode of learning could not continue. These events have created an alarming situation that threatens traditional music. There is still a generation of professional musicians educated in the oral tradition, but the younger generation is being educated in other ways. I have been told of conservatory teachers who write out an improvisation and give it to a student to memorize, then they give him a different improvisation of the same piece, followed by a third one, but when they ask the student to provide a fourth, he is unable to do so. Nor can the teachers explain the principle underlying what they have done. When they stop to correct a student, they cannot tell him why he is off; they only say "do it this way." Furthermore, professional musicians have told me that there is no composer left who can write a "fixed melody," which is their basis for improvisation. They say there is no one alive today who can write in the old classical tradition. The new pieces that are being written betray little knowledge of even the fundamental notions of that tradition. So we can say that within a generation the traditional practice will disappear; it will become the mere residue that I think it has already become in other places.

Schott: In this situation we would expect to see new traditions emerging. What is to fill the vacuum that is left by this disappearance of tradition? The Beatles?

Hood: Not entirely. The Beatles are there already, of course. My point is that unless something happens within twenty years or even less, the old classical traditions which today are still realized beautifully are going to be destroyed in a very awkward way.

Schott: But with their basic drive to make music, they will make music no matter what happens.

Hood: There is no question about that, nor do I deny them the right to change their style.

Van Solkema: How would you account for the fact that the tradition is dying out in Java and Bali when it seems not to be dying in Africa—at any rate not in the parts of Africa that Profesor Nketia discussed here? I have the impression that acculturation is not affecting the traditional music of Africa to any very great extent, at least not to the extent people worried about twenty years ago, for example.

Hood: It is not yet dying out in Java—that sounds too final. Very ancient traditions are hanging on. But I do think that there is a tradition that is still in flower and, since the carriers of that tradition themselves are concerned, we, too, should be concerned. Let us put it in a different frame of reference: suppose we had no manuscripts from the Classic period and we felt it slipping away, would you not feel rather desperate? The traditional music of Java is a great literature; its disappearance would be a great loss. It is not that they may not have new traditions, but it would be a great pity if they lost a tradition such as I do believe has been lost in Thailand. I think one of our jobs may be to try to anticipate what appears to be a real crisis.

SUPPLEMENTARY READING

Hood, Mantle, "The Enduring Tradition: Music and Theater in Java and Bali," in *Indonesia*, ed. Ruth T. McVey (New Haven, 1963).

Music and Cult:
The Functions of Music in
Social and Religious Systems

FRANK LL. HARRISON

*T*HE ORIGINAL title of this series of lectures, "Perspectives and Lacunae in Musicological Research," suggests that its planners had two main aims: to elicit ideas about the kind of additions to the established structure of musicological research that may be desirable or are likely to be made in the foreseeable future, and to uncover lacunae in the structure as it exists. I propose in this paper to deal with these topics in reverse order, taking first the subject of lacunae, and second the possibilities of extension into new areas of investigation and into research techniques not hitherto associated with orthodox musicology.

It is an inescapable implication of my title that musicology is not a subject, but only part of a subject. In the course of the past century musicology acquired its name, and with a name it eventually gained a local habitation (in Shakespeare's sense) in the university household. There, happily, it flourished and still grows, as the inauguration of this doctoral program bears witness. In speaking of lacunae one is implicitly accepting for the moment the established framework, while seeking gaps in information and defects of interpretation. In considering perspectives one must question the existing framework, since its contrived separation of disciplines forces most of us into studying the material residues of human behavior while ignoring the behavior that produced them. In a university context perspectives involve the question, What does the future need from, or have to do with, the past?—precisely one of the questions that are burning up young minds in universities here and elsewhere. As far as traditional musicology is concerned, we may defend the position that it should continue to be the same interminable scratching around in a selected patch on the Western cultural pile; alternatively, we may suggest valid approaches to a kind of musicology that bears more relation to the realities of human behavior in the present as well as in the past.

Liturgiology, the scientific study of Christian religious observances, has developed fully only in the present century, so it is just about the same age as musicology. The most comprehensive single work on Christian liturgies is Anton Baumstark's *Comparative Liturgy*, originally a series of lectures given in 1932, a revised form of which is available in an English translation by F. L. Cross.[1] Baumstark's book deals with all the Christian rites of Europe, southwest Asia, and northwest Africa. He was familiar not only with the Latin and Greek liturgies, but also with the Christian rites of the Near East and India, whose texts are in a great number of different languages. The geographical scope of Eastern Christian liturgiology in this full sense ranges, as Baumstark observed, "from the Mediterranean to the gates of China and from Turkestan to the foot of India." When the various European rites, both obsolete and continuing, are taken into account, the number of Christian liturgies with distinct geopolitical characteristics which originated before the sixteenth century is about eighteen. In addition the Western rites include the more or less distinct liturgical practices of monastic orders, first the Benedictine and later the Cistercian, Dominican, and Franciscan. One must also mention archaisms such as those surviving in Toledo, Lyons, and Braga. Baumstark's book, readable although densely packed, is most enlightening on the range and aims of the comparative method in Christian liturgiology. Its English translation is provided with a comprehensive bibliographical appendix covering text editions and secondary literature of most of these liturgies, and also has an index of manuscripts as well as a general index.

Those in need of descriptive treatments of the history and content of the separate rites will find the various books by Archdale King the most useful. His four volumes, in a series called Rites of Western Christendom, have the titles *Liturgies of the Religious Orders*,[2] *Liturgy of the Roman Church*,[3] *Liturgies of the Primatial Sees*[4] (this is on the rites of Lyons,

1. Anton Baumstark, *Comparative Liturgy*, trans. F. L. Cross (London, 1958).
2. Archdale A. King, *Liturgies of the Religious Orders* (London, 1955).
3. Archdale A. King, *Liturgy of the Roman Church* (London, 1957).
4. Archdale A. King, *Liturgies of the Primatial Sees* (London, 1957).

Braga, Milan, and Toledo), and *Liturgies of the Past*.[5] King had earlier published *The Rites of Eastern Christendom*.[6]

Both the comparative and descriptive approaches to Christian liturgical usages depend on the availability of original documents and texts. The first period of collecting and editing earlier texts and interpretations of the Christian liturgy was the sixteenth century, when would-be reformers of the medieval rites, both Catholic and Protestant, wanted to know about earlier Christian liturgical practices. The first large compilation of this kind was made is 1568 by the anti-Protestant Melchior Hittorp of Cologne,[7] who had the object, as he says in his title, of "refuting the heretics of our time who calumniate the rites and ministries of the Catholic Church." Michael Praetorius began his *Syntagma Musicum* (1614–15) with a history of choral and instrumental music in the Jewish, Egyptian, Asiatic, Greek, and Latin churches. This was intended to justify the rich ritual and musical practices of the Lutheran church. Earlier, Praetorius had prefixed to the first part of his *Musae Sioniae* (1605) the complete text of Martin Luther's *Encomion Musices* of 1538, in the course of which Luther justified instrumental music in church with the flat statement that the church fathers had used instruments in their sacred songs. In the prefaces to some later volumes of church music, Praetorius deployed at considerable length his knowledge of general and liturgical history, with copious references. The curious dedication of the *Hymnodia* (1611) to James I of England consists of two abbreviated histories. One, of Christianity in the British Isles, has among its more striking inaccuracies the statement that Saint Patrick died at the age of 122. He concluded the other, which is on sacred hymnody, with the wish that under the protection of James's "honest laws and by the will of God, the indigenous and not superstitious arts of the liturgy and of the sacred hymnology of the country may be favored and fostered."

Praetorius's opinions on ritual and its history supported the Lutheran position that all available musical means were meant by God to be used to praise Him and expound his gospel. John Calvin's deductions from the same historical facts were quite the opposite. To him the use of elaborate and instrumental music in the rituals described in the Old Testament made them a part of the Old Dispensation, whose ceremonies were designed for less developed minds. In the New Dispensation of the Christian church, instruments of various kinds were appropriate only for civil pomp (*legalis ceremonia*) and for teaching the young (*legalis paedagogia*).[8] The Roman

5. Archdale A. King, *Liturgies of the Past* (London, 1959).

6. Archdale A. King, *The Rites of Eastern Christendom* (Rome, 1947, 1948).

7. Melchior Hittorp, *De divinis Catholicae Ecclesiae officiis et mysteriis varii vetustorum aliquot ecclesiae patrum de scriptorum ecclesiasticorum libri quorum Catalogum pagina decimasexta complectitur* . . . (Paris, 1610).

8. *Die Musik in Geschichte und Gegenwart, s.v.* "Calvin, J."

church and the reformed Anglican church in the sixteenth century were mainly concerned with modernizing and standardizing their liturgies. Neither took an official position on the use of musical media, and neither church has since then attempted seriously to enforce one.

The point I particularly wish to stress here is that at no time in the course of the liturgical controversies of the Reformation and Counter Reformation were questions of musical usage discussed on the basis of such criteria as suitability, adaptability, or availability. They were treated only in the light of nonmusical sanctions of a religious or social character. This raises the question of the meaning and usefulness of common historical stylistic terms like Renaissance, mannerist, and Baroque. Are these true entities, or are they merely concepts imposed much later, as the result of incomplete study of behavior whose criteria were primarily social and religious?

During the Reformation and Counter Reformation, the subject of liturgy and ritual was caught up in the polemics of political and religious controversy. But from the mid-seventeenth century until the end of the eighteenth the history of Christian worship, both Eastern and Western, was studied in a more disinterested way by scholars seeking adequate documentation. Two of the most productive scholars of Western liturgies were Maurist Benedictines of Saint-Maur-des-Fossés, a community especially interested in ecclesiastical history: Jean Mabillon (d. 1707) edited Roman ordinals and documents of the Gallican liturgy,[9] while Edmund Martène (d. 1739) printed Rituals and Ordinals.[10] Lodovico Muratori (d. 1750), a pioneer of Italian historiography who was ducal archivist at the Este library in Modena, published Roman and Gallican Sacramentaries,[11] and the Jesuit scholar F. A. Zaccaria (d. 1795) made available a great variety of liturgical materials in his *Bibliotheca ritualis*[12] and *Onomasticon rituale*.[13] Martin Gerbert, abbot of Saint Blaise and well known to musicologists, is notable not only for his *Scriptores* and *De cantu et musica sacra*, but also for his 1777 collection of *Monumenta veteris liturgiae Alemmanicae*.[14] He also anticipated the nineteenth-century revival by restoring plainsong to his community's services. This may remind us that the history of plainchant between the sixteenth and nineteenth centuries—its submergence, its partial survival, and the various metamorphoses imposed on it—has been infrequently written about, at least in English. The story would begin with the uses of mensuralized plainsong in the late fifteenth and early sixteenth centuries, Renaissance attempts to reform it, and so on,

9. Jean Mabillon and M. Germain, *Musaeum Italicum*, 2 vols. (Paris, 1724).

10. Edmund Martène, *De antiquis ecclesiae ritibus* . . . (Antwerp, 1687, 1689).

11. Lodovico A. Muratori, *Liturgia romana vetus*, 2 vols. (Venice, 1748).

12. Francesco A. Zaccaria, *Bibliotheca ritualis*, 2 vols. (Rome, 1776–81).

13. Francesco A. Zaccaria, *Onomasticon rituale selectum*, 2 vols. (Faenza, 1787).

14. Martin Gebert, *Monumenta veteris liturgiae Alemmanicae*, 2 vols. (Saint Blaise, 1777–79).

to such curiosities as its *galant* ornamentation and figured-bass setting in the eighteenth century.

Still confining this brief bibliographical survey to Western liturgies (since I am not competent to do otherwise), the next phase of liturgical study was initiated in post-Revolutionary France by Dom Prosper Guéranger (d. 1875), founder of Solesmes. The object of the Solesmes restudy of Western ritual monophony was to restore to the Roman rite a usable, standardized conflation of medieval rituals. Its significance to liturgical scholarship lies mainly in the series of facsimiles of plainsong manuscripts entitled *Paléographie musicale grégorienne*, founded by Dom Mocquereau (d. 1930). The Solesmes principles of plainsong performance rest on no such historical foundation, and it is perhaps not surprising to learn that Dom Pothier (d. 1923), their chief architect, had studied cello at the Paris Conservatory.

In England, the nineteenth-century ritual revival was due initially to the new theological outlook of the Oxford movement. It was only later that it took directions more useful to scholarship with the founding of the Henry Bradshaw Society and the Alcuin Club, both for the publication of liturgical documents, and of the Plainsong and Medieval Music Society for music publication and performance. In France, Canon Ulysses Chevalier (d. 1923) directed the mainly documentary series *Bibliothèque liturgique*, and Michel Andrieu (d. 1956) published editions of fifty Roman Ordines of the High Middle Ages.[15] German and Austrian scholars since the mid-nineteenth century have been strong in text collections of a comprehensive kind.

It may be most useful for our present purposes to attempt here a cross section, by types, of the pre-Reformation liturgical materials of most concern to musicologists that are available today. The general catalogues of European libraries and the printed census of manuscripts in libraries in the United States[16] naturally include liturgical source material. Some libraries' holdings of manuscripts and early prints with music have been separately catalogued, and these publications are usually available in musicological collections. Kathi Meyer-Baer has described some early liturgical prints with music.[17] The enormous number of liturgical manuscripts preserved in the public libraries of France are listed and briefly described in the

15. Michel Andrieu, *Les "Ordines Romani" du haut moyen âge*, 5 vols. (Louvain, 1931–61).

16. Seymour de Ricci and William J. Wilson, *Census of Medieval and Renaissance Manuscripts in the United States and Canada*, 3 vols. (New York, 1935–40); Supplement by C. U. Faye and W. H. Bond (New York, 1962). For an example of effective use of United States resources in liturgical manuscripts see Jacquelyn A. Mattfeld, "Some Relationships between Texts and *Cantus Firmi* in the Liturgical Motets of Josquin des Prés," *Journal of the American Musicological Society*, XIV (1961), 159–83.

17. Kathi Meyer-Baer, *Liturgical Music Incunabula: A Descriptive Catalogue* (London, 1962).

admirable official series *Catalogue générale des manuscrits des bibliothèques publiques de France*. This is organized by cities and towns, whose libraries usually contain at least some of the surviving liturgical books of the local churches. Under this enlightened system many local liturgical sources are locally preserved, adequately catalogued, and accessible on request. The information in these catalogues is greatly augmented by Victor Leroquais in his books on several types of liturgical manuscripts. For musicologists, his six-volume work on the breviaries is likely to be the most useful.[18] The chief bibliographical item of this kind for Britain is Walter Howard Frere's *Bibliotheca Musico-Liturgica*,[19] which lists and briefly describes liturgical manuscripts containing music in many libraries in Great Britain and Ireland. Richard B. Donovan's *The Liturgical Drama in Medieval Spain*[20] has a bibliography of manuscript and early printed liturgical sources in that country, including not only those directly related to his subject but also "other medieval liturgical manuscripts which are extant or may be extant." For Portugal, researchers may consult the discussion of manuscript sources in Chapter V of Solange Corbin's *Essai sur la musique religieuse portugaise au moyen âge*,[21] and also the material in Bertino Daciano's *Bibliografia Musical Portuguesa*.[22]

Under the heading of facsimiles with music, in addition to the substantial *Paléographie musicale* series, a Rouen Gradual[23] and a Leipzig Gradual[24] are available, and the Salisbury Antiphonal[25] and Gradual[26] have been published, each with an Introduction by W. H. Frere. At least three Sequentiaries—which are usually called *Prosaria*—have been published: those of the Sainte-Chapelle, of Aix-la-Chapelle, and of Utrecht.[27]

Modern editions of liturgical documents include in the first place Ordinals and Customaries, and in the second place service books such as Missals and Breviaries, which have little or no music. For the early medieval liturgy there are critical surveys of the sources and content of the Gradual and of the Mass Antiphonal, and a text edition of the Mozarabic

18. Victor Leroquais, *Les Bréviaires manuscrits des bibliothèques publiques de France*, 6 vols. (Paris, 1934).

19. Walter Howard Frere, *Bibliotheca Musico-Liturgica*, 2 vols. (London, 1894).

20. Richard B. Donovan, *The Liturgical Drama in Medieval Spain* (Toronto, 1958).

21. Solange Corbin, *Essai sur la musique religieuse portugaise au moyen âge (1100–1385)* (Paris, 1952).

22. Bertino Daciano, *Bibliografia Musical Portuguesa* (Porto, 1947), 147–56.

23. Henri Loriquet, Joseph Pothier, and Amand Collette, *Le Graduel de l'Église cathédrale de Rouen au XIIIᵉ siècle*, 2 vols. (Rouen, 1907).

24. Peter Wagner, *Das Graduale der St. Thomaskirche zu Leipzig*, 2 vols. (Leipzig, 1930–32).

25. Walter Howard Frere, ed., *Antiphonale Sarisburiense* (London, 1901–26).

26. *Id.*, ed., *Graduale Sarisburiense* (London, 1894).

27. *Le Prosaire de la Sainte-Chapelle* (Macon, 1952) and *Le Prosaire d'Aix-la-Chapelle* (Rouen, 1961), both ed. Dom Hesbert; *The Utrecht Prosarium*, ed. N. de Goede (Amsterdam, 1965).

Antiphonal.[28] For the early and High Middle Ages, the most comprehensive series is that of the Henry Bradshaw Society (which has not confined itself to British liturgies) and for France the *Bibliothèque liturgique* of Chevalier. Ordinals published independently of these series include those of Chartres,[29] of Évreux,[30] and of Salisbury.[31] Modern editions of all the service books of the Use of York have been published by the Surtees Society, which specializes in the publication of documents connected with the ecclesiastical history of York and Durham.[32] The Salisbury Missal and Processional have been published outside of the established series.[33]

Most modern editions of Ordinals and service books have text indices to facilitate research in local usage and in the ritual context of liturgical items. For sacred metrical texts of the Middle Ages the vast fifty-five-volume collection *Analecta hymnica medii aevi* by Clemens Blume and Guido Dreves has outshone and virtually replaced earlier anthologies like H. A. Daniel's *Thesaurus hymnologicus*[34] and F. J. Mone's *Lateinische Hymnen des Mittelalters*.[35] Another formidable and enormously useful work is Chevalier's *Repertorium hymnologicum*,[36] which occupies six volumes of his *Bibliothèque liturgique*. The *Repertorium hymnologicum*, like the *Analecta hymnica*, is much more comprehensive than the brief form of its title implies. It is an index of first lines of 42,000 items of medieval Latin sacred metrical verse, including hymns, sequences, tropes, conductus, and rhymed offices, organized alphabetically and by number. Chevalier's *Repertorium* is complemented by Hans Walther's two-volume *Initia carminum ac versuum medii aevi posterioris latinorum*,[37] an

28. *Le Graduel Romain, édition critique par les moines de Solesmes*, 4 vols. (Solesmes, 1959–1962); *Antiphonale Missarum Sextuplex*, ed. Dom Hesbert (Brussels, 1935); *Antifonario Visigotico mozarabe de la catedral de Leon*, ed. Dom Louis Brou and Dr. José Vives (Barcelona-Madrid, 1959).

29. Yves Delaporte, *L'Ordinaire chartrain du XIIIe siècle* (Chartres, 1953).

30. R. Delamare, *Ordo servicii de l'insigne cathédrale d'Évreux* (Paris, 1925).

31. Walter Howard Frere, ed., *Use of Sarum*, 2 vols. (Cambridge, 1898, 1901).

32. *Missale ad usum insignis Ecclesiae Eboracensis*, 2 vols. (Newcastle, 1874) and *Manuale et Processionale . . .* (Newcastle, 1875), both ed. W. G. Henderson; *Breviarium . . .* , ed. S. W. Lawley, 2 vols. (Newcastle, 1880, 1882); *Horae Eboracenses*, ed. Christopher Wordsworth (Durham, 1920).

33. John Wickham Legg, ed., *The Sarum Missal* (London, 1916 [edited from three MSS]); Francis H. Dickinson, ed., *Missale ad usum insignis et praeclarae ecclesiae Sarum* (Burntisland, 1861–83 [edited from printed sources]); W. G. Henderson, ed., *Processionale ad usum Sarum* (Leeds, 1882).

34. Herman A. Daniel, ed., *Thesaurus hymnologicus*, 5 vols. (Leipzig-Halle, 1841–56).

35. Franz J. Mone, *Lateinische Hymnen des Mittelalters*, 3 vols. (Freiburg im Breisgau, 1853–55).

36. Cyr Ulysse Chevalier, *Repertorium hymnologicum: Catalogue des Chants, Hymnes, Proses, Séquences, Tropes en usage dans l'Église Latine depuis les Origines jusqu'à nos jours*, 6 vols. (Louvain and Brussels, 1892–1920).

37. Hans Walther, *Initia carminum ac versuum medii aevi posterioris latinorum*, 2 vols. (Göttingen, 1959).

alphabetical and numbered list of later medieval poetry, which takes into account research since Chevalier's *Repertorium*. Both Chevalier and Walther give references to modern prints of the texts they list. Musicologists should always give Chevalier or Walther numbers, if they exist, for metrical Latin texts quoted or cited in their studies or editions.

There is as yet little study material in the form of liturgical genres with both text and music. An especially honorable mention and best wishes for successful completion go, therefore, to Bruno Stäblein's series *Monumenta monodica medii aevi*, whose first volume, containing hymns, has been followed by volumes of Graduals and Alleluias.[38]

Under the heading of reference works, books, and monographs, perhaps the most remarkable item is the *Dictionnaire d'archéologie chrétienne et de liturgie*,[39] which was fifty years in the making. Designed to cover on a generous scale Christian archeology to about A.D. 800 and liturgy to modern times, this work was largely written single-handedly by Henri Leclercq, formerly of Solesmes, who spent a great part of his life in the British Museum. Though the *Dictionnaire* has weaknesses of content and balance (the coverage under the later letters tails off markedly), it is useful for some aspects of liturgical history. A list of standard works on the history of Christian liturgy would begin with Louis Duchesne's pioneering book *Origines du culte chrétien*, and would include Pierre Batiffol's *Histoire du bréviare* and Josef A. Jungmann's *Missarum sollemnia*, which was written in German. All three of these basic works are available in English translation.[40] The collected papers of two noted English liturgiologists have been reprinted in Edmund Bishop's *Liturgica historica*[41] and in a book entitled *Walter Howard Frere, a Collection of His Papers on Liturgical and Historical Subjects*.[42] Special studies of the music of at least two medieval monastic orders have been published: *Le Graduel des prêcheurs* (on the Dominican chant) by Dominique Delalande[43] and S. R. Marosszéki's *Les Origines du chant cistercien*.[44] The

38. Bruno Stäblein, ed., *Monumenta monodica medii aevi*, I: *Hymen* (Kassel, 1956); II: *Die Graduale-Gesänge der Hs. Vat. lat. 5319*, with M. Landwehr-Melnicki (Kassel, 1970); VII: *Alleluia-Melodien I (bis 1100)*, ed. Karlheinz Schlager (Kassel, 1968).

39. Fernand Cabrol and Henri Leclercq, *Dictionnaire d'archéologie chrétienne et de liturgie* (Paris, 1907–57).

40. Louis Duchesne, *Christian Worship, Its Origin and Evolution*, trans. M. L. McClure (London, 1927); Pierre Batiffol, *History of the Roman Breviary*, trans. A. M. Y. Baylay (London, 1912); Josef A. Jungmann, *The Mass of the Roman Rite*, trans. W. F. A. Brummer, 2 vols. (New York, 1951–55).

41. Edmund Bishop, *Liturgica historica* (Oxford, 1918).

42. *Walter Howard Frere, a Collection of His Papers on Liturgical and Historical Subjects* (London, 1940).

43. Dominique Delalande, O.P., *Le Graduel des prêcheurs* (Paris, 1949).

44. Solutor R. Marosszéki, *Les Origines du chant cistercien*, Analecta Sacri Ordinis Cisterciensis, VIII (Rome, 1952).

Origins of the Modern Roman Liturgy, by Stephen van Dijk and Joan Hazelden Walker,[45] is a study of the close historical relationship between the medieval Franciscan liturgy and the postsixteenth-century Roman rite. Finally, the long and distinctive history of the religious practices of Ethiopia, whose music urgently needs investigating, is the subject of a full-length study by Edward Ullendorf.[46]

It may be asked, What value have liturgical history and documentation for the musicologist, and what kind of information may he expect to find in them? The honest answer is that you can't tell until you look. You may spend a lot of time before you are lucky enough to see something that gives you the sensation Sir Maurice Powick once described as "sitting on the cat." This characterizes exactly the feeling I had when I first looked into the 1337 Ordinal of Exeter Cathedral.[47] The first and musicologically most useful volume of the Exeter Ordinal was published by the Henry Bradshaw Society in 1909; though it has been available for some fifty years, I believe I was the first musicologist to quote extensively from it in print. Ordinals rarely tell us exactly which parts of the services could be polyphonically sung or played and when—but the Exeter Ordinal does.[48] John Grandisson, who was responsible for it, was an unusual bishop—he didn't have cloth ears. In the section on chants for the Ordinary of the Mass, his Ordinal has an expression about musical quality of a kind which is very rare in medieval writing: "Let us drop utterly," he says, "that disagreeable Kyrie which has one very long phrase and one very short phrase; it has a weak tune, although it is among those customarily sung in the Use of Salisbury."[49] It is not my intention here to dig out musicological nuggets from British liturgical sources, but rather to suggest that there is plenty of research still to be done on the music history of the British liturgies. This is particularly true of the liturgies of pre-Norman churches, both secular and monastic, in all parts of the British Isles. We know from the Winchester Troper[50] that polyphony was cultivated there before the end of the tenth century, nearly a hundred years before the Norman conquest. But we don't know to what extent Winchester was typical or exceptional, and we know very little about the musical characteristics of Anglo-Saxon rituals and of those of Pre-Norman Ireland and Scotland. The fact that what seems to be the earliest known specimen of three-part polyphony was

45. Stephen J. P. van Dijk and Joan Hazelden Walker, *The Origins of the Modern Roman Liturgy* (Westminster, Md., 1960).

46. Edward Ullendorf, *Ethiopia and the Bible* (London, 1968).

47. John N. Dalton, ed., *Ordinale Exon*, 4 vols. (London, 1909–40).

48. *Ordinale Exon*, I, 19–20: "De modo psallendi et modulandi discantandi aut organizandi."

49. *Ordinale Exon*, II, 468.

50. Walter Howard Frere, ed., *The Winchester Troper* (London, 1894); Andreas Holschneider, *Die Organa von Winchester* (Hildesheim, 1968).

written in Ireland before the Anglo-Norman invasion[51] suggests that we should be cautious of making wide general statements on a small amount of evidence—further evidence may drastically alter the picture. This kind of discovery also suggests that the orthodox terminology of central and peripheral spheres of musical culture is not necessarily applicable to the Middle Ages.

Research into certain kinds of medieval liturgical documents provides insights into the psychology of professional executants, an important and neglected subject in the music of any society and period. A twentieth-century performer of my acquaintance once described his profession as that of "going through a routine in order to produce ecstasy in somebody else." Similarly, musicians taking part in ritual acts are not necessarily engaged in worship, but in servicing professionally someone else's act of worship. In a ritual situation in the pre-Renaissance West or in a non-Western society, both worshipers and service providers are likely to have a highly matter-of-fact attitude toward religion. The Ordinal of Laon Cathedral tells us that after the Gloria of the Mass on Christmas Day two canons sang the Laudes to the bishop, who thereupon gave each of them twelve pence. While two subdeacons sang the Gradual in the *pulpitum maius* (that is, in the rood loft), the subdeacon who had read the Epistle went for his pence to the bishop. After the Alleluia, presumably during the singing of the sequence, the two subdeacons who had sung the Gradual and the two deacons who sang the Alleluia went ceremonially in turn for *their* money. After the bishop had begun the Credo, the cantor, subcantor, and some others got their money from the bishop while the Credo was being sung. After Sext, everyone went to the refectory singing *Salve festa dies* on the way, and while the bishop feasted the singers sang for his entertainment. After the meal two canons sang before the bishop's table an item whose title is given as *Pascis visceribus* and when they finished it they received money.[52] Routines of this kind, in which the bishop paid out money during Mass on festivals, are described also in the Ordinals of Rheims[53] and Bayeux.[54]

Ordinals give us information about the performance practices of medieval rituals that no other sources do—for example, on how the sequence at Mass was performed. This was not always the same throughout the year. At Bayeux in Advent, the verses were sung alternately with two singers to

51. See Frank Ll. Harrison, "Polyphony in Medieval Ireland," in *Festschrift Bruno Stäblein* (Erlangen, 1967).

52. Cyr Ulysse Chevalier, ed., *Ordinaires de l'église cathédrale de Laon* (Paris, 1897), pp. 51–52.

53. Cyr Ulysse Chevalier, ed., *Sacramentaire et Martyrologe de l'Abbaye de Saint-Rémy; Martyrologe, Calendrier, Ordinaire et Prosaire de la Métropole de Reims (VIIIe–XIIIe siècle)* (Paris, 1900), p. 33.

54. Cyr Ulysse Chevalier, ed., *Ordinaire et Coutoumier de l'Église cathédrale de Bayeux (XIIIe siècle)* (Paris, 1902), p. 296.

each verse until the last half-stanza, which all four sang together. An exception was made for the sequence *Qui regis sceptra* for the third Sunday in Advent, which was sung straight through by two singers.[55] The reason for this appears if you examine this unusual sequence, which is not in paired half-stanzas as one expects a sequence to be, but has only six lines, all of different lengths.[56]

In Bayeux, Advent apart, singers who had been picked out in advance by the ruler of the choir on each side gathered in two bunches (the Latin word here is *conglobare*), one in front of the dean and the other in front of the cantor's stall, and sang the sequence in alternating half-stanzas until the last half-stanza, which all sang as they walked back to their seats.[57]

It is clear that a sequence was sung only by those who had memorized it. The Salisbury procedure for singing a prose, which is a trope of an Office respond cast in the same double-verse form as a sequence, carries the same implication. While the verse of the respond was being sung, the rulers went to each person in the two upper rows, saying to each, "Domine, ad prosam?" Those who wished, joined in the prose in two facing rows in mid-choir, while the main body of singers repeated the tune after each verse, vocalizing it to the vowel of the last syllable of the first verse.[58] Apparently, singers who were not prepared to sing the text of the prose from memory could recall and repeat the tune on one hearing. The idea is similar to that of "lining-out" in the hymn singing of post-Reformation congregations.

The extent to which plainsong was sung from memory is directly relevant to the understanding of medieval musical practice as a whole. Even if books were provided, they were obviously of no use at a night Office without lights, and the lighting of candles was meticulously regulated, chiefly on the ground of expense. A statute of the dean of Laon of about 1200 implies that at Matins two psalters and two antiphonals were provided for the whole choir, but says firmly that candles may not be lighted "unless from evident necessity, and when this is over the candles shall be extinguished."[59] It was clearly prudent to provide for the possibility that a singer or small group might break down completely in the verse of a respond. At Bayeux in the thirteenth century, the proper of the Mass was sung from books, but everything from the Antiphonal had to be sung from memory, except on the feasts of Saint Stephen, Saint John, and the Holy Innocents.[60] The services on these feasts just after Christmas were

55. *Ibid.*, p. 27.

56. Francis H. Dickenson, ed., *Missale Sarum*, cols. 27–28.

57. *Ordinaire de Bayeux*, p. 58.

58. Francis Proctor and Christopher Wordsworth, eds., *Breviarium ad usum insignis Ecclesiae Sarum* (Cambridge, 1886), III, cols. 17–18.

59. *Ordinaires de Laon*, p. xxiv.

60. *Ordinaire de Bayeux*, pp. 11, 369.

carried out in most secular churches by particular groups—by the priests on Saint Stephen's Day, the deacons on Saint John's Day, apart from Mass, and the boys on Holy Innocents. None of these groups ever otherwise ran a complete service, and would have needed books to do so.

Most Ordinals have a section on the use of bells. At Bayeux, on the principal feasts all the bells were rung simultaneously before Matins—an effect that was called *tumultus*. At the beginning of the *Te Deum* at the end of Matins, the smallest choir bells (*campana minima in choro*) were sounded two or three times, and then two medium-sized bells in the tower were rung continuously throughout the singing of the *Te Deum*. From the words "aeterna fac" (that is, during the last nine verses), all the bells in the choir were sounded.[61] In Exeter, all the tower bells were sounded together (this was called *classicum* there) during the last six verses—from the words "Per singulos dies."[62] The other part of the liturgy where bells were sounded was during the sequence, except in Advent. At Bayeux, two larger bells in the choir were sounded all through the sequence;[63] in Exeter, two medium-sized bells in the tower were rung during the sequence.

Bells, or pseudobells, have been used in modern performances of medieval polyphonic music, but there seems to be confusion here between two kinds of bells, and between their ritual use and pedagogical use. The various bells used in a medieval church community were clearly enumerated in the twelfth century by John Beleth, whose *Rationale divinorum officiorum*[64] is the only systematic discussion of Western liturgy surviving from that time. Beleth says there are six bell-type instruments: *tintinnabulum*, played in the refectory and other eating rooms; *cymbalum*, played in choir; *nola*, played in monastic churches; *nolula*, a clock bell; and *campanum*, a tower bell. Joseph Smits van Waesberghe, in his admirably documented monograph *Cymbala*,[65] says that at first bells were "intended to distinguish the intervals in teaching music," and advances the theory that "when the organ began to be established as a liturgical musical instrument they were used in the churches of monasteries and chapters to accompany the chant." *Cymbala*, he believes, "must have been first used for those chants in which the organ also played a part, primarily for the *Sequentia*." But in Bayeaux, as we have seen, two bells in the choir were sounded, and at Exeter two bells in the tower. The bell routines at Saint Augustine's in Canterbury are even more specific. There were bells in the campanile and also in the tower, and the more important bells in the

61. *Ibid.*, p. 59.
62. *Ordinale Exon*, II, 536.
63. *Ordinaire de Bayeux*, p. 53.
64. J. P. Migne, ed., *Patrologia Latina*, CCII, cols. 13–166.
65. Joseph Smits van Waesberghe, *Cymbala*, American Institute of Musicology, Studies and Documents, I (Rome, 1951).

tower had names. On Christmas Eve the bells called Absalon Major and Matheus were rung during the sequence (*ad prosam*), and at the *Te Deum* two larger bells in the campanile were rung. At the beginning of the sequence in the main Christmas Mass, two small bells in the campanile were sounded, then four bells together.[66] It is quite clear that none of these ritual bell-uses called for bells tuned scalewise, which in medieval iconography have always a pedagogical implication. The David initial of a twelfth-century Psalter, for example, depicts a set of fifteen small hanging bells. The first six beginning from the left and the first six beginning from the right are both marked with the syllables *Ut* to *La*; the three in the middle are *B fa*, *B mi*, and one bell unmarked.[67] There can be no doubt that this depicts a teaching situation, not a ritual one. In some illuminations with tuned bells, David is using them to teach his attendant musicians. This use of tuned bells seems to be a uniquely Western practice, connected with music as an art and a science. In the thirteenth-century French poem *La Bataille des VII Ars* (The Battle of the Seven Arts), by Henri d'Andeli, music is introduced as "Ma dame Musique aus clochetes" (Lady Music, she of the little bells).[68] The magic and ritual function of bells predates by many millennia the scientific use of bells as pitch reference. There are many survivals in historic times—for example, the bells on the garments of Jewish high priests and of some Celtic Christian clergy, in the Coptic church, and in modern survivals of Dionysiac religion.

When medieval liturgical documents mentioned the organ, which is not often, they generally did so in the most casual way. This is frustrating for most musical researchers, whose hindsight inclines them to regard the use of the organ as more than a peripheral subject. In the Ordinal of Bayeux, the organ is mentioned in a list of church appurtenances, including crosses, chalices, glass vessels, and bells, whose care was the responsibility of a lay custodian.[69] In the Customary of Saint Augustine, Canterbury, organs, bells, and soap are associated in a passage which provided payments (and sometimes nonpayments) for the functioning of the organ and bells on certain festivals. The organ blowers were to get extra payment "if the organ was used three times during one festival." It is not specified in this passage what these three occasions were, but elsewhere, again quite incidentally, the information is given that the organ was used for the sequence on Saint Michael's day; in still another place we read that on the

66. Edward M. Thompson, ed., *The Customary of the Benedictine Monasteries of St. Augustine, Canterbury and St. Peter, Westminster* (London, 1904), II, 292–93.

67. Frank Ll. Harrison and Joan Rimmer, *European Musical Instruments* (London, 1964), Pl. 44.

68. Louis J. Paetow, ed., *La Bataille des VII Ars of Henri d'Andeli* (Berkeley, 1927), p. 49.

69. *Ordinaire de Bayeux*, p. 302.

feast of Saint Augustine the organ was sounded *both* at Vespers *and* during the sequence.[70] It appears, therefore, that either the organ or ritual bells or both participated in the performance of a sequence, except in Advent, and that ritual bells, and perhaps also the organ, sounded during the *Te Deum*. Precisely how the organ was used in these contexts is still uncertain; more extensive research in liturgical and related sources than has hitherto been done may eventually give at least a partial answer. A chronicler of Saint Alban's Abbey, for example, relates that in 1396 their new abbot was welcomed with the ceremonial singing of the *Te Deum*, with the organ alternating (*alternantibus organis*). During the *Te Deum* at another fourteenth-century reception of an abbot at Saint Alban's shawms were played (*sonantibus chalamis quos "burdones" appellamus*), the bells in the clock were rung, and all the tower bells were sounded together.[71]

As far as research into liturgical performance goes, one can hardly even speak of "lacunae"—"a large void" would be more accurate. Present-day performance of pre-sixteenth-century liturgical music is frequently a sorry affair, done in quavery, self-pitying style, which is perhaps intended to suggest ancient piety, or boosted with instruments in order to add color, which is absent from the singing. The specific questions that must be asked about liturgical performance practice are those which must be asked about any performance practice. First, what was the appropriate tempo? Second, what was the nature of the vocal timbre and pronunciation? Third, what were the acoustic circumstances of performance, the forces used, and their disposition? Fourth, if instruments were involved, what were they and what were their techniques? These are interrelated questions, and if we are far from having answered them about profane music in the Middle Ages, we have hardly begun to *ask* them about liturgical music.

The results of not asking them can produce musical incongruities such as would not be tolerated in the performance of any other kind of music. This may be illustrated by comparing the two available performances of an English version of the Latin sequence *Stabat mater Christi crucem, stabat videns veram lucem*, whose vernacular form is set to a tune identical with that of the liturgical sequence. The English poem, beginning "Stond wel, moder, under rode," is not, as is its Latin prototype, a meditation on the crucifixion of Jesus, but a dialogue, truly dramatic in impact, between Christ on the cross and his mother below. The ludicrously slow tempo of one of these performances (its six stanzas take eight minutes and fifteen seconds as compared with the other performance's three minutes) completely distorts the song's verbal-cum-melodic shape and destroys the dra-

70. *Customary*, II, 29–94, 259, 268.
71. Henry T. Riley, ed., *Gesta Abbatum Monasterii S. Albani*, 3 vols. (London, 1867–69), III, 434, I, 520.

matic sense of the dialogue. Has anyone, in fact, investigated the subject of when, where, and why very slow singing started?

It was a basic principle in medieval Christian liturgical practice that men and women did not sing in the same choir. Quite apart from this original sanction, standard present-day women's voices on the upper parts of medieval polyphony seriously unbalance the texture. This is particularly true in hocketing. Pronunciation, too, is a matter that fundamentally affects timbre. Modern Italianate pronunciation is quite alien to most of the sounds of medieval Latin. No contemporary singer, to suggest a possible analogy, would sing a Charles Ives song in broad Cockney.

Until about 1400, most polyphonic vocal liturgical music was performed from a single book by a small group of from two to about five singers. Depending on the ritual situation, this was done either on the choir screen (the singers facing the altar), at the center of the choir floor, or at the first step (*gradus*) leading to the altar. The acoustical circumstances were further determined by the fact that this took place in a fully enclosed choir space within the larger space of a Gothic church. This may still be heard in many Spanish cathedrals. In the later Middle Ages, most liturgical polyphony was sung by larger forces in quite different acoustical circumstances. Few present day concert-hall and recorded performances take account of the varied sonority requirements of different genres of medieval music, or use recording techniques to achieve some degree of likeness to the original sound.

Finally, a great many performances of medieval liturgical music rescore the original for a variety of often quite anachronistic instruments. Enough research has been done on this subject to show how completely unhistorical and invalid it is to use, for example, flutes, recorders, violins, cornett, reed organ, shawms, and trombone in Machaut's *Messe de Notre Dame*. There are two assumptions, still commonly held, on which performances of medieval liturgical music are frequently posited. One is that any instrument co-existing in time with any kind of music is, therefore, usable in its performance; the other is that any "old" instrument is usable in any "old" music, even though many centuries and great differences of specialization separated the existence of instrument type and music genre. These assumptions are of a naïveté rarely encountered in the performance of music of any other period.

I propose to begin the second part of this discussion with some definitions. Though these have been partly assumed in what I have already said, it may be well to formulate them rather precisely as we move into the wider context of social and religious systems in general. The word "liturgy" signified originally—that is, in ancient Greece—"a public office or duty discharged by the richer citizens at their own expense."[72] This

72. Definitions in quotation marks are from the *Shorter Oxford English Dictionary*.

meaning is exactly the same as that attached to the word *cargo* in a Spanish or Latin-American context. In certain Christian-Indian communities in Central America, the social and religious rituals that are indispensable to their society are carried on in turn by members of the community who take on a *cargo* for one year.[73] The word "liturgy" has come to mean "a collection of formularies for the conduct of public worship." I use it in this wide sense, to cover everything that goes on in organized religious observance. I use the word "ritual," when speaking of pre-Renaissance Europe or of non-Western societies, in a more restricted sense, for "a prescribed order of performing religious or other devotional service." "Prescribed" is the key word here, the implication being that the order is obligatory, and that the efficacy of the ritual depends on its exact observance. The word "use" connotes a liturgy which is in some degree localized, in the sense of being "the distinctive ritual and ceremonial of a particular church, diocese, community, etc.," which is, however, only a local modification of a standard liturgy. The sense of the Latin word *cultus* is "worship," and the word cult has come to be used for special devotion to a particular person or thing; its object was generally a religious one in a pre-Renaissance context.

It has often been remarked that the Christian West is unique in having developed a musical science based on part-music, with "laws" of counterpoint and harmony. Used initially for religious purposes, this was ultimately transferred to the neutral surroundings of the concert hall, where only a minimal religious element occasionally intrudes. Attempts have been made to account for this unique development in terms of the West's intellectual heritage from Greece and the Arab world. This is both a *post factum* kind of explanation and one that relates musical happenings to subsequent theory rather than to characteristic features of the behavior of the people concerned. The thing which differentiated medieval Christian religious observance most sharply from that of other major religions was its capacity for constructing elaborate and ostentatious devotions around an original core of magical and propitiatory rites. For some twelve centuries, from the recognition of Christianity until the Reformation, plainsong was the fixed musical component of the prescribed ritual, whose other components of language and movement were prescribed with equally rigorous sanction. From about the ninth century onward, however, the standardization imposed by Charlemagne in the Empire and by the Cluniacs in Spain was accompanied and followed by large-scale interpolations and proliferations. None of these was essential for ritual efficacy, and uniformity was not, therefore, imposed on them. Hence, John Beleth, in describing liturgical books in the twelfth century, said of a Troparium that "it has not got a fixed beginning"—he meant for the purpose of listing by the

73. See Frank Ll. and Joan Harrison, "Spanish Elements in the Music of Two Maya Groups in Chiapas," *Selected Reports*, II (1968), 2 ff.

initial words of the second folio, as manuscripts always were—"since its contents are sung *ad placitum.*" "No one," he went on, "considers that this or that Kyrie should be sung on any particular feast. On the other hand, an Antiphonal has a fixed beginning, namely *Aspiciens a longe,* and a Gradual likewise, namely *Ad te levavi.*"[74] By the High Middle Ages, the Western liturgy had acquired a great number of elaborations and accretions; polyphonic music was superimposed on some ritual genres, using their prescribed plainsong, and interpolated between others, adapting or not a plainsong motif. The largest single body of accretions was connected with the cult of the Virgin Mary, for whom there was created a complete liturgy, paralleling the canonical Mass and Hours, which was universally observed, although not ritually prescribed. In the main, the superimpositions and accretions had a social rather than a religious reason for their existence; they were largely public demonstrations of piety, intended to be judged and measured by their amplitude and elaboration. Many of the artistic happenings of the Western Middle Ages—whether fan vaulting, or church decoration, or sacred motets—were part of this essentially social impulse which acted under the guise of a religious one. The history of these happenings in art seems coherent in these terms, as it does not in terms of a supposed evolutionary developing toward retrospectively intellectualized norms of technique and structure.

It was exclusively in social and ritual terms, moreover (as we noticed earlier), that the reformers of the Western liturgy saw the technique and structure of sixteenth-century music. To the English Protestants, the magico-ritual element, most of the accretions, and the whole concept of florid artistic elaboration were all devilish. Absolute uniformity of relatively simple liturgical formularies was imposed, for social and political reasons. To Martin Luther, all of the liturgy, except a part involving what may now seem a relatively minor theological difficulty, was to be turned to God's purpose as a means of teaching. His overriding criterion was that it should be understood, whatever the language in which it happened to be pronounced; otherwise, he imposed no uniformity at all. John Calvin's rejection of the ritual and its accretions was almost total, but he did have an ear for a well-made and memorable tune; this made him one of the most effective people in public music in the sixteenth century, although he is seldom seen in this light. In Pope Pius V's reformed Breviary and Missal, most of the medieval liturgical interpolations were excised, but none of the cultic accretions. The Council of Trent's observations on musical superimpositions were inconclusive, and composers, like Vincenzo Ruffo, who tried to translate them into practice—Palestrina, too, though not entirely for the same reasons—became the victims of an historical dead end. (In using the words "dead-end" in connection with Palestrina, I am naturally thinking of what actually happened in the sixteenth and early

74. *Patrologia Latina,* CCII, col. 65.

seventeenth centuries, not of the retrospective evaluations of musicologists and pedagogues.)

It has become increasingly clear that orthodox musicological research methods do not in themselves bring useful results in the study of social and ritual aspects of music. Not only is a broadening of the range of research needed, but also new methods of pursuing research, new attitudes to the time-honored but largely outworn questions of musical esthetics and criticism, and new kinds of objective and historical questions about people's *uses* of music. These questions should embrace not only the kinds of music we have been accustomed to call "masterworks" and to tell people they *ought* to use, but also the kinds we often pontifically tell them should be beneath the notice of cultivated persons.

When Guido Adler laid the foundations of modern musicology,[75] he asserted that the focus of the new musical learning was the "musical work of art itself," and that the central aim of all research in music (by which he meant written European music) was to elucidate its theoretical and esthetic principles in the various periods of its history. Since for Adler the focus of musicological study was something called a "musical art work," he began with a premise that excluded material he could not bring himself to regard as "art music." Not that he disregarded what he called "the simple natural products" of so-called folk music; the program he suggested, however, was to observe closely what he called "the organic processes of art—how nature and culture [which, by implication, he dichotomized] unite, blend, balance each other, and so combined, reach full fruition from time to time"—not, of course, in any product of simple nature but in what he called a "musical work of art." In suggesting some possible guidelines for new perspectives—if you want a new term, I suggest "Anthropomusicology"—I shall try to shift the focus of attention from an isolated art object to what I can only call for the present a "musical occasion." Thinking along these lines about musical occasions leads naturally to *the* fundamental question, What is music being used for on this occasion? What is it for?—as well as What is it? No adequate or even preliminary answer to this kind of question can be attempted without examining the full *context* of the occasion.

The almost exclusive preoccupation of most musicologists with written music and its structure has tended to make them neglect much of the evidence of living processes of musical acculturation offered by music that is improvised, unwritten, or only partly coded. A second fundamental question about a musical occasion would, therefore, be this: Was the music (a) wholly improvised, or (b) partly improvised, or (c) produced in as nearly as possible exact conformity to an established model, whether written or unwritten, and whether a written form was before the players or

75. Guido Adler, "Umfang, Methode und Ziel der Musikwissenschaft," in *Vierteljahrsschrift für Musikwissenschaft*, I (1885).

not? The research procedures of Adlerian musicology, based as they were on the establishment of once-and-for-all definitive written versions, whose existing variants must be regarded as deviants, have found difficulty in coping with this kind of question. Merely to ask the question implies that frozen and therefore fossilized, copyrighted and therefore canonized, musics are only a portion, though admittedly a characteristic one, of the music used in modern industrial societies. Orthodox musicological techniques have so far failed to provide adequate ways of recording and studying the intricate processes of collision, assimilation, adaptation, and acculturation that are taking place in much unwritten or partly written music of today. The reasons are not only technical but sociological, since many of us are unwilling to concede that any uses of music but those associated with nineteenth-century European patterns, which are almost exclusively those of the concert hall and opera house, are worthy of attention.

While concert-hall music is fossilized in content and function, music in other surroundings often reveals the living process of adaptation at work. Music whose structure and content are thoroughly familiar may be transferred from its original context to a significantly different one. A case in point is such an innocuous evangelical hymn as *Onward, Christian Soldiers* when played by a flute band in the fiercely anti-Catholic ceremonies of the Orange cult in Northern Ireland, especially on July 12. By association, this social ritual gives the music an explosive political connotation; it becomes an identifying part of a ritual that exerts a major influence in government.

The Orange hymn is a case of transference of music from one use to another within a society. Cases where music has been transferred from one society to a different one, there to fill the same or a different function, are more complex to analyze. On-the-spot research in southern Mexico has shown that certain music belonging to Spanish social and religious rituals of the sixteenth century became without significant change the ritual music of Christianized Indians, whose own civilization had used formal liturgies at least as elaborate as those of Christians in Spain.[76] The processes whereby some techniques of the polyphonic music of three-and-a-half centuries ago, and instruments identical with those on which it was played, can be observed in continuing social use today is of considerable musicological interest. Analysis in depth of this music, which one can validly describe as frozen Baroque with Indian elements, involves about equal parts of field work (chiefly in recording, examining, and measuring instruments, and in interrogating musicians and others) and library work (in the history of early Spanish Baroque institutions, music, and instruments, in the relevant history of the conquest of New Spain, and in the present-day social structure of this Indian community).

In the course of the fiesta of San Sebastian in Zinacantan, southern

76. See footnote 73 above.

Mexico, a change-over of *cargo* from two outgoing to two incoming
Alfereces—the highest rank in their social and religious hierarchy—was
marked by a dance outside the west door of the church, in which all four
men participated. The music of this Alfereces dance was played on a
three-hole pipe and two long tabors of medieval European type. We
know from various sources, mainly the iconography of ceremonials and
surviving or still current instruments, that some kinds of block flute and
some forms of drum were indigenous to the American continent, but we
also know that they were not these kinds. This is another case of frozen
European music several centuries old being used in a specific context in a
very different social system.

I should like to branch out from here for a few moments in order to
indicate, in the briefest way, how widely ranging may be some of the religious and social implications of musical usage. Rodney Needham, the
Oxford social anthropologist, has pointed out—more in an inquiring than
in an asserting spirit—that a noise produced by striking or shaking is
widely used in order to communicate with the other world.[77] He mentions in this connection drum, gong, bell, cymbal, tambourine, xylophone,
metallophone, rattle, rasp, stamping tube, concussion sticks, sticks on
stretched mats, resounding rocks, and clashing anklets. Mircea Eliade, to
whose work he refers, has summarized usefully the sound-making usages
of shamans in northern Europe and Asia, in North and South America,
and in other places, in her book *Le Chamanisme et les techniques ar-
chaïques de l'extase*. She says (and I quote from the revised edition in English) that "there is always some instrument that, in one way or another, is
able to establish contact with the world of the spirit."[78]

That this phenomenon has historical depth as well as geographical
spread is suggested by the musical usages of present-day popular religion
in Thrace, which seems to preserve some of the chief characteristics of
ancient Dionysiac cults. In these orally transmitted rites, "songs and
rhythms are pre-determined by inherited ancestral ritual. In accordance
with this ritual, on the evening of the 20th May, the initiates gather
together ... in the Konaki, and the lyre-player begins a song of pure con-
trition, accompanying himself on the lyre; next, the drum adds its stimulating beat, which, during the vigil that is to continue till midnight, pro-
vokes the first manifestations of ecstasy."[79] (Organological footnote: the
instrument here translated as "lyre" is the Greek bowed lira.)

Someone may ask, Do not these "perspectives" for musicologists in-
fringe on territory that has been pre-empted by ethnomusicologists? They

77. Rodney Needham, "Percussion and Transition," *Man*, II (1967), 606–14.

78. Mircea Eliade, *Shamanism: Archaic Techniques of Ecstasy*, trans. W. T. Trask
(New York, 1964), p. 179.

79. Katerina J. Kakouri, *Dionysiaka: Aspects of the Popular Thracian Religion of
Today*, trans. H. Colaclides (Athens, 1965), p. 119.

do. As I have observed elsewhere, it is in my opinion "the function of all musicology to be in fact ethnomusicology, that is, to take its range of research to include material that is termed 'sociological.' " In Allen M. Garrett's *Introduction to Research in Music*, the author thus forecast the shape of things to come in musicology and ethnomusicology: "At the present time comparative musicology is regarded as a subdivision of musicology; but it is not beyond the bounds of conjecture to suggest that the broader scope of the present-day researcher in that subdivision will be the normal point of view of the musicologist of the future."

If one looks at the social ritual of the concert hall a little more objectively than is usually done, it becomes clear that its peculiarly ambiguous nature, whose characteristic setting is the anonymous urban culture of industrialized societies, has given rise to a correspondingly anomalous musicology, whose accepted materials are largely bound to an artificial set of contexts for musical use. Concert-hall music is produced in an aura of priestly ritual whose highest validity comes from its conformity to a canonized procedure and musical text, while the present-day conductor is an expert in the form of a latter-day priest "in whose hands ritual procedure becomes more and more of a consciously studied discipline." One result of modern music-making rituals is that musicologists tend to discuss music originating outside the context of the modern concert hall in terms entirely unrelated to the actual occasions which regulated its technical features. The obverse of this situation is that in which the structure of so-called masterworks is studied in complete isolation from their use. It is manifest that a Brahms symphony played under the composer's direction at Ramburg in 1878 is in many significant musical respects quite a different thing from the same score brought to sound by an American symphony orchestra in 1969. We should obviously delude ourselves if we thought that a study of the structure of a recipe could take the place of eating the meal based on the recipe. And we should be poor gastronomes if we were to disregard dishes whose recipes have never been written down or have been merely coded.

The enormous area of unwritten or only partly written musical practice, of many kinds and with many uses, of other cultures as well as our own, is not so much underresearched as not yet productively related to our special concerns—one of the most urgent of which is historical validity in the performance of old European art music. For this purpose much of the research already done and reported upon needs reconsidering, and new research and observation along lines which I have called "anthropo-musicological" needs programming. The connecting link and underlying principle of the reassessment of past research and a program for the future is, I suggest, the idea of "occasion," in all its complex totality. Occasions separated in time may appear identical—but a concert-hall performance in 1969 is not the same as one which used the same score in 1928, for many operative features of the context are different. Similarly, occasions removed in space and in our notion of culture may be allied by identity of function and similarity of behavior. The chief guideline is that our curiosity and increasing awareness of music and musical behavior should be man centered and not thing centered. From this point of view, the "musical work of art itself" is an illusion. If anthropology be properly defined as "the study of man as a unit in the animal kingdom," anthropomusicology is the study of man's musical behavior in the context of his total behavior. Our study, to paraphrase a sentence written long ago by Jacques Handschin, should be not music in and for itself, but man in his capacity as a user of music.

DISCUSSION

MRS. HAMPTON: Professor Harrison, you propose the term "anthropomusicology" to shift attention from the work of art itself to the musical occasion of that work, and I find this thought-provoking, particularly as applied to nineteenth-century American music. Here, we do not have masterpieces so much as musical occasions; it is the total body of work that is of interest. Yet almost no one considers nineteenth-century American music as being of any significance, simply because there is no Mozart or Beethoven among its composers. Would you not say this is a particularly relevant field for the anthropomusicologist?

HARRISON: Indeed, yes. The word that seems to get in the way is value. What is the interest in making value judgments? This piece is a fine work of art and this other one is what German musicologists call *Trivialmusik*, which is not an apologetic category. It is considerably more urgent to find out what happened rather than what we wish might have happened.

Musicology, and other fields as well, until recently, seem to be based on judgments of what we ought to like or value highly from the past. As I said in my lecture, Palestrina was a dead end, historically speaking. He simply was of no use to anyone for a century and a half after his death. Then he was artificially revived by a pedagogue who used him to teach counterpoint. In other words, North American music in the nineteenth century is as valid a subject to study as any other, if the purpose is to establish and understand what actually happened, without regard to a hierarchy of values.

What we are trying to find out is about people, not things, and what people did is important. The only question is, What is your basis for selectivity when you are writing history? It seems to me that you are just not writing history at all if you set up value judgments about music on any basis whatsoever, even if you take a technical basis. Nobody can write history without technical analysis. But much more subtle methods of technical analysis need to be developed. It seems to me that our analytical tools need to be sharpened, since analysis does lead to value judgments.

VAN SOLKEMA: I think we will want at some point to say that a collection of music that includes works showing the musical imagination of a Haydn or Mozart is more important than a group which does not.

HARRISON: Now you have got to define the musical imagination of a Haydn or Mozart. In what terms will you define that?

SCHOTT: In preparing for a career in musicology, I do not think I want to make myself into a sort of research vacuum cleaner; this seems to be the ultimate thrust of what you have been saying. You seem to be denying any kind of normative function in musicology; you seem to be dehumanizing the musicologist and turning him into a kind of computer which receives information, sorts it, and puts it in record form, which can then be assimilated by people. I do not think any human can indulge in any activity without making value judgments. I think attempts in other fields, such as the social sciences, to deny this have proven completely idle.

HARRISON: Can you find the basis for a value judgment in the efficacy of music to do what people want it to do, for the use they want to make of it? That is to say, would it be possible ever to relate music and use in the sense of "this is more useful than that" or "this does its job better than that"?

SCHOTT: Palestrina was more churchly than Barnby?

HARRISON: We should say, "Does he fill in the space needed for a motet between the offertory and the elevation with something that is functional, or that has an effect on the situation, or that does something to people?" You see, I am going to get myself out of this picture you have made of me.

SCHOTT: I exaggerate the picture, of course, purposely.

HARRISON: I am thinking of Hindemith's term. His final approval in composition study was in the words "This is in order." He would say, in teaching composition, "You and I are not discussing esthetics." He would discuss esthetics as a question in terms of history or philosophy—but not music in terms of esthetics. Nonetheless, he would say that you and I ought to be able to sit down together and agree by analysis, because we are both professionals and craftsmen, that this is a well-made piece of music, just as we might discuss this chair without necessarily agreeing on any esthetic question whatever.

HARMS: But he was taking this position as a teacher, not as a performer or artist. Certainly value judgments are made by listeners and by the composer himself on the basis of "I like it" or "I do not like it." One would say, "This composition of mine is well made and this other one is equally well made, but I happen to like the first work more."

HARRISON: Is this really a value judgment? For example, suppose we make an analogy with cooking. I may agree that a certain dish represents an excellent bit of cuisine, but I just do not like it. It is a matter of taste, not a matter of value.

BUSHLER: I think we make a mistake in separating a composition from the listener. The work and listener interact. The listener hears the work in terms of his own past experiences and associations. To say that a piece is good or not good is really quite fallacious. If we can say that a certain number of people followed the work over a period of time and that the piece gave satisfaction, maybe of a nonverbal kind, that is enough. I do not like the term "value judgment," since value implies that we can spell out what it is worth. I believe we should focus on what it is we are trying to evaluate and then say it does or does not meet the conditions we are looking for. A piece is thereby neither damned nor saved, but merely commented upon. Would this not clarify matters?

HARRISON: Yes, I like that sort of statement.

MRS. JORGENS: I think we have come back to the original point of "occasion." In the case of Palestrina, we must consider the people who listened to him, the people for whom he was writing. What do we know about these people? We may know that priests in charge of music chose the music to be performed, but we do not really know whether the people in a congregation liked it or not, whether they felt uplifted by it or not.

HARRISON: This has been a question in general history for a long time. Trevelyan and others steered away from great men and politicians and the whole "great" complex in favor of what the ordinary chap did, thought, and felt during any given period in the past. We have to do that sort of thing with music. We have to widen our vacuum-cleaner opening a bit. If you say the general consensus of listeners in the last century is that Mozart was a genius, the question is, What options did they have? Did they hear anyone else? One has to say yes; when they went into a concert hall they heard Mozart, but elsewhere they heard other music. And what was that something else? When music is played in a supermarket, who chooses the music that makes people enjoy buying more than they ought to? What kind of music is it? A musicologist is a music historian, and his subject is people behaving musically.

BROOK: You have edited music and made recordings; on what basis do you choose the works for such a purpose?

HARRISON: Perhaps I make a value judgment as between this piece of Machaut and that piece of Machaut, based on technical analysis and imagination of how it sounds and how it can be made to sound—the effect on me and others. This kind of analysis is of supreme importance. If that is making a value judgment, one is making a judgment on the basis of having to select a number of pieces to fit into twenty-four minutes of music and

trying to represent a certain composer by, say, two rondeaus, or two vire-
lais, or two lais. You do have to decide that this rondeau—for me, for this
purpose, with these other pieces—is preferable to that one.

MRS. JORGENS: But you have also chosen Machaut over lesser composers
who are not as well known or as highly regarded.

HARRISON: We have come to the question of survival. Medieval music is
a field where nobody makes value judgments in the Mozart sense at all. If
one finds a piece of music from the fourteenth century that was never
noticed before, it is completely irrelevant what its value is; it is a new
piece of evidence in a period where every laundry list, so to speak, is of
inestimable value because of its uniqueness.

BROOK: We are now close to the subject of the Kerman-Lowinsky
exchange on the goals of American musicology. You remember that
Kerman suggested that we should follow the lead of literary critics of
twenty years earlier in being concerned above all with the great work of
art and its esthetic evaluation. In response, Lowinsky held that musicology
should embrace not only esthetic judgment but a multitude of other
approaches, presumably including that which you have now called
anthropomusicology. I am heartily in agreement with the latter view. Historical evaluation of the occasion, in order to understand the history of
music in society, must be one of our fundamental concerns, It is important
in tracing American history to study what music existed, and how it functioned. This is not a vacuum-cleaner operation at all. When we study historical processes, we cannot limit ourselves to what is attractive to us personally.

HARMS: Such an approach could lead us very far afield. If we begin by
taking into consideration the cathedral a composer wrote for, the wars
going on, and so forth, we end up by including all of world history.

HARRISON: There are two problems: one's own career, which must be
specialized nowadays, and the aims of musicology as a whole. I, for one,
constantly try to imagine myself as the director of an institute of research
in musicology trying to see in what direction I would want to guide any
such group, or musicology generally. Given the necessity for specialization while maintaining a sense of direction for the profession as a whole, I
think collaboration with other experts, such as linguists or architectural
historians, is becoming more and more necessary.

MRS. PERSHING: There may be another reason for placing specialities
within as large a context as possible for musicologists who engage in
teaching. Musicological research not only relates to social and historical
events of the period investigated but must be made clearly relevant to the
students themselves.

HARRISON: Relevance is the key word, isn't it? To use an extreme case,
there is a group of students in England, notably in the London School of

Economics, who say that the function of universities is to build a future, not to retain the past. This seems to wipe out musicology altogether, doesn't it? Is this an indication of the kind of thing you are referring to?

MRS. PERSHING: It is not as simple as that. Relevant to what? The future does not exist in a vacuum. Everything is related to both the past and the future.

MRS. HAMPTON: May we take up the word "ritual," which you defined in your lecture [p. 322] as a prescribed order for performing religious and devotional services; you applied it also to the procedures of the concert hall today. Can we discuss this term in connection with the rise of polyphony in Western music? In your *Music in Medieval Britain* you note that polyphony developed in sections of the service that were not strict ritual. Some sections had to be done in a wholly prescribed manner in order to achieve "ritual efficacy." Other sections seem designed to make an impact on people who were listening, which is quite a different idea. In other words, polyphony is not necessary to the ritual.

HARRISON: The relationship between polyphony and ritual is extremely interesting. This would explain the use of polyphony, in its early European history anyhow. Whether there was an even earlier polyphony is another very interesting question. There may have been a collision of two practices, one outside and one inside the church, the result of which was adapted for church use: organum, we call it. This is a big historical question, which may indeed involve a meeting between Northern oral traditions of poetry and music (which Irish scholars are now studying intensively) and Christian ritual (which was taught to many more people after Charlemagne than before). In such a situation, notation probably became a necessity, a necessary part of the social machine. It is an anomaly of Christianity that the whole phenomenon of the rise of polyphony and its notation had a social impulse, not a religious one. This is a subject that needs a lot of work.

LEAVITT: You referred earlier to techniques of analysis, which you say should be expanded and refined. Would you recommend any new paths we should take in this area?

HARRISON: Yes, take the business of tunes: How do we decide which tune is better than another? We say, this one is made of a little idea here, three notes, and these three pop up again here, and they unify, so it is a good tune. Now there may be something in this, but it is only a beginning of a very complex process of analyzing things like difference, similarity, recurrence, repetition, and so on.

How were tunes put together in the Middle Ages? What is sometimes wrongly called harmony is really the technique of medieval composition. People talk about tonality in the fourteenth century, and the term just does not apply. We have fairly good tools, I think, for tonal analysis from, say, 1750 to 1900. But what happens before 1750—before 1600—or before 1400? What were the criteria with which the composer worked and what were his procedures?

VAN SOLKEMA: I would like to broaden Mr. Leavitt's question somewhat. I find the prospect of your imagined institute an exhilarating one. Supposing you were to have a group of twenty musicologists at your disposal, what tasks would you set for them? I have in mind your statement that all musicology is in a sense ethnomusicology. Could you project twenty years from now to predict any radically different way of training musicologists?

HARRISON: You are giving me a graduate musicological institute with twenty people?

BROOK: Twenty people and twenty million dollars.

HARRISON: I accept. We are assuming, of course, that our twenty lucky people have a solid humanistic and technical education. I think that with twenty million dollars I would start by collecting a basic library. Then I would buy a big, comfortable ship, and we would all go on it, with crew and captain and lots of the very latest tape recording, film, and other documentation equipment. The director would have the option, in consultation with the faculty, of picking out where to go, for two or three years, beginning perhaps with Veracruz (not Acapulco) and down the other coast of South America, to Peru, across to Indonesia, Singapore, Hong Kong, Persia, using the equipment and the library when necessary.

BROOK: What would happen to your current investigation of fourteenth-century music?

HARRISON: I would be seeing "frozen" fourteenth-century music all over the world—music that is still being used as it was in the fourteenth-century, not ever identically perhaps, but similarly. I would have a chance to see how epics are sung today in North Africa, in Colombia, in Persia, in Burma. I could see what they use their harps for, while here I can only see the instrument in the museum.

LEAVITT: You imply that we are better observers outside of our usual cultural context. Is this what you mean?

HARRISON: Don't you think so? It is very difficult to see one's particular context objectively, especially in the use of an art. I wonder whether it wouldn't be useful for a while to study other people's present rather than our own past.

MRS. PERSHING: This kind of "anthropomusicological" tour may well sharpen our observation of the music of our own society in our day, but I don't see, given your own definition and requirement of "occasion," how this sort of observation can sharpen our analysis of the music of an earlier day, since that was a different music with a different function.

HARRISON: I think you exaggerate the differences. We tend to believe, before we have investigated, that musical occasions and, hence, musical functions differ drastically from culture to culture. I have found that phenomena widely separated geographically and chronologically can often show extraordinarily close parallels. I think our "anthropomusicological" cruise could develop two means of sharpening our analytical tools in dealing with our own earlier music. One would be new criteria altogether for the musical occasion. The other would be the observation of music in societies where it may still today be fulfilling functions it used to fulfill in our society two hundred or more years ago. In our own Middle Ages, we can observe musical processes that go back three millennia or more. Fresh insights and new analytical tools for dealing with these are among the rewards one could hope to find by going on our good musicological ship.

READING LIST

Eliade, Mircea, *Shamanism: Archaic Techniques of Ecstasy*, trans. W. T. Trask (New York, 1964).

Expert, Henri, ed., *Le Psautier huguenot du XVIᵉ siècle* (Paris, 1902).

Harrison, Frank Ll., *Music in Medieval Britain*, 2nd ed. (London, 1963; New York: Dover), Chs. 1–3.

Harrison, Joan E., *Prologomena to the Study of Greek Religion*, 6th ed. (New York, 1959).

Ricard, Robert, *The Spiritual Conquest of Mexico*, trans. L. B. Simpson (Berkeley, 1966), Chs. 5, 6, 10–13.

Rimmer, Joan, *Ancient Musical Instruments of Western Asia in the British Museum* (London, 1969).

Sahagún, Fray Bernardino de, *Florentine Codex: General History of the Things of New Spain*, II: *The Ceremonies*, trans. A. J. O. Anderson and C. E. Dibble (Santa Fe, N.M., 1951).

Stevenson, Robert, "Church Music: A Century of Contrasts," in *One Hundred Years of Music in America*, ed. Paul Henry Lang (New York, 1961), pp. 80–108.

Musicology as a Discipline:
A Selected Bibliography

Compiled by B.S.B.

Abraham, Gerald, "Musical Scholarship in the 20th Century," *University of Western Australia Studies in Music*, I (1967), 1–10.

Adler, Guido, *Methode der Musikgeschichte* (Leipzig, 1919).

―――― "Musik und Musikwissenschaft," *Peters Jahrbuch*, V (1898), 27–39.

―――― "Umfang, Methode und Ziel der Musikwissenschaft," *Vierteljahrsschrift für Musikwissenschaft*, I (1885), 5–20.

Albrecht, Hans, *see* Wiora, Walter, and Hans Albrecht.

Allen, Warren D., *Philosophies of Music History* (New York, 1939; 2nd ed., 1962).

Allorto, Riccardo, and Claudio Sartori, "La Musicologia del 1945 a oggi," *Acta Musicologica*, XXXI/1 (1959), 9–17.

Benestad, Finn, "Musikforskning och musikundervisning," *Musikrevy*, XIV (1959), 80–81, 89.

Berger, Donald Paul, "Ethnomusicology—Past and Present," *Music Educators Journal*, XLIV/7 (March, 1968), 77–79, 127–31.

Blume, Friedrich, "Historische Musikforschung in der Gegenwart," in *Report of the Tenth Congress, Ljubljana, 1967*, ed. Dragotin Cvetko, 13–25. English trans. J. M. Wolff, *University of Western Australia Studies in Music*, II (1968), 1–14, under the title "The Present State of Musical Studies, I: Historical Musicology."

―――― "Musicology in German Universities," *Current Musicology*, IX (1969), 52–63.

―――― "Musikforschung und Musikleben," in *Kongressbericht Bamberg 1953* (Kassel), pp. 7–23.

——— "Musikforschung und Musikpraxis," in *Festschrift Fritz Stein zum 60. Geburtstag* (Braunschweig, 1939), pp. 13–25.

——— "Zur Lage der deutschen Musikforschung," *Die Musikforschung*, V/2–3 (1952), 97–109.

Bose, Fritz, "Südamerikanische Musikforschung," *Acta Musicologica*, XXIX/1 (1957), 43–45.

Brailoiu, Constantin N., "Musicologie et ethnomusicologie aujourd'hui," in *Bericht über den siebenten internationalen musikwissenschaftlichen Kongress Köln 1958* (Kassel, 1959), pp. 17–29.

Brockhaus, Heinz Alfred, "Musikwissenschaft als Leitungswissenschaft," *Musik und Gesellschaft*, XVIII (1968), 747–54.

——— "Zur Problematik der Musikhistoriographie; Musikgeschichte in *Reclams Universal-Bibliotek* 1867–1967," in *Hundert Jahre Reclams Universal-Bibliotek* (Leipzig, 1967), pp. 306–46.

Brook, Barry S., "On Graduate Study and Standards in Musicology," *Current Musicology*, II (1966), 156–60.

——— ed., "Computer Applications to Music and Musicology: Bibliography," in *Musicology and the Computer* (New York, 1970).

——— ed., "Musicology 1966–2000: A Practical Program," *ibid*. Includes: Luther Dittmer, "Western-European Music of the Christian Era before 1400: Research and Publication" (p. 190); Jan LaRue, "New Directions for Style Analysis" (p. 194); Edward Lippman, "History of Theory" (p. 198); Lewis Lockwood, "Utopian Proposals" (p. 204); Claude V. Palisca, "Stylistic Change and the History of Ideas" (p. 211); Franklin Zimmerman, "Musical Biography and Thematic Cataloguing: Two Opposing Aspects of Musicology in the 21st Century" (p. 216); Arthur Mendel, Discussion (p. 222).

Brook, Barry S., and Leon B. Plantinga, eds., "Patterns in the Historiography of 19th-Century Music. IMS—Colloque—St. Germain," *Acta Musicologica*, XLIII/3–4 (1971), in press. Includes contributions by William Austin, Barry S. Brook, Vincent Duckles, Vladimir Féderov, Georg Knepler, François Lesure, Lewis Lockwood, Rey M. Longyear, Fritz Noske, Pierluigi Petrobelli, Leon B. Plantinga, Alexander L. Ringer, Boris Schwarz, Miloš Velimirović, and Robert Wangermée.

Bücken, Ernst, "Grundfragen der Musikgeschichte als Geisteswissenschaft," *Peters Jahrbuch*, XXXIV (1927), 19–30.

Bukofzer, Manfred, "Historical Musicology," *Music Journal*, IV (Nov.-Dec., 1946), 19–27.

——— *The Place of Musicology in American Institutions of Higher Learning* (New York, 1957).

Burjanek, Josef, *Otakar Zich; studie k vývoji ceského muzikologického myšlení v první třetině našeho století* [A study of the development of Czech musicological thought in the first third of our century] (Brno-Praha, 1966).

Carpitella, Diego, "Rassegna bibliografica degli studi di etnomusicologia in Italia dal 1945–a oggi," *Acta Musicologica*, XXXII/2–3 (1960), 109–13.

Chailley, Jacques, *Précis de musicologie* (Paris, 1958).

Chartier, Yves, "La Musicologie à l'université—méthodes et expériences," *Revue de l'Université d'Ottawa*, XXXVIII/3 (July, 1968), 405–30.

Chodkowski, Andrzej, "Les Études musicologiques en Pologne," *Musique en Pologne*, II (July, 1967), 17–22.

Chomiński, Józef Michał, "Radziecka muzykologia," *Muzyka*, V/4 (1960), 3–11.

Chrysander, Friedrich, Preface, *Jahrbücher für musikalische Wissenschaft*, I (1863).

Claro, Samuel, "Hacia una definición del concepto de musicología; contribución a la musicología hispano-americana," *Revista musical chilena*, XX/101 (July-Sept., 1967), 8–25.

Clercx-Lejeune, Suzanne, "La Musicologie en Belgique depuis 1945," *Acta Musicologica*, XXX/4 (1958), 199–214; XXXI/3–4 (1959), 130–32.

Cvetko, Dragotin, "Les Formes et les résultats des efforts musicologiques yougoslaves," *Acta Musicologica*, XXXI/2 (1959), 50–62.

Dahlhaus, Carl, "Historismus und Tradition," in *Zum 70. Geburtstag von Joseph Müller-Blattau*, Saarbrücker Studien zur Musikwissenschaft, 1 (Kassel, 1966), pp. 46–58.

Dent, Edward J., "The Historical Approach to Music," *Musical Quarterly*, XXIII/1 (Jan., 1937), 1–17.

———— "Music and Music Research," *Acta Musicologica*, III/1 (1931), 5–8.

———— "The Scientific Study of Music in England," *Acta Musicologica*, II/3 (July, 1930), 83–92.

Devoto, Daniel, "Panorama de la musicología latino-americana," *Acta Musicologica*, XXXI/3–4 (1959), 91–109.

Dolflein, Erich, "Historismus und Historisierung in der Musik," in *Festschrift für Walter Wiora zum 30. Dezember 1966*, ed. Ludwig Finscher and Christoph-Hellmut Mahling (Kassel, 1967), pp. 48–56.

Donà, Mariangela, "La Musicologia in Italia," in *Studi de musicologia in onore di Guglielmo Barblan in occasione del LX compleanno* (Firenze, 1966), pp. 94–101.

Duckles, Vincent, "Patterns in the Historiography of 19th-Century Music," *Acta Musicologica*, XLII (1970), 75–82.

———— *Music Reference and Research Materials: An Annotated Bibliography*, 2nd ed. (New York, 1967).

Eggebrecht, Hans Heinrich, chairman, "Symposium: Reflexionen über musikwissenschaftliche Forschung heute. Internationalen musikwissenschaftlicher Kongress. Bonn, 1970," (Kassel, 1972), in press. Preprint distributed at the symposium included the following summaries: Carl Dahlhaus, "Über historische und systematische Musikwissenschaft"; Michał Bristiger, "Strukturelle und genetische Perspecktive"; Zofia Lissa, "Tradition in der Musik"; Hans-Werner Heister, "Musikwissenschaft als Sozialwissenschaft"; Hans Heinrich Eggebrecht, "Konzeptionen"; Clytus Gottwald, "Musikwissenschaft und Kirchenmusik"; Lars Ulrich Abraham, "Musikgeschichte bestimmt Musikpädagogik"; Kurt von Fischer, "Über die Verantwortung des Musikwissenschaftlers"; Hans-Peter Reinecke, "Studiengange der Musikwissenschaft"; Harald Hackmann, "Wissenschaftliche und ausserwissenschaftliche Bereiche in der Musikologie"; Konrad Boehmer, " 'Musikwissenschaft'—Voraussetzungen ihrer Zukunft."

Elschek, Oskár, "Hudobnovedecká systematika a etnoorganológia" [Systematization of musical science and ethnoorganology], *Musicologica slovaca*, I/1 (1969), 5–41.

Engel, Hans, "Musikwissenschaft und ihr Studium," *Aspekte*, II/6 (May, 1969), 32–40.

—————— "Die Entwicklung der Musikwissenschaft 1900–1950," *Zeitschrift für Musik*, CXI/1 (1950), 16–22.

Erdely, Stephen, *Methods and Principles of Hungarian Ethnomusicology*, Uralic and Atlantic Series, 52 (Bloomington, Ind.-The Hague, 1965).

Ernst, Viet, "Über die Einheit von historischer und systematischer Musikwissenschaft," *Beiträge zur Musikwissenschaft*, IX/2 (1967), 91–97.

Federhofer, Hellmut, "Gegenwartsprobleme der Musikforschung," *Musikerziehung; Zeitschrift der Musikerzieher Österreichs*, XXII (1969), 147–49.

Fellerer, Karl Gustav, *Einführung in die Musikwissenschaft* (Münchberg, 1953).

—————— "Musik und Musikwissenschaft," in *A Ettore Desderi nel suo 70. compleanno* (Bologna, 1963), pp. 61–69.

Franck, Wolf, "Musicology and Its Founder, Johann Nicolaus Forkel (1749–1818)," *Musical Quarterly*, XXXV/3 (Oct., 1949), 588–601.

Gallagher, Merellyn Martha, "The State of Musicology in American Universities," *Student Musicologists at Minnesota*, II (July, 1967), 1–51.

Geering, Arnold, "Musikwissenschaft in der Schweiz," *Österreichische Musikzeitschrift*, XXIV (1969), 177–79.

Gerson-Kiwi, Edith, "Musicology in Israel," *Acta Musicologica*, XXX/1–2 (1958), 17–26.

Goldthwaite, Scott, "The Growth and Influence of Musicology in the United States," *Acta Musicologica*, XXXIII (1961), 72–79.

Graf, Walter, "Neue Möglichkeiten, neue Aufgaben der vergleichenden Musikwissenschaft," in *Festschrift für Erich Schenk* (Graz, 1962), pp. 231–45.

Grasberger, Franz, "Musik und Forschung. Ein historischer Rückblick," *Österreichische Musikzeitschrift*, XXII/11 (Nov., 1967), 641–46.

Griffel, Michael, "Musicological Method in American Graduate Schools," *Current Musicology*, VI (1968), 7–50.

Grout, Donald Jay, "Current Historiography and Music History," in *Studies in Music History: Essays for Oliver Strunk* (Princeton, 1968), pp. 23–40.

Gurlitt, Wilibald, "Hugo Riemann und die Musikgeschichte," in *Musikgeschichte und Gegenwart* [collected essays by Gurlitt, edited by H. H. Eggebrecht], Beihefte zum Archiv für Musikwissenschaft, II (1966), 103–22.

—————— "François-Joseph Fétis und seine Rolle in der Geschichte der Musikwissenschaft," *ibid.*, 123–39.

Haapanen, Toivo, "Gegenwärtiger Stand der Musikwissenschaft in Finnland seit 1923," *Acta Musicologica*, I/3 (April, 1929), 46–48; I/4 (July, 1929), 53–54.

Handschin, Jacques, "Der Arbeitsbereich der Musikwissenschaft," in *Gedenkschrift Jacques Handschin. Aufsätze und Bibliographie* (Bern-Stuttgart, 1957), pp.23–28, Also, "Vom Sinn der Musikwissenschaft," pp.29–37.

—————— "Belange der Wissenschaft," *ibid.*, pp. 60–69.

—————— "Gedanken über moderne Wissenschaft," *ibid.*, pp. 51–59.

—————— "Humanistische Besinnung," *ibid.*, pp. 376–84.

—————— "Über das Studium der Musikwissenschaft," *ibid.*, pp. 38–50.

—————— "Musicologie et musique," in *Report of the Fourth Congress of the*

International Musicological Society, Basel, 1949 (1951), pp. 9–22; *Revue internationale de musique* (1950–51), pp. 220–32.

Harap, Louis, "On the Nature of Musicology," *Musical Quarterly*, XXIII/1 (Jan., 1937), 18–25.

Haraszti, Emile, "La Musicologie, science de l'avenir," in *Encyclopédie de la Pléiade. Histoire de la musique*, ed. Roland-Manuel, II (Paris, 1963), 1549–92.

——— "Fétis fondateur de la musicologie comparée," *Acta Musicologica*, IV/3 (1932), 97–103.

Harran, Don, "Musical Research in Israel: Its History, Resources, and Institutions," *Current Musicology*, VII (1968), 120–27.

Harrison, Frank Ll., Claude V. Palisca, and Mantle Hood, *Musicology*, Princeton Studies in Humanistic Scholarship in America (Englewood Cliffs, N.J., 1963). Includes: Frank Ll. Harrison, "American Musicology and the European Tradition"; Mantle Hood, "Music, the Unknown"; Claude V. Palisca, "American Scholarship in Western Music."

Haydon, Glen, *Introduction to Musicology* (New York, 1941; reprint, Chapel Hill, N.C., 1959).

——— "Musicology in the United States: A Survey of Recent Trends," in *Proceedings of the Music Teachers Association* (1947), pp. 321–41.

Heckmann, Harald, "Musikwissenschaftliche Unternehmungen in Deutschland seit 1945," *Acta Musicologica*, XXIX/2–3 (1957), 75–94.

——— ed., *Elektronische Datenverarbeitung in der Musikwissenschaft* (Regensburg, 1967).

Heinz, Rudolf, *Geschichtsbegriff und Wissenschaftscharakter der Musikwissenschaft in der zweiten Hälfte des 19. Jahrhunderts. Philosophische Aspekte einer Wissenschaftsentwicklung*, Studien zur Musikgeschichte des 19. Jahrhunderts, 11 (Regensburg, 1968).

Herbst, Kurt, "Musikpsychologie und Musikwissenschaft. Eine grundsätzliche Betrachtung über E. Kurths 'Musikpsychologie,'" *Acta Musicologica*, III/2 (1931), 64–68.

Hibberd, Lloyd, "Musicology Reconsidered," *Acta Musicologica*, XXXI (1959), 25–31.

Hickmann, Hans, "Über den Stand der musikwissenschaftlichen Forschung in Ägypten," in *Report of the Fourth Congress of the International Musicological Society, Basel, 1949* (Basel, 1951), pp. 150–54.

"History and the Present," *Sovetskaja muzyka*, XXXII/3 (March, 1968), 9–23. In Russian. Notes on a discussion by Soviet musicologists of Walentina Konen's article (*see* Konen, Walentina).

Hoerburger, Felix, and Wolfgang Suppan, "Die Lage der Volksmusikforschung in den deutschsprachigen Ländern: Ein Bericht über die Jahre 1945 bis 1964," *Acta Musicologica*, XXXVII/1–2 (1965), 1–19.

Hood, Mantle, *The Ethnomusicologist* (New York, 1971).

Hood, Mantle, *see* Harrison, Frank Ll., Claude V. Palisca, and Mantle Hood.

Hughes, Anselm, "Ninety Years of English Musicology," in *Liber amicorum Charles van den Borren* (Anvers, 1964), pp. 93–97.

Husmann, Heinrich, *Einführung in die Musikwissenschaft* (Heidelberg [1958]).

Iselin, D., "Die Musikwissenschaft an den schweizerischen Universitäten," *Acta Musicologica*, I/2 (Jan., 1929), 27–32; I/3 (April, 1929), 39–46.

Jankovič, Ljubica S., "La Situation actuelle de l'ethnomusicologie en Yougo-slavie," *Acta Musicologica*, XXXII/2–3 (1960), 94–102.

Jelescu, Paur, "Ce înseamnă a prelucra folclorul?" [What does the processing of musical folklore mean?], in *Naţional şi universal în muzică* (Bucharest, 1967), pp. 181–92.

Kabalevskij, Dimitrij, "K aktuàlnim otázkim hudebni vedy a kritiky" [On the current problems of musicology and music criticism], *Hudebni rozhledy*, III/11–12 (1951), 28–29.

Kastner, Macario Santiago, "Veinte años de musicología en Portugal (1940–1960)," *Acta Musicologica*, XXXII/1 (1960), 1–11.

Katzarova-Koukoudova, Rayna, "L'Ethnomusicologie en Bulgarie de 1945 à nos jours (1959)," *Acta Musicologica*, XXXII/2–3 (1960), 77–89.

Kerman, Joseph, "A Profile for American Musicology," *Journal of the American Musicological Society*, XVIII (1965), 61–69.

———— "Rebuttal to 'Reply' by Lowinsky," *Journal of the American Musicological Society*, XVIII/3 (1965), 426–27.

Kier, Herfrid, *Raphael Georg Kiesewetter (1773–1850): Wegbereiter des musikalischen Historismus*, Studien zur Musikgeschichte des 19. Jahrhunderts, 13 (Regensburg, 1968).

King, Alexander Hyatt, "Musikwissenschaft in England. Ursprung und Quellen," *Musik und Zeit*, IV/1 (1953), 57–62.

Kinkeldey, Otto, "Musical Scholarship and the University," *Musica Disciplina*, I (1948), 10–18.

Knepler, Georg, "Reaktionäre Tendenzen in der westdeutschen Musikwissenschaft," *Beiträge zur Musikwissenschaft*, II/2 (1960), 3–21.

Kolinski, Mieczyslaw, "Recent Trends in Ethnomusicology," *Ethnomusicology*, XI/1 (Jan., 1967), 1–24.

Konen, Walentina, "Zur Verteidigung der historischen Musikwissenschaft," *Kunst und Literatur*, XVI/2 (1968), 199–207.

Kremljow, J., "Über einige Fragen der sowjetischen Musikwissenschaft," *Musik und Gesellschaft* (June, 1952), 184–86.

Kretzschmar, Hermann, *Einführung in die Musikgeschichte* (Leipzig, 1920).

———— "Kurze Betrachtungen über der Zweck, die Entwicklung und die neuesten Zukunftsaufgaben der Musikhistorie," *Peters Jahrbuch*, XIV (1907), 83–96.

Krohn, Ernst C., "The Development of Modern Musicology," in Lincoln Bunce Spiess, *Historical Musicology* (New York, 1963).

Kümmel, Werner Friedrich, "Die Anfänge der Musikgeschichte an den deutschsprachigen Universitäten," *Die Musikforschung*, XX/3 (July-Sept., 1967), 262–80.

———— *Geschichte und Musikgeschichte*, Marburger Beiträge zur Musikforschung, 1 (Kassel, 1967).

Kunst, Jaap, *Ethno-Musicology. A Study of Its Nature, Its Problems, Methods and Representative Personalities to Which Is Added a Bibliography* (The Hague, 1955).

Lang, Paul Henry, "Musical Scholarship at the Crossroads," *Musical Quarterly*, XXXI (1945), 371–80.

———— "Musicology for Music," *Modern Music*, XIX (Jan.-Feb., 1942), 92–95.

—— "On Musicology," *Musical Quarterly*, XXXIII (1947), 557–64.

LaRue, Jan, "Codetta: Some Details of Musicology in the United States," *Acta Musicologica*, XXXIII/2–4 (1961), 79–83.

Lenaerts, René, "Wegen en doelstellingen der muziekwetenschap," in *Mélanges Ernest Clossen. Recueil d'articles musicologiques offerts à Ernest Clossen à l'occasion de son 65ᵉ anniversaire* (Brussels, 1948), pp. 139–44.

Lesure, François, "Musicologie et sociologie," *Revue musicale*, CXXI (1953), 411.

—— "La Musicologie française depuis 1945," *Acta Musicologica*, XXX/1–2 (1958), 3–17.

Liess, Andreas, "Aktuelle Probleme der Musikgeschichtsschreibung. Integratio—Proviso—Deliberatio," *Neue Zeitschrift für Musik*, CXXX/3 (March, 1969), 139–41.

—— "Zur Problematik der Musikgeschichte als Wissenschaft und Unterrichtsfach," *Musikerziehung*, XXII/1 (Sept., 1968), 6–11; XXII/2 (Nov., 1968), 55–60.

—— *Protuberanzen*, I: *Zur Theorie der Musikgeschichte* (Vienna, 1970).

Lincoln, Harry B., "The Current State of Music Research and the Computer," *Computers and the Humanities*, V/1 (Sept., 1970), 29–36.

—— ed., *The Computer and Music* (Ithaca, N.Y., 1970).

Lippman, Edward A., "What Should Musicology Be?," *Current Musicology* (Spring, 1965), 55–60.

Lissa, Zofia, "Uwagi o metodzie marksistowskiej w muzykologii" [Notes on the Marxist Method Applied to Musicology], in *Księga pamiątkowa ku czci Prof. Adolfa Chybińskiego w 70-lecie urodzin. Rozprawy i artikuły z zakresu muzykologii* (Kraków, 1950), pp. 50–119.

—— *Wstep do muzykologii* [Introduction to musicology] (Warsaw, 1970).

Lockwood, Lewis, Revue, *Musicology* by Harrison, Hood and Palisca, *Perspectives of New Music*, III/1 (1964), 119–27.

Lönn, Anders, "Trends and Tendencies in Recent Swedish Musicology," *Acta Musicologica*, in press.

Lowinsky, Edward, "The Character and Purpose of American Musicology: A Reply to Joseph Kerman," *Journal of the American Musicological Society*, XVIII (1965), 222–34.

McAllester, David Park, "The Present State of Ethnomusicological Studies," *University of Western Australia Studies in Music*, II (1968), 15–20.

Machabey, Armand, *La Musicologie* (Paris, 1962; 2nd ed., 1969).

McPeek, Gwynn S., "Musicology in the United States: A Survey of Recent Trends," in *Studies in Musicology . . . in Memory of Glen Haydon* (Chapel Hill, N.C., 1969), pp. 260–75.

Maillard, Jean, "The Many Faces of Medieval Musicology," *University of Western Australia Studies in Music*, IV (1970), 1–18.

Marcel-Dubois, Claudie, "Ethnomusicologie de la France 1945–1959," *Acta Musicologica*, XXXII/2–3 (1960), 113–21.

Mendel, Arthur, Curt Sachs, and Carroll C. Pratt, *Some Aspects of Musicology* (New York, 1957). Includes: Arthur Mendel, "The Services of Musicology to the Practical Musician"; Curt Sachs, "The Lore of Non-Western Music"; Carroll C. Pratt, "Musicology and Related Disciplines."

————— "Evidence and Explanation," in *Report of the Eighth Congress of the International Musicological Society, New York, 1961* (Kassel, 1962), V/2, pp. 3–18.

Merriam, Alan P., *The Anthropology of Music* (Evanston, Ill., 1964).

————— "Ethnomusicology Revisited," *Ethonomusicology*, XIII (1969), 213–29.

Meyer, Ernst Hermann, "Über die wechselseitige Beziehung musikwissenschaftlicher und kompositorischer Tätigkeit," *Beiträge zur Musikwissenschaft*, XI/3–4 (1969), 235–44.

Meyers, Charles S., "The Ethnological Study of Music," in *Anthropological Essays Presented to Edward Burnett Tylor in Honour of His 75th Birthday, Oct. 2, 1907* (Oxford, 1907), pp. 235–53.

Moberg, Carl-Allan, "Musik und Musikwissenschaft an den schwedischen Universitäten," *Acta Musicologica*, I/4 (July, 1929), 54–70; II/1 (Jan., 1930), 10–26.

————— "Musik und Musikwissenschaft an den schwedischen Hochschulen," *Acta Musicologica*, II/2 (April, 1930), 34–44.

Moser, Hans Joachim, "Über den Sinn der Musikforschung," in *Festgabe für Hans Joachim Moser zum 65. Geburtstag 25. Mai 1954* (Kassel, 1954), pp. 158–70.

————— "Über die Zukunft der Musikwissenschaft," in *50 Jahre Gustav Bosse Verlag* (Regensburg, 1963), pp. 113–16.

————— "Musikwissenschaft und Gegenwart," *Zeitschrift für Musik*, CXIV/7 (1953), 389–93.

————— "Die Zukunft der deutschen Musikforschung," *Die Musikforschung*, XII/2 (1959), 178–80.

Muradjan, Matevos, "Die Entwicklung der armenisch-sowjetischen Musikwissenschaft," *Beiträge zur Musikwissenschaft*, X/1–2 (1968), 3–15.

Naegele, Philipp, "August Wilhelm Ambros: Historical and Critical Thought," Diss. Princeton 1954.

Nettl, Bruno, *Theory and Method in Ethnomusicology* (New York, 1964).

Nomura, Francesco Yosio, "Musicology in Japan since 1945," *Acta Musicologica*, XXXV/2–3 (1963), 47–53.

Nováček, Zdeněk, "Úkoly slovenské hudebni védy," *Hudebni rozhledy*, III/10–12 (1951), 89.

Osthoff, Helmuth, "Die Anfänge der Musikgeschichtsschreibung in Deutschland," *Acta Musicologica*, V/3 (1933), 97–107.

Palisca, Claude V., *see* Harrison, Frank Ll., Claude V. Palisca, and Mantle Hood.

Petzoldt, Richard, "Musikforschung heute," *Der Musik-Almanach*, I (Munich, 1948), 381–402.

Pietzsch, Gerhard, "Zur Pflege der Musik an der deutschen Universitäten," *Archiv für Musikwissenschaft*, I, III, VI (1936–41).

Pirro, André, "L'Enseignement de la musique aux universités françaises," *Acta Musicologica*, II/1 (Jan., 1930), 26–32; II/2 (April, 1930), 45–56.

————— "Pour l'histoire de la musique," *Acta Musicologica*, III/2 (1931), 49–52.

Plantinga, Leon B., *see* Brook, Barry S., and Leon B. Plantinga, eds.

Pratt, Carroll C., *see* Mendel, Arthur, Curt Sachs, and Carroll C. Pratt.

Pratt, Waldo S., "On Behalf of Musicology," *Musical Quarterly*, I/1 (1915), 1–16.

Redlich, Hans Ferdinand, "Musik als akademische Disziplin diesseits und jeneseits des Ärmelkanals," *Studium Generale*, XI (1958), 318–22.

———— "The Meaning and Aims of Musicology" (Percival lecture).

———— "Musical Research in Germany—East and West of the Iron Curtain," *Music Review*, XIII/4 (1952), 294–96.

Reeser, Éduard, "Musikwissenschaft in Holland," *Acta Musicologica*, XXXII/4 (1960), 160–74.

Reich, Othmar, "Was ist eigentlich 'das Material der Musik'? Ein Beitrag zum materialproblem der Musikwissenschaft," *Acta Musicologica*, X/2 (1938), 118–29.

Reinecke, Hans-Peter, "Musikforschung als Aufgabe," *Jahrbuch des Preussischen Kulturbesitz*, V (1968), 250–54.

Reinhard, Kurt, *Einführung in die Musikethnologie*, Beiträge zur Schulmusik, 21 (Wolfenbüttel-Zurich, 1968).

Reinhold, Helmut, "Musik, Wissen und Musikwissenschaft," in *Festgabe zum 60. Geburtstag von Willi Kahl am 18. Juli 1953* (Cologne, unpublished typescript), pp. 130–39.

Riedel, Friedrich Wilhelm, "Zur Geschichte der musikalischen Quellenüberlieferung und Quellenkunde," *Acta Musicologica*, XXXVIII (1966), 3–27.

Riemann, Hugo, *Grundriss der Musikwissenschaft* (Leipzig, 1908).

Ringbom, Nils-Eric, "Die Musikforschung in Finnland seit 1940," *Acta Musicologica*, XXXI/1 (1959), 17–24.

Rokseth, Yvonne, "Musical Scholarship in France during the War," *Journal of Renaissance and Baroque Music*, I/1 (1964), 81–84.

Ronga, Luigi, "Musicologia e filologia musicale," *Rassegna musicale*, XX/1 (1950), 1–12.

Rosenberg, Herbert, "Musikwissenschaftliche Bestrebungen in Dänemark, Norwegen und Schweden in den letzten ca. 15 Jahren," *Acta Musicologica*, XXX/3 (1958), 118–37.

Rouget, Gilbert, "L'Ethnomusicologie," in *Encyclopédie de la Pléiade. Ethnologie générale*, I (1968), 1339–90.

Rusu, Liviu, "Perspective și preocupări teoretice în istoria muzicii românesti," *Studii de muzicologie*, II (1966 [1967]), 229–67.

Rybarič, Richard, "Slovenská historiografia a deformácie," *Slovenská hudba*, XII/9–10 (Dec., 1968), 398–405.

Sachs, Curt, *see* Mendel, Arthur, Curt Sachs, and Carroll C. Pratt.

Sartori, Claudio, *see* Allorto, Riccardo, and Claudio Sartori.

Schanzlin, Hans Peter, "Musikwissenschaft in der Schweiz (1938–1958)," *Acta Musicologica*, XXX/4 (1958), 214–24.

Schenk, Erich, "Musikwissenschaft an der Universität Wien," in *Sborník Prací Filosofické Fakulty Brněnské University* (Brno, 1969).

Schering, Arnold, "Musik und Musikforschung," *Acta Musicologica*, III/3 (1931), 97–99.

Schiedermair, Ludwig, *Einführung in das Studium der Musikgeschichte* (Bonn, 1947).

Schneider, Frank, "Die Musikwissenschaft in der DDR," *Beiträge zur Musik-wissenschaft*, XI/3-4 (1969), 163–75.

Schrade, Leo "Eine Einführung in die Musikgeschichtsschreibung älterer Zeit," in *De scientia musicae studia atquae orationes*, ed. Ernst Lichtenhahn (Bern, 1967).

Schultz, Helmut, *see* Zenck, Hermann, and Helmut Schultz.

Schweizer, Gottfried, "Die Musikwissenschaft der Schweiz," *Zeitschrift für Musik*, CXII/6 (1951), 295–96.

Seeger, Charles L., "Music and Musicology in the New World," *Hinrichsen's Musical Yearbook*, VI (1949–50), 36–56.

———— "Systematic and Historical Orientations in Musicology," *Acta Musi-cologica*, XI (1939), 121–28.

———— "Systematic Musicology," *Journal of the American Musicological Society*, IV (1951), 240–48.

———— "Toward a Unitary Field Theory for Musicology," *Selected Reports, Institute of Ethnomusicology*, I/3 (1970), 171–210.

Semzovskij, J., "Heute und Morgen der Musikfolklore-Forschung," *Kunst und Literatur*, XVI (1968), 640–48.

Sessions, Roger, "Musicology and the Composer," *Bulletin of the American Musicological Society*, V (Aug., 1941), 5–7.

Skyllstad, Kjell, "Noen metodologiske grunnproblemer i musikkforskningen" [Some methodological problems in musicology], in *Festschrift til Olav Gur-vin*, ed. Finn Benestad and Philip Krømer (Oslo, 1968), pp. 162–67.

Sohor (Sochor), Arnold Naumovič, "50 Jahre sowjetische Musik im Spiegel der sowjetische-russischen Musikwissenschaft," *Beiträge zur Musikwissen-schaft*, IX/3–4 (1967), 181–96.

———— "Studying, Criticizing and Propagandizing," *Sovetskaja muzyka*, XXXI/12 (Dec., 1967), 20–26. In Russian.

Sonneck, Oscar, "The Future of Musicology in America," in *Essays Offered to Herbert Putnam by His Colleagues and Friends on His Thirtieth Anniversary as Librarian of Congress, 1 April 1929*, ed. William Warner Bishop and Andrew Keough (New Haven, 1929), pp. 423–28.

Spiess, Lincoln Bunce, *Historical Musicology* (New York, 1963). A reference manual for research in music, with articles by Ernst C. Krohn, Lloyd Hib-berd, Luther A. Dittmer, Tsang-Huaei Shu, Tatsuo Minagawa, and Zdeněk Nováček.

Strunk, Oliver, "The State and Resources of Musicology in the United States," *Bulletin of the American Council of Learned Societies*, XIX (1932), 76 p.

———— "The Historical Aspect of Musicology," in *Papers of the American Musicological Society* (1936), pp. 14–16. One of "Twelve Papers on Various Phases of Musicology."

Supičič, Ivo, "Muzikologija i estetika," *Zvuk*, XCV (1969), 197–205.

Suppan, Wolfgang, "Volkslied. Seine Sammlung und Erforschung," in *Realien-bücher für Germanisten, Abt. E.: Poetik X* (Stuttgart, 1966).

Suppan, Wolfgang, *see* Hoerburger, Felix, and Wolfgang Suppan.

Szmolyan, Walter, "Die Musikwissenschaft an Österreichs Universitäten," *Österreichische Musik-Zeitung* (Oct., 1966), 55–63.

Tischler, Hans, "And What Is Musicology?," *Music Review,* XXX/4 (Nov., 1969), 253–60.

Torrefranca, Fausto, "Musica e storia della musica," *Acta Musicologica,* IV/1 (1932), 3–4.

Treitler, Leo, "On Historical Criticism," *Musical Quarterly,* LIII/2 (April, 1967), 188–205.

––––––– "The Present as History," *Perspectives of New Music* (Spring-Summer, 1969), 1–58.

Vetter, Walther, "Voraussetzung und Zweck in der Musikwissenschaft," in *Festschrift A. Orel zum 70. Geburtstag* (Vienna, 1960), pp. 207–12.

Vitányi, Iván, "A Magyar zenetudomány kezdetei. Kovács Sándor és Molnár Antal" [Beginnings of Hungarian musicology. Sándor Kovács and Antal Molnár], *Muzsika,* XI/11 (Nov., 1968), 12–20.

Vysloužil, Jiří, "K počátkům českého hudebního dějepisectví" [The beginnings of Czech musicology], *Hudebni rozhledy,* VIII, X (1967), 234–36, 296–98.

Wagner, Peter, *Universität und Musikwissenschaft* (Freiburg, 1921).

Wangermée, Robert, *François-Joseph Fétis, musicologue et compositeur* (Brussels, 1951).

––––––– "La Musique ancienne contre la musique d'aujourd'hui," *Polyphonie,* III (1949), 12–29.

Watanabe, Ruth T., *Introduction to Music Research* (Englewood Cliffs, N.J., 1967).

Weber, Edith, "La Musicologie dans les universités françaises," *Revue historique,* CDXC (April-June, 1969), 373–80.

––––––– "L'Enseignement de la musicologie en France. Historique, organisation, activités et réalisation, perspectives d'avenir," *Annales de l'Université de Paris,* XXX (1960), 398–407.

Wellek, Albert, *Musikpsychologie und Musikästhetik; Grundriss der systematischen Musikwissenschaft* (Frankfurt am Main, 1963).

––––––– "Gegenwartsprobleme systematischer Musikwissenschaft, Sammelreferat über Musikpsychologie und -ästhetik," *Acta Musicologica,* XLI/3–4 (1969), 213–35.

Wessely, Othmar, "Die österreichische Musikforschung nach dem zweiten Weltkrieg," *Acta Musicologica,* XXIX/4 (1957), 111–19.

Wiora, Walter, "Musikgeschichte und Urgeschichte," in *Studier tillägnade Carl-Allan Moberg 5 juni 1961* (Stockholm, 1961), pp. 375–96.

––––––– "Musikwissenschaft und Universalgeschichte," *Acta Musicologica,* XXXIII (1961), 84–104.

––––––– "Grenzen und Stadien des Historismus in der Musik," in *Die Ausbreitung des Historismus über die Musik,* Studien zur Musikgeschichte des 19. Jahrhunderts, 14 (Regensburg, 1969), pp. 299–327.

––––––– ed., *Die Ausbreitung des Historismus über die Musik,* Studien zur Musikgeschichte des 19. Jahrhunderts, 14 (Regensburg, 1969).

Wiora, Walter, and Hans Albrecht, "Musikwissenschaft," in *Die Musik in Carl-Allan Moberg 5 juni 1961* (Stockholm, 1961), pp. 375–96.

––––––– "Musikwissenschaft," in *Die Musik in Geschichte und Gegenwart,* IX, cols. 1192–1220.

Wolf, Johannes, "Musik und Musikwissenschaft," in *Von deutscher Tonkunst. Festschrift zu Peter Raabes 70. Geburtstag* (Leipzig, 1942), pp. 38–44.

────── "Musikwissenschaft und musikwissenschaftlicher Unterricht," in *Festschrift Hermann Kretzschmar zum siebzigsten Geburtstag* (Leipzig, 1918), pp. 175–79.

Wolff, Hellmuth Christian, "Die Geschichte der Musikwissenschaft an den Universitäten Leipzig und Berlin," in *Sborník Prací Filosofické Fakulty Brněnské University* (Brno, 1969).

────── "Grenzen der Musikwissenschaft," in *Festschrift für Walter Wiora zum 30. Dezember 1966*, ed. Ludwig Finscher and Christoph-Hellmut Mahling (Kassel, 1967), pp. 661–72.

Zemkovskij, Izalij, "Musical Folklore Studies of Today and Tomorrow," *Sovetskaja muzyka*, XXXI/12 (Dec., 1967), 26–32. In Russian.

Zenck, Hermann, and Helmut Schultz, "Die Musikforschung in Leipzig und ihre Neuorganisierung," *Acta Musicologica*, II/2 (April, 1930), 56–61.

Index